The Economic Organization of East Asian Capitalism

Nicole, Marco, and Gary
Seattle, October 1994

Marco Orrù
1954-1995

The Economic Organization of East Asian Capitalism

Marco Orrù
Nicole Woolsey Biggart
Gary G. Hamilton

SAGE Publications
International Educational and Professional Publisher
Thousand Oaks London New Delhi

For information address:

SAGE Publications, Inc.
2455 Teller Road
Thousand Oaks, California 91320
E-mail: order@sagepub.com

SAGE Publications Ltd.
6 Bonhill Street
London EC2A 4PU
United Kingdom

SAGE Publications India Pvt. Ltd.
M-32 Market
Greater Kailash I
New Delhi 110 048 India

Printed in the United States of America

Library of Congress Cataloging-in-Publication Data

Orrù, Marco, 1954-1995
    The economic organization of East Asian capitalism / Marco Orrù
Nicole Woolsey Biggart, Gary G. Hamilton.
        p. cm.
    Includes bibliographical references and index.
    ISBN 0-7619-0479-4 (alk. paper). — ISBN 0-7619-0480-8 (pbk.:
alk. paper)
    1. Organizational behavior—East Asia—Case studies.
    2. Capitalism—East Asia—Case studies. I. Biggart, Nicole
Woolsey. II. Hamilton, Gary G. III. Title.
    HD58.7.O77   1997
    338.095—dc20   96-10136

This book is printed on acid-free paper.

97 98 99 00 10 9 8 7 6 5 4 3 2 1

Acquiring Editor:	Peter Labella
Editorial Assistant:	Frances Borghi
Production Editor:	Michèle Lingre
Production Assistant:	Sherrise Purdum
Typesetter/Designer:	Janelle LeMaster
Indexer:	Will Ragsdale
Cover Designer:	Candice Harman

Contents

Preface

his book represents the fruits of our decade-long, three-way collaboration with the late Marco Orrù, investigating the institutional underpinnings of Asian capitalism. When we began this research, Asia was very much a mystery to most Westerners. It was clearly a vibrant, dynamic entrant into the global economy, but just as clearly, its economies violated our presumptions of how successful markets should be organized. The chapters included in this volume represent our efforts to theorize Asian capitalism and analyze the economic organization of East Asia. Part III, which contains the last work completed by Marco Orrù before his untimely death in September 1995 at the age of 41, represents an important comparative extension of the Weberian economic sociology we have collectively worked to further.

We present different dimensions of a Weberian perspective in the three sections of this book. The three chapters in Part I describe our approach in theoretical terms. Chapter 1 outlines the institutional foundations of our approach, Chapter 2 summarizes the historical and civilizational dimensions of our perspective, and Chapter 3 suggests how a Weberian approach would alter the theories currently being developed by the new institutional economists and would lead to an alternative approach to economic sociology in its own right.

The six chapters in Part II represent applications of this approach to the analysis of capitalism in East Asia. Chapters 4, 5, and 6 present a comparative framework that we use to distinguish and contrast the three capitalist economies of East Asia: the Japanese, the Taiwanese, and the South Korean. Chapters 7, 8, and 9 examine each of these economies individually and in more detail. In these chapters, we show not only that these economies are different, one from another, but that the capitalistic origins, operations, and trajectories of development of these economies are also all distinct from each other.

Part III of the book, the part Marco wrote on his own, extends the comparative framework developed in the intra-Asian comparisons to incorporate a comparison between Asian and European countries. In Chapters 10, 11, and 12, Marco shows in considerable detail the significant array of similarities in the economic organizations of the three pairs of European and Asian countries. Despite having extremely different cultures and historical patterns of development, each paired set—the German and the Japanese economies, the Italian and the Taiwanese economies, and the French and the South Korean economies—have many parallel economic organizations and many similar economic institutions that are not shared by their closest geographic neighbors.

We believe that Marco's findings, empirically outlined in Part III, have extremely important implications for economic sociology. With these results, Marco shows that radically different forms of social and cultural institutions can lead to economies that are organized and work in remarkably similar ways. Currently important perspectives in economic analysis, such as Granovetter's (1985) embeddedness approach and Williamson's (1975, 1985) transaction cost economics, tend to generate theories of economic organization from the bottom up. Marco's findings suggest that a more complex view of economic organization is required than one narrowed to the interaction among firms or among people in social networks. Marco initially made this comparative leap between Europe and Asia as a result of his first trip to Asia in 1989. Having grown to adulthood in Italy—in Sardinia during his youth and in northern Italy during the formative years of his education— Marco heard, in the chaotic streets of Taipei, the echoes of Italy in his youth. He could not shake this sense of similarity everywhere he visited—in the flexibly organized family firms, in the homes of our Taiwanese colleagues, in the restaurants where we had banquet after banquet, or in the streets filled with motorbikes and vendors of all types. Unwilling to write this feeling off as nostalgia, Marco returned to Asia in the following years, traveling to Japan and South Korea as well as to Taiwan. Then he returned to northern Italy, where he investigated factory networks. He gradually began to piece together the similarities and differences and to discern the deep structural and institutional parallels between economies that are otherwise entirely different. Underlying these institutional patterns, Marco recognized systemic processes that tie firms together into a division of labor that is, on a firm-by-firm basis, not entirely of their own making. In a 1993 study of small-firm networks in Italy, Marco called this form of organization "organic isomorphism." The matrix of similarities and differences among economies that the three of us discuss in this book leads us to suggest a most Weberian interpretation. The growth of capitalism from at least the nineteenth century onward has not been a country-by-country phenomenon, but rather a global one. The organization of whole economies is not cut off from economic development elsewhere. To understand patterns of economic activity in any one location, it is necessary to see that activity as being pulled by rationalizing economic forces, such as capital accounting systems and global commodity chains, as well as being pushed by socially embedded people to want to earn a good living, if not get rich. Economic organization represents a compromise between the two, between the people tied to a place and to a way of life on the one hand and the global conditions of their economic work on the other. In searching for ways to fashion business organizations, states and societies have a limited array of possible configurations. Very different societies may in the end arrive at structurally similar solutions to economic organization.

We dedicate this book to the memory of our collaborator and friend, Marco Orrù.

—Nicole Woolsey Biggart
—Gary G. Hamilton

Acknowledgments

e have been working on this and related projects for many years, and have incurred many debts to colleagues, friends, and supporting institutions. Collectively we have been aided by the Institute for Governmental Affairs at the University of California, Davis; Pacific Rim Grants of the President's Office of the University of California; and National Science Foundation funding. Gary was also a recipient of Guggenheim and Fulbright Fellowships that aided this research.

A number of people have worked on this project with us. We thank Chen Chu-po, Chung Wai-Keung, Cindy Chu, Ho Dwanfan, Kim Wan-Jin, Lai Chi-Kong, Lim Eun Mie, Lin Holin, Mariko Suzuki, Pat Woelk, Moon-Jee Yoo, Yu Sheunn-Der, and William Zeile for their efforts in helping us to collect and analyze the data we present in this volume.

We have relied, too, on the advice and encouragement of colleagues in the United States and abroad. Asian colleagues include Kao Chung-shu and his team of researchers at Tunghai University, especially Chang Wei-an, now a professor at National Tsing Hua University; Jai Ben-ray; Chen Chieh-hsuan, now a professor at Tunghai University; Professor Wong Sui-lun and Gordon Redding, University of Hong Kong; Professor Edward K. Y. Chen, president of Lingnan College, Hong Kong; Eddie C. Y. Kuo, Nanyang Technological University; and Tong Chee Kiong, National University of Singapore.

We also want to acknowledge the assistance of colleagues at the University of California at Davis, including Robert Feenstra, Martin Kenney, Kwang-Ching Liu, Benjamin Orlove, Jean Stratford, Juri Stratford, and Alan

Olmstead. Marco Orrù's colleagues at the University of South Florida, Jennifer Friedman and Frasier Ottanelli, helped us gain access to Marco's research files after his death. The preparation of this manuscript was made possible by the care and skill of Josephine Chu.

PART

Theoretical Perspectives

1

Explaining Asian Economic Organization

Toward a Weberian Institutional Perspective

NICOLE WOOLSEY BIGGART

n the world of business and economics, the empirical phenomenon of the decade clearly has been the remarkable growth and development of Asian nations into world-class economic powers, particularly the Northeast Asian economies of Japan, South Korea, and Taiwan, but also Hong Kong and Singapore. These coun-

AUTHOR'S NOTE: This chapter is reprinted here with kind permission Kluwer Academic Publishers from "Explaining Asian Economic Organization: Toward a Weberian Institutional Perspective," by Nicole Woolsey Biggart, *Theory and Society,* 1991, vol. 20, pp. 199-232. Copyright 1991. This chapter has benefited from presentation before several audiences who challenged my logic and discourse. I appreciated the give-and-take of seminars at the University

tries have emerged from an array of political and social challenges that include world and civil wars, massive migration, external occupation and colonization, and substantial destruction of their economic capacities to become, in little more than a generation, extraordinarily successful players in the world economy. Indeed, Japan now has the second-largest economy in the world after the United States, Taiwan the largest per capita foreign reserves in the world, and Singapore a per capita income second only to Japan in Asia. Remarkably, all these nations have achieved success despite poor natural resources.

This dramatic empirical phenomenon has naturally excited an array of explanations from observers, including scholars, businesspeople, journalists, trade negotiators, and policy analysts. The explanations have ranged from the polemical, such as *The Japanese Conspiracy* (Wolf, 1983), to the tactical, including Clyde Prestowitz, Jr.'s *Trading Places* (1988), in which the author argues for a tougher U.S. stance toward trade with Japan. Although the polemical and tactical, as well as a range of other discussions of Asian economic prowess, are sometimes well informed and even well written, it quite naturally has remained to the scholarly community to provide a more dispassionate and sustained analysis of Eastern economic structure and practice.

The volume of recent research on Asia is large and growing and uses a diverse array of theoretical tools to explain the economic patterns of Asia. Four perspectives, however, have guided most of the recent scholarship on Asia: a political economy approach that emphasizes the role of the state in economic development; a market approach that concentrates on economic factors; a cultural approach that focuses on the socially constructed character of economic organization; and my own chosen framework, an institutional approach that argues for the centrality of institutionalized authority relations (Table 1.1). These four theoretical paradigms are familiar to students of economic organizations and have been used to explain industrial practices and arrangements in the West; they now face the challenge of explaining like phenomena in the East.

I have both a general and a particular purpose in this chapter. The general purpose is to take an accounting of current theories of economic organization

of Lancaster, England; Stanford University; Australia National University; and the Cardiff Business School, University of Wales College at Cardiff; as well as at the annual meetings of the American Sociological Association held in San Francisco, August 1989. I appreciate, too, the comments of George Bittlingmayer, Marco Orrù, and three *Theory and Society* reviewers who read the manuscript with care.

Table 1.1 Four Perspectives on Organization

	Market	*Cultural*	*Political Economy*	*Institutional*
Key variables	economic	values, symbols	state	ideology, authority
Social action	individual utilitarianism	collective action	class and interest groups	dialectic of structure and individual action
Social order	invisible hand/ self-interest	enacted solidarity	stratification (repression, majority rule)	domination
Social change	market forces	continuity	institutional contradictions/ interest politics	historical development
Organization	most efficient structure	symbolic expression of cultural values	expressions of bureaucratic and market power	structure of economic domination utilizing cultural understandings

by discussing their underlying assumptions and suggesting their strengths and limitations in explaining Asian, as well as Western, industrial patterns and organizational processes. I use examples from the literature on Asian economies, and occasionally Western economies, to illustrate the distinctive characteristics of the different approaches.

In addition to my general purpose of theoretical assessment, I have a particular purpose in arguing for the utility of an institutional perspective rooted in Weberian sociology in the study of non-Western societies. Although the political economy, market, and cultural approaches are all useful in important ways, institutional theory, unlike any one of the other three perspectives, accounts well for both ideal and material factors, may be used to explain both micro- and macro-level patterns of organization, may allow for the agency of actors, readily allows comparison, and has no inherent Western bias. Whereas the first three characteristics may be important to theorizing in any geographic sphere, the last two—comparability and absence of a Western bias—are crucial to studies that hope to make sense of economic activity in an international arena. These five criteria are my choices for a "good" theory of economic organization, but I believe they are widely shared.

In this chapter, I first characterize in turn the political economy, market, and cultural approaches to economic organization. Although there are variations within these theoretical traditions, I focus on the assumptions that are broadly associated with each perspective. Second, I assess the strengths and weaknesses of the theories in accounting for economic organizations. Finally, I argue for a form of institutional theory, suggesting how it builds on the other perspectives while avoiding their limitations. Throughout the discussion, I use recent analyses of Asian economies to provide illustrations of the ways in which each perspective tries to account for organized economic action and arrangements. Theories that account well for Asia, I believe, may result in better theories of the West.

The Political Economy Approach

Political economists do not usually discuss firms or markets per se; rather, they focus on the relation between the state and the economy. Political economists are concerned with macrostructural political institutions and their consequences for social outcomes—for example, the routes to modern state formation in different countries, the role of bureaucratic state arrangements in political and economic affairs, the influence of democratic institutions on state functioning, and the fiscal crises of capitalist regimes forced to satisfy competing claims on state resources.

There are different theories of the state—Alford and Friedland (1985) identify three basic types—but political economy theories generally assume that the character and policies of the state are determined by the character of the economy, with other institutions (e.g., educational, ideological, family) shaped by their role in sustaining political economic relations. To oversimplify, socialist states, mercantilist states, corporatist states, and fascist states necessarily maintain different social institutions to support their different characteristic economies.

Political economy theories support structural analyses. Capitalist societies, they argue, structure relations between owners and workers, between officials and citizens, in predictable ways. To understand the dynamics of a given capitalist society, one must understand the way in which power is structured between major social groupings. Individuals act in terms of their structural—often described as class—location: Managers act as they do because of the interests and powers inherent in their class position. Likewise, workers and officials act as they do because of their different interests and locations in the structure of power. Moreover, states themselves have relative positions in the world economic structure. A state's structural location—for example, as a developed core state, or as a clientelist dependent state—shapes its policies and behavior.

Structural theories of this sort rarely examine the activities of individual firms or economic decision makers because these are assumed to act in ways that express their social position within the market structure. But theories of the state have been employed frequently to explain, at a general level, economic patterns and outcomes.

For example, several theorists account for Asian development through largely structural analyses. The main arguments focus on one or more of three basic components: the state, multinational corporations (MNCs), and the local bourgeoisie. Political economists typically emphasize the similarities between, for example, Taiwan and South Korea—both countries are thought to occupy a position of political and economic dependence in relation to developed nations (especially the United States and Japan), and their success is equally attributed to a dependent relation. Bruce Cumings (1984), for instance, argues that Taiwan and South Korea are economic-military protectorates of the United States and economic vassals of Japan. The path of development for both countries was drawn by the larger industrial powers: Declining sectors in Japanese industry are cyclically passed on to Korean and Taiwanese industries (Cumings, 1984, p. 3). Both countries, Cumings asserts, share the common features of "bureaucratic-authoritarian industrializing regimes" (p. 28) (state autonomy, central coordination, bureaucratic planning, private concentration in big conglomerates, military strength, and authoritarian repression). Cumings acknowledges that "what could be done with economic incentives in Taiwan required coercion in Korea" (p. 11) and that "Taiwan produced a weak nationalist impulse, Korea an extraordinarily strong one" (p. 12). Still, he equates the two, contending that "by the 1960s both Taiwan and South Korea possessed strong states that bear much comparison . . . to the bureaucratic-authoritarian states in Latin America" (p. 28).

Focusing directly on the state, Thomas Gold (1986) proposes a less deterministic version of Taiwan's dependent development, resorting to Cardoso and Faletto's "historical-structural methodology." In Gold's words, this approach allows one to appreciate how "economic relationships and the social structure that underlies them arise as a result of human activity, and how they can be transformed through social action" (p. 15). Although Gold offers good insights into the changing posture of the Taiwan state over the decades, his final analysis remains that "the KMT state controlled the way Taiwan incorporated into the world system in a way few other countries have" (p. 126). Similarly, Alice Amsden (1985) argues that "the balance of power between the state and both labor and capital was weighted far more to the state's advantage" (p. 98), and she concludes that the state "can be said both to have transformed Taiwan's economic structure and to have been transformed by it" (p. 101). In his analysis, Ramon Myers (1984, p. 516) places importance on a partnership between the Taiwan state and MNCs, particularly in the development of new economic sectors such as electronics.

Japan, no less than Taiwan and South Korea, has been subject to analysis by political economists. In addition to scholarly treatments of the sort I describe above, popularized treatments embracing a political economy logic have explained Japanese economic success as a product of the organizing skill of the Japanese state. These arguments often describe Japan's government as "Japan, Inc.," portraying officials as managers of the economy. Some Western writers have suggested that state officials and industrial managers, more than orchestrating the economy, have conspired to protect Japanese firms from international competitors (in addition to Wolf, 1983, see Brandon, 1983; Taylor, 1983).

Political economists, for the most part, do not have a theory of social action. Actors are unimportant factors—they play the roles assigned them by their place in society. Structural factors, especially the state in its role as guardian of economic interests, are causal. The economy is a political arena whose operation reflects the relative power of domestic and multinational economic actors and the nation's position in the world economy: Economy produces and reflects structures of power.

The Market Approach

The market approach, which has several variants, explains industrial structure as a response to economic conditions. Its most famous expression lies in the work of economic historian Alfred D. Chandler. In *The Visible Hand* (1977), Chandler chronicles the replacement of traditional forms of enterprise in the United States by the modern "multiunit business enterprise," or divisionalized firm. His explanation for the development of new organizational forms centers on market factors: the growth of markets made possible by new technologies of production and transportation, and the development of professional managers to coordinate within the enterprise activities previously conducted in the marketplace, for example, financing and distribution. New enterprise forms replaced the old because of lower costs and improved coordination. Chandler argues that firms developed and took the forms they did because they were economically and technologically superior.

Related, but more abstract and ahistorical, economic explanations are found in the work of industrial organization (IO) economists. One important variant is elaborations of the work of Oliver E. Williamson and his "markets and hierarchy" thesis.[1] According to Williamson, every economic transaction—production, purchasing, hiring, distribution—contains costs, including those that ensure that each party to an exchange lives up to the terms of the parties' agreement. Entrepreneurs will go to the marketplace to conduct business as long as their transaction costs are low, but when costs associated with maintaining contracts, searching for skilled labor, guarding against cheating, and other diseconomies become too great, entrepreneurs will organize these activities within a firm or "hierarchy" where they have managerial control. Hierarchies have their own maintenance costs but also countervailing economies, for example, economies of scale and ease of monitoring. Whether economic activity takes place in a market or in a hierarchy depends on which means of doing business has the lowest transaction costs. Moreover, the structure of an organization—whether a company vertically integrates or merges with another—depends on a calculus of the most efficient (i.e., least expensive) way to conduct business. The organizing strategies of business-people, according to both Williamson and Chandler, can be traced to the rational weighing of economic costs and benefits. Organization—whether large, small, vertically integrated, or divisionalized —is the efficient product of entrepreneurs' rational response to market conditions.

Although a Western theoretical perspective (and, in the case of Chandler, derived from the American experience), the Chandler-Williamson form of market explanation has been used to interpret Asia's business structure. For example, Sherman Cochran (1984) explains the changing form of Chinese business enterprise involved in interregional trade from 1850 to 1980 using a transaction cost model. According to Cochran, traditional native-place associations, later protomodern sales organizations, and, finally, bureaucratic state commercial companies successively dominated trade in tobacco and textiles. He explains the development of each subsequent form of organization as a solution to transaction cost problems imposed by changing requirements of the Chinese government. In another work,

Cochran (1982) echoes Chandler's argument about the growth of firms as a response to the geographically larger markets made possible by new transportation technology: "The large enterprises that introduced vertical integration into China in the early twentieth century responded to technological opportunities for controlling space not available to their predecessors."

A complementary market explanation is found in the work of strategy theorists such as Michael Porter and the related "structure-conduct-performance" school of IO that derives from the work of Bain and Mason (see, e.g., Bain, 1968; Mason, 1960; Porter, 1980). These theorists explain organizational form and functioning as a consequence of industry structure.[2] The structure of the industry, concentration rates, barriers to entry, product diversity, and demand influence a firm's conduct (quality, price, capacity), which in turn influences performance—allocative efficiency (profitability) and technical efficiency (cost minimization). The form and functioning of firms, then, is explained by firms' rational response to an industry's structure of opportunity and constraint.

Several theorists have used variants of the structure-conduct-performance model to explain Asian business organization and strategy. One of the most prominent, Ian D. Little (1979), for example, attributes Taiwan's spectacular success to market conditions that approximate economists' hypothesized "perfect market," that is, a market characterized by many small autonomous firms with few barriers to entry. Little argues that a laissez-faire state did not saddle the economy with inefficient regulations and state agencies, and stimulated the economy through low taxes and high interest rates. Market structure favored the entrepreneurial response of many individuals who formed small competitive firms, with resulting strong economic performance for the economy as a whole.

Economists have proposed other theories to explain organization and management practice. For example, agency theory posits that firms are legal fictions—a firm is "really" the sum of contracts among owners, employees, managers, and suppliers. The structure and performance of a firm can be predicted by the nature of its contracts and the monitoring (control) devices used to maintain adherence to contractual terms (see, e.g., Fama & Jensen, 1983; Jensen & Meckling, 1976).

The market approach as I define it, however, is not limited to economists. Others, including anthropologists and sociological exchange theorists, have embraced logically similar models—seeing social organization emerging from a utilitarian calculus.[3] A market approach, in all its disciplinary variants, however, is commonly characterized by assumptions of economic rationality and sees the atomized individual—whether a firm or a person—as the crucial economic actor. Market theories further assume that the economic system is an aggregated outcome of the production, exchange, and consumption of goods and services. Through the self-interested and rationally calculated pecuniary activity of individuals, social order, including organization, emerges: Economy produces society.

The Cultural Approach

The cultural approach reverses the market theory's hypothesized causal relation, viewing the economic system as a product of the social order: Society produces economy. In addition, most culturalists reject the structuralism and materialism of political economy and market theory.[4] Instead, they see economies as the subjectivist product of social action. Structure—if it is acknowledged at all—is merely the aggregation of meaningful interactions.

In the culturalists' vision, economic exchange materially sustains society to be sure, but, more important, the patterned circulation and use of goods is an idealist accomplishment, a celebration of common beliefs and social solidarity. Economic institutions emerge from, are possible only because of, society. Anthropologist Mary Douglas (1979) expresses a cultural view of economic activity in her discussion of consumption:

> Consumption has to be recognized as an integral part of the same social system that accounts for the drive to work, itself part of the need to relate to other people, and to have mediating materials for relating to them. Mediating materials are food, drink, and hospitality of home to offer, flowers and clothes to signal shared rejoicing, or mourning dress to share sorrow. Goods, work, and consumption have been artificially abstracted out of the whole social scheme. (p. 4)

A cultural approach explains organizational structure and practice as a collective enactment of beliefs and values or of shared cognitive structures.[5] Although it does not deny the material constraints or benefits of organizing, it explains organizational patterns as driven by shared ideas and understandings. Viviana Zelizer (1988) argues in a review essay that culture-based theories have a moral impulse to them, a reaction against theories that see the market only in rational-material terms.

The cultural approach has often been used to explain Asian business. For example, Japanese organizing practices, such as the subordination of individuals to the group, seniority systems that reward continuity of participation, collective exercises and singing, and consensual decision making, are explained as expressions of the widely held Japanese belief in *wa*, or harmony (see, e.g., Abegglen, 1958; Benedict, 1946). Similarly, Chinese business practices and structure are explained as derivations of Confucianism (see, e.g., Hu, 1984; Silin, 1976). The self-discipline of workers, the loyalty to superiors, the preference for patrilineal relations as business partners—all these and more are explained as organizational outcomes of a Confucian belief system.

Western organizations have also been examined by culture theorists. Among the most scholarly studies have been Foucault's (1965, 1979) sophisticated analyses of asylums and prisons in France, which he describes as representations of European beliefs about the nature of madness and crime, and further about what is socially deviant and normal. The objective purposes of these organizations—isolation and incarceration—are secondary factors in Foucault's explanation of why they have been structured and operated as they have been. According to Foucault, forms and practices say more about society than about the institutions or their tasks. Other scholars have looked at contemporary organizations in Sweden, Yugoslavia, England, and France, seeing factories and offices in each nation as shaped by cultural traditions (Blumberg, 1973; Crozier, 1964; Dore, 1973; Tannenbaum, Kavcic, Rosner, Vianello, & Weisner, 1974).

Until recently, the cultural perspective was the province of scholars— ethnographers and comparative culture theorists—but in the 1980s managerial consultants and applied researchers embraced this approach to understanding corporate organization. The phenomenal success of *In Search of Excellence* (1982), by Thomas J. Peters and Robert H. Waterman, Jr., demonstrated how attractive and sensible a cultural explanation is to people who work in modern American enterprise. Similarly, strategic management theorist William Ouchi's popular book on Japanese management, *Theory Z* (1982), explains consensual decision making and the promotion of cohorts rather than individuals as expressions of Japanese "groupness." These widely read books repudiate rational approaches to organizing—management by numbers—and focus instead on organizations as cultural systems. According to these authors, the promotion of shared beliefs and meaningful interaction, as much or more than financial analysis, is the crucial management task.

Their works and the work of other corporate culture writers have established the cultural perspective as an alternative to the economic rationality paradigm in popular management literature.

Assessing the Political Economy, Market, and Cultural Perspectives

The political economy, market, and cultural perspectives have all proven useful in explaining economic arrangements. Although I have emphasized their often logically opposed assumptions, in fact they have rarely been pitted one against the other as alternative forms of explanation. For the most part, political economy, market, and cultural models have been used for different purposes—political economy to explain patterns and rates of development, market models for regulatory prescription and economic prediction, and cultural models for ethnographic description. Each has largely been suited to its respective scholarly tasks. Each has distinctive abilities and limitations for the comparative analysis of economic patterns and organization. The institutional approach I describe in the pages ahead attempts to employ the strengths of all three in contributing to international comparative analysis of economic action while avoiding some of their limitations for this purpose.

Political economy models have several advantages for performing the kind of comparative analysis necessary to understanding economic action in a multinational environment. First, political economists— unlike market and cultural theorists—focus our attention on the state as a crucial force in advanced capitalist societies. It is difficult to imagine an explanation for patterns of Asian (or other) capitalism that does not account for the states' roles in development policies, the regulation of markets, and the maintenance of political stability necessary for foreign and domestic investment. Second, political economy models recognize the importance of both material and ideal factors in explanation. Market models are concerned with materialist explanation, and cultural models are concerned largely with such ideal factors as values and beliefs, but neither accounts well for the other factors. Political economists take seriously material factors, usually expressed as group interests or class location, as well as ideal factors such as democratic values, class consciousness, and capitalist ideologies. Third, political economy theories are sensitive to the connections among social institutions. Although the state is usually seen as the most important institution in economic maintenance, connections among the polity, culture, and economy are assumed and examined. Finally, political economy explanations are sophisticated about the role of power in social outcomes. Although one might argue with political economists' conceptualization of power as merely structural, neither the market nor the cultural approach conceptualizes power as well as a political economy approach (for discussion of this point, see Hamilton & Biggart, 1985).

There are limitations to the political economy perspective, however. First, the structure of the economy is assumed to be the determining factor in all societies. This may be true of any given case, but such an assumption prejudges the character of social relations in a society, assumptions that should be the object of investigation. Second, political economy arguments are open to the charge of functionalist teleology: State theories categorize a type of state—for example, capitalism—and then conceptualize the structures essential to a capitalist society—for example, a bourgeoisie and a proletariat. To have a capitalist society one must, by definition, have ownership and working classes, because it is in the nature of capitalism to have them. This creates a circular, undisprovable logic: Functional necessity "causes" workers and owners to act as they do; if they did not, then there would be no capitalism.

Third, and related to the above, political economy theories have oversocialized conceptions of social action. Individuals act as agents of their classes or interest groups: Industrialists act like industrialists, and state officials act according to the functional needs of their position in running a capitalist state. Social action, in this conceptualization, becomes depersonalized and stylized, with individuals portrayed as unknowledgeable automatons. Although political economists study Asia and other non-Western locales, the characters of the societies being explained are often unimportant; it is supranational concepts and processes, such as the logic of capital formation, that are really being explained. Finally, and crucial to my argument for an institutional approach, the state is usually conceptualized in terms of the Western state. Recent scholarship suggests that although Japan, for example, has a parliamentary democratic state form, power in fact is diffused through an array of institutions quite different from Western counterparts (see, e.g., the popular work by Karl van Wolferen, *The Enigma of Japanese Power,* 1989).

The macrostructural orientation of political economy is excellent for bringing attention to the effects of structure on social relations, but it conceptualizes crudely the link between structure and action. It fails to see how organizational structures, including the state, institutionalize and appropriate social relationships, including economic relationships. Political economy models may suffer Western biases.

Market models make very strong assumptions about economic action and market structure. Typically, they assume that atomized individuals are economic decision makers and have complete information on offers to buy and sell in the marketplace. They assume that commodities are homogeneous, that firms act independently, and that no firm is sufficiently large or powerful to dominate a market. These presuppositions, which have the status of disciplinary dogma among economists, produce clear and elegant models that allow the contrast of real-world economies with an assumed perfect market (Stigler, 1968). Deviations are explained through the discovery of what market theorists call "imperfections," deviations from a hypothesized ideal of autonomous actors. Social relations, for example, are seen as "friction" that interrupts the smooth relations of the impersonal, hypothesized ideal.

Strong, widely shared assumptions about economic action and structure have produced a tradition of clear, elegant models. These models would seem to be ideally suited to comparison—the same assumptions underlie economic research wherever it is conducted, and "imperfections" may be compared readily. Moreover, at the macrostructural levels at which economic models have been most often applied, the relatively crude characterizations of people and social processes—a common criticism of a market approach—are probably adequate. At least it would seem that the hypothesized economic calculus of atomized individuals has some validity in Western economies: In the West the social ideal of individualism is widespread, and educational and legal institutions sustain individual rights and responsibilities in, for example, contract law (Biggart & Hamilton, 1990).[6]

Importantly, it seems, the market approach correctly draws our attention to economic factors—market concentration, labor costs, technology, competitive advantages—factors that obviously have effects on the development of an economy and are all too often overlooked by psychological, sociological, and anthropological theories. Poor resources, outdated industrial processes, and barriers to market entry clearly make an economic difference. Economically rational social action is widespread in a capitalist economy; it would be amazing if it were not. However, I believe, and have argued before, that economic factors better explain patterns of *growth* than patterns of *organization* (see Hamilton & Biggart, 1988). An abundance or scarcity of resources speaks to whether an economy expands or stagnates rather than to the precise structure of organizations it utilizes to transform and distribute the resources it has.

The success of a market model in the discipline of economics generally has in recent years stimulated criticism, some by economists, as rationalistic models have been applied to more micro-level settings, including organizations. Four critiques are worth noting. First, the evolutionary model proposed by Chandler and the related markets and hierarchies thesis of Williamson posit that firms develop because they are more efficient or effective than other forms of enterprise. Perrow (1981) has charged that efficiency is a possible but not necessary explanation of firm development: Firms better control labor and may be "efficient" insofar as they are effective means of extracting productivity from workers. Where Chandler and Williamson attribute the effectiveness of vertically integrated capitalist firms to their efficiency, Perrow attributes it to their control of the workplace. Second, and relatedly, William G. Roy, while applauding Chandler's historical scholarship, has attacked his logic. Roy (1987) charges that "Chandler's narrow technological focus ignores important empirical factors, especially political factors. This omission is not merely myopic but derives from the logical error of equating causes and consequences" (p. 5). Chandler's functionalist logic, akin to political economy explanations, explains firm development as a necessary consequence of technological advance —necessity was the mother of invention. His causality is teleological and does not leave open either the possibility of an alternative outcome or an explanation of why an economically superior firm was socially and politically possible. Roy deals only with Chandler's work, but a similar critique can be made of Williamson's argument: How can we know that all existing structures are the most efficient— that is, have the lowest transaction costs—if only the fittest survive? A functional logic does not leave open the possibility of refutation.

Third, market models have been criticized—most persuasively by Mark Granovetter (1985)—as providing an undersocialized conception of human agents who everywhere act alike, rationally pursuing unspecified interests. Market models cannot account for the impact of social networks, gender, class, culture, religion—the entire panoply of social life that so apparently influences what people want and how they go about getting it. Despite recent attempts by market theorists to incorporate a more sensitive model of individual decision making, the result has been too often the joining of a naive psychology with a reified methodological individualism.[7] Concrete social relations—the economic networks that characterize most real-life market activity—are absent from market models, even those with a psychologized component.

Finally, as I have argued elsewhere, the neoclassical model is fundamentally ethnocentric, based as it is on the institutional conditions and presuppositions of Western society, most notably autonomous, self-seeking actors uninfluenced by social relations.[8] Although individualism, and the social institutions that flow from it, such as individually binding contracts, antitrust regulations, and antinepotism norms, are not universal in the West, they are common and can be traced historically to Christian and Enlightenment thought on individual rights and responsibility. Scholars must question the applicability of the neoclassical model, based as it is on the primacy of individual actors (including firms as fictive individuals), to explain Asian economies where individualism is unimportant ideologically and institutionally, and was never a factor in the historical development of Eastern civilization. Organizations and markets and other forms of social organization in Asia are built on groups and networks—of people and firms—not on the individual actors hypothesized by Western market theorists.

This factor causes economic theory difficulty in characterizing Asian business networks, the single most important market structure in Asia, and leads market theorists to see Asian economies as distorted despite their obvious success. The neoclassical paradigm can conceptualize only two efficient economic structures, markets of autonomous actors, and hierarchies or autonomous firms, which may arise under certain conditions, for example, to achieve economies of scale. Networks of social relations among economic actors can be conceptualized only as aberrations that arise due to imperfections of the hypothesized perfect market. For example, Chandler (1982) characterizes the Japanese *zaibatsu,* the pre-World War II business networks that are precursors to modern business groups, as "organization[s] comparable to the M-form," or multidivisional firms, that originated in the United States. Chandler characterizes a network of socially interdependent Japanese companies as a single firm, although each constituent company has its own management, employees, and stockholders. He explains the rise of Japanese business groups as a technical response to "undeveloped" capital markets in Japan; *undeveloped* is a comparative term using the West as a benchmark. Chandler and other market theorists look at the East through the lens of the West when they employ the neoclassical paradigm to explain Asia and in so doing find it "imperfect" and "distorted." [9]

Cultural models, in contrast to political economy and market models, are filled with the stuff of social life. They are often detailed, close-up examinations of people going about their business and working together in organizations. Cultural models put society back into an organizational explanation: Society is not just an epiphenomenon, and organizations are not just instrumental by-products of the pursuit of economic utilities. Rather, society provides the very means by which organized economic activity can be sustained—common understandings, social values and rewards, ideologies of work and management. As Mary Douglas (1986) puts it, "For discourse to be possible at all, the basic categories have to be agreed on. Nothing else but institutions can define sameness. Similarity is an institution" (p. 55). Beliefs, categories of sameness—what political economists describe uncritically as "interests" and the market model either assumes without question or dismisses as "friction" and "imperfection"—the cultural model sees as central problems for explanation. Moreover, social actors are taken seriously by the cultural perspective; they are the central figures in any research program.

Despite, and perhaps because of, the richness of many culture studies of organizations, this perspective also has limitations. Often the studies have been so particularistic that generalization of features, and hence comparison, is problematic. Even explicitly comparative culture studies when conducted in the same cultural arena—for example, Japan and Taiwan—cannot explain differences. Cultural continuities such as the influence of a Confucian ethic throughout East Asia cannot explain why Japanese and Taiwanese businesses are organized so differently. It can explain only why there are similarities—for example, obedience to superiors and a disciplined orientation to work.

The cultural approach also has difficulty explaining changes over time, even within the same society. Culture is relatively constant, transforming only slowly. How then can a culture theory explain Japanese labor practices before World War II—when seniority systems and lifetime employment in core industries were not widespread—as well as the postwar practices we now associate with Japanese management (Jacoby, 1979)? If seniority systems and other management policies are expressions of group-oriented Japanese culture—as they surely are—how can we explain their emergence at a particular historic moment? Moreover, how can a culture model explain differences in a society in a given period—that is, account today for Japan's large organizations and small, those privately held as well as those publicly traded? Culture is too much a background factor, important to be sure, but by itself insufficiently specific to explain differences in organizational structure and functioning. And finally, where market theories suffer from an undersocialized conception of actors, culture theorists, like political economists, often err in the opposite way, seeing actors as unwittingly propelled by values and social pressures.

The above characterizations of the political economy, market, and cultural perspectives are just that, characterizations that capture neither the variety of viewpoints within the perspectives nor the substantive merits of the research produced by each, which are admittedly considerable. Rather, my purpose has been to sketch the theoretical underpinnings of these alternative explanations in an attempt to create an approach to industrial patterns that avoids some of their shortcomings.

I am not alone in this endeavor. Indeed, the development of economic theories that account better for political and, especially, social and cultural factors is something of a boom industry at the moment, not least among economists. In addition to the psychologizing of economic models, some economists have embraced social structural and cultural concepts in recent years. Two examples suggest the direction of these efforts.

First, IO economists have attempted to introduce an explicitly cultural variable into their models. William Ouchi (1981, 1982) has joined with Williamson in arguing that the most efficient form of organization may be that in which solidarity norms are strong. Mission-oriented firms—"clans," in these authors' terminology—will arise in situations where markets "fail" and hierarchies have high costs, perhaps because of the complexity of work and the difficulty of monitoring or enforcing contract compliance. "Culture" becomes the grease that reduces the costly friction of social relations.

Another important attempt by economists to integrate social structural variables is represented in institutional economic history (to be distinguished from the institutional school of organizational analysis described below), best developed in the writings of Douglass North (1981). North takes seriously the historically developed institutions of a society, including the state and social ideology. For example, he writes that "strong moral and ethical codes of a society [are] the cement of social stability which makes an economic system viable" (p. 47). More important, North's project is concerned with how institutions are constraints upon the hypothesized neoclassical model. How can economic rationality—an unquestioned assumption—proceed given social and political formations? North and his colleagues examine historical market settings and "fit" the neoclassical model within them.

Institutional economists have come far from the formal neoclassical models of mainstream economics in an attempt to account for the social and cultural factors that so obviously influence economic organizations. They do so in a way, however, that preserves the primacy of the economic over the social. Williamson, Ouchi, and North all see social variables as outcomes of, or constraints upon, the economic. They do not, however, ask why economic factors such as property rights—a social and political institution—are made possible by the institutions of the state or come to be understood as efficient.

I do not intend to argue with the culturalists that economic activity presupposes shared meanings, with the economists who see culture emerging from exchange, or with political economists who see the economy as a consequence of state structure. Rather, I develop an institutional theory that regards political, market, and culture factors as crucial variables in any explanation of economic organization. I believe economic rationality is widespread in market societies, as economists assume, but not that it is a state of human nature from which all else, including organization, follows. Rather, I suggest that economic rationality is socially produced and culturally maintained. For economic rationality to exist requires social and cultural underpinnings of the sort that capitalist societies maintain—legal, educational, political, and ideological institutions. Moreover, economic rationality is not everywhere the same, an undifferentiated force of social nature; it varies substantively with the history, culture, and institutions of a society and may have variable expression. Although a merchant in imperial China may have been just as profit seeking as a contemporary Wall Street investment banker, and just as "economically rational," his reasons for pecuniary pursuit, his norms of exchange, his networks of financial relations, his conceivable strategies of accumulation—his entire orientation to gain—were strikingly different. A sociological "institutional theory" draws on state, market, and culture factors to explain these differences, but in a way that makes none logically prior.

What Is an Institutional Explanation?

The institutional school of organizational analysis is a loose agglomeration of theoretical approaches that vary considerably.[10] They largely, however, reject explanations for organizational structure and functioning that rest solely on technical causes such as task requirements, size, and market factors. Moreover, institutionalists tend to view organizations as socially constructed —a product of actors' subjective realities—rather than as objective, material artifacts. Institutionalists do not deny the material impulse behind organizing, such as an orientation to profit, but seek further than economic rationality for explanations of the structures people manufacture in their pursuit of gain. It is not my purpose here to review the variation or detail in the institutional perspective, which has been ably described by others (e.g., W. R. Scott, 1987; Zucker, 1987). Rather, because of the diversity in this perspective and the debates between practitioners (see, e.g., Zucker, 1988), I want to suggest what I intend as an "institutional theory" and to make explicit the assumptions on which it rests. There are four elements to the institutional theory of economic organizations that I propose, each of which is a derivative of Weberian sociology: economic action as social action, the embeddedness of economic activity in institutional settings, institutional logic as a crucial concept, and the necessarily multilevel nature of an institutional argument.

Economic Action Is Social Action

The economic man of neoclassical economics is an avaricious hermit, a supersmart, selfish individual without history or tradition, without friends or enemies. This character is the useful fiction employed by economists to depict decision making in market settings. Few, if any, economists would argue that real people act like the miserly loner of their models. The advantage of the fiction is not to mirror reality but to simplify it, to reduce to essentials the general orientation of people as they buy and sell goods and services in a market.

This simple fiction yields the virtue of elegance in microeconomic model making, but it is not without critics. David Teece (1984), an IO economist, for example, acknowledges that real markets are not peopled with "faceless economic agents." He argues that "the abstraction [of hyperrational decision makers] may be appropriate for framing certain problems but it is . . . not a characterization of individual behavior and, even more so, of organizational behavior." Social characteristics, such as reputation and experience, "are the very stuff which permits markets to operate efficiently" (pp. 91-92). Market theorists such as Teece recognize that economic actors indeed have histories, suffer forgetfulness, and are propelled by desires. While acknowledging that economic man is a useful caricature for modeling the behavior of populations of actors, they understand the limits of the caricature for describing the activities of real people close-up.

At the heart of this limitation, I believe, is the presumption that economic action is asocial, that is, conducted without consideration of others. Although it is possible to conceive of asocial economic activity, it is so evidently rare in enduring conditions of exchange, as Teece suggests, as to be a weak basis for theory building. Rather, I propose constructing theories of economic action based on observed reality: Economic action is social action.

What is social action? According to Weber (1978), it is action oriented to others and includes both failure to act and passive acquiescence. It may be oriented to the past or the future, as well as the present. Social action may be motivated by revenge, peer pressure, desire for power or gain, the memory of one's ancestors—any motivation that considers or expects the response, intentions, feelings, beliefs, or attitudes of others.

> The "others" may be individual persons, and may be known to the actor as such, or may constitute an indefinite plurality and may be entirely unknown as individuals. (Thus, money is a means of exchange which the actor accepts in payment because he orients his action to the expectation that a large but unknown number of individuals he is personally unacquainted with will be ready to accept it in exchange on some future occasion.) (Weber, 1978, p. 22)

Not all human action is social: "Social action does not occur when two cyclists, for example, collide unintentionally; however, it does occur when they try to avoid the collision or sock one another afterwards or negotiate to settle the matter peacefully" (p. 23). Intention is crucial.

It is clear, however, that much of what we consider economic action is social action. Haggling over price, forming a partnership, purchasing a gift, negotiating a contract, hiring a worker, attempting to outwit a competitor, regulating a market—all of these anticipate the actions or feeling states of others and make some judgment of how those others will react in given circumstances. Much business activity, and all organized enterprise, is social action.

Weber has described four forms of social action—instrumentally rational, value-rational, affectual, and traditional. Instrumentally rational action involves an individual's calculation of a course of action in the pursuit of a rationally determined end, for example, profit or market share. This, of course, is the economic rationality of market models, but in Weber's conceptualization it includes a calculus of more than price; it considers as well the likely actions of others as an individual pursues profit or other rational goals.

Instrumentally rational social action predominates in market societies, but it is not the only form of social action involved in the economy. Value-rationality is action oriented toward beliefs or values. Ethically constrained economic behavior and economic activity that is prompted by religious beliefs, such as tithing, are examples of value-rational economic activity.[11] Americans, for example, have no objection to the burial of their dead overseas (e.g., thousands of U.S. servicemen are buried in Korea); this is at least in part an expression of belief that when an individual's life is over it is appropriate for survivors to look to the future. Costly funeral arrangements are generally regarded as unseemly. Asians, however, have a sense of themselves in a temporal continuity that should remain unbroken, and burial anywhere but in ancestral soil is unthinkable. This sense has prompted a range of economic behaviors that would seem wasteful to many Westerners. For example, a Japanese battleship sank in 1943, and "at the end of World War II it was refloated at enormous cost, and the crew's remains recovered and cremated, then presented to relatives" (Hayashi, 1988, p. 84).[12] Such expense borne by an impoverished Japanese state was considered there to be wholly appropriate. One of the important functions of Chinese merchant guilds in imperial China was to maintain accounts to return deceased members' bodies to ancestral tombs for burial (Liu, 1987).

Affectual social action is oriented toward feeling states, particularly emotions. Economic activity that is motivated by revenge or the anticipation of pleasure is an affectually driven form of social action. Charitable contributions may be motivated by beliefs but also by the pleasure that attaches to giving. Finally, traditional social action is prompted by habit, often the habits of generations. For example, the economic patterns of European craft guilds in the Middle Ages were oriented more toward custom than toward the maximization of profit; religious and economic activities were entwined.[13] Guilds in imperial China similarly maintained customary rituals. "The Ningbo guild in Shanghai built up its strength through the Buddhist All Souls' Day festivals it cosponsored with numerous small Ningbo fellow-provincial societies affiliated with various trades in the city, devoted to filial piety, to philanthropy, and to the veneration of literacy" (Le Goff, 1980, p. 68). Economic organization and traditional practices may be entwined, each informing the other and influencing the acts of individuals and groups.

The four types of social action described above are ideal types, models of human orientations to activity, that in fact are always combined in some way. But it is clear that real economic action is not merely "economically rational" in an abstract, impersonal way. The economy is filled with more than greedy hermits; it includes people moved by ethics, regulations, hate, status aspirations, and custom. Economic action—not all of it, but most of it—is social action. An institutional explanation of the sort that I describe begins with the assumption that people consider others when they do business; they are not the isolated individuals of market models.[14]

The Embeddedness of Economic Activity in Institutions

If economic action is rarely the autonomous activities of atomized individuals, then it is the relations of mutually aware persons. Where does this "awareness" come from, and what consequences does it have for the development of firms and other organized economic structures?

It is evident that individuals do not reconstruct norms of exchange each time they meet; rather, they develop mutually agreeable means for the repetitive conduct of business. With time, these patterns become routinized, taken-for-granted understandings of "the way things are done." Indeed, social order of any form, not just economic order, cannot proceed without shared interpretations of action. "These interpretations, or 'typifications,' are attempts to classify the behavior into categories that will enable the actors to respond to it in a similar fashion. The process by which actions become repeated over time and are assigned similar meanings by self and others is defined as institutionalization" (W. R. Scott, 1987, p. 495). It becomes difficult, if not impossible, for an individual to pursue economic action in disregard of the institutionalized behavior patterns of others, particularly if the efforts or goods of others are necessary to the actor's project.

Persons who have had a part in the formation of institutionalized economic norms or who become knowledgeable about them develop a stake in their maintenance; established norms make continuous exchange predictable and simpler than constant negotiation of the terms of exchange. In this sense of making action "simpler," institutionalized norms are "efficient"; they provide previously negotiated, ready-made means for taking care of business. Clearly, efficiency in this sense is not measured against a "most efficient" abstract standard, but actors who disregard institutionalized patterns will certainly meet with social friction of the type hypothesized by market theorists. The most efficient form of economic action from the point of view of an actor is institutionalized action—that is, action knowledgeable in the ways of insiders.[15]

Moreover, patterns and structures that develop over time for purely instrumental purposes may become infused with value, as Selznick (1957) notes: "They are products of interaction and adaptation; they become the receptacles of group idealism; they are less readily expendable" (p. 22). Institutionalized patterns and structures then have both instrumental and value components, technical and ideal qualities. Failure to act in ways that accord with institutionalized norms, even if more abstractly efficient, may signal that the actor is outside the system morally as well as instrumentally, and not to be trusted (for discussion of this point, see Biggart & Hamilton, 1984). For example, in 1983 a member firm of the Toshiba business group violated a U.S.-Japan agreement barring the sale to the Soviet Union of machine tools that could be used for military purposes. When the sale was uncovered in 1987, the president of the largest Toshiba group company resigned in shame, although his firm had no part in or even knowledge of the illegal sale by a smaller independent but affiliated firm (Prestowitz, 1988, p. 154). Because this man served as senior representative of the "community" of Toshiba firms, however, his act was considered proper, even required, given the moral standards of firm behavior in Japan, which is based on communitarian norms. No such act, of course, would be expected in the United States, where firms are embedded in institutions that sustain their autonomy, not their community.

Organizational and ideological arrangements develop to sustain the patterns that have been worked out by actors. The lending and borrowing of money, for example, become routinized in economic organizations such as banks and equity markets. Despite the common need for these services in all industrialized societies, financial concerns are structured and operate differently depending on the institutional setting. Banking laws in the United States—for example, the Glass Steagall Act—prevent banks from investing in corporations, an institutionalized expression of the importance of firm independence for market order. No such laws exist in Japan, where interfirm networks are widely believed to be crucial for maintaining economic stability. Banks, in fact, are important members of Japanese business groups and may be leading investors in corporations (Orrù, Biggart, & Hamilton, 1991). In contrast, banks of any sort are relatively unimportant in Taiwan, where financial activities, including the raising of investment capital, tend to be conducted among families and friends. In a society dominated by family firms, not publicly traded corporations, a range of private financing arrangements have become institutionalized (Jacobs, 1985). When seen in the light of local institutions, Chandler's previously cited characterization of Japan's capital markets as "undeveloped" is clearly ethnocentric, an application of American economic standards to an alien institutional arena.

From an institutional perspective, economic and organizational activities are viewed not as apart from society, but as embedded in it. The particular character of that embeddedness—networks of relations, social beliefs, gender and family structure, and other institutionalized forms of social order such as the state and religion—varies across societies. The extent to which, for example, the polity and the economy are mutually supportive, relatively autonomous, or overtly antagonistic is a subject of institutional explanation and not an a priori assumption. For the most part, however, institutionalists expect that societal sectors have connections of some sort and, in particular, that intrasocietal social relations will frequently partake of similar organizing logics.

Organizational Logics

In what ways are societal sectors connected to each other and, in particular, to the economy? There is no easy answer to this question, and indeed the answer will vary across societies. My own studies and those of others suggest, however, that supraorganizational norms and patterns that express those norms serve as common resources for the structuring of social relations in a society. In their article "The Iron Cage Revisited" (1983), Paul DiMaggio and Walter W. Powell highlight the phenomenon of organizational isomorphism—the tendency of organizations within an institutional environment to resemble each other because of similar constraints and resources (e.g., state regulation, professional group norms). I would argue further, however, that isomorphism results from the application of common organizational logics both across and between societal sectors. By *organizational logic,* I mean a legitimating principle that is elaborated in an array of derivative social practices. In other words, organizational logics are the ideational bases for institutionalized authority relations.

For example, the U.S. economy is based on an institutional logic of autonomous firms and independent actors. Accounting regulations, hiring practices, antitrust regulations—all are expressions of a belief in the correctness of individualism and autonomy (Biggart & Hamilton, 1990). In contrast, in my study of direct-selling organizations in the United States, I noted the widespread use of an alternative, even oppositional, logic frequently expressed as a family metaphor (Biggart, 1989). Direct-selling companies use the model of a patriarchal family to provide both a structure of meaning and a pattern of interaction for distributors; the organizational logic of family is immediately apprehensible and acceptable to women with little paid work experience. Direct selling, as opposed to firms, is characterized by nurturing and diffuse relations, and a number of business practices in the industry are familial in character. The logic of one institution, the patriarchal nuclear family, is used to inform another, a business.

Similarly, in my study cited above with Marco Orrù and Gary Hamilton, we noted the differing logics that organize business groups in Asia (Orrù et al., 1991). Japanese firms enact a communitarian logic, Korean firms a patrimonial logic, and Taiwanese firms a patrilineal logic.[16] Although all are network logics, they differ qualitatively and have important implications for how workers are organized, the character of subcontracting relations between firms, investment patterns, and a host of other economic relations. Each of these logics informs not only business relations but social relations in other institutions in each society. For example, the patrimonial logic of Korean business groups is reproduced in the relations between the state and business, and within Korean families. Patrimonialism has deep historic roots in Korea and provides a readily understood basis on which to organize social relations of various types (Biggart, 1990). Different spheres—the family, the polity, the economy—may use the same or related logics to organize members and to pattern interaction.

Institutional logics may be challenged, and the tenacity of a dominant logic in the face of changing environments is variable, according to recent studies. D. Eleanor Westney (1987) found that industrializing Japan in the late nineteenth century adapted organizational forms from Europe and the United States, but not in a wholesale manner: "In the early Meiji period, Western models provided both inspiration and legitimation; later they continued to supply inspiration, but the grounds for legitimation were increasingly sought in the Japanese tradition and environment" (p. 220). The research of Richard Florida and Martin Kenney (1991) suggests that organizational logics may be deeply rooted in legitimation and practice and survive transplant to an alien institutional arena: Japanese auto companies in the United States reproduce the communitarian relationship they have with subcontractors in Japan.

If actors construct social order, including the economy, by employing intersubjectively meaningful logics, then it is clear that those meanings exist only for those within the bounds of the social order. This basic premise of an institutional argument has important consequences for research methods and causal explanation.

Explanations for institutional structure and practice must be adequate at the level of meaning, that is, understandable from the points of view of participating actors. Organizations, from an institutional perspective (and similar to a cultural perspective), are the consequences of people working out routine means for handling repetitive economic functions. Arrangements are not the "best adapted" or "most efficient" in an instrumentally abstract way. Nor are they "necessary" outcomes of a stage of economic development, as Chandler's theory of the firm suggests. Institutional arguments reject the above forms of explanation as limited by functionalism—that is, confusing consequences with causes.

Rather, I argue that institutional factors such as values, networks of relations, and socially constructed rules shape organizations by limiting possibilities, making some forms of action likely or more "reasonable" because they have the force of understanding and acceptance in the community. But institutional factors do not "cause" organizations in the sense implied by the form of analysis expressed by market models and other explanations that seek answers in the correlation of ahistorically conceived variables such as size, industry characteristics, and product diversity.[17] Any method that relies on high levels of abstraction and seeks to find universal laws will have difficulty uncovering institutional logics where the context is crucial.

This is not to suggest that generalization is impossible in an institutional explanation. But generalization is of a limited form, for example, the ideal types of Weberian analysis. Ideal types summarize common elements of a limited number of real instances of a phenomenon, such as bureaucratic organization or rational capitalism. Generalization is possible at an intermediate level between the hypothesized universal laws of market theories and the unique explanations of some forms of cultural and historical analysis. There can be institutionalized "laws," of course, in the sense that individuals may act as though such laws exist. In an institutional explanation, for example, there is no necessary law of marginal utility or other impersonal system of laws that works to produce the economy; individuals may enact a "law" of marginal utility by assuming the individualistic, calculating orientation that such a law implies. This does not, of course, mean that the "law" has status independent of actors who produce and reproduce it through social interaction. Actors make social and economic systems and, through their knowledgeable reproduction of those systems' patterns, maintain them or change them incrementally through the course of history.

Institutional Analysis
Is Multilevel Analysis

Market theories and some forms of political economy explanation locate crucial explanatory factors in supraorganizational phenomena—for example, the state, industry structure, or economic resources. Cultural analysis often locates the crucial factors at the intraorganizational level—in the minds of actors or in patterns of interpersonal relations. An institutional analysis, because of its concern with both structure and action, by necessity is a multilevel analysis. Indeed, it must not only examine micro- and macro-level phenomena, but must do so in a way that shows their simultaneity: the structure that shapes action, the actions that reproduce structure.

Although institutional research is concerned with both micro and macro levels of analysis, the focus is primarily on the middle range of social life. Institutionalists are concerned mostly with the organized relations and practices that are common to the economy—the structures of business ethics, the networks of ownership and production, the concrete arrangements that direct investment and trade in particular ways. It is in the intermediate range that we are best able to see the impact of both large-scale influences, such as state regulation, and the acts of individuals, such as investment decisions. An institutional theory, therefore, can build on both the more and less abstracted market, cultural, and political economy analyses even while recognizing their sometimes limiting (for the purposes of institutional inquiry) assumptions.

Conclusion

Social theorists are challenged to explain an increasingly complex economic order. It is clear that old theories that posited a developmental sequence from "undeveloped" to "industrialized" cannot explain the diverse patterns of industrialization that exist. Certainly, Japan is as developed as Western nations, but its patterns of development, its economic norms, and its industrial practices are substantially different from those of the United States and even its Asian neighbors in Taiwan and South Korea. For example, the fact that Japan has the largest banks in the world and Taiwan has relatively few and weak ones (despite the world's largest per capita foreign reserve holdings) cannot be explained only through recourse to market or state factors, although each plays a role. Both countries were practically awash in money in the 1980s, and both countries are clearly capitalist societies where banking institutions are assumed to be critical to economic development, as they have been in the West. But more than market and political economy factors are at work here.

In Japan, historically developed institutional factors, dating from before the Meiji Restoration and industrial revolution, created conditions for business group self-financing. Modern-day *keiretsu,* such as Sumitomo and Mitsui, with their huge banks as centerpieces, trace their origins to preindustrial merchant houses under family ownership. Inheritance practices in Japan are based on primogeniture, inheritance of the entire fortune by the eldest son. This practice has allowed merchant family fortunes to remain intact under the stewardship of the heir. Successful families thus have had huge sums of money available to finance the businesses of affiliated branches operating under the "badge" of the mother house. The descendants of the *zaibatsu* merchant houses, the *keiretsu,* continue to rely on their own sources of finance, now institutionalized in banks that serve their credit and other financial needs. Seeing large banks encapsulated within business networks as only the outcome of distorted market conditions, or as only the result of a powerful business class, misses their institutional origins and overlooks the contemporary institutional underpinnings of the Japanese banking system.

Ironically, the weakness of Taiwanese banks can also be traced to a strong family system. Chinese societies practice partible inheritance, that is, division of a family estate equally among all sons. As a result, families divide their fortunes every generation, which militates against the development of large sums of money. Instead, there is great pressure within families to develop multiple businesses, so that at the death of the family head, each son can claim an independent enterprise. Because all Chinese families face the problem of setting up children in business (being an employee is not a desirable status in Taiwan as it is in Japan), a range of informal lending arrangements have arisen within families and among friends to generate investment capital. Strong social norms dictate that one assist financially a kin member or close friend. Banks play a relatively minor role in Taiwan because alternative institutional arrangements, also with preindustrial origins, have obviated the need for banks for some financial functions. Again, an understanding of market factors is important to an understanding of the strong curb market and weak formal banking system in Taiwan, and political economy factors, notably the absence of a strong central bank, are also significant. An institutional explanation, however, integrates these factors into an explanation that begins with the character of the society being explained.

We need theories that can account for difference without reducing cases to unique instances, that do not presume the individualistic character of Western social orders, and that are sensitive to an array of ideal as well as material factors operating in different locations. Although political economy, market, and cultural theories all have contributions to make, an institutional perspective of the type I have outlined here may be especially suited to the comparative analysis of emerging world economic organization. I think, ironically, that a sensitivity to institutional factors may yield better theories of the West. Rather than assume that the United States and Europe are the exemplars of advanced capitalism, the closest empirical instances of the idealized competitive market, Japan and other Asian nations are suggesting that the West is simply one form of capitalist economic development, an expression, no doubt, of the West's own institutional heritage. When we relinquish ethnocentric perspectives, we can begin to look at ourselves and our own institutional heritage more clearly.

Notes

1. The most elaborate treatment of Williamson's perspective is found in his book *The Economic Institutions of Capitalism* (1985).

2. IO economics assumes homogeneous firms whose behavior is dictated by market structure, for example, whether a market is concentrated or has barriers to entry. Porter and other economists interested in strategy take IO economics from the point of view of a focal firm, to argue that a firm should foster structural "imperfections" in a market to its own competitive advantage. Chamberlinian economics, on the other hand, assumes heterogeneous firms and argues that firms behave in ways that exploit their competitive advantages, such as patents and technical know-how. For reviews of these and related market perspectives, see Barney and Ouchi (1986).

3. In earlier work, Gary Hamilton and I discuss the logic of sociological exchange theories (see Hamilton & Biggart, 1985).

4. This is a generalization with important exceptions, however. Although cultural studies are *primarily* concerned with such subjectivist phenomena as language, discourse, symbolism, and meaning, there are certainly cultural studies that see these as embedded in or creating the foundation for social structure. Cultural structuralists such as Foucault, however, typically see culture as the basis for structure, not the reverse, and assume that structure and culture are socially constructed. For a discussion of these issues, see Wuthnow, Hunter, Bergesen, and Kurzweil (1984).

5. The number and variety of cultural theories of organization are large and include conceptualizations of culture as a regulatory mechanism, as a system of shared cognitions, as a

symbolic system, and as a universal infrastructure of the mind's unconscious. For a review of cultural theories and their application to organization theory, see Smircich (1983).

6. In Biggart and Hamilton (1990), we explain in some detail the ethnocentric logic of neoclassical economics and trace its origins in the history of the West.

7. Decision theorists and some economists have in recent years acknowledged that economic models of human decision making are simplistic (see, e.g., Brown & Oxenfeld, 1977; Tversky & Kahneman, 1974). Economists' response to improving their models of economic action for the most part has been to construct laboratory experiments of economic behavior, not to examine economic action as it actually occurs in social life.

8. This observation has been made before by both culture theorists and economists. For an example of the former, see Chie Nanake's (1970) analysis of group structures in Japan and Gary Hamilton and Kao Cheng-Shu's (1987a) discussion of the importance of lineages to Chinese firms. Economists, even while embracing individualist models, also recognize the importance of business groups to Asian economies (see, e.g., Caves & Uekusa, 1976).

9. There are others, besides economists, who use the same logic. For example, U.S. trade negotiators demand that Japan restructure its market to conform more closely to the patterns of the United States, and some political economists describe the "developmental state" in Asian societies as having been responsible for creating systematic market distortions. Both assume the logic of a perfect, Western-style market as the basis of "good" economic organization.

10. The institutional school has emerged from organizational sociology, but its explanatory power is not limited to formal organizations or economic matters. It has potential for explaining all sorts of established social practices and institutions, from cultural expressions to family structure.

11. In earlier work, I have described an entire industry based on value-rationality (Biggart, 1989). In direct selling, distributors believe that the products and services they sell have special, nonmaterial qualities and that selling is an exalted activity that affirms a range of beliefs and values.

12. Hayashi (1988) also compares Eastern and Western notions of time.

13. In the ninth to thirteenth centuries in Europe, an era when trade was growing in new towns and cities, the church sustained a prejudice against the trades, which were oriented toward secular activities. In an attempt to gain legitimacy, trade guilds adopted patron saints and clothed their economic activities in religious robes (Le Goff, 1980, p. 68).

14. My argument for an institutional theory premised on social action differs from those of theorists who describe institutions as taken-for-granted ways of acting in the world. In this latter conceptualization, institutions obscure the interests of actors by promoting uncritical modes of behavior. It is far more useful to see *the extent to which* actors are active agents channeled (but not necessarily determined) by the institutional environments in which they are embedded. For a good discussion of this issue, see DiMaggio (1988).

15. John Meyer and Brian Rowan (1983) made this discovery in studying the organization of schools. Schools display a number of organizational features that cannot be explained as abstractly efficiency enhancing, but failure to have these "modern" features can bring down the wrath of regulators—clearly inefficient from the schools' points of view.

16. Richard Whitley (1990b), using somewhat different terminology, notes these patterns as well.

17. For an excellent discussion of these issues, notably the logical differences between variable and case analysis, see Ragin and Zaret (1983).

2

On the Limits of a Firm-Based Theory to Explain Business Networks

The Western Bias of Neoclassical Economics

NICOLE WOOLSEY BIGGART
GARY G. HAMILTON

he leading business success story of the past two decades cannot be disputed: the tremendous growth and economic development of the East Asian economies. During the 15-year period from 1965 to 1980, Japan and the newly industrialized countries (NICs) of South Korea, Taiwan, Hong Kong, and Singapore grew

AUTHORS' NOTE: This chapter is reprinted here by permission of Harvard Business School Press from "On the Limits of a Firm-Based Theory to Explain Business Networks: The Western at an average annual rate of 8.8%. At the same time, the U.S. economy grew 2.9%. In the period from 1980 to 1985, a time of world recession, Japan grew 3.8%, while the Asian NICs "slowed" to 6.6%. The comparable figure for all industrial market economies for that 5-year period was 2.5%.

Both the popular and the scholarly presses have lauded the economic development of Asia, using such hyperbole as "miracle" and "astounding" to describe nations whose economies were little more than rubble after World War II and the Korean War. Observers have marveled at the ability of countries with poor resources not only to grow, but to become world-class competitors in the most advanced industrial sectors, including automobiles, steel, shipbuilding, electronics, and pharmaceuticals.

It is no small irony that precisely those countries that Westerners have marveled at have come under severe attack for their patterns of economic development and international trade practices. Analysts and trade negotiators describe Japan and its neighbors as being "unfair" in bilateral trading relations and as suffering "imperfections" that "distort" their domestic economies. These criticisms are most often leveled at the dense networks of ties between firms in Asia, ties that look like cartels to Westerners. Network ties link major industrial firms into groups, such as Sumitomo in Japan and Samsung in Korea, as well as the myriad small manufacturers in the Taiwanese economy.

Why the paradox? Why should Asian economies that have been extraordinarily successful by every economic measure at the same time be described as unprincipled and distorted? Is it merely a reflection of Westerners' sense of fair play or perhaps even their own inadequacy in the face of vigorous economic competition? Or is it a fundamental misunderstanding of the patterns of Asian capitalism?

Although it is no doubt frightening to have one's economic well-being challenged by other nations' competitive success, we do not believe that this is the primary reason for the strong American critique of Asian economies. For example, the United States has had substantial trade deficits with its second-largest trading partner, Canada, for years with little public outcry. The recent heavy investment by the Japanese in the United States has met with far more invective than has U.S. investment by the British or the Dutch, two economies that have higher levels of American investment than Japan does.

We believe, rather, that the response to Asian capitalism as unfair and distorted is primarily the result of ethnocentrism, a Western-based view of the proper organization and functioning of a market economy. American economic thinking is largely grounded in the neoclassical economic tradition, which views competition between autonomous economic actors, both individual capitalists and firms acting as fictive individuals, as a necessity of mature capitalism. In numerous ways, the United States has institutionalized competitive individualism in its market structure. Asian economies, in contrast, are organized through networks of economic actors that are believed to be natural and appropriate to economic development. Likewise, Asian nations have institutionalized policies and practices that flow from a network vision of correct market relations.

We argue two points in this chapter. First, Western academic and popular conceptualizations of Asia, particularly those based on the neoclassical model, are biased portrayals of Asian economic dynamics. A Western perspective leads analysts to conclude that Asia's network capitalism rests on market imperfections, and therefore that the vibrant capitalism of the region has been artificially induced and maintained. Second, and more important, the successful network structure of Asian capitalism reveals the neoclassical model to be not a general theory of capitalism, but rather an ethnocentric model developed from Western experience and applicable only to Western economies. We will not argue that neoclassical economics is wrong, merely that its utility is limited to settings where its institutional assumptions are in force.

Markets Are Not All Alike

The neoclassical economic paradigm conceives of ideal conditions for perfect competition: a large number of firms making substitutable products so that buyers have no reason to prefer one firm's output over another's, independent and dispersed firms, and complete knowledge of all offers to buy and sell (Stigler, 1968).

This model of competitive economic relations conceives of actors as isolated units. Capitalists, both buyers and sellers, ideally are independent and mindless of one another and indifferent as to the parties from whom they buy or to whom they sell. Price is the only criterion for a transaction. This is an asocial conceptualization of economic action (Abolafia & Biggart, 1990) in the sense that it believes meaningful social relations are unimportant to competitive outcomes under idealized conditions. Where social relations are recognized to occur, they are viewed pejoratively and called "friction." Social relations in a market can lead only to such anticompetitive practices as price-fixing, restriction of output, and other forms of collusion. Keeping economic actors apart is a crucial condition of capitalism in the neoclassical view.

Western markets, particularly the Anglo-American economies, attempt to approximate tenets of the neoclassical paradigm at the levels of both firms and individuals. Laws, including corporate and employment regulations, stress individual rights and obligations. Contracts, for example, are binding only on the parties involved and not on their families or communities. Employers for the most part hire, promote, and otherwise reward workers based on their personal efforts. Seniority, to many Americans, does not seem a just way of determining pay or promotion. Affirmative action laws similarly express a belief that employment decisions should be made regardless of social characteristics or connections; individual competence and effort should be the bases of selection.

Americans are fearful of hiring spouses, blood relatives, and even friends into the same company. Many firms have antinepotism rules to limit the effects of personal relations in the workplace, effects assumed to be detrimental. Employers may require disclosure of stock ownership and other ties, even through relatives, to outside firms. Disclosure guards against favoritism in awarding contracts, something most Americans think is wrong.

An individualistic institutional structure exists at the corporate level as well. State regulatory agencies, such as the Federal Trade Commission, prevent firms from colluding with each other. Strong antitrust laws enforced by the U.S. attorney general limit monopoly power and the formation of cartels, except under very unusual situations (such as public utilities, where there exists what economists call a "natural" monopoly). The role of the federal government in the U.S. economy is largely a regulatory one. Government does not have a coordinated planning role and does not have a strategic management plan for the place of the United States in the world economy. Its primary function is to maintain competitive—that is, autonomous—conditions between economic actors.

At both the level of individuals and the level of corporations, people in the United States act to maintain an "open" market in which independent buyers, sellers, and workers can pursue their own interests in arm's-length transactions. In the United States, *open* means free from social relations between individuals and firms.

Market Conditions in Asia

The free market conditions that Westerners think are crucial technical requisites for a successful capitalist economy are frequently not in evidence in Asia. In fact, they are often not even presumed to be necessary. Asian economies espouse different institutional logics from those of Western economies, logics rooted in connectedness and relationships: Asians believe that social relations between economic actors do not impede market functioning, but rather promote it. Just as Western economies have institutionalized ways of maintaining autonomy between actors, Asian economies are rooted in institutions that encourage and maintain ties.

For example, the crucial economic actor in Asian societies is typically not the individual, but rather the network in which the individual is embedded. In major Japanese firms, cohorts are often hired, compensated, and promoted, with individual performance differences having little import until late in a career (Clark, 1979). Korean firms encourage workers to nominate their friends and relatives for vacant jobs; Koreans believe that social relations exert pressure on workers to perform well and to work hard for fear of embarrassing their nominators. The major sources of venture capital in Taiwan, a country noted for its economy of small-scale entrepreneurial concerns, are friends and relatives (Biggs, 1988a). Impersonal sources of funds, such as banks and unknown investors, are far less important in Taiwan than in Western societies. In all three countries, buyers favor suppliers with whom they have established relations, rather than least-cost suppliers. They routinely violate the neoclassical expectation that price is the critical factor in purchase decisions.

Although relationships are manifested in multiple ways at the interpersonal level in Asian business, they are seen dramatically and most importantly in business networks linking Asian firms. It is impossible to overestimate the importance of business networks—sometimes called enterprise or business groups—to the development of Asian capitalism. The Japanese economy is dominated by *kigyo shudan,* modern-day descendants of pre-World War II *zaibatsu,* family-controlled conglomerates. *Kigyo shudan* are networks of firms in unrelated businesses that are joined together, no longer by family ties, but by central banks or trading companies. Michael Gerlach (1992) has recently argued that these intermarket networks constitute a form of capitalism that he calls "alliance capitalism." Many of the largest firms in Japan are members of these major business networks: Mitsubishi, Mitsui, Sumitomo, Fuji, Dai-Ichi, and Sanwa. Other forms of networks also link Japanese businesses; for example, a major manufacturer and its affiliated subcontractors (e.g., the Toyota "independent group") and small neighborhood retailers (*gai*) may invest together (Orrù, Hamilton, & Suzuki, 1989).

The South Korean economy is dominated by networks that on the surface resemble Japan's, but in fact have substantial differences (Amsden, 1989a; Biggart, 1990; Hamilton & Biggart, 1988; Kim, 1991; Orrù, Biggart, & Hamilton, 1991; Whitley, 1990a). South Korean *chaebol* are networks of firms owned and controlled by single persons or families and organized through central staff, which may be holding companies or "mother" firms. By far the most powerful actors in the Korean economy are the major *chaebol* networks, which include Samsung, Hyundai, Lucky-Goldstar, and Daewoo.

The Japanese and Korean economies are ruled by networks of medium-sized to very large firms. Networks are important in Taiwan, too, but they link smaller numbers of smaller firms (Hamilton & Biggart, 1988; Hamilton & Kao, 1990; Numazaki, 1986). The leading economic actors in Taiwan, although occupying a less central position than the *kigyo shudan* or *chaebol,* are the family firms and family-owned conglomerates, which are called *jituanqiye.* Chinese business networks are usually based on family and friendship ties between owners and partners who often cross-invest in businesses, hold multiple positions throughout the network, and act as suppliers or upstream producers to downstream firms.

What the American economy works so studiously to prevent—connections between individuals, links between firms—Asian economies accept as appropriate and inevitable. Moreover, Asian nations have institutionalized networks and built economic policies around the presence and presumption of social relations among market actors.

Explaining Differences

With the extraordinary success of Asian economies, both businesspeople and scholars have attended to the apparent differences between Asian and

Western business practices. Analysts hope to understand the differences in order to explain success, to project patterns of growth, and to predict likely competitive outcomes of Asian economic practices. There are diverse explanations for Asian economic differences from the West, but three types of theories are most influential: development theories, culture theories, and market imperfection theories.

Development Theories

Development theories are concerned with the factors that aid or impede economies in their presumed march toward industrialization. In their earliest form, "modernization" theories assumed a linear progression that all nations passed through on the path toward development into modern capitalist economies, epitomized by the United States and industrialized Europe. There was a presumption that stages of development were more or less alike and that at some unspecified future moment there would be a convergence, with all market economies having similar market institutions—for example, a capitalist class, a freely accessible money and banking system, and a rational orientation toward economic matters.

More recent versions of modernization theory argue that learning is possible; countries can skip stages by observing and emulating more advanced nations, or by having "modern" economic practices imposed on them —through colonial subjugation, for example, or as a precondition for development loans. Alice Amsden's *Asia's Next Giant: South Korea and Late Industrialization* (1989a) is in this genre, arguing that South Korea was able to industrialize rapidly, leapfrogging early development stages, by appropriating technologies and processes formulated by more advanced nations.[1]

Alternatively, another set of development theories, conventionally labeled "dependency" theories, argues that the more developed industrial economies are systemically linked to and impede the development of the less developed economies (Evans & Stephens, 1988). Powerful advanced nations maintain the dependency of less developed economies by enforcing, for example, unfavorable trading relations or lending policies. A web of political relations shapes nations' differential possibilities for advancement.

There are a number of criticisms of development theories (e.g., Evans & Stephens, 1988). It is increasingly clear, for example, that there is no convergence toward a single model of capitalism as exemplified by the West.

It is also equally apparent that the world economy is neither a monolithic economic system nor easily divided into core and peripheral areas (Gereffi & Hamilton, 1990). Moreover, Asia's differences, as well as those of some other industrializing nations, are not disappearing as these nations become more developed (Orrù et al., 1991). Although it is certainly true that nations can learn from more developed economies, the learning thesis is not especially useful because it cannot predict which countries can or will learn, or indeed which models they will choose to emulate. For example, both Taiwan and South Korea were colonies of Japan, and both received substantial economic aid and policy directives from the United States. Neither economy looks very much like the United States or Japan, although Korea has adopted some elements of Japanese industrial organization.

One branch of development economics, the endogenous growth models, does ask why differences in the fact and rate of economic growth and well-being persist over time. Neoclassical economic models predict that capital, both labor and financial, flows to the most efficient locales, eventually limiting nation-state differences. In fact, there is great diversity in per capita economic well-being and national growth rates, and the differences endure. Endogenous growth models posit that variations are attributable to differences in trade policies and human capital differences—that is, the differential investment in learning by various labor forces. Labor forces are not all the same in their approach to hard work, learning, and productivity. Endogenous growth models go beyond an earlier individualistic approach to human capital, which focused on the returns on investment in learning by individuals to posit that there are social returns or effects, at the level of groups such as families and firms, to the acquisition of new skills and orientations by labor. It seems to us that this perspective is important in raising the unit of observation from the individual to the group, showing the cumulative effects of individual economic decisions (for example, to invest in schooling rather than to take a low-skilled job). By focusing on effects, however, endogenous growth models do not seek answers as to why observably different patterns are pursued in different locales, whether they be trade policies or human capital decisions. R. E. Lucas (1988), for example, dismisses the possibility of identifying the social impulse for human capital acquisition: "We can no more directly measure the amount of human capital a society has, or the rate at which it is growing, than we can measure the degree to which a society is imbued with the Protestant Ethic" (p. 35).

Culture Theories

Culture theories do precisely what the endogenous growth models leave aside: attempt to account for the differential bases for economic action and organization. They are popular in journalistic accounts of Asian management practice, but they also have academic standing (e.g., Berger & Hsiao, 1988). Culture—the beliefs, values, and symbols of a society—is understood to be the basis for economic practices and institutions. For example, the Japanese penchant for involving all members of a firm in decision making is seen to be an expression of a belief in the importance of consensus and harmony (*wa*) (Alston, 1986). In contrast, the American CEO is expected to make independent decisions, probably after consulting subordinates, but ultimately to take individual responsibility. The two sets of decision-making practices, common in their respective economies, are explained by culture theory as respective expressions of the cultural values of communitarianism and individualism.

Cultural explanations have much truth in them; clearly, a preference for groupness or individualism will be reflected in commercial practices. Culture, however, is a problematic basis for comparative analysis (Hamilton & Biggart, 1988, pp. S69-S74). American culture, even if one could define it, cannot explain the differences in business practices one encounters in the United States. Is IBM's strong hierarchical management style the "true" organizational expression of American culture? Or is Apple Computer's decentralized and team-based system the "real" exemplar of American ideals? When comparing Japan with the West, which Western practices form the basis of comparison? Culture theories, by building up from rich and diverse data in a single society, make generalizations—and hence comparisons—difficult.

Market Imperfection Theories

Market imperfection theories are based on the logic of neoclassical economics and offer the most important explanation of Asian distinctiveness. Under perfectly competitive market conditions, optimal firm size is a function of the demand for and the economies of scale to produce a product (Stigler, 1968, p. 1). When markets are not fully competitive—that is, when they suffer from constraints—firm size is influenced by the constraints as well as by production and demand requirements. For example, when there is no market, as in a socialist command economy, decrees by the state will influence the size and structure of the firm. Although economists recognize that a fully competitive market is an ideal condition that does not exist anywhere in reality, they use this conception of the ideal market and the optimal firm as a model against which to assess real conditions. They can then compare actual markets and firms to see how well they conform to the ideal. Deviations are either more or less "perfect."

This conceptualization of the perfect market, with its conditions of autonomy and impersonality and its resultant "optimal" firms, was developed as a means to understand the structure and functioning of Western societies, primarily the British and American economies. Economists, however, do not regard this model as an abstract, ethnocentric representation of these economies, but rather as a general model of capitalism that can be applied worldwide.

According to neoclassical theory, there are only two forms of economic organization: markets and firms (also called hierarchies). Economists have difficulty applying this model of markets and firms to Asia, with its developed interfirm networks (Aoki, 1984b, 1990; Goto, 1982). Networks are neither independent market actors nor hierarchically governed firms. Nonetheless, Western economists attempt to interpret Asian economic organization in terms of this dualistic neoclassical conceptualization. Alfred Chandler (1984), for example, describes the Japanese *zaibatsu,* the historical precursor to the *kigyo shudan,* as an "organization comparable to the M-form," or multidivisional firm that originated in the United States (p. 22). Nathaniel Leff (1976, 1978) writes that Asian firms, as well as firms in other non-Western societies, actually constitute a single firm organized on a "group principle." "The group is a multicompany firm which transacts in different markets but which does so under common entrepreneurial and financial control" (Leff, 1978, p. 664). Others endorse the idea that despite some differences, the Asian business group is the functional equivalent of the Western firm. Like Western firms, some groups are large and monopolistic, whereas others are small or operate in competitive markets in which the group principle allows economies of scale without actually expanding the size of firms.

Several Japanese economists have slightly qualified this view (e.g., Aoki, 1984b; Goto, 1982). Knowing Japan well, they argue that Japanese business groups are neither firms nor markets, but constitute an intermediate phenomenon that exists between the two. They argue that Japanese business groups do not operate like a single firm. They have neither a single set of owners nor a tightly integrated system of financial controls. They are not independent, competitive firms, nor do they constitute a single megafirm. They are networks, according to Goto (1982), that buffer and channel market forces.

Despite some disagreement about how to categorize Asian business groups, economists do concur on how to explain their presence. Virtually all use a theory of market imperfections that to neoclassical economists seems self-evident. As Leff (1978) notes:

> The group pattern of industrial organization is readily understood as a microeconomic response to well-known conditions of market failure in the lessdeveloped countries. In fact, the emergence of the group as an institutional mode might well have been predicted on the basis of familiar theory and a knowledge of the environment in these countries. (p. 666)

Chandler (1984) explains the differences between the Japanese *zaibatsu* and the M-form American and European conglomerates by citing "undeveloped" capital markets in Japan. Even Goto (1982) explains Japanese business group networks the same way:

> The group is an institutional device designed to cope with market failure as well as internal organizational failure. Under certain circumstances, transactions within a group of firms are more efficient than transactions through the market or transactions through the internal organization of the firm. (p. 69)

More recently, but using the same logic, Jorgensen, Hafsi, and Kiggundu (1986) have argued that in developing countries, a category in which they place Japan, market imperfections occur in the course of "striving for self-sufficiency" and the absence of an adequate "density of market transactions" (p. 424). In promoting a "rational," risk-controlling policy for industrialization, governments promote such market "distortions" as tariffs to protect infant industries, exchange controls to create price advantages, and administrative hierarchies to coordinate resource allocation and other forms of market imperfections (p. 426). They note four common "aberrations" in developing economies: the entrepreneurial family firm, the industrial cluster, the multinational corporation subsidiary, and the state-owned enterprise (pp. 427-432). All four of these so-called aberrations are common in Asian economies, even the most developed, and are not disappearing.

There are other variants of the market imperfections thesis. Political economists emphasize the importance of the "developmental state" in creating systemic distortions, both in the economy and in the society, that allow for concentrated capital accumulation and rapid development. Such theorists thus create a link between market imperfection and development theories. American trade negotiators likewise argue that Japan has created "structural impediments" to "free" trade that prevent American access to Japanese markets; most notable of the alleged impediments are business groups that limit competition. Although they focus more on political factors that create distortions, the logic of both political economists and trade negotiators is much the same as the market imperfections thesis: Asian economies deviate from the Western ideal and therefore suffer imperfections.

We believe that market imperfection theories, like development and culture theories, do not explain the Asian "difference" very well. The neoclassical paradigm is a framework that assumes one fundamental "perfect" economy against which real economies can be gauged. Although it does not exist anywhere in reality, the model is an approximation of the market economies that developed during Western industrialization. It is not a theory of Asian capitalism but a theory of Western capitalism applied to Asia, and its logic is akin to the logic of Henry Higgins's question in *My Fair Lady:* "Why can't a woman be more like a man?" Answers to a question so framed can only detail the ways in which a woman deviates from a man; they cannot lead to discovery of what a woman is. A market imperfection theory can describe the ways in which Asian capitalism deviates from the neoclassical ideal, but it cannot discover the principles of Asian capitalism.

Evidence of the economic vitality of Asia leads us to advance two points. First, a model of Asian capitalism based on Asia's institutional foundations is overdue. It stretches credibility to describe Japan, the world's second-largest economy, as "imperfect" or "deviant," even for analytic purposes. Second, the poor fit of the neoclassical model to the Asian case suggests to us not an imperfect economy, but rather an inappropriate theory. Asia calls into question the presumption that this model is a general theory of capitalism. We will argue that the neoclassical model is more suited to the institutional arena that it was developed to explain: England and the United States. In fact, neoclassical economics rests on an institutional theory of firm autonomy that displays great power in explaining Western economic dynamics. It is not, however, a general theory of capitalism.

The Development of Markets in the West

The neoclassical model is based on a central idea: the autonomy of economic actors, both individuals and firms, who seek their self-interest in economic matters. Actors go into the marketplace and, mindless of all social and moral considerations, rationally calculate exchanges based only on price. This portrait of economic actors as individuated, asocial, and rational is the useful fiction that economists have drawn to provide a parsimonious behaviorist model of economic action. Although few economists would argue that any real person acts exactly this way, it is assumed that this is the ideal that most people, at least in the aggregate, approximate.

Homo economicus is a generic individual distinguished not by sex, ethnicity, religion, age, or any other social characteristic. The presumption is that any person, in any place, at any time would behave more or less the same way—that is, as a rational individual. In building on this central idea, neoclassical economics assumes that social relations and characteristics do not make significant differences in economic choice. To the extent that these assumptions have a universal reality, they support claims that the neoclassical paradigm is a general theory of capitalism.

Recently, a number of scholars have attempted to question tenets of the neoclassical paradigm. For example, the individual decision-making studies of psychologists Tversky and Kahneman (1974) suggest that people are not the hyperrational actors assumed by the model. Economic sociologist Amitai Etzioni (1988) has marshaled substantial evidence that people consider moral as well as economic factors in making economic choices. Anthropologist Richard Schweder's (1986) anthropological studies of a community in India demonstrate that economic rationality is based on substantive beliefs, not abstract calculus. Similarly, Mark Granovetter (1985) has argued that the economy is embedded in social relationships and is not the aggregate activity of isolated individuals. Our own studies have suggested, as we do in this chapter, that Asian economic action is based on different principles of social action, principles developed through the historical experience of Asian nations (see Hamilton & Biggart, 1988; Orrù et al., 1991).

Although these and other studies question crucial elements of the neoclassical model, particularly as they apply to non-Western locales, it remains clear that the model does describe in important ways the aggregate dynamics of Western economies, especially those of the United States.

We believe that it is possible to reconcile the power of the neoclassical paradigm for understanding much of the West with its limitations in explaining microeconomic phenomena, especially in non-Western settings: The neoclassical model assumes and tacitly incorporates many of the features of the Western societies it was developed to explain. Its "ideal typical" premises aptly characterize the institutional setting in which Anglo-American capitalism developed.[2]

The Institutional Foundations of Western Markets

The rise of markets in Western Europe followed what Barrington Moore (1966) calls the "routes" that Western nations took in moving from feudalism to modernity. At the beginning of this period, sometime before the thirteenth century, markets were embedded in an *oikos* economy dominated by aristocratic households. A market city either constituted a part of the manor and was actually owned by the lords of the land (Koebner, 1964) or existed as a free city, characterized by Weber (1968a, pp. 1212-1236) as a "nonlegitimate" enclave located at the margin of a manorial economy. Although it varied from region to region, the feudal economy was embedded in the political structure of Western Europe, and when that structure began to change decisively with the rise of absolutism, market economies also began to change.

Absolutism gradually moved the organizing locus of the economy from manors to cities, particularly national cities such as London and Paris that were dominated by kings. Mercantilism followed an economic policy designed to fill royal treasuries, which were used mainly to pay for navies and land armies needed to defend or expand territory. When European kings had difficulty gaining revenues from territory owned by their fellow aristocrats, they tried to compensate by creating royal companies, such as the East India Company, designed to generate royal surplus from overseas adventures. Mercantilistic policies created national urban-centered, consumer-oriented economies. Urban-centered consumption in turn fostered an integrated marketing system linking urban, rural, and overseas areas and nurtured rural industries that produced raw resources and handicraft items for urban consumption (Jones, 1987). Although commercial markets were certainly growing and prospering, the mercantilistic economy rested on royal institutions, including the kings' courts and the kings' companies.

The revolutionary period, starting in the last half of the eighteenth century, entirely changed the institutional structure of Western economies and accelerated the growth of "free market" capitalism. Social scientists have described the changes from a mercantilistic to a free market economy as a "great transformation" (Polanyi, 1957). The phrase is somewhat hyperbolic for economic activity but quite accurate for the institutional change that occurred after these revolutions, a period in which all the major economic institutions that we associate with capitalism first developed.

The change in government from absolutism to democracy marked a pivotal switch from an institutional environment based on centralized public spheres to one dispersed through decentralized private spheres. With great insight, Michel Foucault (1979) has described this shift in connection with the institutions for criminal justice, but an even larger and more profound shift occurred in the regulation and conduct of the economic activity. Isomorphic with the shift in other institutional spheres, the shift in the economic sphere in Western Europe and the United States moved from centrally instituted economies through royal banks, companies, courts, market taxes—all institutions against which Adam Smith (1991) inveighed in his *Wealth of Nations*—to a "self-regulating" economy. The economic counterparts of Bentham's panopticon that so intrigued Foucault (1979) were the commodity and equity markets created in the same period as circular panopticon prisons. Both institutional structures embodied the principles of self-regulation: In the circular market pit, where all buyers and all sellers exchange simultaneously, everyone sees everything.

The Institutionalization of Firm Autonomy

Underlying self-regulation in markets, as in prisons, was the notion of the autonomy of individual units. In the criminal justice system, as in society in general, rested the presumption that every individual was distinct and responsible for his or her own actions. The same principles applied in the economy: Every firm was distinct and responsible for its own actions.

This belief in individual autonomy, as applied to both people and their businesses, arose out of an intellectual tradition that is characteristically Western. The strands of this tradition can be traced to antiquity, particularly to the Roman legal system, which had decisive effects on modern Western European state structure, citizenship, and commercial law, and to Christianity, which conceptualized each individual as a distinct soul-bearing entity.

Despite the many strands, however, the institutionalization of individual autonomy did not occur until after absolutism gave way to democracy.

The cornerstone of self-regulating markets based on firm autonomy came from the Enlightenment philosophers' reconceptualization of private property. In Western Europe, with the enactment of the constitutional state based on natural laws, ownership and control of property were not so much an economic issue as a political issue with economic implications. Property rights became a crucial principle in the articulation of democracy, an idea used by citizens to claim rights over jurisdictions that formerly had been held by absolutist monarchs. The writings of eighteenth-century philosophers such as John Locke and, slightly later, Adam Smith are rife with the notion of private property and its implications for individual political control vis-à-vis an authoritarian state. Therefore, when constitutional states were enacted, the right to property was embodied in individualism, in the very conception of what an individual is.

The idea of individual autonomy in a society is the principle of nineteenth-century democracy, and the idea of firm autonomy in the economy is the principle of self-regulating markets in a democratic society. These ideas were not only abstract philosophies, but also working principles gradually instituted throughout society to conform to changing social and economic conditions. Such abstract ideas have a very technical dimension when they are used to order everyday reality.

The legal assignment of private property rights requires a clear delineation of who claims ownership and what is owned. When nonstate businesses in the West were subsumed under the legal definition of private property, business firms became in principle separate, distinct, and independent. They became conceptualized as persons—as autonomous, legally indivisible units that could form contractual links with people and with other firms. The clearest demonstration of this occurred in the United States, where under the Fourteenth Amendment corporations were held to be persons and could not be "deprived of life, liberty, or property" without due process.

In the early nineteenth century, when businesses were small and individually or family owned, firms were equated with property and due process applied to their owners, and not to the firms as separate entities. With the growth of American capitalism and large firms with multiple owners, the firm itself took on the status of an individual. The test case in the U.S. Supreme Court in 1882 was a conflict between a California county and the

Southern Pacific Railway Company. The issue was who owed taxes to the government. The Court upheld the idea, already established, that "incorporation" created a unified entity—literally, a body—that had an existence over and above the parts that made it up.

This legal formulation had far-reaching effects on the development of Western business practices. Importantly, the law required the individuation of firms. Each firm was conceptualized as a corporate body, a single entity distinct from all others. Business practices conformed to this principle, not because it was efficient or necessary, but because it was the law and deeply rooted in Western political and social ideas. The principle of individual corporateness established an institutional environment that formed a basis for Western capitalism's organizational structure and dynamics.

As legislated by most Western countries, and independently by states in the United States, laws of incorporation require firm autonomy and require the specification of ownership and corporate assets. National and state laws of taxation demand accounting procedures that delineate ownership and income. Capital markets assume that firms are autonomous: The loan provisions of the banking system, the equity provisions of the stock markets, and the insurance provisions of industry all have institutionalized the principle of firm autonomy. Antitrust legislation, in working to prevent the formation of cartels and monopolies, provides sanctions to sustain autonomous corporations.

Firm autonomy has been institutionalized in many ways. A part of this process has been to work out legally and procedurally modes of legitimate interfirm linkages. That firms are really autonomous from all other firms or that individuals are entirely independent of one another is, of course, a fiction. But it is a fiction that was created historically as a means to specify institutionally the interrelations among people in the creation of a democratic political order. The fiction of autonomy became true, with time, for firms as well as for people. Interrelationships between businesses and people in the West are specified in legal terms, through contracts—that is, through autonomous entities exercising their free will to make agreements. Firm autonomy and personal autonomy are not independent of the institutions that reinforce such autonomy.

Therefore, to see firm autonomy as a universal element of capitalism, as something inherent to it in all times and all places, is really a misreading of history and of economies. It is a profoundly ethnocentric point of view.

The Development of Markets in Asia

It is incorrect to think that Asian economies "matured" only after being exposed to Western capitalism. Although it is certainly the case that they changed considerably after the nineteenth-century opening of Chinese and Japanese economies, it is not the case that the respective economies were undeveloped before the nineteenth century. The dazzling innovation in, and virtual explosion of, Western societies and economies after the seventeenth century has obscured the fact that Asian societies were economically quite advanced and quite complex. Although neither was heading toward industrial capitalism, both Japanese and Chinese economies were quite dynamic and quite old. They had been mature for a long time.

The organization of these economies, like the organization of society, rested on principles quite different from those found in the West. The great historian of Chinese science Joseph Needham has clarified these differences by contrasting Chinese "associative thinking" with what he calls the Western "billiard ball" conception of reality. Westerners, he says, see their world in terms of "rational" cause and effect: Like billiard balls bouncing off each other, one motion causes another motion, which causes another motion in turn. Had he written later, he might have called this the "rational choice" model of human behavior: reduced to individual units, causative, and lawlike.

According to Needham (1956a, pp. 279-291), a Chinese worldview is completely unlike a Western one. Although highly developed and more advanced than Western science until the seventeenth and eighteenth centuries, Chinese science did not rest on correlations based on cause and effect, on first principles, or on lawlike assertions. Instead, Chinese science rests on a conception of order. In the Chinese thinking, order rests on a stable relationship among things. There is order in a family when all the relationships in a family are obeyed; there is order in a country when all the reciprocal relationships between subjects and rulers are fulfilled; there is order in the universe when humankind fulfills its relationship with heaven and earth. Needham compares this Chinese notion of order to a dance that has no beginning and no ending and in which all partners dance in time to the music, "an extremely and precisely ordered universe, in which things 'fitted' so exactly that you could not insert a hair between them" (p. 286). Everything causes everything else. Therefore, what is essential in life is not the individual cause and effect, but the order in the group as a whole.

In Asian societies the principle informing human behavior is not for people to obey the law, whether God's laws or natural laws or economic laws. Instead, it is for people to create order by obeying the requirements of human relationships as these are manifest in a situational context. The person in Asia is always embedded in ongoing relationships and is not an abstract entity that exists outside society, not even for purposes of rational calculation.

Just as individualism is institutionalized in Western societies, social relationships are institutionalized in Asian societies. Legal codes in Asia, as many have argued, are in fact codifications of morality embedded in social relationships. For instance, the Tang Dynasty legal codes, which influenced Japan's legal codes and were passed down more or less intact through all the remaining dynasties in China, made unfilial behavior to one's parents one of the "Ten Abominations" and a crime punishable by death. Other relationships, such as those outlined in the *wulun* (five relationships: parent-child, emperor-subject, husband-wife, older sibling-younger sibling, and friends), were upheld in the magistrate's courts as well as in quasi-legal settings such as the lineage, village, and merchant associations. Because everyone has a responsibility for order in a group, failure to uphold one's responsibility in a relationship could lead not only to personal punishment, but also to the punishment of others in one's group. In this way mutual surveillance has come to be an essential part of the institutionalization of social relationships in East Asian societies. The Western concept of an individual's "right to privacy" has no meaning in an Eastern setting.

The eminent Chinese sociologist Fei Xiaotong (1992) shows that this relational logic produces a society that rests on social networks. Every person is a part of multiple networks: family, friends, neighbors, coworkers—the list goes on and on. Each person is not an independent, self-willed actor, but rather is responsible simultaneously for the order within multiple networks. Fei shows that network ties are ranked, with family ties taking precedence over more distant kinship ties, which in turn may (or may not, depending on the context) have priority over ties with other types of people. Fei also shows that every institutional sphere, including the economy, is based on a structure of networks of relationships.

The Institutional Foundations of Asian Markets

Using these insights, we can show that network organization is an institutional feature of Asian capitalism. These networks precede the modern era.

For instance, in China during the Ming and Qing Dynasties (extending from the sixteenth century to the twentieth century), commercial activities and handicraft industries were highly developed, with a level of production and a volume of movement exceeding all other locations in the world until the eighteenth century. This level of complexity was achieved without support from the state, even in such matters as maintaining a currency, establishing weights and measures, and creating commercial laws. In short, creating order within the worlds of merchants and artisans was not a function undertaken by the imperial state, but one that remained in the hands of those actually engaged in business.

Through *huiguan,* associations of fellow regionals, merchants and artisans themselves established and enforced economic standards that created pre- dictability and continuity in the marketplace (Hamilton, 1985). *Huiguan* were literally meeting halls, places where people from the same native place would congregate. As a number of researchers have shown, all the main merchant groups in late imperial China were out-of-towners organized through *huiguan* (Fewsmith, 1983; Golas, 1977; Hamilton, 1979; Skinner, 1977). Within the *huiguan,* people with common origins were pledged to a moral relationship (*tongxiang guanxi*) that generated sufficient trustworthi- ness for them to monopolize an area or areas of business for themselves. They would set and enforce standards for the trade as well as moral standards for fellow regionals in the trade.

Although the regional associations mediated the trading relationships, the actual firms engaged in business were always family firms. The family firms, through their ties with other firms, often owned by fellow regionals, stretched beyond any one locale. In fact, through using native-place ties as the medium of organization, merchants were able to monopolize commerce in a commodity for an entire region, as the Swatow merchants did for the sugar trade for all of China. The success of the overseas Chinese in South- east Asia in the nineteenth century was organizationally based on regional networks.

In the premodern era, Japanese merchants were organized quite differently from the Chinese merchants. Japanese merchants were organized as mem- bers of city-based guilds. Unlike Chinese firms, which would come and go, Japanese merchant and artisan firms were members of stable communities of firms, each one of which would be passed from father to eldest son or to a surrogate for him. Whereas Chinese firms would often be dissolved at the death of the owner because of partible inheritance, many Japanese firms continued intact for generations. Moreover, as members of stable networks of urban-based firms, Japanese merchants often developed long-term creditor-debtor relationships with members of the samurai class.

In the modern era, the same general network configurations persist both in overseas Chinese communities, including Taiwan, Hong Kong, and Southeast Asia, and in modern Japan. Continually changing patrilineal networks of small firms that connect near and distant kin, and frequently friends, into production-and-supply networks characterize modern Chinese economies. Likewise, relatively stable business networks of large firms dominate the modern Japanese economy. Neither Asian social sphere has ever had a legacy of autonomous firms comparable to those of the West, nor are they likely to develop. Recent scholarship confirms that the institutional environments that support associative network relationships remain strong in Asia at the interpersonal, business, and state levels.

Conclusion: The Neoclassical Paradigm as an Institutional Theory

The fundamental assumptions of neoclassical economics include the idea that economic actors are rational and autonomous, and that they seek their self-interest independent of social relations or characteristics. Even a brief examination of the history of Western Europe demonstrates that these characteristics of individuals, to the extent that they are true now, were not always evident. In feudal society, people were not autonomous but were bound by traditional ties of fealty and homage. In absolutist Europe, people belonged to the "body politic" that was personified by the king himself (Kantorowicz, 1957). Kings "embodied" nations, so that individuals within those jurisdictions were presumed to have no ultimate autonomy. Only after the institutionalization of the constitutional states in the West did an order arise in which the building blocks of societies and economies—people and firms—became rationally and systematically individuated.

The factors that neoclassical economics assumes are universal traits of the human condition are, in fact, part of the development of the modern West. Western institutions are embodiments of beliefs in individual autonomy and economic rationality. Now institutionalized, these principles are reproduced by individuals and firms who go about acting "rationally" and "autonomously." Neoclassical economics captures, at least at some level, institutional characteristics of American and European societies, and it would be surprising if this theory did not work well in explaining important aspects of Western economic activity. Nonetheless, this paradigm cannot sustain a claim to universal status. It fits poorly the Asian economies that do not have the same institutional heritage. Asian societies have never had a Western-style legal system that treated each person as a separate entity, equal to all others. Asia has had no salvationist religion from which to derive a principle of individual rights. Individuals are not the basic social, economic, or political units in Asia. Rather, networks of people linked together through differentially categorized social relationships form the building blocks of Asian social order and derive from Asia's institutional history. Individuals play roles in these networks, to be sure, but it is the networks that have stability. The presence of networks—of kin, of friends, of fellow regionals— is institutionalized in business and other social practices. Persuasive explanations for the success of Asian business will ultimately come from an institutional analysis of Asian societies and the economies that are embedded in them. Explanations will not come—indeed, cannot come—from attempts to apply a theory rooted in Western experience to an alien institutional arena. That can result only in explaining Asia as "imperfect" and "distorted."

Notes

1. Earlier versions of this theory are found in the work of Marion Levy (1972) and the very sophisticated treatment of Ronald Dore (1973) as applied to Japan.

2. This point requires a short digression into the methods of what Milton Friedman calls "positive economics." Friedman (1953) makes it clear that not even those economists who believe fully in the utility of models of perfect competition would argue for the universality and the validity of these theories. Friedman argues for the utility of economic models, but at the same time says that they are not valid or universal in an absolute sense. In this regard, economic models resemble Weberian ideal types more than they resemble natural laws. Economic models represent a slice of reality from which a few causal factors or processes are reformulated on a more abstract plane and are made more precise and internally logical. The model is then applied back to the same or like contexts from which the main elements have been abstracted in order to see how well the model predicts the actual behavior. "The ideal types," says Friedman, "are not intended to be descriptive; they are designed to isolate the features that are crucial for a particular problem" (p. 36). In this role economic models, logically, neither make a truth claim nor require an assumption of universality. The model merely has to meet the test of usefulness.

3

Varieties of Hierarchies and Markets

An Introduction

GARY G. HAMILTON
ROBERT C. FEENSTRA

Varieties of Markets and Hierarchies

Institutional economics and economic sociology have developed rapidly and in tandem in recent years. Both subfields have moved from positions of peripheral concern to positions of central concern in their respective disci-

AUTHORS' NOTE: This chapter is reprinted here by permission of Oxford University Press from "Varieties of Hierarchies and Markets: An Introduction," by Gary G. Hamilton and Robert C. Feenstra, *Industrial and Corporate Change,* 1995, vol. 4, pp. 51-91. Copyright 1995 by Oxford University Press; all rights reserved. We gratefully acknowledge the research assistance of Wai-Keung Chung and Eun Mie Lim, and the support of the Ford Foundation for this research project. We also wish to thank Richard Swedberg for his comments on an earlier draft.

plines. In the development of both subfields, no distinction has been more formative than that between "market" and "hierarchy," between the "invisible hand" of market forces and the "visible hand" of authoritative organizations. In most of the literature this distinction is formulated as a continuum connecting polar opposites, with markets at one end and hierarchies at the other. Economists and sociologists enter the discussion about these concepts from opposite poles, with both trying to make their poles of orientation representative of the entire continuum. Economists argue that rational maximizing logics carry over into nonmarket situations, and sociologists argue that nonmarket social relations permeate all situations, including markets. Turning on alternative visions of societal order, this debate is less about the distinction between markets and hierarchies than about which interpretation of the world is correct. Because rational calculation and social relationships always coexist, this debate, though interesting and sometimes fruitful, is unending. More perniciously, however, rigid adherence to one interpretation over the other undermines the integrity of making the distinction between markets and hierarchies in the first place. As Williamson (1991) quips in a paraphrase of Clausewitz's aphorism, hierarchies are "a continuation of market relations by other means" (p. 271).

In this chapter we want to reformulate the markets-versus-hierarchies debate by reconceptualizing the notion of hierarchy in line with what Coase (1937, pp. 403-404) regards as the "essential" feature of economic organizations: their authoritative structure. Economic organizations ("firms" in Coase's classic article, but viewed more broadly here as economic organizations) are, above all, authoritative organizations that structure relationships according to established rules of conduct and allow, in the context of such organizations, owners and managers of resources to decide how to participate effectively in the marketplace. In most of the recent literature, hierarchy is treated very narrowly, as a "governance structure" that is internal to the firm but that derives wholly from external market conditions. The narrowness of this characterization of hierarchy, however, produces many ambiguities that limit the clarity and precision of economic and sociological analyses, particularly those having a comparative or a historical focus. One such ambiguity is the necessity to propose omnibus "hybrid," intermediate or network types of economic organization to analyze those many economic situations that are characterized by neither markets nor firms (Powell, 1990; Thorelli, 1986; Williamson, 1991).

In order to clarify the distinction between markets and hierarchies, we will supplement Coase's original distinction and subsequent writings on economic organization, particularly those by Williamson (1975, 1985, 1991), with the nearly identical distinction that Weber (1978, pp. 941-948) made more than 70 years ago between economic power and "authoritative" power. Weber, a legal and economic historian who was highly suspicious of the speculative sociology of his time and who "avoided the concept of society" in his own work (Schluchter, 1989, pp. 3-4), developed a sophisticated typology of authority structures specifically for the purpose of demonstrating the interrelationship between what we would today call markets and hierarchies.

Using reformulated concepts of markets and hierarchies, we will make three theoretical points. First, markets and hierarchies are not opposites and, therefore, should not be seen as being located at opposite ends of a continuum. Rather, they should be seen, conceptually, as mutually creating and mutually reinforcing aspects of any economic system. Markets and hierarchies exist in a dynamic, creative tension with each other. Conceptualizing them as opposites obscures their mutuality. Second, distinct and different market and hierarchy configurations exist empirically and vary historically and geographically. To conceptualize these in an initial way, we discuss vertically and horizontally structured network hierarchies and their market affinities. Third, we will illustrate the utility of our approach with an analysis of two very different economic systems: the capitalist economies of Taiwan and South Korea.

The Background to "Markets and Hierarchies"

The market/hierarchy distinction has had several independent origins, but in the current revival of interest in economic organization, writers universally trace the present version to Coase (1937). In a sweeping theoretical manner, Coase (p. 390) asks the question of why firms emerge in market economies. Neoclassical theorists suggest that the price mechanism, a function of supply and demand, "organizes" the economy. Firms, in theory, are merely production units that result from demand for a product and from the economies of scale needed to produce that product efficiently. Coase observes, however, that in the real world firms are quite variable, and often function in ways that supersede the price mechanism. Firms vertically integrate their production, thereby bypassing price-fixing markets for many inputs and for many steps leading to the finished product. Therefore, he asks why firms exist in market economies. He answers that there "is a cost of using the price mechanism" (p. 390), a transaction cost that occurs as a result of needing to negotiate exchanges, of ensuring satisfactory compliance with the terms of the negotiations and of the necessity of marketing the finished goods. Firms can potentially avoid some of these costs by "forming an organization and allowing some authority (an 'entrepreneur') to direct the resources." In Coase's vision, therefore, the crucial aspect of the firm is the authoritative ability of "some authority" to direct resources efficiently in the production or marketing of goods (pp. 403-405).

Coase's definition of the firm makes it a two-sided concept. On the one side is the authoritative ability to direct resources effectively. On the other side, this ability to direct resources effectively presupposes that whoever is in charge has the legitimate (e.g., legal) authority to do so. In his original article, Coase (1937) is quite clear on this point.[1] He states that the defining quality of the firm is the specific content of the "relationship" between the "master and servant" or "employer and employee." The subordinate "must be under the duty of rendering personal services to the master or to others on behalf of the master, otherwise the contract is a contract for the sale of goods or the like," and the "master must have the right to control the servant's work, either personally or by another servant or agent" (p. 430).

Both sides of Coase's definition of the firm are essential in making the firm analytically distinct from the market. In the marketplace, decision making presumes calculations based on information about prices. In firms, decision making has more latitude because it presumes the ability of the decision makers, based on an established structure of power and obedience, to direct resources authoritatively to their best advantage. In both markets and firms, of course, decision makers would pursue and, theoretically at least, attempt to maximize their own interests, however they define them, but the contexts of making decisions substantially differ, markets having price and firms having authority over others as the calculative backdrop.

Coase's original distinction between markets and firms has served as the foundation for a huge and still-expanding literature on economic organiza-tion.[2] Much of the literature focuses on debate about the nature of the firm (e.g., Holmstrom & Tirole, 1989; Putterman, 1986; Williamson & Winter, 1991). The most influential interpretations, including agency theories, moral hazard theories, incomplete contracting theories, and transaction cost theories, all tend to treat the size and structure of economic organizations (i.e., the firm) as being contingent on external market conditions. Transaction cost theories, especially the version developed by Williamson, constitute arguably the most influential interpretation and the one on which we will focus. In fact, it was Williamson (1975) who popularized *hierarchy* as a generic term for the firm.

Hierarchy, however, has a specific meaning in Williamson's transaction cost theory that problematizes only half of Coase's original distinction (Dow, 1987). To Williamson, hierarchy is a governance structure that arises in order for firms, as transactional units, to gain greater efficiency in the marketplace.[3] Hierarchy is effective centralized decision making relative to an external market,[4] and not authoritative control within the organization. Williamson is very clear on this point, because he views his version of transaction cost theory as being directly challenged by a group of scholars he labels the "Radical Economists." The Radicals (Bowles, 1985; Edwards, 1979; Marglin, 1974; Stone, 1974) argue that firm organization is a system of control to extract labor from workers, a system that is necessarily exploitative whether or not it is efficient. Williamson (1985) replies to their arguments by asserting that "hierarchy serves to economize on transaction costs" (p. 210). Hierarchy cannot, however, be equated with power and authority per se, because power is "so poorly defined that power can be and is invoked to explain virtually anything" (Williamson, 1985, p. 238).

Because power is, to Williamson, an undefined concept, he has left the authoritative side of hierarchy analytically undeveloped.[5] A brief look at the debate between Williamson and the Radicals suggests the reasons for this. The two sides in the debate are looking at different phenomena but using the same terminology to describe what they see. The Marxist economists look at the rise and character of the capitalist economy as a whole. They approach this topic from a structural point of view. Looking out at the economic landscape of Western capitalism, they see the central importance of large, vertically integrated firms, containing large numbers of laborers grouped together for the purpose of mass production. With this sight in view, they ask what holds this economic structure together and what makes it different from the preceding traditional structures? They answer that it is power, the power of capitalists to direct labor and the derivative power of a state that establishes legal and political institutions that legitimate the centralized decision making of the capitalist class.

Along with most transaction cost theorists, Williamson is examining a different economic terrain. He sees transactions as the basic units of observation. He looks at the level of transactions to understand how one set of exchanges differs from another set. In an exercise in theoretical induction (i.e., theory from the bottom up), he generates categories of transactional differences, classifications of governance structures, and microeconomic explanations to account for the resulting array. The nature of transactions tends to constitute the independent variables and the nature of firms the dependent variables. From this perspective, power is an amorphous concept, a result rather than a cause of structure, and is, more or less, a background factor consistently present throughout the field of observation. To explain the classificatory differences that he observes, such as why some firms in some industrial sectors tend to be more vertically integrated than others, something more than just power must be evoked. According to Williamson, the differences emerge as a result of the exigencies encountered in doing business in competitive economies. Different types of businesses have different transactional requirements that lead, in turn, to a specific range of organizational decisions about how to handle them, such as how to obtain standard but specialized inputs for manufacturing a product. When the process of exchange grows too difficult, too expensive, or too unpredictable, for whatever reasons, firms must decide whether or not to expand their boundaries to organize authoritatively those areas once managed through exchanges based on price. Hierarchies, Williamson maintains, grow and change in response to the dynamics of transactions, not in response to the dynamics of power.

Many scholars have criticized the thesis that hierarchy is an outcome of efficiency. Some attack the thesis empirically, by arguing that efficiency was not the cause for the waves of vertical integration that occurred in the United States and Europe from the 1890s on (Fligstein, 1985, 1990, 1991; Perrow, 1981, 1990; Roy, 1990).[6] Instead, capitalist greed, politicians' connections, legal justifications, and simple imitation serve as more reasonable explanations for vertical integration than considerations about efficiency. Others attack the thesis more theoretically, suggesting that hierarchy provides new sources of opportunity rather than only efficiency, that markets are more structured and hierarchies less authoritative than the distinction would suggest, and that making an outcome (greater efficiency) the cause of a prior condition (hierarchy) is overly functionalist and tautological (Dow, 1987; Granovetter, 1985; Perrow, 1990).

For sociologists, the most important critique of Williamson's transaction cost theory comes from Granovetter (1985), who directly criticizes the market/hierarchy distinction by arguing that "social relations between firms are more important, and authority within firms less so, in bringing order to economic life, than is supposed in the markets and hierarchies line of thought" (p. 501). Accepting Williamson's equation of hierarchy with firm, Granovetter maintains that systems of interfirm relations, based on some form of power, are important determinants of market structure. However, he does not provide a way to conceptualize these interfirm power relationships.

Most of these criticisms do not really engage Williamson's transaction cost theory on its own terms, as a way to understand theoretically the organizational outcomes of firm-level decision making in a competitive environment. Some of the critics would like to dismiss the entire relevance of a transactional level of analysis, preferring instead a more top-down structuralist perspective. Others would substitute other factors, such as social relationships, for transaction costs and make these decisive for interfirm relations. We believe, however, that in the study of economic organization, a transactional level is necessary because it represents a level of analysis in which economic action can be conceptualized in subjectively meaningful terms.[7] However, without an adequate conceptualization of authority underpinning the concept of hierarchy, the subjective aspect of control within an economic organization is played down in preference to a subjective recognition of external market conditions. With such an emphasis, hierarchy becomes a derivative concept, a tautological outcome of external market conditions, an outcome of market efficiency. In this role, hierarchy is always a dependent rather than an independent variable, a consequence rather than an independent cause, of market conditions. It is the duality of market and hierarchy, a duality between price and the entrepreneur as independent but interrelated modes for organizing market activities, that serves as the basis of Coase's original conceptualization, and without the duality, the conceptualization is strictly a one-handed approach to economic analysis.

Rethinking the Market/Hierarchy Distinction: The Problem of Boundaries

Putterman (1986) has identified two key steps that need to be taken in order to make the market/hierarchy distinction more useful. Firms and markets, he writes, are "woven, together, into the cloth that is the economy as a whole. The task of analyzing the economic nature of firms ultimately must include both an understanding of the forces shaping the boundary between firms and markets . . . and a sense of the way in which firm and market fit together in the larger system" (p. 15). The need to define the boundary lines is logically the first step. This requirement is satisfied, analytically at least, by defining the reach of authority, for it is authority that determines the extent of economic organization, the limits of authoritative economic action.

In his development of Coase's market and hierarchy distinction, Williamson, following Coase's lead, makes two assumptions that undermine the independent role of authority relations in economic organizations. First, he equates the entrepreneur's authoritative control over resources with the "governance structure" internal to a firm. In fact, a large part of the recent literature in institutional economics is an attempt to define the economic nature of the firm, instead of the economic role of authoritative organizations. Williamson equates hierarchy with the firm, the modern corporation in particular, and when he discovers that a significant portion of economic activity is organized outside the firm, he posits an organizational category between firms and markets, the hybrid, in which he deposits everything that does not fit into one of the two extremes (Williamson, 1991).

There is no a priori reason to think, however, that structures of authoritative control are necessarily contained in or limited to the firm. If the ability to make authoritative decisions regarding economic resources is a defining feature of hierarchy, then theory requires that the boundaries of economic organization be defined empirically, in terms of the structures in which authoritative actions take place, rather than arbitrarily assigning those boundaries to that of the firm.[8] Moreover, as Biggart and Hamilton (1992) have argued, the firm does not have the same empirical and conceptual significance throughout the world; rather, it is a prominent feature of what Davis and North (1971) call an institutional environment—"the social and legal ground rules that establish the basis for production, exchange and distribution" (pp. 6-7)—only in modern Western societies, but not, for instance, in Asian societies.

The second assumption about hierarchy that Williamson makes, again following Coase, leads to misplaced emphasis on the role of contract and law. In Williamson's view, markets operate through contracts that bind participants in economic exchanges. The legal system provides the rules to the game, but is often inadequate to ensure timely, cost-effective compliance with the contracts. Within economic organizations, however, contracts give way to the "efficacy of administrative controls" (Williamson, 1991, p. 280). As a number of critics have maintained, however, relations within firms are also contractual and legalistic, and compliance is just as much a problem in firms as it is in markets (e.g., Granovetter, 1985). The nature of the contracts, the application of laws, and the maximization of individual interests in the two locations, however, differ substantially. Instead of understanding the differences, Williamson generalizes (and categorizes) the contractual nature of markets, making them, theoretically, a variable feature of all markets. Although he repeatedly claims that transaction cost theory is necessarily comparative, he fixes the very features that do, in fact, differ in intermarket comparisons.[9] For instance, legalistic and contractual thinking and assumptions of firm-based autonomy characterize a particular system of authority (the "institutional environment" in North's terms) in which both markets and hierarchies exist in the United States (Biggart & Hamilton, 1992). It is an empirical question whether the same institutional environment also obtains in other locations. Our research on East Asia shows that legalistic and contractual thinking does not form the foundations of these market economies in the same way.

The distinction between markets and hierarchies can be greatly strengthened by supplementing it with Weber's distinction between economic power and authority.[10] Weber makes this distinction one of the key dividing lines motivating his analysis in *Economy and Society,* sometimes regarded as his magnum opus. In this work, Weber (1978, pp. 63-211) systematically develops an extended typological analysis of the formal and informal constraints on economic action.[11] A market-versus-authority distinction serves as the dividing line in this analysis for precisely the same reason that it does in Coase's article: because it distinguishes calculation based upon market conditions from calculation based upon authority. To interpret rational economic calculations, Weber developed an institutional theory similar in spirit and scope to that developed recently by North (1990). Weber assumed that participants in market economies reach decisions based on rational means end calculations of interests. These calculations occur in institutionalized contexts, where only a range of specific options and an array of specific economic organizations are present. In such contexts, economic calculations are conditioned by the fact that economic actions are "carried" by an existing set of "economic organizations" (i.e., corporations, cartels, and business groups) and are channeled by an existing set of "economically regulative organizations," a category including everything from "medieval village associations" to "the modern state" (Weber, 1978, p. 74). Developmental economic changes over time tend to move economies toward greater means-end systematization. In Weber's terminology, the economy becomes increasingly rationalized, in terms of both the exchange processes and the institutions (including the state) that support them. One of the key features of this economic rationalization is the "power" of economic actors to control and dispose of economic resources, which implies a system of property relations.[12]

Extrapolating from Weber's discussion of economic action, one can easily see that Weber's analysis could go in the direction pioneered by Williamson. Weber is clear that in any given institutional environment, economic organizations attempt to dictate the terms of exchange, and those in charge of these organizations, if they have the ability, will quickly alter their organizational structures to achieve greater market power. Weber's notion of economic power and Williamson's concept of efficiency are very similar in this regard: The hierarchies that are efficient to Williamson become recognized as economically powerful by other actors who calculate their personal interests in exchanging with them. To Weber, increasing the market power of a firm through vertical integration ("hierarchy," in Williamson's terms) is a rational response to external market conditions.[13]

Weber, however, makes an additional crucial distinction that Williamson does not make: Hierarchy in relation to a market is not the same thing as hierarchy inside an organization.

> In addition to numerous other types, there are two diametrically contrasting types of domination, viz., domination by virtue of a constellation of interests (in particular, by virtue of a position of monopoly), and domination by virtue of authority, i.e., power to command and duty to obey. . . . In its purest form, the first is based upon influence derived exclusively from the possession of goods or marketable skills guaranteed in some way and acting upon the conduct of those dominated, who remain, however, formally free and are motivated simply by the pursuit of their own interests. The latter kind of domination rests upon alleged absolute duty to obey, regardless of personal motives or interests. (Weber, 1978, p. 943)

He illustrates this distinction between the two types of domination with an example of two interfirm networks:

We shall not speak of formal domination if a monopolistic position permits a person to exert economic power, that is, to dictate the terms of exchange to contractual partners. Taken by itself, this does not constitute authority any more than any other kind of influence which is derived from some kind of superiority, as by virtue of erotic attractiveness, skill in sport or in discussion. Even if a big bank is in a position to force other banks into a cartel arrangement, this will not alone be sufficient to justify calling it an authority. But if there is an immediate relation of command and obedience such that the management of the first bank can give orders to the others with the claim that they shall, and the probability that they will, be obeyed regardless of particular content, and if their carrying out is supervised, it is another matter. Naturally, here as everywhere the transitions are gradual. (p. 214)

In these two examples of interfirm networks, the distinction between power in the market and power in an economic organization rests only on a small difference in the nature of the relationship among the banks, but this difference, according to Weber, is all-important. In the first example, the hierarchy is established among independent economic organizations, with the relations among banks being determined by independent calculations of interest. In the second example, however, the hierarchy is internal to the economic organization and rests on the presumed right of command and the presumed duty to obey. The structure of the first networked hierarchy grows out of market conditions, but the structure of the second hierarchy, although perhaps influenced by the market, is determined by the substantive content of authority relationships.

Weber took such care in making this distinction because it served as a dividing point in his analysis: he certainly acknowledged that economic organizations were shaped internally by external economic processes, but they were also and more significantly influenced by the character of authority embodied in the organizations themselves. The calculative logic internal to authoritative organizations turns on the "principles" used to legitimate the exercise of control within the organization. The internal structures of authoritative organizations, therefore, necessarily articulate the basis of their legitimacy. Weber recognized that even normal routines of action within the organization would reflect specific norms of authority. He illustrated this theoretical conclusion with an extended historically detailed discussion of the three "pure types" of domination and the characteristic structural arrangements that grow from the organizational logic of each type: legal-rational domination giving rise to variations of bureaucratic organizations, traditional domination giving rise to variations of patrimonial organizations, and charismatic domination giving rise to variations of organizations based on discipleship (Weber, 1978, pp. 212-301, 941-1211).

In *Economy and Society,* Weber discusses authoritative organizations at such length because he concludes that authoritative organizations influence the structure of the economy more than the economy influences the organizations.[14] This assessment is based on a wide-ranging historical and comparative analysis. The profit-oriented corporation, the legal system from which it is derived, and the market system in which it is located are all part of a distinctly modern developmental process that originated only in the West.[15] Other types of economic organizations existing historically and comparatively also have a great impact on economic endeavors and can also be rational and efficient, given their historical context. In fact, Weber was by no means certain, and expressed profound reservations, that these Western patterns would prevail in the long run despite the process of bureaucratic and economic rationalization.

In summary, Weber's particular perspective on economic organizations provides three very useful additions to Coase's and Williamson's market/hierarchy distinction. First, when hierarchy is defined in terms of both authority and economically "effective" action, the boundaries of economic organization are determined by the reach of authoritative power and are not arbitrarily equated with the firm. With the reformulated definition of hierarchy, the boundaries of economic organizations expand to match the extent of the authority relationship. To the extent that a network of people or firms is linked together by the exercise of binding norms, the network functions as an economic organization. To the extent that a network of people or firms is linked together only by individual economic interests, the network does not constitute an organization in its own right. The key point in this definition is participants' subjective recognition that they are bound to the authoritative norms of the organization, that they are not formally free to act in other ways, and that there is a coercive means to enforce the normative rules.[16] With this distinction, most intermediate types, hybrids, and network organizations (Powell, 1990; Thorelli, 1986; Williamson, 1991) would become either market-oriented voluntarist networks or authoritatively grounded networks that are economically active.

Second, no longer attached to historically specific terms (e.g., the firm, laws, exchange contracting), the new concept of hierarchy as economic organization facilitates comparative analyses on the exact nature of the interaction between markets and hierarchies. This, of course, is Putterman's second point of correction: Both markets and hierarchies constitute the larger economic system. One must understand how they function together to analyze the larger whole. Weber's key addition to this view is that the structure and array of economic organizations in a given economy create parameters for economic performance. Economic activities in the marketplace, in turn, feed back on the structure, substantiating essential roles and systematizing those roles to achieve greater efficiency relative to the goals being sought. In this sense, markets and hierarchies are mutually creating and mutually reinforcing.

Third, the revised distinction provides a way to add Granovetter's (1985) embeddedness perspective to transaction cost theory without relinquishing the theoretical claims of either approach. Interfirm networks that rest on strongly normative social bonds are better understood as economic organizations in their own right instead of as a residual or intermediate category. Embedded networks, rather than the firms that constitute them, become units of economic action. What Redding (1991) has observed about Chinese interfirm networks is true of all such embedded networks: The network linkages are stronger than the firms that make up the networks. Firms come and go, but the networks persist over time.

Two Types of Network Hierarchies

In this section we want to examine these three additions more systematically by analyzing two types of networked economic organizations and their modes of incorporation into economic activities. Network hierarchies obviously differ in how they link people together. With some oversimplification, some types of social networks link people in vertically arranged configurations. For instance, patronage systems in Hispanic societies tended historically to arrange people of power and wealth at the top of the hierarchy, and people of lesser wealth and power were connected to those at the top through some form of clientage, as represented by the *ladifundia* system of allocating rights to land. Other types of social networks, however, are much less hierarchical, and instead horizontally link people who are held to be normatively equivalent.

As we have discussed, one of the main factors influencing economic organization is the nature of authority relations linking people together.

Verticality tends to build on inequalities in power. Such inequalities can occur in the most diverse historical settings, ranging from bureaucratically defined chains of command common in modern organizations to clearly defined rankings of dependent status positions in patrimonial groups. Horizontal ties, however, tend to develop where relative (but not absolute) equality is normative. Colleagueship among faculty members of the same department or the same college and cooperation among members of a football or baseball team are examples of relations among participants who may have very different functional roles and levels of income but still are accorded formal equality within particular organized settings.[17] It is important to stress that the sociological content of either the vertical or the horizontal bonds differs greatly from context to context, and that these differences will certainly influence the resulting network configurations. However, despite differences in the sociological content, the vertical or horizontal dimensions greatly influence how authoritatively structured networks can be adapted to organizing economic endeavors and how economies, in turn, adapt to them.

One of the clearest illustrations of these differences is presented by Geertz (1963), who examines economic development in two Indonesian cities. In one of the cities, in Java, the economy is primarily a "bazaar economy" dominated by Islamic and Chinese merchants, the peddlers. As Geertz describes it, merchant households are typically coterminous with the firm, and these family firms are very small. The interlinkages among firms, however, are horizontal chains through which capital and commodities flow easily. The networks are characterized by their commercialism, by equality among participants, and by their loosely coupled character, which in turn creates a "hyperflexible marketing system" (p. 69).[18]

In the other city, in Bali, the economy is organized through aristocratic households, the princes. The elites use their long-standing authority over lower-ranked households to organize interhousehold networks for the purpose of commodity production. These princes overlap authority derived from the traditional social structure with the pursuit of modern economic goals. Differentially ranked households provide the nuclei for vertically integrated economic networks producing such commodities as textiles and tires. Geertz notes that "in organizational terms there is little doubt that the firms [organized by the princes] are much more impressive than those [organized by the peddlers]," and are capable of "bringing together hundreds of villages in a common effort" (p. 121).

Using this illustration as a starting point, we want to offer a hypothesis, an organizational rule of thumb. The way an economic organization can be made cohesive—that is, the way it can be grounded in authoritative norms—creates a finite range of possibilities for organizing economic action. When adapted to economic purposes, vertically cohesive groups have an affinity for establishing vertically integrated systems of commodity production, systems whose organization expands along links in commodity chains. Horizontal ties, when adapted directly to economic purposes, do not lead to vertical integration; rather, they are segmental and lead to what we will call *market integration*.[19]

Vertically Controlled Networks

Vertically arranged hierarchies occur in the most economically diverse settings. In precapitalist societies, economies often developed into what Weber (1978) calls *oikos* or manorial economies. *Oikos* economies rest on the economic activities of elites, who authoritatively and patrimonially organize subordinate groups—serfs, slaves, and other forms of bound labor—into cohesive economic organizations. Although often agrarian based, *oikos* economies can also be urban and oriented toward handicraft production (Weber, 1978, pp. 381-383). The elites or their agents are the economic decision makers and, as Weber argues, these decision makers normally sought "want satisfaction" and not profits or efficiency. In some settings, however, such as in seventeenth- and eighteenth-century England or in the plantation economies of the Americas and Asia in the same period, *oikos* economies could become intensely market oriented and could produce goods efficiently relative to the market conditions of the time.[20] In all of these cases, the economic organizations, the manors or the plantations, were not firms in a conventional sense. They encompassed many diverse households of unrelated people and placed them under the centralized direction of people in positions of recognized authority.

Authoritatively controlled vertical networks remain important forms of economic organization in modern capitalist societies as well. Geertz's example of princely households from Indonesia's developing economy might be considered a premodern example, except for the fact that such elite households in Indonesia and elsewhere have continued to grow and to flourish in a fully capitalist era (e.g., Robison, 1986). In many parts of the world, such elite households have organized extensive networks of legally independent firms that are known in the literature as "business groups" (Granovetter, 1994; Hamilton, Zeile, & Kim, 1990; Leff, 1976, 1978). Such business groups normally share some form of common ownership. Systems of ownership and control vary, however. The most common system of control is family ownership of at least the top tier of firms. Family members typically exercise their control through a central holding company or family foundation that owns all or a substantial portion of the firms in the group. In addition, many of these business groups intermix modern professional management with systems of control that manipulate ethnicity, status, and other features common to patrimonial economies. Variations of such family-owned, vertically integrated business groups are found in India (Encarnation, 1989), Latin America (Aubey, 1979; "The Economic Groups," 1991; Ostiguy, 1990; Strachan, 1976), and, to a lesser degree, in such countries in Western Europe as France and England (Encaoua & Jacquemin, 1982). The South Korean *chaebol,* which we will describe below, is also an example of this type of vertical network.

Japanese business groups, the *keiretsu,* represent another type of vertically controlled hierarchical networks (Fruin, 1992; Futatsugi, 1986; Gerlach, 1992; Hamilton et al., 1990; Orrù, Hamilton, & Suzuki, 1989). In these networks, the large firms at the top of the hierarchy are mutually owned through overlapping shareholding. Corporate control and economic decision making, however, are not centralized as in most family-owned business groups, but rather are somewhat decentralized and tend to be coterminous with production sequences (i.e., commodity chains) leading to the production of a common group of products (Aoki, 1988, 1990). These very large corporatized and mutually owned networks dominate the markets for intermediate inputs, labor-intensive operations, and services. These networks therefore have positions of considerable economic power vis-à-vis the thousands of small and medium-sized firms that supply goods and services to them on a long-term noncontractual basis under conditions generally favorable to the *keiretsu* firms. As Orrù (1993) has shown, a similar hierarchical network structure has also developed in the German economy.

In both the family- and corporate-controlled networks, the business strategies of the group have an affinity for vertical integration in the production of commodities and the delivery of goods and services. These economic organizations build upon systems of authority that facilitate the formation of very large, authoritatively controlled groups. The possibilities for creating vertically controlled networks precede their formation and, at least in an economy influenced by capitalism, such possibilities create an affinity for vertical integration in relation to commodity production.[21]

Horizontally Controlled Networks

Horizontally arranged network hierarchies also occur in the most diverse historical locations, but differ in most economic respects from vertical ones. In precapitalist periods, horizontal networks were primarily organized linkages joining independent, economically engaged households into functionally diverse but organizationally encompassed economic endeavors. The best examples of such economic organizations are guilds, *landmanschaften* or *huiguan,* and other types of trade and merchant associations. As Greif, Milgrom, and Weingast (1994) argue in the case of medieval guilds in Europe, the guild was the main organizational unit of medieval commerce, the "nexus of contracts," rather than the households of individual merchants and artisans. The same conclusion also applies to late imperial China, where the *huiguan* and artisan associations were the organizational focus of all trade and handicraft production (Hamilton, 1985; Rowe, 1984). As a rule, these associations were organized as "collegial bodies" (Weber, 1978, pp. 271-282), emphasizing the equivalence among members, usually by recognizing a common identity. They were usually brotherhoods of fellow townsmen, fellow regionals, or fellow ethnics. These associations, when formalized, as were the European guilds and the Chinese *huiguan,* typically had two foci of control (Hamilton, 1985). First, they had associational rules aimed at defining the terms of doing business and the quality of products and services. Second, they regulated entry into the associations themselves. These associations endeavored to monopolize their economic spheres and punished those who violated either set of rules.

In the case of some religious and ethnic groups whose members specialized in long-distance trade or became nonlocal merchants in many locales, horizontal networks worked more informally in the sense that the network had no geographic location, no visible building—not even a meeting site. Though more informal, these networks still operated as authoritative economic organizations in the sense that the behavioral expectations rested on sanctionable social rules.[22] Among Jewish and Chinese merchants, business dealings implied a commonality, such as kinship ties or common origins or a common middleman, that preceded transactions and gave the transactions a predictive normative structure that was not intrinsic in the transactions themselves. Violations of the normative expectations could also be sanctioned by expulsion, shunning, and others means familiar in close-knit groups for dealing with noncompliance. Such groups handled trade relationships at great distances and in conditions of considerable uncertainty with relative ease.

In capitalistic societies, horizontally arranged networks continue to be a source of important economic organizations. Stock markets and commodities exchanges are modern counterparts to the medieval guilds and other forms of market organization. They represent organizationally encompassed firms, the brokerage houses with seats on the exchange, that work under a common set of rules defining the terms of trade and the conditions of entry (Abolafia, 1984). Even though they differ by size, wealth, and functional specialization, the brokerage houses are equivalent in formal terms, each occupying a seat and each possessing rights and duties that ensue from that fact. Actions violating the common rules can be and are punished by the group itself, in addition to any other punishment that might result from legal action in a civil or criminal court.

Another particularly important variation of horizontal networks in capitalist societies is found in the household-based economies established by such groups as the overseas Chinese—the Chinese living outside the People's Republic of China. In the next section we will discuss one such economy, the Taiwanese economy.

Horizontally networked economic organizations interact with market forces in ways very different from those found in vertical networks. Horizontal networks are segmented into conceptually equivalent units that all act according to the same organizational rules. These rules may be defined in many ways, in terms of ritual decorum, ethnic pride, or bureaucratic professionalism. Internally, because the equivalent units act similarly in conformity to known rules, they are highly predictable. Moreover, they are inherently antimonopolistic. Even though the organizations themselves may monopolize their spheres of economic activity (e.g., the commodity exchange for silver), organizational rules forbid monopolization of that activity by anyone internal to the groups (e.g., a specific brokerage house) (Abolafia & Kilduff, 1988). Associational rules do not facilitate individual strategies leading to vertical and horizontal integration, in part because transaction rules are defined collectively and in part because monopolistic strategies threaten the groups themselves. Because of their organizational characteristics, these organizations and groups occupy economic niches intersecting commodity chains. They have an affinity for being market intermediaries instead of market producers. Guilds and stock markets act as organizational interfaces between buyers and sellers. Long-distance merchant groups played much the same role. In capitalist Taiwan, as we will show below, horizontally arranged networks of family firms, wedged in a global economy between big buyers and retail sellers, also play functionally similar roles, although under very different conditions of production and distribution.

To illustrate more precisely the relation between these two types of networked hierarchies and their associated market economies, we will summarize the paired comparisons that we have made between the industrial structures of Taiwan and South Korea.

Business Groups in South Korea and Taiwan

South Korea and Taiwan are two rapidly industrializing economies; they are located in the same part of the world, about 2 hours' flight time from each other; they have developed in roughly the same years at roughly the same rapid rates; they have had similar historical influences, both having been socially and culturally dominated first by China and then, in the colonial period, by Japan; and both have used similar economic policies to develop, first supporting a strategy of import substitution and then adopting an aggressive strategy of export-led industrialization. Moreover, in both locations, most private firms, even those making up the largest business groups, are family owned and controlled, and, significantly, in both locations, family authority and practices draw on Confucian ideology to sustain the patterns of relationships within and among families. In all these background variables —economic, social, and cultural—Taiwan and South Korea are as nearly the same as could be imagined between any two countries in the world today. Yet the economies of these two countries are organized in radically different ways, Korea through vertically controlled networks and Taiwan through horizontally controlled networks. We first will outline the economic differences and then account for these differences in terms of the underlying networked hierarchies.

The economies of both countries are structured through networks of legally independent family-controlled firms.[23] Korean business groups, called *chaebol* (or money cliques), play prominent and decisive roles in organizing systems of commodity production and distribution in the total economy. The *chaebol* networks encompass the organization of commodity chains. By contrast, the Taiwanese business groups, sometimes called *guanxichiye* (related enterprises), do not encompass commodity chains; they have niche roles in the economy and are primarily suppliers of intermediate products and services sold domestically in an economy that is predominantly export oriented. Table 3.1 gives a comparison of the top business groups in both countries. As is apparent, Korean business groups on balance are much larger than their Taiwanese counterparts. Table 3.2 describes the shares by industrial sector of the largest business groups in Korea and Taiwan quantitatively. It is clear as well that Korean business groups account for much larger proportions of the total output in the economy than do those in Taiwan. Even so, the Taiwanese business groups are still substantial.

Vertically Arranged Business Networks in Korea

To what degree do the *chaebol* networks represent vertically integrated networks, "one setism," as such networks are known in the literature on Japanese business groups (Gerlach, 1992, p. 85)? We can measure this quite precisely. The degree of vertical integration within the networked group can be conceptualized as the degree to which firms within the group supply the demand for intermediate inputs and essential services necessary to produce and distribute a finished commodity. The more vertically integrated the interfirm networks, the more likely it is that the firms in the group will transact their business with other firms in the same group. We can therefore conceptualize one setism as the internalization of transactions within a business group.

To measure the rate of internalization for the South Korean case, we use self-reported accounting data that were compiled for Korean Investors Service (Lim, Feenstra, & Hamilton, 1993).[24] These data contain, among other things, the interfirm transactions for all the firms within each *chaebol* (these data are presented in Appendix 3.1). In Table 3.3 the degree of internalization for the top 43 *chaebol* is summarized as the ratio of internal sales of firms in a group to total demand for intermediate inputs.[25] The average rate of internalization for the 43 *chaebol* is a little more than 17%. This figure represents the amount of the total demand for intermediate inputs that is supplied by firms within the business groups. Table 3.3 also shows that the degree of internalization is correlated with the total size of the *chaebol*. The

Table 3.1 East Asian Business Group Comparative Statistics

	Total Sales ($U.S. millions)[a]	Total Assets ($U.S. millions)[a]	Total Firms	Firms per Business Group (by internal)	Total Workers	Workers per Business Group (by internal)	Workers per Firm (by internal)
South Korea (1983)							
Top 5 *chaebol*	35,360	24,872	123	25	322,876	64,575	2,625
Top 10 *chaebol*	47,317	33,772	202	16	425,872	20,599	1,304
Top 20 *chaebol*	58,187	44,078	328	13	550,458	12,457	989
Top 30 *chaebol*	64,509	49,611	412	8	688,385	13,793	1,641
Top 50 *chaebol*	70,772	56,391	552	7	798,976	5,530	780
Taiwan (1983)							
Top 5 business groups	5,084	5,547	90	18	85,719	17,144	952
Top 10 business groups	7,488	9,660	180	18	164,129	15,682	871
Top 20 business groups	10,444	13,744	283	10	220,413	5,628	546
Top 30 business groups	12,084	16,002	375	9	251,616	3,120	339
Top 50 business groups	14,027	17,902	494	6	289,787	1,908	321
Top 96 business groups	15,842	19,763	743	5	330,098	876	162

SOURCES: For South Korea, Hankook Ilbo (1985); for Taiwan, China Credit Information Service (1985).
a. Exchange rate per $U.S.: Japan, 233 yen; Korea, 772 won; Taiwan, 40 NT$.

Table 3.2 Business Group Shares in the Manufacturing Sectors of the Economies of South Korea (1989) and Taiwan (1988)

Manufacturing Sector	South Korean Business Group %	Taiwan Business Group %
Food products	34.79	13.60
Beverages	31.87	0.22
Textiles	46.73	42.26
Garments and apparel	1.17	6.40
Leather products	4.63	0.00
Lumber and wood products	11.21	5.20
Pulp and paper products	13.54	22.24
Printing and publishing	7.16	0.40
Chemical materials and plastics	38.62	15.80
Chemical products	6.18	4.54
Petroleum and coal products	91.20	0.00
Rubber products (not footwear)	29.05	12.80
Nonmetallic mineral products	26.72	25.90
Basic metals	36.93	4.00
Metal products	19.05	17.10
Machinery	21.14	18.50
Electrical and electronic products	63.14	11.65
Shipbuilding and repairing	74.16	2.40
Transportation equipment	50.39	28.70
Precision machinery	13.95	0.20
Miscellaneous industrial products	2.43	6.14

SOURCES: Manufacturing sector classifications are based on Directorate-General of Budget, Accounting and Statistics (1989) (with minor modifications). South Korean business group data for 1989 are based on Korea Investors Service (1990) and *Hankuk Kiop Chongnam* (1989). Taiwan data are based on China Credit Information Service (1990).

larger the *chaebol* in total sales and assets, the higher the rate of internalization becomes.

How high is this rate of internalization? One can think of a network of firms in which there are no internal sales at all; each firm produces products and sells to firms outside the group. The degree of internalization for such a group would be zero. At the other extreme would be a situation in which a group of firms buys no intermediate goods from any outside source—no electricity, no gas, no raw products of any kind—sells 100% of their intermediate products to other firms in the group, and at the end of the day produces a final commodity that is sold outside the group. The degree of internalization in this group would be 100%, but in today's manufacturing economy such a group is clearly impossible.

Table 3.3 Internal Transactions for Korean Business Groups
(trading companies excluded)

Degree of Internal Transaction (%)

Measured relative to total sales of the business groups	21.98
Measured relative to total input demand (as weighted average)	17.53

Correlation	Year.1	Year.S	Sales Figure	Asset	Number of Companies
Internal transaction as proportion of each business group's total sales	−0.0513	0.0169	0.4051	0.3571	0.2977
Internal transaction as proportion of each business group's total input	−0.352	0.0349	0.3961	0.3512	0.2962

SOURCES: Korea Investors Service (1990), *Hankuk Kiop Chongnam* (1989), and Business Korea (1992).
NOTE: Internal transaction = degree of internal transaction of each business group (%) being measured in two different ways; Year.1 = number of year of establishment of each group's first company; Year.S = number of year of establishment of each group's biggest company (in terms of sales figure); Sales Figure = total sales figure of each business group; Asset = total asset of each business group; Number of Companies = total number of companies in each business group.

In comparative terms, the 17% figure represents a substantial degree of internalization. First of all, this figure does not measure the vertical integration that occurs within firms, only between firms, and we know that the largest firms in the largest *chaebol* are themselves highly vertically integrated (Amsden, 1989a). The 17% figure therefore is in addition to such vertical integration as occurs at the firm level. Recognizing this fact, one can compare the Korean rate to the rate of internal transfers within U.S. corporations that have accounting procedures based on multiple internal profit centers. In a survey of 237 U.S. corporations engaging in pricing internal transfers, Vancil (1978, p. 176; also cited by Eccles, 1985, pp. 106-113) found that more than 77% of these corporations had 15% or less of their total cost (or total sales) for intermediate inputs satisfied by divisions within their own corporations. Within Japanese automobile manufacturing groups, J. H. Dyer (in press) cites MITI statistics showing that 31% of the costs of the products sold are manufactured internally by firms within the group, compared with 45% of the cost for the more vertically integrated U.S. automobile manufacturing firms. Considering just the interfirm transactions of the Hyundai group, Korea's top automobile manufacturer, these figures fall between the Japanese and the U.S. cases. However, if both intra- and interfirm sources of vertical integration were included, the Hyundai group would likely be even more vertically integrated than the U.S. automobile makers are. For business groups in Japan as a whole, Gerlach (1992, pp. 143-149) reports that the rate of internal transactions within the intermarket groups has been variously calculated to be around 10% or less.

Based on these rather inexact comparisons, it would appear that Korean *chaebol* networks would rank very highly among the world's most vertically integrated economies. Additional evidence for this impression comes from our comparisons of the Korean and Taiwanese imports into the United States (Feenstra, Yang, & Hamilton, 1993). Data from U.S. Customs show that Korean imports are predominantly high volumes of a limited number of finished consumer products. The *chaebol* networks tend to make automobiles, VCRs, television sets and computers rather than only the component parts for these products. The firms in the *chaebol* are the principal upstream suppliers for the big downstream *chaebol* assembly firms. For instance, we have been told in interviews that in Samsung electronics, most of the main component parts for the consumer electronics division are manufactured and assembled in the same compound by Samsung firms. Our statistical data correspond to what we have been told: For Samsung, nearly 25% of all intermediate demands are filled by Samsung firms—almost 32% if we count the contribution of the Samsung trading company.

Horizontally Arranged Business Networks in Taiwan

In contrast with the *chaebol*'s vertical networks, Taiwan business networks are highly segmented in distinct economic niches and show little evidence of vertical integration even within those niches. Our measurement of the rate of internalization for Taiwan's largest business groups is an estimation.[26] This estimate, based on sales figures for member groups, reveals much lower levels of internalization. The estimates we arrive at for each business group are presented in Appendix 3.2. As shown in Table 3.4, when adjusted for value added, the average of these estimates for the top 96 business groups is only a little more than 4%.

Our calculations suggest that only 6 of the 96 business groups had a rate of internalization of 17% or above, which was the average rate for the top 50 Korean *chaebol*. Moreover, unlike in the Korean case, there was no correlation between size, as measured in assets or sales, and the rate of

Table 3.4 Internal Transactions for Taiwanese Business Groups

Degree of Internal Transaction (%)

Measured relative to total sales of the business groups	2.05
Measured relative to total input demand (as weighted average)	4.41

Correlation	Year.1	Year.S	Sales Figure	Asset	Number of Companies
Internal transaction as proportion of each business group's total sales	0.0345	−0.0561	−0.0777	−0.0726	−0.0268
Internal transaction as proportion of each business group's total input	−0.129	−0.0915	−0.0452	−0.049	−0.0531

SOURCE: All calculations are based on 1988 data reported by China Credit Information Service (1990).
NOTE: Out of the 100 biggest business groups recorded, 4 have been deleted from this study because of some analysis problems. Internal transaction = degree of internal transaction of each business group (%) being measured in two different ways; Year.1 = number of year of establishment of each group's first company; Year.S = number of year of establishment of each group's biggest company (in terms of sales figure); Sales Figure = total sales figure of each business group; Asset = total asset of each business group; Number of Companies = total number of companies in each business group.

internalization. Nor was the rate correlated with the age or the number of firms in the business groups.[27] Figure 3.1 displays the comparison of business group internalization between Korea and Taiwan. The low rank of internalization matches other data from Taiwan showing that neither state enterprises nor large business groups are vertically integrated producers of finished products.[28] State-owned enterprises primarily supply infrastructure and basic initial goods and services, such as electricity, gasoline, and steel. They sell to all firms, regardless of size. The largest business groups predominantly produce intermediate products and sell their products to all firms, regardless of size. Table 3.2 shows this tendency in comparison with Korean business groups. Whereas the *chaebol* command a large share of the manufacturing sectors having final export products as well as the basic upstream sectors required to produce those products, Taiwanese business groups have significant shares only in intermediate product categories: textiles, but not garments; chemical materials, but not plastic products. Even in automobile production (Taiwan has 27 automobile manufacturing firms, all for domestic sales), the largest business groups have only a 28% share of the automobile manufacturing market, compared with the *chaebol*'s near-100% domination in this sector. Simply examining the business sectors of the firms in the

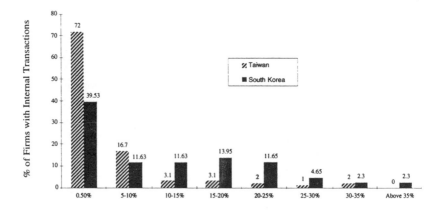

Degree of Internalization

Figure 3.1. Rates of Internalization for Taiwanese and South Korean Business Groups

largest 10 business groups in Taiwan reveals that only one of them—Tatung, a conglomerate producing electrical appliances and electronics goods—engages in sizable exports of finished products, and even Tatung specializes in producing component parts for the export market (Hamilton, Chapter 9, this volume). The rest of the top 10 business groups specialize in separate service or upstream manufacturing niches. For instance, Formosa Plastics, by far the largest business group in Taiwan, primarily supplies plastic material to domestic manufacturers who, in turn, make plastic products for the export market. Our estimate shows that the rate of internalization (the demand for inputs that are supplied by member firms) among the 18 firms in the Formosa Plastics group is considerably less than 1%.

In light of these figures, it is important to remember that Taiwan is aggressively export oriented. Taiwan's manufactured exports as the percentage of total GNP is 51%, compared with South Korea's 37.5% and Japan's 16.4%. Government statistics show that 65% of these exports are produced by firms having fewer than 300 employees, a percentage that has been steadily increasing for past two decades. Moreover, if we examine these exports we see that the products differ substantially from products produced by Korean *chaebol*. Our analysis of Taiwanese exports into the United States shows conclusively that, in comparison with Korea, a country twice its size,

Taiwan exports a much wider variety of products in all industrial categories except one, transportation equipment (Feenstra et al., 1993). Specializing in a high volume of a few big-ticket consumer items, Korea exceeds Taiwan only in certain categories of high-value final goods. In all other categories, Taiwan beats Korea.

It is obvious that production of exports is not handled through vertical integration. In Taiwan, small and medium-sized firms use the intermediate goods and services supplied by larger Taiwanese and foreign firms to manufacture the products that Taiwan exports.[29] Unlike in Japan and Korea, large firms and large networks of large firms do not organize the production of small firms by creating a demand structure for intermediate goods and services. In Taiwan, the reverse is true. Every level of the economy, from upstream producers to downstream manufacturers, is segmented and driven by downstream demand. Looking at the distribution of firm size, one must conclude that the small-firm tail wags the entire economy.

The networks that form in this economy are not, typically, vertical networks that link upstream and downstream firms. Instead, our research shows that two types of networks are common. One is an ownership network of family enterprises. As we have shown from the internalization measures, the embedded networks of the largest Chinese family-owned business groups are not vertically integrated, but, rather, are highly diversified conglomerates. Our analysis of the development strategy of these business groups over time reveals that their typical mode of development is to intensify production in a core area in order to satisfy existing and future demand for the product or service, and then, using the profits from the core business, to diversify into unrelated areas, often into real estate or finance. In short, in Taiwan, embedded networks of family ownership and commodity chains are not coterminous.

The second type of networks are production networks. These networks, sometimes called satellite assembly systems, consist of independently owned small, medium-sized and some large firms joined together to manufacture products for the export market. These assembly systems typically work with local and foreign buyers, who supply the specifications for the products needed. Network organizers put together the needed firms to manufacture the product in the amount required.

What makes these production networks so successful rests on two features. First, Taiwan's production networks represent the production end of a global commercial network. As Gereffi (1993) shows, the rise of the Taiwan economy corresponds to the rise of the mass-marketing retail revolution that has been orchestrated by "big buyers," such as the Gap, Reebok, the Price Club, Walmart, and other mass merchandisers that never owned or stopped owning their own factories in preference for global sourcing. These supply-on-demand production networks occupy a niche between global buyers and mass merchandisers. They are more commercial than industrial. Second, the networks are so successful because they organizationally encompassed household-based production systems that run according to the rules of Chinese society, as we will explain below.

In summary, conceptualizing production and distribution networks as a commodity chain, we can say that in South Korea the large *chaebol* are the main organizing nodes in the economy's system of production and distribution. These are "producer-driven" networks (Gereffi & Hamilton, 1992) and are structured so that the larger firms in the networks create the demand for the smaller firms outside the networks. Through research and development, advertising, and aggressive merchandising by their own trading companies, these large firms also promote, if not create, final consumer demand for their products as well. In this sense, efficient production in these networks is based on achieving economies of scope and scale, a sort of "network-based Fordism." In economic terms, these are "demand-creating" networks.

By contrast, in Taiwan the large firms and large business groups are not organizing nodes in commodity chains. Big businesses are upstream suppliers of intermediate goods and services, responding to the demands generated by manufacturing networks of the small and medium-sized firms that, in turn, respond to the demands of buyers external to the producing networks. Gereffi (1993) calls this type of network "buyer driven." Production in these networks relies on external markets. The responsiveness to buyers makes Taiwan's small-firm economy highly integrated in the global economy. These networks, therefore, can be termed *demand responsive*.

Embedded Networks Hierarchies

What factors account for the huge differences in the industrial structures of Taiwan and Korea? As we noted previously, the two countries share many similar features. Most observers, so bent on explaining the success of Asian economies in general, have in fact missed the major differences in industrial structure and economic performance between them.[30] In suggesting an explanation for these differences in general terms, most analysts would be inclined to look for some peculiar difference in the timing of industrialization or in the action of the state. Such differences can certainly be located, but are these differences that explain the difference? We do not believe the differences can be explained idiosyncratically as a set of events or a group of persons that created a path-dependent trajectory, in part because of the general patterns of organizational isomorphism within each economy (Orrù, Biggart, & Hamilton, 1991). The few transaction cost theorists who have examined the differences in the economies have concluded that transaction costs are lower in Taiwan than in Korea, and therefore the Korean economy is more vertically integrated (Levy, 1988, 1991). But for the explanations, the end result is projected backward in time and made the cause of the imputed outcome. In other words, transaction costs are as much a consequence of hierarchies as a cause of them.

It is our hypothesis that the differences in industrial structure can best be accounted for by differences in the network hierarchies between the two locations that stem, in turn, from differences in social structures growing out of the transmission and control of family property. In South Korea, the kinship system supports a clearly demarcated, hierarchically ranked class structure in which core segments of lineages acquire elite rankings and privileges. These are the "great families" (*dajia*). As Biggart (1990) describes, this pattern hearkens back to the social structure of the Yi Dynasty (1392-1910), when the rural-based ruling class, the *yangbang,* consisted of privileged clans that competed for control of society. The lineage was centrally controlled by the eldest son of the dominant segment of the lineage. The clan head inherited from his father all the communal clan landholdings and his own dominant share (about 60%) of the father's private estate, with the younger sons dividing up the rest. This system preserved the aristocratic clan as the principal unit of political and economic action.

These inheritance practices are still in force, and a highly privileged, lineage-based class hierarchy was reinstituted after the Korean War, especially after the Park Chung Hee coup in 1961, as a direct consequence of Korea's industrial policy (Kim, 1991, 1994). At that time, Park tried to stimulate the economy aggressively by selecting certain successful and politically trustworthy businessmen to create large, family-owned business groups similar to the *zaibatsu* in prewar Japan. Precedents for Park's action were there in Korea's history. Park acted on an affinity for elites (i.e., deference patterns and class expectations) that existed in Korean society; it was a logical and rational choice and, in retrospect, it is clear that this choice led to a reincorporation of patrimonialism in the management of Korea *chaebol* (Biggart, 1990).

In Taiwan, however, the Confucian family was situated in a very different social order. In China's early dynastic period, roughly from 221 B.C. until the end of the Sung period in 1280 A.D., Chinese social structure also rested on privileged lineage groups. Especially in the middle period, during the Sui (589-618) and Tang (618-907) Dynasties, the great families controlled the countryside and vied with the emperor's family for aristocratic prestige. After the Mongol victory in 1280, however, the corporate, aristocratic lineages gave way to a segmented patrilineal kinship system in which households, not lineages, were the key building blocks in rural society (Hamilton, 1991; Twitchett, 1959, pp. 131-133). Internal segments would cut across class lines. Unlike in Korea (and in the early Chinese dynasties), where the eldest son inherited the lion's share of the estate and all the lineage's communal holdings, in late imperial China the Chinese practiced partible inheritance, in which all sons equally split the father's estate. Also, communal lands of lineages tended to be very small. This set of practices preserved the household and made it the key unit of action, rather than the lineage itself. Lineage became a ritual community, as opposed to a key unit of action. Over time, partible inheritance and associated practices of lineage segmentation led to an economy that mirrored the society. Landholdings were divided into small plots and were dispersed in space. Large landowners did not have contiguous holdings. Instead of managing their agricultural resources, they rented their land to tenants, who fully appropriated usage rights to the topsoil.

Taiwan was largely settled during the Qing Dynasty (1644-1911) with migrants from Fukien province. The landholding patterns were based on a southern Chinese model of strong segmented patrilineages, with some households in a lineage having substantial holdings and others in the same lineage being landless or becoming tenants tilling their kinsmen's land. This pattern of landowning continued largely in place even after the Japanese takeover of Taiwan in 1895, a concession from the Sino-Japanese War. However, in the 1950s, after Chiang Kai-shek and his Kuomintang forces had taken control of Taiwan, the Kuomintang instituted a comprehensive land reform that distributed the land in small plots to the people who tilled the soil. A similar reform occurred in Korea, but unlike in Korea, in Taiwan the government did not at the same time attempt to create an industrial structure based on elite holdings. Instead, the Taiwan government tried to stimulate the private sector of the economy by nourishing Chinese family economic practices, a solution that favored the reinstitutionalization of a household-based economy that became filled, in time, with commercially oriented industrialists.

A number of analysts have described Chinese economic practices and have argued that Chinese patrilineal kinship patterns produce strong pressures on the Chinese to develop enduring working relations with equally ranked people outside of their immediate kinship groups (Fei, 1992; Hamilton, 1991, 1992, 1995; Hwang, 1987; King, 1991). These horizontal ties become the chief vehicle for individuals to marshal resources, including economic resources, for the purposes of household and personal advancement. The strength of these horizontal ties further undermines the influence of the lineage group over its members and enforces the norms that favor the household (*jia*) to be the central nodes in extensively organized horizontal networks.

In summary, although based on similar kinship principles, Korean and Chinese kinship systems operate in very different ways.[31] In South Korea, kinship norms can be used coercively to incorporate people and groups beyond the household, creating the cohesion necessary to form and maintain large groups. To the extent that these relational norms are used as models for managing extrakin groups, the organizations formed are, by definition, patrimonial.[32] And in this sense, the Korean *chaebol* are patrimonial. In the Chinese society of Taiwan, kinship norms do not apply to people beyond the household, but apply rigidly to members of the household. Outside the household, reciprocal norms based on some form of commonality (*guanxi*) tie people together authoritatively in horizontal networks (Fei, 1992; King, 1991). Large, far-flung, but narrowly cohesive networks result, but these lack the coerciveness of authority possessed by groups organized through patrimonial and bureaucratic means. In both cases an affinity for economic action is present, but this affinity pushes people to go in very different directions when they organize efficiently to achieve "rational" economic goals.

Conclusion

Williamson (1991) writes that vertical integration is a "paradigm problem" for transaction cost theory. We have argued in this chapter, however, that hierarchy needs to be a two-sided concept, one that deals with more than simply organizational efficiency in the economy. Although one side of the definition should stress the organization's effective integration in a market economy, the other should stress the authoritative structure of the organization and its basis of legitimacy. When conceptualized in this way, hierarchy becomes a way to organize groups that cohere on the basis of subjectively held and coercively enforced rules of conduct. Depending on the internal structure of such authority, economically active groups have a prior affinity for size and scope. As preexisting groups interact within a market environment, they create, based on their repertoire for action, their own sources of transactional efficiency. Out of this interaction between market and hierarchy comes an industrial structure, a lineup of economic organizations that operative effectively in the marketplace.

Applying this reasoning to the East Asian cases, we would argue as follows: The current shapes of the market structures of Taiwan and South Korea have been greatly influenced by several decades of success in the global economy. The early and continuing success of these two economies in larger economic arenas has had substantial impact on the development of their economic structures. The early decisions, however, based on social structural affinities, have led not only to a path of development, but also to an organizational environment that feeds back on itself (path dependence), creating an economic system that has an internal dynamic and institutionalized rules of the game. It is the organizational dynamic, rather than specific features of embeddedness, that produces and sustains market structures. Embedded structural features provide direction to trajectories of economic development, but structure should not be confused with economic development itself. For an analysis of the dynamic interaction between markets and hierarchy, we feel that transaction cost theory has many contributions to make, but a theory of transactions is not, at the same time, a theory of hierarchies.

Appendix 3.1   Rate of Internalization in Korean Business Groups

Group[a]	Number of Companies	Rate of Internal Transactions (%)[b]
1. Hyundai	30	25.83
2. Samsung	37	24.24
3. Lucky-Goldstar	46	20.18
4. Sunkyong	16	19.63
5. Daewoo	25	13.11
6. Ssangyong	15	16.55
7. Korea Explosives	19	6.48
8. Han Jin	11	3.72
9. Hyosung	20	3.74
10. Daelim	12	5.29
11. Doosan	18	15.69
12. Lotte	23	12.20
13. Kolon	14	5.08
14. Han Yang	4	1.60
15. Kumbo	8	.66
16. Sammi	5	33.94
17. Dongbu	8	21.15
18. Kia	10	21.06
19. Dong Ah Construction	12	1.84
20. Donkuk Steel Mill	10	4.51
21. Miwon	13	8.10
22. Hanil	12	11.57
23. Tong Yang	5	16.74
24. Taihan Electric Wire	3	4.04
25. Donkuk Corporation	7	1.43
26. Samyang	5	2.12
27. Kangwon Industries	12	39.58
28. Byucksan	18	.95
29. Hanbo	3	2.66
30. Daesung Industries	8	2.45
31. Jinro	10	3.60
32. Tongil	10	6.51
33. Oriental Chemical Ind.	9	13.03
34. Poongsan	6	4.42
35. Kohap	6	17.20
36. Life Construction	4	2.53
37. Kuk Dong Construction	4	.32
38. Kukdong Oil	3	21.64
39. Halla	7	15.02
40. Woosung Construction	6	2.85
41. Anam Industrial	5	14.08
42. Kyesung Paper	5	26.62
43. You One Construction	2	0.00

SOURCES: Korea Investors Service (1990), *Hankuk Kiop Chongnam* (1989), and Business Korea (1992).
a. Ranked by total sales.
b. Ratio of internal sales/intermediate inputs.

Appendix 3.2   Rate of Internalization in Taiwanese Business Groups

Group[a]	Number of Companies	Rate of Internal Transactions (%)[b]
1. Formosa Plastics	11	0.27
2. Hua Lon	8	0.42
3. Lin Yuan	5	0.0075
4. Shin Kong	18	0.63
5. Far Eastern	14	2.5
6. China Trust	15	8.50
7. Tatung	5	1.68
8. Yue Loong	11	32.50
9. President	13	2.40
10. Wei-Chuan Ho-Tai	20	1.00
11. National Electric	13	0.0005
12. Chi Mei	7	2.33
13. Tuntex	14	1.26
14. Pacific Wire & Cable	12	0.43
15. Teco Electric	8	2.98
16. Tainan Spinning	17	0.57
17. Sam Shin Trading	7	0.00
18. China General Plastics	7	0.50
19. Chung Shing	9	6.26
20. Yuen Foong	7	3.30
21. Acer	4	0.011
22. Sampo	6	5.41
23. China Rebar	—	—
24. Taiwan Cement	8	1.22
25. Yeu Tyan Machinery	7	0.37
26. Cheng Loong	6	24.26
27. San Fu Motors	5	1.77
28. Chun Yuan	5	0.24
29. Chang Chun	5	0.82
30. Sun Moon Star	11	7.47
31. Foremost	8	1.22
32. Yieh Loong	4	8.47
33. Lien Hwa Industry	6	0.00
34. Chen Zhen	—	—
35. Hsiu Chu Trucking	8	0.22
36. Walsin Lihwa	7	0.00
37. Shung Ye Trading	5	4.84
38. Shin Lee	9	0.27
39. Shih Lin Paper	4	8.47
40. Kuo Chan	7	0.37
41. Prince Motors	6	2.95
42. Taiwan Glass	9	0.00
43. Mercuries & Associates	2	0.00
44. Nam Chow Chemical	9	0.27
45. Lien-I Textiles	6	15.03
46. Ve Wang	3	0.20

Appendix 3.2   Continued

Group[a]	Number of Companies	Rate of Internal Transactions (%)[b]
47. Hwa Eng. Wire & Cable	4	11.73
48. Tah Tong Textile	13	8.47
49. Ve Dan	7	3.40
50. Pou Chen	3	0.26
51. Lily Textile	5	6.06
52. Great Wall	—	—
53. Fwu Sow Grain Products	6	3.27
54. Tah Hsin	6	0.00
55. Ocean Plastics	3	0.00
56. Ta Ya Electric Wire	3	7.55
57. Tung Ho Steel	3	9.11
58. Microtek	—	—
59. Formosan	2	0.00
60. Tai Roun	7	1.47
61. International Auto	3	2.58
62. Chu Che	3	5.93
63. Kung Hsue She Co.	3	0.00
64. Lee Tah	3	0.00
65. Associated	11	0.00
66. Far East Machinery	4	0.00
67. Ho Cheng	7	4.19
68. Tung-Kuang	5	8.07
69. Southeast Cement	5	12.30
70. Pievue	4	0.00
71. U-lead	3	0.00
72. Kwong Fong	4	0.41
73. Chun Yu Works	5	6.40
74. Ever Fortune	3	0.00
75. UB	6	0.00
76. Tai Hwa	4	3.34
77. Rexon Industry	8	7.95
78. Lien Fu	5	2.64
79. Hui Shung	8	1.00
80. Sino-Japan	5	1.01
81. San Yu	3	0.98
82. Chih Lien Industry	7	17.00
83. China Chemical	5	6.40
84. Ability	7	1.95
85. Fu Tai Umbrella	6	6.95
86. Nice	3	0.00
87. Fu I Industrial	6	14.67
88. Victor	6	0.00
89. Kaisers Plastic	6	0.19
90. Sun Wu	4	15.50

(continued)

Appendix 3.2   Continued

Group[a]	Number of Companies	Rate of Internal Transactions (%)[b]
91. Tong Hsing	4	0.00
92. Fong Kuo	3	0.54
93. Cosmos	7	0.00
94. Typhone	4	2.49
95. Ye Shan Mu	5	0.00
96. Trans-world	3	0.29
97. OEMEC	3	0.00
98. Cheng Hong	7	0.00004
99. Chin Ho Fa Steel & Iron	4	9.36
100. Tai Hsin	4	0.00

SOURCE: China Credit Information Service (1990).
NOTE: Out of the 100 biggest business groups recorded, 4 have been deleted in this study because of some analysis problems.
a. Rankings are based on the size of the business groups' total sales (China Credit Information Service, 1990, p. 2).
b. The rate of internal transactions is the proportion of total estimated demand (input) of the business group that is internal transactions. It is interpreted as the proportion of demand (input) that is satisfied by the companies within the group.

Notes

1. In recent comments on his 1937 paper, Coase (1991) seems to back off from his emphasis on the authoritative relationship within the firm: "I consider that one of the main weaknesses of my article stems from the use of the employer-employee relationship as the archetype of the firm" (pp. 64-65). However, he wants to expand the basis of the relationship by clarifying what, in Weberian sociology, would be called the "basis of legitimacy," which in the case of the modern firm is its contractual and legalistic character. Coase explains, "As a result of the emphasis of the employer-employee relationship, the contracts that enable the organizers of the firm to direct the use of capital (equipment or money) by acquiring, leasing, or borrowing it were not examined, perhaps because, fifty years ago, I did not know enough to be able to handle these problems." In making this qualification, however, Coase seems to be embracing Cheung's (1983) interpretation of the firm as the "nexus of all contracts." Although this qualification accords with a Weberian reinterpretation, its consequence has been to divert attention away from domination within economic organization to extensive debates on the character of and differences among contracts within and between firms.

2. The extent of this literature and its contents are well represented in Schmalensee and Willig (1989).

3. "By governance structure, I refer to the institutional setting within which the execution of transactions is accomplished and their integrity is decided" (Williamson, 1986, p. 155).

4. "When the responsibility for effecting adaptations is concentrated on one or a few agents, hierarchy is relatively great. Where instead adaptations are taken by individual agents or are subject to collective approval, hierarchy is slight" (Williamson, 1985, p. 221).

5. Williamson (1991) has recently acknowledged this fact when he "dimensionalizes" governance by adding the "hybrid" type of governance structure between the market and hierarchy extremes.

6. We should note that, for these scholars, Chandler's *The Visible Hand* (1977) is the first target of criticism, with Williamson coming second.

7. This level of analysis allows what Weber calls a *verstehen* interpretation of action, action conceived in terms of the subjective meaning intended by the actors.

8. Economists sometimes equate the concept of firm with every level of economic organization that acts authoritatively, whether that is a business group (Leff, 1978), a guild (Greif, Milgrom, & Weingast, 1994), or the modern corporation.

9. Williamson notes frequently that his approach is comparative, but comparative methodology for transaction cost theory means the generation of typologies and classifications of differences in transactions and in governance structures. It implies cross-market or even cross-societal comparisons.

10. Although rarely used by either the new institutional economists or the new economic sociologists, Weber's writings on the economy played a formidable role in the thinking of the earlier generation of institutional economists, notably Knight, who translated Weber's *General Economic History* of 1923 in 1961, and Schumpeter, briefly a colleague of Weber, who "was greatly influenced by Max Weber's attempt to create a new and broad type of transdisciplinary economies, call *Sozialosonomil,* or 'social economics' " (Swedberg, 1991, p. 2). Among sociologists, of course, Weber is regarded as a founder of economic sociology (Swedberg, Himmelstrand, & Brulin, 1990), but his contribution is often restricted to his controversial thesis about the Protestant origins of capitalism and to his formulation of bureaucracy as an ideal type. Despite his relative neglect in both economics and sociology, Weber's writings constitute a highly sophisticated institutional theory of economic activity. Weber's major contribution to institutional economics came in the decade after he wrote his book on the Protestant ethic, between 1908 and 1920, when he undertook the task of editing and himself writing large portions of a handbook he titled *Outline of Social Economics.* With this handbook, Weber aimed to correct the theoretical excesses of neoclassical economists in his own day by spelling out the relationships between the economy and socially organized groups. As time went on, Weber's contribution to the volume grew as other scholars failed to provide manuscripts of sufficient quality. In the end, Weber himself wrote the main section, which he provisionally titled "The Economy and the Societal Orders and Powers." Dying of pneumonia in 1920 before he had the opportunity to prepare the final manuscript for publication, Weber left several versions that were subsequently compiled, edited, and published posthumously as *Economy and Society.* See Schluchter's (1989) definitive account of the development of this book.

11. This typological analysis formed a conceptual framework that allowed Weber to develop, in a series of studies on world civilizations, an explanation for the rise of Western capitalism.

12. In the most modern era, says Weber (1978), "a modern market economy essentially consists in a complete network of exchange contracts, that is, in deliberate planned acquisitions of powers of control and disposal" (p. 67).

13. For Weber, a "typical measure of rational economic action" is similar to what Williamson regards as the calculative motive for vertical integration: "The systematic procurement through production or transportation of such utilities for which all the necessary means of production are controlled by the actor himself. Where action is rational, this type of action will take place so far as, according to the actor's estimate, the urgency of his demand for the expected result of the action exceeds the necessary expenditure, which may consist in (a) the irksomeness of the requisite labor services, and (b) the other potential uses to which the requisite goods could be

put; including, that is, the utility of the potential alternative products and their uses. This is 'production' in the broader sense, which includes transportation" (Weber, 1978, p. 71).

14. Weber (1978) argues that, once the capitalist process began, market processes would further systematize economic organizations: "All material means become fixed or working capital; all workers become 'hands.' As a result of the transformation of enterprises into associations of stock holders, the manager himself becomes expropriated and assumes the formal status of an 'official' " (p. 148).

15. For extended discussion of Weber's analysis of modern capitalism, see Collins (1980), Schluchter (1989), and Hamilton (1994).

16. In real life, of course, participants often do both at once. They often recognize that they are bound by organizational authority and act in a self-interested way in violation of the organizational norms. Also, in real life, the boundaries of who should obey, when obedience is required, and what the content of compliance should be are highly ambiguous.

17. See Hamilton (1978, 1985) for discussions of several types of economic action arising from particular groups in which the participants formally regard themselves as equals.

18. We should note that Geertz (1963) does not explicitly identify the horizontal networks that are present in this case and in the case of other overseas Chinese traders in Southeast Asia. What Geertz observes are individuated households, with each actor making independent economic decisions, a condition that indicates, to him (p. 47), an absence of organization. What he describes, however, is a highly organized system of horizontal networking in which "traders . . . treat each other in precisely formulated and technically restricted terms" (p. 46). "A trader contracting even a fairly petty agreement will look for others to go in with him, and, in fact, there is widely felt normative obligation on the part of traders to allow other people to cut into a good thing. . . . The individual trader, unless he is very small indeed, is the center of a series of rapidly forming and dissolving one-deal, compositely organized trading coalitions" (p. 40). Made up of repeat players, these coalitions are the short-term manifestations of the perduring horizontal networks that make up this economy.

19. For the purposes of this chapter, organizations supporting market integration, the opposite of vertical integration, correspond to what Geertz (1963) calls "interstitial" groups that intersect commodities chains. These groupings form an interface between sets of economic actors, such as buyers and sellers, producers and merchandisers, in those situations where an organization forms a condition in which each link in a commodity chain is independently constituted and controlled and forms a distinct transaction with its own costs and efficiencies.

20. Weber's (1978) evaluation of the *oikos* is worth quoting in this context: "[The *oikos*] is not simply any large household or one which produces on its own various products, agricultural or industrial; rather, it is the authoritarian household of a prince, manorial lord or patrician. Its dominant motive is not capitalistic acquisition but the lord's organized want satisfaction in kind. For this purpose, he may resort to any means, including large-scale trade. Decisive for him is the utilization of property, not capital investment. The essence of the *oikos* is organized want satisfaction, even if market-oriented enterprises are attached to it. Of course, there is a scale of imperceptible transitions between the two modes of economic orientation, and often also a mode of less rapid transformation from one into the other" (p. 381).

21. The United States is an exception to this pattern because vertical integration primarily occurred within the boundaries of a legally defined firm instead of occurring within a network of firms. See Biggart and Hamilton (1992) and Hamilton and Sutton (1989) for discussion of the exceptional nature of the United States.

22. There are many examples of informal, short-term financial associations that are organized on this basis. The rotating credit associations common throughout many parts of the world

constitute one example. Another example is the *compagnia* of medieval Italy (Lopez & Raymond, 1955, pp. 185-187).

23. All the researchers who have studied ownership patterns among large firms in Taiwan (Greenhalgh, 1988; Hamilton & Biggart, 1988; Mark, 1972) have emphasized the importance of family (*jia*) ownership and family control. An analysis of the 1983 and 1986 data on Taiwan business groups, as well as interviews with core people in some of the business groups, substantiates this finding. Majority ownership and control of business group firms are in the hands of core family members and heads of households. Our colleagues in Taiwan who are also working on this project have determined, on a group-by-group basis, that 84 of the top 97 business groups in 1983 can be strictly classified as family-owned business groups (Peng, 1989, p. 277). Of these, 23 are primarily owned by a single head of household; the remaining 61 have multiple family members classified among the core people in the group, and most of those family members (54 out of the 61) are of three types: fathers and sons, brothers, and brothers and their sons (Peng, 1989, p. 278).

24. Our source for these data is Korea Investors Service (1990). These data have been recompiled in *Business Networks in Korea, 1989* (Lim et al., 1993).

25. The total demand figure is reached by subtracting value added for each group (i.e., labor costs plus profits) from the total sales of the group. The remainder approximates the amount of purchases made by firms in a *chaebol* in order to produce final products. The calculations at every level have been adjusted to eliminate any double counting of purchases and sales of the trading companies within the *chaebol*. All of the largest *chaebol* have trading companies. Unlike their Japanese counterparts, the *sogo shosha*, the *chaebol* trading companies primarily distribute group products, usually in foreign markets. In the data on interfirm transactions, *chaebol* trading companies are usually among the main buyers of goods sold by other firms in the *chaebol*, and they are the main seller of products in a final form. In order not to double count a purchase and a sale of the same goods within the *chaebol* network, we decided to eliminate all possibility of double counting by subtracting the internal purchases but not the sales of *chaebol* trading companies. This precaution lowers the rate of internalization, sometimes substantially.

26. Although we have reported accounting data on the sales and assets for the firms in Taiwan's 100 largest business groups, as well as whether or not firms in a business group make transactions with each other, we do not have exact figures on the amounts of those transactions. The source for our Taiwan business group data is the China Credit Information Service's *Business Groups in Taiwan* (1990). From this and from official government statistics, we have compiled a database to estimate the internalization rate for the business groups in Taiwan (Chung, Feenstra, & Hamilton, 1993). Lacking precise data on interfirm transactions within business groups, we have estimated the amount of internal transactions by using the "input-output tables" published by the Taiwan government. These tables come from comprehensive government-run surveys on the state of the economy. A part of the survey compiles the transaction levels between economic sectors. For our estimate, we categorized each firm in a business group into the sector of its business. Then we used the general rate of transaction among sectors in the economy to estimate the amount of transactions among firms in business groups.

27. The only correlation we could discover was with the sector of business. Business groups specializing in textiles showed marginally higher rates of internalization than did other groups.

28. These data are discussed at greater length in Chapter 9 of this volume.

29. This is the reason Taiwan runs such a huge trade deficit with Japan.

30. For one of the best exceptions to this general pattern of reporting, see Scitovsky (1985).

31. Transaction cost theorists might be tempted at this point, and profitably so, to argue that the analytic way to explain the differential outcomes is to apply transaction cost theory to the

family structures themselves. For a transaction cost approach to family and households, see Pollak (1985).

32. The distinction between patrimonialism and patriarchalism is crucial in this comparison. Weber (1978, pp. 1006-1069) defines patriarchalism as the authority of the master over his household, and patrimonialism as the extension of patriarchal principles beyond the household. In the latter case, patrimonial authority within groups is created through the manipulation of relationships so that the loyalty and dependence of household members is approximated in individuals outside the household.

PART

Capitalism in East Asia

Explaining Asian Business Success

Theory No. 4

NICOLE WOOLSEY BIGGART
GARY G. HAMILTON

he business phenomenon of the decade is obvious: the growth of Asian economies—particularly Japan, Taiwan, and South Korea. Both Japan and Taiwan were destroyed by World War II, and Korea was leveled by a civil war that killed 1.3 million people. Yet all three of these countries—ravaged by war—are booming after

AUTHORS' NOTE: This chapter is reprinted here by permission from "Explaining Asian Business Success: Theory No. 4," by Nicole Woolsey Biggart and Gary G. Hamilton, *Business and Economics Review*, 1990, vol. 5, pp. 13-15. Copyright 1990 by Business and Economics Review; all rights reserved.

little more than a generation. In 1984, Japan's gross national product was the second highest in the world, and Japan has growth and investment rates twice those of the United States. Taiwan's GNP grew an average of 10.6% a year in the decade 1963-1972, and from 1973 to 1982—a period that included a world recession—it still grew 7.5%. South Korea did not begin industrializing until the 1960s, but from 1963 to 1972 its manufacturing exports grew an amazing 52%. From 1962 to 1984 South Korean industrial production increased 17%. In comparison, the U.S. gross domestic product grew an average of 3.2% between 1976 and 1985. In the same period, Great Britain's grew 1.8%. The figures are clear and confirm our observations: Asians have become world-class manufacturers and exporters.

The second-biggest business phenomenon of the decade is related to the first: the explosion of books and theories that try to explain Asian business success. One can go into any bookstore, and many supermarkets, and find a dozen books that claim to unlock the secret to Asian management. Although there are many theories, we can put them into three categories.

Theory No. 1: Culture

First, there is Theory No. 1, the culture theory. This theory claims that the Confucian ethic is the key to understanding Asia, and it is certainly true that most Asian nations have been influenced by Confucianism. Confucianism stresses the importance of family, of obedience to superiors, of hard work and self-discipline. It is also an ethic that promotes education. Anyone who has been to Asia cannot help but be impressed by the willingness of people there to work extremely hard for very long hours, often for very little pay. The crime rates are low and literacy rates are high, consistent with the Confucian values of self-control and obedience to authority. Clearly all of these factors help the economy.

Culture theory books usually have two lessons for people in the West. The first lesson is that success comes to those who are willing to work for it. Second, Westerners are exhorted to return to traditional values of family thrift, hard work, and education. Europeans and Americans had better revive the Protestant ethic if they are going to compete with the Confucian ethic according to this perspective.

Theory No. 2: Management

Theory No. 2 explains Asian success in a different way. This theory argues that the problem really is not cultural differences. After all, many people in the West work very hard, too, and Western nations also have high literacy rates. The problem is not laziness and disinterest, but rather poor organization and management. According to Theory No. 2, the large and small enterprises of Europe and America are simply not put together correctly. The problem is simply one of misorganization and economic mismanagement.

For example, there are books like William Ouchi's *Theory Z* (1982) that discuss the effectiveness of Japanese consensus management, of getting everyone involved in decision making. Or of the *kanban* system, the just-in-time inventory system that reduces production time and links assembly plants with smaller subcontractors who are outside their back doors. Here the lesson is that Westerners must reorganize factories and even whole economies—if Western organizational arrangements were efficient, like those in Asia, then presumably they would remain competitive in world markets.

Theory No. 3: Government

The next explanation, Theory No. 3, is not so popular, perhaps, but still important. It argues that although there are certainly differences between Asian and Western cultures, and between Asian and Western business organizations, these differences are not decisive. What is decisive is the relationship between government and business. In all Asian countries, Theory No. 3 argues, the government takes a prominent role in planning and executing economic policy. The government coordinates the domestic economy, controls crucial economic institutions such as banking, and actively promotes industries that are on the rise in the world economy. The lesson is that Asian governments, through smart industrial planning and economic coordination, have created their own economic successes.

What is the message of Theory No. 3? It is grim for people in the United States, whose federal system is hopelessly outdated. They have no economic planning, no centralized mechanism to promote selected industrial sectors, and—if Americans could somehow agree on a plan—virtually no mechanism to coordinate the economy. Instead, the U.S. government is constitutionally divided, with checks and balances that prevent centralized decision making. Branches of government—Congress, the White House, the judiciary—are pitted against each other. State governments contend against Washington, and cities and counties fight with each other and with states for a share of revenue. The United States, where economic coordination is institutionally impossible, must confront capitalist economies that are highly coordinated and strategically planned.

European nations have more centralized authority and planning structures than the United States, and the anticipated unified European economy could be a powerful force. But countries such as Britain and France have a tradition of debate, of loyal opposition, that makes the orchestration of political and management decisions difficult. It also remains to be seen if nations as diverse as Spain, the Netherlands, Germany, and Greece will coordinate their economies.

So what is the solution for politically fragmented societies committed to public debate? Books espousing Theory No. 3 often argue for major political reform.

Which Culture?

We have described above three different theories about what is right with Asia and, implicitly, what is wrong with the West. We, however, believe that Theories 1, 2, and 3 are built on shaky premises—not that they're all wrong, but they make generalizations that simply do not hold when Asia is closely examined.

Consider again Theory No. 1, the culture theory. This explanation assumes that Asian cultures are all alike. Japan, Taiwan, and South Korea share a Confucian and Buddhist heritage. Through trade, ideas and practices have diffused throughout Northeast Asia for millennia. China, especially, has had an influence in the region. For example, Japanese writing uses Chinese script, as did Korean writing until the sixteenth century. It is also true that as Confucian countries, they all place great emphasis on family, work, education, obedience, and self-discipline.

It is not true, however, that they are culturally all alike any more than England, Italy, Sweden, and France are the same. The Japanese, Koreans, and Taiwanese all speak different languages that are mutually unintelligible.

They have different cuisines, different political systems, and different dress and manners.

For example, they all believe in the importance of family, but "family" means something quite different in each nation. In Japan the eldest son inherits everything. He keeps the family wealth intact, whereas younger sons must establish their own fortunes. If a man does not have a son, he will frequently adopt one in order to pass on his wealth. Japanese family relations tend to be harmonious or at least strive toward that ideal.

In Chinese societies such as Taiwan, wealth is divided equally among all sons, so families are often concerned with building a separate business for each male heir. Unlike in Japan, adoption is rare in China—only blood relations have a place in the lineage. No one ever accused the Chinese of harmony: Families squabble and rivalries among sons are commonplace.

The Koreans are different yet. Like the Chinese, they are outspoken and do not adopt outsiders into the family. But they give the lion's share of the inheritance—usually about two-thirds—to the oldest son, and smaller shares to younger brothers. The Korean inheritance pattern is like neither the Chinese nor the Japanese.

One could continue by comparing education, hours of work, and other cultural expressions, and would find that they, too, differ substantially among the three countries. The point is that although there are certainly cultural continuities throughout East Asia, just as there are throughout Europe, Asians are not culturally all the same. Therefore, one cannot explain the success of Japan, Taiwan, and South Korea using a cultural argument— there is no single culture that explains their common success.

Which Asian Management?

Theory No. 2 suggests that Western businesses, and Western economies, need to reorganize and adopt Asian management practices. Usually this means Japanese management practices. But in fact, the Korean and Taiwanese economies are organized very differently from the Japanese and seem to be doing well without adopting consensual decision making or just-in-time inventory systems.

The Japanese economy is dominated by large business groups such as Sumitomo and Mitsubishi. The Sumitomo business group, for example, is a group of firms in insurance, banking, heavy industry, shipping, and a variety of other industries. Other business groups, like Mitsubishi and Mitsui, also have member companies in diversified businesses. These business group firms are all legally independent, but they work together to aid each other by pursuing joint ventures, lending managers to each other, and financing promising ideas initiated by member firms. It is as though the U.S. companies AT&T, Xerox, Bank of America, and Chevron had formed a mutual aid society.

The large firms in Japanese business groups are linked to smaller subcontracting firms through very stable long-term relations. They try to help each other by improving product designs and sharing economic downturns. In sum, the Japanese economy is characterized by networks of large companies connected to each other by stable relations and to smaller companies through similarly stable subcontracting ties. Even the large business groups like Sumitomo and Mitsubishi have ties to each other through the common ownership of financial institutions.

Koreans also have large business groups, such as Daewoo, Hyundai, and Lucky-Goldstar. But these are not networks of companies that come together for mutual assistance, as in Japan. Instead, each of these business groups is a giant conglomerate owned by a single patriarch and his family. None of the firms in the Hyundai group—or *chaebol,* as such groups are called in Korea—would think of meeting together in the absence of the patriarch. These are highly centralized groups of firms that report only to the man at the top, who runs them with a very authoritarian management style. There is no consensus management in South Korea, no subcontracting relations of any importance, and Korean *chaebol* compete fiercely with each other.

Taiwan is organized differently yet. Taiwan has business groups also, but they tend to be networks of small to medium-sized family firms. There are almost no large companies in Taiwan that could rival those in Korea and Japan. Firms are established in one generation only to break apart and re-form in the next. The stability of Japanese companies and the size of Korean companies are unthinkable in Taiwan.

When books based on Theory No. 2 espouse that the United States organize its economy like Asian economies, or that U.S. firms borrow Asian management practices, one must ask which Asian economy and practices—Japan's, South Korea's, or Taiwan's? They differ dramatically one from the other, and yet each has been successful.

Consider again Theory No. 3, which says Asians have been successful because their governments are active participants in economic planning. In fact, in all of the three countries we are considering, government and business have very different relationships. In Japan, the state acts as a negotiator of business interests. Businesses are reluctant to depart from government plans, but agreement is reached through negotiation and consensus building, not through direct orders. The Japanese government does not run the economy, although it plays an oversight function and encourages investment in promising industries.

In South Korea, government does run the economy. It targets industries for development, picks the companies that will develop them, approves their plans, and lends them money. Until recently, Korean businesses could not get money without going to the government—the state owned all the banks. If the government disapproves of the way an industry is run, financing dries up.

In Taiwan, the government takes care of industrial infrastructure such as transportation and energy. As in Korea, the Taiwanese government was authoritarian throughout the period of rapid industrialization. But aside from providing infrastructure and a lot of rhetoric, it tends to keep out of the economy. Milton Friedman, the conservative American Nobel laureate in economics, is said to approve of Taiwan's free market environment.

So, if one is going to explain Asia's success according to Theory No. 3, government activism in the economy, which government is to serve as a model? Each is different from the others.

Theory No. 4

So what are we left with? If it's not culture, management, or government that explains Asia's obvious business success, what is it?

We believe that Japan, Taiwan, and South Korea have done very well not because they have been attempting to do the same Asian thing, but because they have been pursuing different industrial strategies. Each has a culture, organizational arrangements, and a government-business relationship that suits its national strategy for success in the world economy.

Theory No. 4 says very simply that Asian economies have worked so well because they have created organizational arrangements and management practices that give them a competitive advantage. Japan, South Korea, and Taiwan all pursue business strategies that suit their social arrangements—their cultures, their traditional ways of organizing and managing, and their government structures. None of these nations attempts to do everything, and none has attempted to imitate the West. Instead, each has focused on industries and processes in which it has a particular social advantage.

Consider Japan first. Before World War II, Japan's economy was dominated by large enterprise groups called *zaibatsu*. *Zaibatsu* were groups of firms owned by families. The firms in the groups kept separate books, but in fact were related to each other through shared investments and common ownership. The *zaibatsu* firms coordinated their business plans with each other, shared personnel, and even entered into common financing arrangements.

The *zaibatsu* grew very large and powerful and in fact dominated the Japanese economy by the time of World War II. When the United States occupied Japan in the late 1940s and helped to orchestrate that country's recovery from war, one of the first things the Americans did was take apart the *zaibatsu*. *Zaibatsu*, from a Western perspective, look like a terrible way to organize. They were essentially cartels and impeded competition. Their management practices were very paternalistic and rewarded seniority, not merit. The Americans made the *zaibatsu* companies independent firms and forbade all but the smallest cross-holdings of shares between companies in Japan. The United States wanted Japan to establish an economy of independent firms that competed aggressively with each other. The Americans wanted a Japanese economy that looked like theirs, then the strongest economy in the world. They attempted to rout out cooperation and collusion among firms.

The *zaibatsu* are gone. There are no more powerful family-owned business groups in Japan that control large portions of the economy. But who dominates the Japanese economy today? Groups of firms like Sumitomo, Mitsui, and Mitsubishi—groups of firms that look much like their pre-war predecessors. In fact, the Japanese did not take long in reconstructing their prewar organizational patterns.

Today's business groups, such as the Sumitomo group, are typically composed of a couple of dozen firms that—although legally independent—act together for their mutual advantage. They enter into joint projects, plan common business strategies, and share personnel. They act like a *zaibatsu* community of firms.

There was a period during the 1960s when this reversion to traditional patterns of organizing, and to traditional paternalistic management practices, was soundly criticized by both Westerners and some Japanese. The critics said that competition and individualism were the only ways to compete successfully in the modern world economy. Critics predicted that Japan would do well only as long as its labor costs were low, but that it could not compete in technologically advanced industries. In fact, Japan did well by adapting its traditional business patterns to a modern economy. Indeed, it is clear that some Japanese methods work especially well in a modern international economy.

What are the competitive advantages of the Japanese pattern? First, there is a commitment to the organization that is conspicuously absent in the West. Paternalism—treating workers as family, as the *zaibatsu* did—develops a loyalty to the products and success of the firm. Quality control experts say that this human commitment—as much as technical superiority—is responsible for the low error rates of Japanese manufacturing. Japan has become known for its high-quality products.

Second, cooperative relations among legally independent firms create financial and managerial synergies. Most of the stock of Sanwa Bank is owned by Sanwa business group firms. If the bank wants to invest in a project that has good long-term payout, it has only to convince the other members of the group that this is a worthy idea. The group will forgo short-term profits and be patient, waiting for a more substantial reward over the long term. Because stock ownership is more diffuse in the West, Western firms feel greater pressure to seek quick returns to keep investors happy.

Cooperative relations—not just competition—can cut costs. For example, just-in-time inventory systems can mean considerable savings. The Japanese keep their subcontractors near the back doors of their assembly plants. They do not need to stockpile, at great expense, large inventories of small parts and materials. This system is possible in Japan because of the close cooperative relations that exist between manufacturers and parts suppliers. A large firm works closely with smaller firms, often helping them out with financial problems. The small firms know that the large firm values their relationship and will work to keep it profitable for both parties.

Contrast this with the West, where competitive bidding dominates. If a given firm can beat last year's supplier by a dollar, there is a new supplier. Suppliers are constantly looking for multiple outlets for their goods, so that in case one company abandons them, they will not go out of business. Companies can lose suppliers, too, if the suppliers find other companies that will pay a dollar more. As a result, in the West there is the just-in-case inventory system—large, expensive stockpiles of parts kept on hand, just in case.

Third, cooperative relations between business and the Japanese government have enabled the country to target areas for development and to direct R&D money to especially promising projects.

These are examples—there are many more—of ways in which cooperative relations and paternalistic management have helped the Japanese to develop a healthy economy. They were given the opportunity to develop Western patterns, but opted for doing what made sense to them culturally. The Japanese have certainly borrowed technology and management techniques from the West, but they have imported new ideas without changing their basic framework.

South Koreans also have large business groups, but they are very different from the Japanese groups. In South Korea, most of the stock of Hyundai, Samsung, Lucky-Goldstar, and each of the other *chaebol* is owned by a single man—a patriarch and his heirs. All of the companies within a *chaebol* report to the man at the top, and most of the firms are run by members of the family, who exert very tight control. There is no consensus decision making in Korea. There is centralization and rigid hierarchy within each *chaebol*.

How did the Koreans come up with these patriarchal conglomerates as a way to organize their economy? After all, Korea was colonized by the Japanese until World War II, and Koreans knew all about *zaibatsu* organization; further, the United States tried to teach them Western management techniques after the Korean War.

In fact, the *chaebol* is reminiscent of preindustrial political organization in Korea. Korean society—for hundreds of years—was organized into patriarchal clans. These clans were located in geographic regions and sent emissaries to the Korean dynastic court in Seoul. It is a very ancient form of organizing that the Koreans reverted to when they planned their economic recovery. Even today, the *chaebol* have regional roots—most of the top executives in any *chaebol* come from the same province as the patriarch who owns it.

Nor does the South Korean government sit down to coordinate national business planning the way the Japanese government does. Instead, the Korean government dictates what business will do in much the way the Korean kings attempted to dictate their political will. The government decides which sectors of the economy will grow and selects businesses to develop those sectors. It lends money to the businesses—the government owns all the banks—and then often tells them what price they can charge.

How can the Koreans have succeeded, given these rigid, hierarchical organizations that are owned by families? What competitive advantages do the *chaebol* offer? First, the *chaebol* are a very effective way to keep large amounts of capital together. These are huge conglomerates with large sums of money under their control—given the watchful eye of government. The *chaebol* have been able to invest in highly capital-intensive industries such as steelmaking, shipbuilding, and automobile manufacturing. The amounts of money these industries require would have been very hard for independent entrepreneurs to raise without the backing of government. The limited amount of competition that the government allows assures that Korea will have viable businesses in some core industries.

Second, worker discipline has been maintained by the rigid hierarchy of Korean management. Americans work about 38 hours a week, Japanese about 42 hours a week, and Koreans nearly 58 hours a week. These are incredibly long hours, often under difficult circumstances. Korean management style stresses self-discipline and obedience to superiors. Unlike the Japanese, who encourage workers to master several jobs, even on assembly lines, the Koreans want dedication to a position.

Is this a good organizational strategy for development? Probably in the short term, yes. South Korea has become a major competitor in capital-intensive industries, such as heavy construction, equipment manufacturing, and steelmaking. It is also giving Japanese shipbuilding a tough time. Moreover, South Koreans have enjoyed a rising standard of living even while working hard.

No doubt there will be a modification of this harsh strategy as workers demand more pay and as Koreans need more advanced technology. Rigid hierarchy and centralization are poor ways to encourage innovation. Nonetheless, the South Koreans have achieved an amazing level of success by using traditional organizing strategies—strategies that made sense to them. They developed a competitive advantage not by copying the West or the Japanese, but by figuring out what they could do well given the kind of society they had.

The Taiwanese borrow organizationally from neither the Japanese nor the South Koreans. The Taiwan example shows that remarkable development can occur in the absence of huge corporations. Although Taiwan certainly has large firms, few Westerners could name a single company there or identify a single Taiwanese brand name. Yet Taiwan's economic success in recent years is second to none, with monetary surplus matching even that of Japan.

Westerners are unfamiliar with Taiwanese companies because the majority of export goods to the West enter under local brand names or are insignificant component parts of larger items. Taiwan sells few expensive consumer items to the West—no cars, robotic systems, supercomputers, high-grade steel, or computer chips. Instead, Taiwan sells inexpensive consumer non-durables such as toys, small electronics, furniture, shoes, and watches.

The typical production system in Taiwan, as in other Chinese societies, is a cooperative network of small and middle-sized firms that join together to produce commodities on demand. These production systems are extremely flexible and respond quickly to market forces. For example, Taiwan is the world's largest producer of bicycles for export, yet has not a single large bicycle factory. Instead, there are firms that manufacture parts and others that assemble them to meet retailers' specifications.

These "satellite assembly systems" dissolve when the orders stop. The individual firms seek new product orders and form a new satellite assembly system with the next wave of orders. Flexible, undercapitalized, and extremely sensitive to market demand, this type of production system creates a sort of capitalism that rolls with market forces and does not attempt to control them. Several people have called the Chinese industrial system "guerrilla capitalism."

Like the Korean and Japanese systems, this type of capitalism rests on the distinctive features of Chinese society. In Taiwan, where each son gets an equal share of his father's estate, animosity among male heirs can be great. Rather than having a large corporation that breaks up at the father's death, it is a reasonable strategy to start several small independent firms so that each son will have a business to manage. Over the centuries, Chinese people have developed social rules that allow for the formation of cooperative networks of related and unrelated people, called *guanxi* networks, which promote the mutual well-being of their members. These network patterns, with origins in imperial China, have been adapted to the modern world economy. Taiwan's competitive advantage in the international marketplace is based on the ability to form socially binding, but economically flexible, production systems quickly and reliably.

Societal Comparative Advantage

Most analysts see comparative advantage as a product strategy, but if we employ a broader conceptualization, it is clear that comparative advantage also applies to societies. Theory No. 4 tells us that different societies have distinctive social patterns that lend themselves to particular organizing strategies.

What lessons are there in Theory No. 4 for the West? First is the obvious point that there is no one necessarily right way to further economic development. Instead, many possible strategies can be successful. This lesson would suggest that Western nations need not be concerned with following Asian management practices because they are "best."

Second is a less obvious point: The Asian cases show that one should organize in a way that makes sense to the people being organized. Culturally familiar organizing strategies promote control, especially self-control, because people can intuitively understand what is expected of them, even if they do not always like it. Asian nations have drawn on their own social and cultural repertoires to create new economic organizations.

The lesson to be understood from this conclusion is that the United States needs to build on its own traditions. We need to diagnose our own weaknesses dispassionately and to understand the sources of our own shortcomings. From that knowledge we should build upon the repertoire that exists within our own society. If we decide a more cooperative and less competitive economy is needed, then we should remember that ours is not a shallow tradition, but is rather a full and complex one that provides many examples of cooperation. Remember it was Alexis de Tocqueville in the 1830s who marveled at the organizational complexity of American society, a society filled with all manner of voluntary associations. Have we lost our capacity to organize such associations, to form groups such as the so-called friendly societies that filled our country in the nineteenth and early twentieth centuries?

The third point is implied by the second. One can adapt techniques and import technologies from other societies, but the success of these in large part depends upon how well they blend into the organizational structure of the host society. After all, the Japanese took their idea for quality circles from the United States, and these were successful in large part because the Japanese have an affinity for techniques that reinforce group solidarity.

Asian societies, however, have uniformly rejected the radical individualism that is characteristic of behavior within and between American firms.

The lesson to learn from this conclusion is that the successful importation of technology is not independent of the social organization of the host society. If Americans expect to import Asian technology and managerial techniques, they should do not do so mechanically and without thinking about how these will fit into or can be adapted to our own society.

Finally, the fourth point is more sobering. The Asian successes ride on the backs of people who earnestly desire to improve themselves and their families. These people desire to raise their own standards of living by raising the standards of their entire societies, by pushing those societies into the ranks of the industrialized nations. They have been successful in part because they were hungry for success, and they were patient and worked hard for small gains. The patience and hard work of Asians have paid off in terms of a more advanced material life for most of these Asian nations' populations. Will that Asian hunger for well-being continue, or will future generations become complacent? That answer is for the future.

The lesson for the United States right now is that Americans must be willing to work for their society's, as well as for their own individual, benefit. No amount of leadership and no management technique will succeed if people will not follow, or refuse to be organized. Are the truly visionary economic and political leaders in the United States without followers? And for the moment have Americans grown weary of working so hard? Have they lost the will and patience to attain difficult goals? These answers, too, are for the future, but in these particular answers lies hidden the secret of America's economic success or failure in the next century.

5

Market, Culture, and Authority

A Comparative Analysis of Management and Organization in the Far East

GARY G. HAMILTON
NICOLE WOOLSEY BIGGART

everal social science disciplines have been interested in the structure and functioning of economic organizations. This widespread interest is largely grouped around three perspectives. Especially in economics (Chandler, 1977, 1981; Teece, 1980; Williamson, 1981, 1985), but also in anthropology (Orlove, 1986) and

AUTHORS' NOTE: This chapter is reprinted here from "Market, Culture, and Authority: A Comparative Analysis of Management and Organization in the Far East," by Gary G. Hamilton and Nicole Woolsey Biggart, *American Journal of Sociology,* 1988, vol. 94 supplement, pp. S52-S94. Copyright 1988 by The University of Chicago; all rights reserved. Versions of sociology (White, 1981), scholars have studied economic decision making in regard to the conditions under which business firms arise and operate in relation to market-mediated transactions. We call this general perspective the *market approach.* The second perspective on economic organization is the *cultural approach,* which suggests that cultural patterns shape economic behavior. This perspective was formerly a preserve of anthropologists (e.g., Benedict, 1946; Douglas, 1979; see also Orlove, 1986), but is now widespread among a large number of scholars from diverse backgrounds. Studies of corporate culture (Deal & Kennedy, 1982; Kanter, 1983; Peters & Waterman, 1982) and comparative culture studies of Japanese (Ouchi, 1982, 1984; Pascale & Athos, 1981; Vogel, 1979), Swedish (Blumberg, 1973; Foy & Gadon, 1976), Yugoslavian (Adizes, 1971), and other nations' industrial practices have increased manifold in the past 10 years. The third perspective is a political economy perspective that we call the *authority approach.* Scholars in all social science fields have worked on economic organization from this wide-ranging perspective, from the seminal work of Marx (1930) and Weber (1958, 1978) to such recent studies as those by Granovetter (1985), Perrow (1981, 1986), Portes and Walton (1981), Haggard and Cheng (1986), Reynolds (1983), and Mintz and Schwartz (1985).

This chapter assesses the relative efficacy of these three approaches in explaining the industrial arrangements and strategies of three rapidly developing countries of the Pacific region—South Korea, Taiwan, and Japan. We argue that, although market and culture explanations make important contributions to understanding, neither is alone sufficient. A market explanation correctly draws our attention to state industrial policies and entrepreneurial responses, but it cannot account for the distinctive and substantially different

---

this chapter have been presented in the following locations: Pan Pacific Conference in Seoul; Tunghai University Seminar Series in Taiwan; Stanford University Organizational Studies Seminar Series; Regional Seminar on Chinese Studies, University of California, Berkeley; and the All-University of California Conference in Economic History at Asilomar, California. We greatly appreciate the helpful comments of many who attended these sessions and thank the following people who carefully read one or more drafts of the chapter: Howard Aldrich, Manuel Castells, Tunjen Cheng, Donald Gibbs, Thomas Gold, Chalmers Johnson, Cheng-shu Kao, Earl Kinmonth, John W. Meyer, Ramon Myers, Marco Orrù, Charles Perrow, William Roy, W. Richard Scott, and Gary Walton. We also wish to acknowledge and thank the following individuals for their help in some part of the research: Wei-an Chang, Ben-ray Jai, Hsien-heng Lu, Hwaijen Peng, Cindy Steams, Moon Jee Yoo, and Shuenn-der Yu. Gary Hamilton also wishes to acknowledge the support of the Fulbright Foundation and the National Science Foundation (SES-8606582), which made this research possible.

organizational arrangements that have appeared in the three countries. A cultural explanation, however, enables us to see, correctly, organizational practices in Japan, South Korea, and Taiwan as generalized expressions of beliefs in the relative importance of such social factors as belongingness, loyalty, and submission to hierarchical authority. But looking at culture alone obscures the fact that business organizations, no matter how well they accord with cultural beliefs, are fundamentally responses to market opportunities and conditions. Enterprise may be culturally informed, but it remains enterprise. Moreover, cultural variables are insufficiently distinguishable in the region to have clear explanatory force.

In this chapter, we argue that the political economy approach with a Weberian emphasis produces the best explanation of the three. This approach incorporates elements of the market and culture explanations but does so from the point of view of the historically developed authority relations that exist among individuals and institutions in each society. We argue that market opportunities do indeed lead to innovations in organizational design, but that these innovations are not simply a rational calculus of the most efficient way to organize. Organizational practices, instead, represent strategies of control that serve to legitimate structures of command and often employ cultural understandings in so doing. Such practices are not randomly developed, but rather are fashioned out of preexisting interactional patterns, which in many cases date to preindustrial times. Hence industrial enterprise is a complex modern adaptation of preexisting patterns of domination to economic situations in which profit, efficiency, and control usually form the very conditions of existence.

We pursue this argument in the following sections. First, we introduce the recent economic history of the three countries of interest and describe their current patterns of industrial organization. South Korea, Taiwan, and Japan offer an unusual opportunity for comparative analysis. The economy of each was virtually destroyed by war, World War II in the cases of Japan and Taiwan and the Korean War in the instance of South Korea. In recent years, all three nations have rebuilt their economies and achieved extraordinary rates of economic growth, yet each has a different dominant form of organizational structure. Second, we employ in turn market, culture, and authority relations explanations, suggesting the distinctive contribution and limitation of each to analyzing the three cases and explaining their differential outcomes. Finally, we suggest how our analysis of these three East Asian economies, and the relative superiority of the authority relations approach,

Table 5.1 Value of Exports in Japan, South Korea, and Taiwan
($U.S. millions)

	Japan	South Korea	Taiwan
1965	8,452	175	450
1970	19,318	835	1,481
1975	55,753	5,081	5,309
1980	129,807	17,505	19,810
1984	170,132[a]	29,153[a]	30,456

SOURCES: Except as noted, figures for Japan are from Japan, Norinsho (1982); for South Korea and Taiwan, Kyongje Kihoegwon, Chosa Tonggueguk (1985).
a. This figure is taken from United Nations (1985).

has implications for industrial analysis, including the American case as it is currently understood.

Recent Economic Development in Japan, Taiwan, and South Korea

More than 40 years ago, at the end of World War II, Japan lay in ruins, its industrial core shattered and its colonial empire of Korea and Taiwan severed. Taiwan, a largely agricultural society, was also leveled by the war, and "three-quarters of [its] industrial capacity was destroyed" (Little, 1979, p. 454). Moreover, Taiwan absorbed fleeing migrants from the Chinese mainland, who arrived with Chiang Kai-shek's armies and government. Taiwan's population jumped from fewer than 6 million people in 1944 to 8 million in 1950, an increase of more than one-third in about 5 years (Kuznets, 1979, p. 32). Similarly, 32 years ago Korea emerged from a civil war that destroyed its economy and killed 1.3 million of its people. The southern agricultural portion of the country was separated from the industrial north. South Korea lost its supply of manufactured goods, hydroelectric power, and the bituminous coal that powered its railroads (Bunge, 1982, p. 24).

Yet, in the 1980s, these three countries are the centerpiece of a rapidly industrializing Asia (Hofheinz & Calder, 1982; Linder, 1986). They have not only rebuilt their economies but have also become the wonder of the developing and developed worlds. Japan's success is the envy of American and European nations: In 1984, Japan's gross national product was the second highest in the capitalist world (Economist Intelligence Unit, 1985), with growth and investment rates double those of the United States (Vogel, 1979). Taiwan's GNP increased an average of 10.6% a year in the decade 1963-1972, and in the decade 1973-1982, a period that included a world recession, it increased 7.5% a year (Myers, 1984). In 1949, Taiwan's per capita income was less than $50 U.S. In 1970 it was around $350, and in 1984, $2,500 (Minard, 1984, p. 36). South Korea's economic development did not accelerate until the 1960s, but in the decade 1963-1972, manufacturing exports grew 52% a year (Little, 1979), and between 1962 and 1984 industrial production increased at an average rate of 17% (Economist Intelligence Unit, 1985). In 1962, South Korea's per capita GNP was $87 U.S.; in 1980 it was $1,503 (Bunge, 1982, p. 109), and in 1983, $1,709 (*Monthly Bulletin of Statistics*, 1985). All three countries' economic success has largely been fueled by exports. Table 5.1 shows the extraordinary growth in the countries' export sectors. In 1984, Japan's trade surplus to the United States was about $40 billion (International Monetary Fund, 1985, p. 242), Taiwan's was nearly $10 billion (more than twice Japan's on a per capita basis) (Council for Economic Planning and Development, 1985, p. 205), and South Korea's was $3.2 billion (International Monetary Fund, 1985, p. 248). By any economic measure, the growth of these Northeast Asian economies is unprecedented and has led many to refer to this economic success story as the "Asian miracle."

The similarities of Japan, Taiwan, and South Korea go beyond economic recovery in the wake of wartime destruction; in fact, other similarities might seem to account for their common economic development (Cumings, 1984; Hofheinz & Calder, 1982). All three countries have few natural, especially mineral, resources. Their success cannot be explained by the discovery of oil reserves, as in some comparably successful developing nations in the Middle East. Nor is land the source of their wealth. Taiwan, South Korea, and Japan are among the most populated countries in the world in relation to cultivable land, "higher even than Egypt and Bangladesh and four times as high as India" (Little, 1979, p. 450). Clearly, these are nations dependent on industry for wealth. They received economic aid and direction from the United States to repair and restart their economies, but the aid alone, which was given to other countries as well, cannot explain the rapid development there (Amsden, 1979; Barrett & Whyte, 1982; Haggard & Cheng, 1986; Hofheinz & Calder, 1982; Little, 1979). Historically and culturally, the three are intertwined. Japan colonized Taiwan in 1895 and Korea in 1910, pursuing similar colonial policies in each (Cumings, 1984; Myers & Peattie, 1984). Although each nation has its own language and ethnicity, China has, historically, had influences throughout the region. Korea and Japan, like Taiwan, have been deeply influenced by Confucian and Buddhist traditions. All three have relied on exports as a means for economic expansion.

In sum, the similarities are substantial. In fact, they are so great and the fate of the three countries so interlinked historically that Bruce Cumings (1984) insightfully argues that "the industrial development in Japan, Korea, and Taiwan cannot be considered as an individual country phenomenon; instead it is a regional phenomenon." He further argues, "When one [country] is compared to another the differences will also be salient, but when all three are compared to the rest of the world the similarities are remarkable" (p. 38).

Despite these similarities, Japan, South Korea, and Taiwan have substantially different forms of enterprise or firm organization, particularly in the export sectors of their economies. Moreover, in each country the firm is embedded in a network of institutional relationships that gives each economy a distinctive character.[1] The important point here is that, if one looks only at individual firms, one misses the crucial set of social and political institutions that serves to integrate the economy. Taking advantage of Granovetter's (1985) very useful discussion, we argue that the firm is "embedded" in networks of institutionalized relationships and that these networks, which are different in each society, have a direct effect on the types of firms that develop, on the management of firms, and on organizational strategies more generally. The particular forms of economic embeddedness in each society, particularly in relation to political institutions, allow for the activation of different organizational designs to achieve industrialization.

Three Patterns of Industrial Organization

In Japan, two interrelated networks of firms are crucial for understanding the operation of the Japanese economy, and particularly the export sector. These networks represent two types of what Caves and Uekusa (1976) call "enterprise groups." One type of enterprise group consists of linkages among large firms. These linkages are usually loosely coupled, basically horizontal connections among a range of large firms. Although such firms differ in terms of size and prestige (Clark, 1979, p. 95), the linkages between them are what Dore (1983) calls "relational contracting between equals" (p. 467).

Table 5.2 Distribution of Assets of Large Japanese Corporations,
by Group Affiliation

Affiliate Group	Percentage of Total Assets		
	1955	*1962*	*1965*
Public corporations whose capital is wholly or partly government owned	62.2	50.1	38.3
Affiliates of long-term credit banks whose capital is partly government owned	2.1	3.3	4.3
Affiliates of *zaibatsu* and large private banks	23.3	28.4	29.2
Mitsui	6.1	3.8	5.0
Mitsubishi	5.0	6.4	7.2
Sumitomo	3.2	5.9	5.4
Fuji Bank (Yasuda)	2.9	3.6	3.8
Dai-Ichi Bank	3.1	3.5	3.2
Sanwa Bank	1.4	2.2	2.6
Giant industrial corporations with vertical and conglomerate structures of subsidiaries and affiliates	5.6	9.5	8.8
Foreign-owned enterprises	1.0	1.4	1.4
Companies outside the affiliate system	5.8	7.3	18.0
Total	100.0	100.0	100.0

SOURCE: Data from Caves and Uekusa (1976, p. 64).

These groupings of firms are intermarket groups and are spread through
different industrial sectors (Vogel, 1979, p. 107). The second type of enterprise group connects small and medium-sized firms to a large firm, creating
what economists (e.g., Nakamura, 1981; Ozawa, 1979; Patrick & Rosovsky,
1976) call a "dual structure," a situation of "relational contracting between
unequals" (Dore, 1983, p. 465). Both types of enterprise groups make centrally located large firms and associations of large firms the principal actors
in the Japanese economy. As a result of these enterprise groups, assets are distributed throughout a range of different types of firms, as shown in Table 5.2.

The best-known networks of large firms, or *grupu,* are the *kigyo shudan,*
or intermarket groups, which are the modern-day descendants of the pre-
World War II *zaibatsu.* These networks are normally groups of firms in
unrelated businesses that are joined together by central banks or by trading
companies (Caves & Uekusa, 1976; Clark, 1979). In prewar Japan, these
groups were linked by powerful holding companies that were each under the
control of a family. The *zaibatsu* families exerted control over the individual

firms in their groups through a variety of fiscal and managerial methods. During the U.S. occupation, the largest of these holding companies were dissolved, with the member firms of each group becoming independent (Bisson, 1954). After the occupation, however, firms (e.g., Mitsui, Mitsubishi, and Sumitomo) regrouped themselves, but this time allowing for only limited concentration of fiscal resources in banks and none whatsoever in family-run holding companies (Caves & Uekusa, 1976; Johnson, 1982, p. 174). In addition to the former *zaibatsu*, another variant of the intermarket groups emerged in the postwar period. This is what Clark (1979) calls the "bank group," which consists of "companies dependent for funds on a major bank" (p. 72) (e.g., Fuji, Dai-Ichi, and Sanwa).[2]

The second type of enterprise group consists of vertical linkages between major manufacturers (*kaisha*) and their related subsidiaries (Abegglen & Stalk, 1985; Clark, 1979, p. 73), linkages that produce a dual structure in the Japanese economy (Nakamura, 1981; Yasuba, 1976). Major firms in Japan are directly connected to a series of smaller independent firms that perform important roles in the overall system of production.[3] According to Nakamura's (1981) analysis, with the exception of some assembly industries (e.g., automobiles), "the prevailing pattern is that large firms are in charge of the raw materials sector while small firms handle the transformation of these materials into manufactured goods" (p. 191). This system of subcontracting allows large firms to increase their use of small firms during times of expansion and to decrease their use during times of business decline. So common are these relations between large and small firms that the "subcontractorization" of small firms by the large has been seen as the "greatest problem" confronting the Japanese economy, because of the inequality and dual-wage system that it spawns (Nakamura, 1981, p. 175).

In sum, the Japanese economy is dominated by large, powerful, and relatively stable enterprise groups. These groups constitute a "society of industry" (Clark, 1979, pp. 95-96), "where *zaibatsu* and other affiliations link industrial, commercial, and financial firms in a thick and complex skein of relations matched in no other country" (Caves & Uekusa, 1976, p. 59).

Unlike in Japan, with its diversity in business networks, in South Korea the dominant industrial networks are large, hierarchically arranged sets of firms known as *chaebol*. *Chaebol* are similar to the prewar *zaibatsu* in size and organizational structure. In 1980-1981, the government recognized 26 *chaebol*, which together controlled 456 firms (Westphal, Rhee, Kim, &

Table 5.3 Contribution to Gross Domestic Production in the Manufacturing
Sector by *Chaebol* in South Korea (in percentages)

Number of Chaebol	1973	1975	1978	1984-1985
4 largest	—	—	—	45.0
5 largest	8.8	12.6	18.4	—
10 largest	13.9	18.9	23.4	—
20 largest	21.8	28.9	33.2	—
50 largest	—	—	—	80.0

SOURCES: Figures for the 4 largest *chaebol* are from Helm (1985); for the 5, 10, and 20 largest, from Koo (1984, p. 1032); and for the 50 largest, from Hankook Ilbo (1985).

Amsden, 1984, p. 510). In 1985, there were 50 *chaebol* that controlled 552 firms (Hankook Ilbo, 1985). Their rate of growth has been extraordinary. In 1973, the top 5 *chaebol* controlled 8.8% of the GNP (Koo, 1984, p. 1032), but by 1985 the top 4 *chaebol* controlled 45% of the GNP (Helm, 1985, p. 48). In 1984, the top 50 *chaebol* controlled about 80% of the GNP (Hankook Ilbo, 1985).

Although the *chaebol* resemble enterprise groups in Japan, the member firms of the *chaebol* are closely controlled by central holding companies, each of which is owned by an individual or a family. In turn, the central holding companies of the *chaebol* do not have the independence of action that the enterprise groups possess in Japan. Instead, they are directly managed by the South Korean state through planning agencies and fiscal controls. Whereas the intermarket groups in Japan are based on a central bank and trading company, in South Korea *chaebol* rely on financing from state banks and government-controlled trading companies. With this type of support, the *chaebol* have developed at a phenomenal rate, as shown in Table 5.3. In addition, in contrast to Japan, outside the *chaebol* networks there are few large, successful independent firms and less subcontracting between large and small firms.[4]

In Taiwan, the family firm (*jiazuqiye*) and the business group (*jituanqiye*) are the dominant organizational forms throughout the economy, especially in the export sector. Unlike in either Japan or South Korea, in Taiwan there are relatively low levels of vertical and horizontal integration and a relative absence of oligarchic concentrations. Family firms predominate, and they are usually small to medium in size (i.e., fewer than 300 employees or total

Table 5.4 Contribution to Gross National Product by Firm Size in Taiwan
(in percentages)

Number of Firms	1980	1981	1982	1983
5 largest	5.52	4.90	5.02	5.45
10 largest	8.70	7.91	7.69	8.23
20 largest	12.66	11.73	10.96	11.85

SOURCE: Diao (1983).

Table 5.5 Contribution to Gross National Product by the Largest
100 Business Groups in Taiwan

Percentage of	1973	1974	1977	1979	1981	1983
GNP	34.0	29.5	29.1	32.8	30.0	31.7
Employees	5.1	5.1	5.0	4.9	4.6	4.7

SOURCE: China Credit Information Service (1985, pp. 46-47).

assets of less than $20 million U.S.). According to Zhao (1982), of the 68,898 firms registered in 1976, 97.33% were small to medium in size. These firms employed about 60% of Taiwan's workers and accounted for 46% of the GNP and 65% of Taiwan's exports. (For GNP contributions of the largest firms, see Table 5.4.) Some of these firms form production, assembly, or distribution networks among themselves, often linking together through informal contracts. Other firms, however, perform subcontracting work for larger firms. *Jituanqiye,* or large business groups, crosscut family firms. Most groups are networks of firms controlled by a single family (China Credit Information Service, 1985). These networks, however, do not rival the size of business groups in Japan and South Korea. Instead, most consist of conglomerate holdings of small, medium, and a few modestly large firms. As shown in Table 5.5, a survey of the 100 largest business groups in Taiwan between the years 1973 and 1983 revealed remarkable stability in the overall economy, especially when compared with the rising corporate holdings in Japan and the phenomenal growth of the *chaebol* in South Korea (China Credit Information Service, 1985). We develop the details of these patterns of business networks as we discuss the market, culture, and authority explanations for these differences.

The Market Explanation

The market explanation for organizational structure is associated most importantly with Alfred D. Chandler's analysis of the American business firm. In *The Visible Hand* (1977), Chandler attempts to account for the development and rapid diffusion of the modern corporation. The invention of the corporation, what Chandler calls "multiunit" business enterprise, accelerated the rate of industrialization in the United States and, as American management ideas spread abroad, in the industrializing world generally. Although Chandler (1984) recognizes local differences in the spread of the multiunit firm to Western Europe and Japan, he attributes such differences largely to market characteristics. The United States was the "seedbed" of managerial capitalism, not Europe, because of "the size and nature of its domestic market" (Chandler, 1977, p. 498).

The logic of Chandler's analysis is a straightforward developmental thesis of institutional change based on changing market conditions.[5] Chandler shows that the preindustrial American economy was dominated by small, traditional organizations: partnerships or family-owned businesses with limited outputs. The traditional business typically received its raw materials and tools from a general merchant, who in turn purchased at wholesale the business's finished goods and distributed them in nearby markets at retail prices. The general merchant was the kingpin of the colonial economy (Chandler, 1977, p. 18). After the colonial period and until the advent of the railways, traditional businesses became more specialized, with the general merchant giving way to the commission merchant. But even with these changes, the essential organization of the traditional firm stayed the same. They "remained small and personally managed because the volume of business handled by even the largest was not yet great enough to require the services of a large permanent managerial hierarchy" (p. 48).

The development of a nation-spanning railroad network in the United States in the mid-1800s had two important consequences for industrial organization (Chandler, 1977, pp. 79-187). First, the railroads, the first geographically dispersed business, were compelled to develop innovative strategies of management; they developed the first multiunit firm organizations. Second, and more important, the railroad made it possible for small, traditional businesses to buy and sell in much larger markets, and larger markets made it possible for them to increase the volume of production manifold. Newly enlarged businesses now found it more efficient to perform

under one corporate roof the multiple services performed by various commission merchants. Each business arranged the purchase of its own raw
materials, the financing of its debts, the production of goods, and the location
of and distribution to markets. Managerial or administrative coordination of
these multiple activities "permitted greater productivity, lower costs, and
higher profits than coordination by market mechanisms" (p. 6). Chandler
argues for the technical superiority of administrative over market coordination under conditions of mass markets created by the development of transportation networks.

Chandler's argument rests largely on technological causes. A related but
much more economy-oriented argument has been developed by Oliver E.
Williamson (1975, 1981, 1983, 1985). Building on the work of earlier economists (Coase, 1937; Commons, 1934), Williamson argues that the basic unit
of economic analysis is the economic transaction—the exchange of goods or
services across technological boundaries (e.g., the transformation of raw
materials into finished goods or the purchase of goods for money). Every
transaction contains costs, and especially those costs associated with ensuring that each party to a transaction lives up to the terms of the agreement.
The more the uncertainty within the marketplace, Williamson (1985) argues,
the greater the likelihood that some parties will cheat, "will act opportunistically with guile" (pp. 30-32, 47-50, 64-67). The more such opportunistic
behavior occurs, the less reliable, the less efficient, and the less profitable
the marketplace becomes. At this point, businesses reorganize to correct the
deficiencies of the marketplace; they expand their organization through
vertical or horizontal integration, thereby creating a "governance structure"
that internalizes transactions, reducing transaction costs and increasing efficiency (pp. 68-162).

Using transaction cost theory, Williamson develops a theory of modern
business organization. Multiunit firms arise when internally conducted transactions cost less than market-mediated transactions. The more complex and
uncertain the economic environment, the more likely it is that businesses will
expand their organization. Expansion reduces uncertainty and transaction
costs and maximizes efficiency. For Williamson, the forms of organization
that survive in specific economic arenas are the ones that deliver products
more efficiently.[6]

To Chandler, multiunit firms offer superior coordination; to Williamson,
they offer lower transaction costs. Chandler acknowledges the influence of
historical factors in explaining organization; Williamson (1981) explains the

variety of organizations according to transactions: "There are so many kinds of organizations because transactions differ so greatly and efficiency is realized only if governance structures are tailored to the specific needs of each type of transaction" (p. 568). Both, however, are efficiency theorists and see organization structure as the calculated expression of economically rational persons pursuing profit (Perrow, 1981, 1986, pp. 219-257).

Chandler's market explanation of multiunit businesses can be applied to Japan, Korea, and Taiwan in a straightforward fashion but with ambiguous results. Williamson's central concepts are more difficult to operationalize, particularly "transaction costs" and "contracts" (Perrow, 1986, pp. 241-247). Although both Chandler and Williamson qualify their theories at various points, they restrict their explanations to decisive economic variables.[7] Therefore, differences in organizational structure necessarily would have to be explained in terms of crucial differences among the three countries. We find, however, that all three countries are very similar in regard to the crucial variables Chandler pinpoints. Moreover, even loosely applied, Williamson's theory does not seem to explain adequately the differences among the three.

First, in all three countries internal transportation and communication systems are well developed, modern, and certainly far beyond what they were in late-nineteenth-century America (see, e.g., Ranis, 1979, p. 225). External transportation and communication systems are also well developed. Second, the three countries possess substantial and growing internal mass markets, which have already risen above the level of early-twentieth-century America. But more important, all the countries have vast external markets. Third, Japan, South Korea, and Taiwan use, have available, or have developed the most advanced technologies in the various industrial sectors. This level of technology, of course, is far advanced over that discussed by Chandler. Fourth, business enterprises in all three countries operate on principles of profit in the marketplace. By any definition, they are capitalist enterprises; they practice cost accounting, depend on free labor, develop through invested capital, and, if unsuccessful, may go bankrupt.[8]

Yet, despite these extensive similarities, as well as the others discussed earlier, among the three countries on all macroeconomic variables, the organizational structures of their business enterprises are quite different. Moreover, even when each country is considered individually without regard to the other two, the enterprise structure is only partially explained by the market approach.

On the surface, Japanese business enterprise would seem to satisfy the conditions of Chandler's interpretation the best. The intermarket groups now include firms ranked among the largest in the world. They are vast, complexly organized, multiunit enterprises. They are successful in the world economy, where each of them has a sizable share of the total market in its respective sector. Moreover, as is well known, these enterprises attempt to control the marketplace through administrative means (e.g., cartelization) insofar as it is possible (Johnson, 1982; Vogel, 1979). When Americans speak of emulating Japanese management practices, it is the management techniques of the intermarket groups, such as Mitsubishi and Sumitomo, or the giant *kaisha,* such as Toyota, to which they refer. In fact, Chandler (1977, p. 499) acknowledges that Japanese corporations satisfy his definition of the modern managerial business enterprise.

The South Korean case fits the market explanation less well than the Japanese case seemingly does. But if one includes the state as an aspect of business organization, then the Korean case might be squeezed into a market explanation. East Asian political organization has, of course, been a "multiunit" organization for centuries, but if one ignores this fact, then one could argue that, because of market conditions and the circumstances of a late-developing economy, the rapid industrialization in South Korea favored the formation of a type of state capitalism.[9] Vertical integration in South Korea occurred both at the level of the *chaebol* and at the level of the state, and both forms of integration were structurally and causally linked. Therefore, unlike the firm in the United States and somewhat unlike the firm in Japan, the South Korean multiunit business firm is not independent from state organization. As we will discuss later, important functional operations of the firm are controlled by bureaucratic departments of government. The firm is not an independent creation of market forces, even though state organization and the managerial corps of the *chaebol* attempt to control the marketplace administratively.

If the South Korean case can be made to fit Chandler's thesis, the Taiwan case obviously cannot.[10] Here we find, relative to the other cases, a conspicuous lack of vertical integration and absence of the oligarchic concentration that occurred in the United States, Japan, and especially South Korea. The unwillingness or inability of Taiwanese entrepreneurs to develop large organizations or concentrated industries appears to have defied even the encouragement of government. Ramon Myers (1984) cites an example: When the government persuaded a successful businessman, Y. C. Wang, to establish a plastics factory, the Chinese impulse was immediately to copy Wang's success. "Three other businessmen without any experience in plastics quickly built similar factories, and many more entered the industry later. Between 1957 and 1971 plastic production grew 45% annually. In 1957 only 100 small firms fabricated products from plastic supplied by Wang's company, but in 1970 more than 1,300 small firms bought from plastic suppliers" (p. 516).

The plastics industry is one of the most concentrated in Taiwan's private sector. The tendency in this industry is the rule elsewhere: the "unusual feature of manufacturing and service firms in Taiwan is their limited size: each operation is usually owned by a single proprietor or family" (Myers, 1984, p. 515). Moreover, the organization of such firms is usually of single units, functionally defined in relation to a finished product. These small firms join together in what is called the *weixing gongchang,* which is a system of satellite factories that join together to produce a finished product. Such interorganizational networks are based on noncontractual agreements, sometimes made between family members who own related firms, but more often between unrelated businessmen. On personalistic terms, these businessmen informally negotiate such matters as the quality and quantity of their products. For instance, in Taiwan, the world's leading exporter of bicycles, the bicycle industry is organized in a vast array of separate parts manufacturers and bicycle assembly firms.[11] Similarly, Myers (1984) reports that Taiwan's television industry is composed of 21 major firms and hundreds of satellite firms: "Since this industry [requires] thousands of small parts such as picture tubes, tuners, transformers, loudspeakers, coils, and antennae, countless Chinese firms sprang up to supply these in ever greater quantities" (p. 517).

Although there are exceptions, the small to medium-sized single-unit firm is so much the rule in Taiwan that when a family business becomes successful the pattern of investment is not to attempt vertical integration in order to control the marketplace, but rather to diversify by starting a series of unrelated firms that share neither account books nor management. From a detailed survey of the 96 largest business groups (*jituanqiye*) in Taiwan, we find that 59% of them are owned and controlled by family groups (China Credit Information Service, 1985). Partnerships among unrelated individuals, which, as Wong (1985) points out, will likely turn into family-based business organizations in the next generation, account for 38%. An example of such a family-controlled business group is the Cai family enterprise, until recently the second largest private holding in Taiwan.[12] The family business included more than 100 separate firms, the management of which was divided into eight groupings of unrelated businesses run by different family members, each of whom kept a separate account book (Chen, 1985).

Taiwan does not fit Chandler's evolutionary, technology-based model of modern business organization, but neither does it seem to fit Williamson's model of business organization. Although the variables for transaction cost theory are more difficult to operationalize than the variables for Chandler's theory, it seems apparent that the growth of large business groups in Taiwan cannot be explained by either transaction cost reduction or market uncertainty, two key factors contributing to the boundary expansion of firms.

In the first place, a normal pattern by which business groups acquire firms is to start or buy businesses in expanding areas of the economy. Often, these firms remain small to medium in size, are not necessarily integrated into the group's other holdings (even for purposes of accounting), and cooperate extensively with firms outside the holdings of the business group. As such, firm acquisitions represent speculation in new markets rather than attempts to reduce transaction costs between previously contracting firms.

Second, uncertainty is a constant feature in Taiwan's economic environment.[13] Family firms, many no larger than the extended household, usually do not have either the ability or the means to seek out or forecast information on demand in foreign export markets. They produce goods or, more likely, parts for contractors with whom they have continuing relationships and on whom they depend for subsequent orders. The information they receive on product demand is second- and thirdhand and restricted to the present. They have limited abilities to plan organizational futures and to determine whether their products will find a market and elicit continuing orders. In fact, misinformation and poor market forecasting are common, as is evident in the high rate of bankruptcy in Taiwan.

Conditions like these are the very ones that Williamson predicts should produce vertical integration. These conditions should prevail especially during business depressions in the world economy, such as those that occurred in 1974-1978 and again in 1980-1981. Tables 5.4 and 5.5, however, show no discernible trend in this direction. If anything, one might argue that in Taiwan uncertainty leads in the opposite direction, away from strategies of vertical integration and toward a strategy of spreading investment.

Chandler's and Williamson's theories do not explain the organizational structure of Taiwan business, but if one looks more closely at the Japanese and South Korean cases, it becomes equally obvious that they do not fit the market explanations well either.[14] Intermarket business groups date from the beginning of Japanese industrialization, in some cases even before. Therefore, growing technology, expanding communication, and the increased volume of manufacturing transactions are not the causes of Japanese industrial structure, because the structure precedes the economic growth.

In the Tokugawa era, from 1603 to 1867, a rising merchant class developed a place for itself in the feudal shogunate. Merchant houses did not challenge the traditional authority structure but subordinated themselves to whatever powers existed. Indeed, a few houses survived the Meiji Restoration smoothly, and one in particular (Mitsui) became a prototype for the *zaibatsu* (Bisson, 1954, p. 7). Other *zaibatsu* arose early in the Meiji era from enterprises that previously had been run for the benefit of the feudal overlords, the *daimyo*. In the Meiji era, the control of such *han* enterprises moved to the private sphere, where, in the case of Mitsubishi, former samurai became the owners and managers (Hirschmeier & Yui, 1981, pp. 138-142). In all cases of the *zaibatsu* that began early in the Meiji era, the overall structure was an intermarket group. The member firms were legal corporations and large multiunit enterprises, and could accumulate capital through corporate means. As Nakamura (1983) puts it, "Japan introduced the [organizational] framework of industrial society first and the content afterward" (pp. 63-68).

Zaibatsu clearly emerged from a traditional form of enterprise. Although they adapted spectacularly well to an international, capitalist economy, they did not develop in response to it. Therefore, Chandler's (1977) assertion that the United States is the "seedbed of managerial capitalism" (p. 498), that this form of organization "spread" to Japan (p. 500), is dubious and at the very least must be substantially qualified.

The organizational structure preceded economic development in South Korea as well. The organizational structure of *chaebol*, as well as state capitalism in general, although encouraged and invigorated by world economic conditions, can be traced more persuasively to premodern political practices, to pre-World War II Japanese industrial policy (Myers & Peattie, 1984, pp. 347-452), and to the borrowing of organizational designs for industrialization from Japan, than to those factors specified by either Chandler or Williamson. At the very best, causality is unclear.

The market explanation neither explains the organizational differences among the three countries nor offers an unqualified explanation for any one country. Still, at one level the market explanation is certainly correct.

Transportation systems, mass markets, advanced technology, and considerations of profit all influence the organization of modern business, and it is inconceivable that modern business firms would have developed as they have in fact developed in the absence of these factors. Nonetheless, to equate these factors with organizational structure, to make them the sole causes of organizational design, is not only theoretically and substantively to misinterpret business organization but also to make a serious methodological blunder. Chandler and Williamson, each in his own way, concentrate their entire causal argument on proximate factors. Their cases are analogous to arguing that the assassination of Archduke Ferdinand caused World War I or that the possession of handguns causes crime. Clearly, important causal links are present in all these relationships, but secondary factors play crucial roles in shaping the patterns of unfolding events. To banish all secondary factors, such as political structures and cultural patterns, is to fall into what David Hackett Fischer (1970) calls the "reductive fallacy," reducing "complexity to simplicity, or diversity to uniformity. . . . This sort of error appears in causal explanations which are constructed like a single chain and stretched taut across a vast chasm of complexity" (p. 172). This is what Chandler and Williamson do in their attempts to derive organizational structure solely from economic principles.

The Culture Explanation

Cultural explanations for the diversity of organizational structures and practice are many. Smircich (1983) identifies no fewer than five ways researchers have used the culture framework. Some analysts, for example, see culture as an independent variable, exerting pressure on organizational arrangements (e.g., Crozier, 1964; Harbison & Meyer, 1959), or as a dependent variable in comparative management studies (Peters & Waterman, 1982). Most important recent approaches see culture as socially created "expressive forms, manifestations of human consciousness. Organizations are understood and analyzed not mainly in economic or material terms" (Smircich, 1983, p. 347). Whereas market analysis sees organizations striving toward maximum efficiency, cultural theorists probe the nonrational, subjective aspects of organizational life. Culture studies tend to link organizational patterns with the cultural practices of the larger society. For example, Nakane's classic study *Japanese Society* (1970) combines cultural and structural analyses to show how the group relations of the Japanese family serve larger social institutions, including Japanese enterprise: "The characteristics of Japanese enterprise as a social group are, first, that the group is itself family-like and, second, that it pervades even the private lives of its employees, for each family joins extensively in the enterprise" (p. 19). Swedish shop-floor democracy can be traced to strong socialist sentiments in the country (Blumberg, 1973). Worker self-management in Yugoslavia is linked to an ideology of social ownership (Tannenbaum, Kavcic, Rosner, Vianello, & Weiser, 1974). Americans' strong central values of individualism and free enterprise lead to segmentalist organizations (Kanter, 1983) and fear of central planning by government (Miles, 1980).

Most culture studies do not concern themselves with the economic implications of corporate culture, but a few more popular works do, often to critique economic approaches to management. Peters and Waterman's *In Search of Excellence* (1982) repudiates the "rational model" of organizations, citing as more successful those organizations that promote shared values and productivity through people-centered policies (pp. 29-54).

William Ouchi's (1981, 1984) recent works are important links between culture studies and the economic tradition.[15] Whereas Williamson describes organizational structures ("governance structure") as emerging from market transactions, Ouchi claims that cultural values, such as "trust," influence whether individuals will resort to contracts and other devices of control to mediate transactions (see Maitland, Bryson, & Van de Ven, 1985).

If the market explanation errs by emphasizing proximate causes, then the culture explanation of organization errs in the opposite direction. By concentrating on secondary causes, primordial constants that undergird everything, the cultural explanation works poorly when one attempts to examine a changing organizational environment or to analyze differences among organizations in the same cultural area. Therefore, to use this explanation to account for differences among organizational structures of enterprise in Japan, South Korea, and Taiwan, one must demonstrate cultural differences that would account for different organizational patterns. Such cultural differences, we argue, are difficult to isolate.

The first step in locating cultural differences is to ask what factors would be included in a cultural explanation and what factors would not (see, e.g., Gamst & Norbeck, 1976). Many scholars define culture as the socially learned way of life of a people and the means by which orderliness and patterned relations are maintained in a society. Although the concept of order suggests its link to a sociological authority relations understanding of society, in practice culture theorists tend to be concerned with the symbolic, rather than the material, impulse behind social life—with norms, values, shared meanings, and cognitive structures (see Harris, 1979, for an exception). Basic culture ideals, and myths and rituals in relation to those ideals, are explored for their ability to integrate persons and to reinforce and celebrate common understandings.[16] Recent works about corporate culture, for example, refer to "weak" versus "strong" corporate cultures: how engaging and encompassing corporate life is for employees. Although culture may be understood as universal to the society and changing only slowly, culture theory tends not to look beyond a culture of immediate interest, and especially not at long-term historical trends. In organizational analysis, culture study is social science writ small: either rich, detailed ethnographies of a single people during relatively short historical periods or, at most, the comparison of a limited number of bounded cases. Without a wider scope, such an approach is of only limited use in explaining differences in business organization among societies. Fortunately, in regard to the cases at hand, there have been numerous attempts to develop more broadly based cultural explanations.

The culture explanation has been used often in attempts to understand Japanese corporate practices (see Abegglen, 1958; Benedict, 1946). Although a number of points of departure have been taken, many share the belief that it is the central Japanese value of *wa,* or harmony, that explains Japanese organizational arrangements. *Wa* denotes a state of integration, a harmonious unity of diverse parts of the social order. The organizational consequences of *wa* are numerous, but most important is the subordination of the individual to the group and the practices to which that leads: the necessity to check with colleagues during contract negotiations; the routine and calculated movement of personnel among functional areas to promote wider understanding at the expense of specialization; the promotion of cohorts, not individuals, up the organization ladder; and the development of lifetime employment, internal labor markets, and seniority systems (*nenko*) to maintain the integrity of the group. The wearing of uniforms, the performance of group exercises, the singing of corporate anthems, and even intercorporate cooperation have been explained as expressions of *wa.* At the societal level, cooperation is orchestrated by the state: "The Japanese government does not stand apart from or over the community; it is rather the place where *wa* deals are negotiated" (Sayle, 1985, p. 35).

As persuasive as the culture approach seems in explaining the Japanese case, it has suffered substantial attack. An analysis of one practice, *nenko* (seniority system), suffices to suggest the nature of the critique. *Wa* and its expression in practices such as *nenko* have been described by culture theorists as part of a cultural continuity extending to preindustrial times. But there are many examples of different practices and of discontinuity. For instance, labor turnover rates were high before 1920 and very high in the late 1930s and early 1940s (Evans, 1971; Taira, 1970). Why, then, were apparently expensive lifetime employment and seniority preferences offered by enterprise group firms? Economics provides the alternative explanation that it is economically rational to maintain a stable workforce and protect training investments. "It appears that some of the industrial features thought to be traditionally Japanese . . . are in fact fairly recent innovations, supported by traditional values to be sure, but consciously designed for good profit-maximizing reasons" (Dore, 1962, p. 120). Jacoby (1979) further argues that, although economic interests are important in understanding the institution of lifetime employment and its adoption before World War II, they cannot explain why it exists only in some firms and not others, applies only to some worker groups within the same organization, and appeared at a given historic juncture. He suggests an explanation in line with an authority relations approach:

> More careful historical research on the circumstances surrounding the introduction of internal labor markets in Japan indicates the importance of the increase in firm size and complexity, the change in skilled labor organization, and the desire to forestall unionization. These factors are causally connected to the emergence of an emphasis on stability and control in input markets, as well as the creation of new pressures to maintain employee effort and loyalty. (p. 196)

That *wa* provides a socially accepted justification for *nenko* and that *nenko* accords easily with Japanese culture cannot be denied. Cultural constants, however, are insufficient to explain changing organizational practices.[17]

Similar culture arguments have been made concerning Chinese management practices (Chen, 1984; Chen & Qiu, 1984; Hou, 1984; Huang, 1984; Silin, 1976; Zeng, 1984). For the most part, they focus on the Confucian belief system and its expression in enterprise. Confucianism promotes individual self-control and dutiful conduct toward one's superiors and particularly toward one's family. At some level, modern Chinese organizations reflect these patterns. Comparative management studies show that Chinese entrepreneurs maintain more distance from workers than do the Japanese and are likely to promote competitive relations, not cooperation, among subordinates (who may be family members) (Fukuda, 1983). But, unlike in Japan, where loyalty to the firm is important, Chinese loyalty is not firm specific and may extend to a network of family enterprises. Because a Chinese businessman can with some assurance trust that people in his family network will respect the Confucian obligation to act with honor toward relatives whenever possible, he conducts business with members of his own kinship network (Chan, 1982; Chen & Qiu, 1984; Huang, 1984; Omohundro, 1981; Redding, 1980). Moreover, Confucianism has been described as a system that promotes strong bonds at the local level, when face-to-face relations are paramount, but is a weak form of social control in mediating broader relations.

Despite an appearance of cohering, the Confucian culture argument, if pressed, falls apart. It is used to explain conduct in large factories (Silin, 1976) as well as in small, premodern commercial activities (Yang, 1970). The question here is why today's enterprise organization in Taiwan is composed of relatively small to medium-sized family-run firms. The Confucian culture argument alone will not work well because the culture is a broadly based underlying cognitive factor (Redding, 1980) that affects the society in general and for that reason explains nothing in particular.

This criticism of the cultural explanation gains force especially when one considers that both South Korea and Japan have been deeply influenced by Confucianism, as well as by Buddhism and various folk religions, which China also shares. In fact, in regard to underlying cultural values, Japan, South Korea, and Taiwan are not three separate cultures, but rather parts of the same great tradition. All societies in East Asia have many cultural traits in common, which can be traced to the long-term interaction between the societies in the region. Some of the intermixing of cultures can be explained politically. Imperial China always considered Korea a tributary state and exacted submission during many long periods. More recently, Japan conquered and colonized both Korea and Taiwan and set out systematically to impose Japanese language and behavioral patterns on Taiwanese and Korean societies.

Intermixing due to politics is only part of the picture, however. A much more significant interaction occurred at the levels of language, elite culture, and religion. The direction of the cultural borrowing was usually from China to Japan and Korea. Both Korea and Japan borrowed and used Chinese script. Chinese was the written language of the Korean court until *hangul* was introduced in the sixteenth century. In Japan, the court language was a mixture of Chinese and Japanese, which itself had been adapted to written expression through the use of Chinese script. Scholars in both locations learned classical Chinese and used it in government and in the arts. Beyond the Chinese script, poetry, painting styles, motifs on all artifacts, literature of all types, elite styles of dress and expression, architecture, and elements of cuisine—all these and more intermixed, so that no aspect of elite life in Japan or South Korea can be said to be untouched by cultural diffusion from China.

Besides politics and elite cultural intermixing, there was religious diffusion that permeated all levels in all three societies. Two religions are particularly important. Confucianism, which contains an elaborate ideology of familism and an equally elaborate ideology of statecraft, was supported by the elites in all three societies. In imperial China, this was more or less the case from the time of the Han period (established in 221 B.C.) to the fall of the empire in A.D. 1911. Confucianism had less continuous influence and came later in the other two societies but was extremely important in Korea and Japan during the most recent dynastic periods. Buddhism entered China from India in the second and third centuries A.D. and later became very important before it was finally proscribed at the state level. Thereafter, Buddhism was primarily a local religion in China, merging with other folk practices. In Korea and Japan, after diffusing from China, Buddhism became an important religion at both the state and local levels. In all three societies, Buddhism and Confucianism continue to be important, with the symbolism and values of each being key components of modern life.

We are not arguing that these three societies have the same culture. In the same way that England and France do not have the same culture, these three societies do not either. But just as France and England belong to the same cultural complex (Western civilization), so do Japan, Korea, and China (Eastern civilization). The decisive point here is that we are not dealing with three distinct cases, but rather three societies that share many of the same cultural patterns. Therefore, using the culture explanation, we can argue, as have others (Berger, 1984; Tu, 1984), that this common culture helps to explain common patterns in all three societies, such as the importance of the family, obedience to authority, high rates of literacy, the desire to achieve, and the willingness to work hard. What the culture explanation is not able to do, however, is to distinguish the many differences that exist among these societies, including the organizational structure of business enterprises. The culture explanation cannot account for changes and differences well because the causal argument is concentrated on secondary factors, especially in primordial constants, and thus the explanation only with difficulty deals with factors that underlie historical changes.

Authority Structure and Organizational Practice

The third approach to understanding organizations that we employ is a political economy approach primarily derived from the work of Max Weber (1978). One of the best examples of this approach is Reinhard Bendix's *Work and Authority in Industry* (1974), a historical study of the development of managerial ideology and practice in England, Russia, and the United States. Bendix covers some of the same territory as Chandler in *The Visible Hand* (1977), but provides an alternative explanatory framework.[18]

Briefly, in the Weberian view, many factors contribute to organizational structure. The structures of armies, tax collection, business enterprises, and officialdoms are influenced most importantly by the task at hand. But even when we consider task requirements, there is much room for variation, and historical and situational factors such as available technology, conditions of membership (Weber, 1978, pp. 52-53), and the class and status composition of the group (pp. 926-939) will have an influence.

But all organizations, no matter what their purpose or historical setting (although related to both), have an internal pattern of command and compliance. Organizations exist only insofar as "there is a probability that certain persons will act in such a way as to carry out the order governing the organization" (Weber, 1978, p. 49). This probability rests in part on normative justifications that underlie given arrangements—who should obey and the distinctive mode of obedience owed to the powers that be. Weber calls the underlying justifications "principles of domination."[19] In this context, principles of domination are not abstractions, but rather serve as the substantive rationale for action. They provide guides, justifications, and interpretive frameworks for social actors in the daily conduct of organizational activity (Biggart & Hamilton, 1984; Hamilton & Biggart, 1984, 1985).

The Weberian approach incorporates economic and cultural factors and allows for historical diversity. Principles of domination are clearly related to culture, but are not reducible to it. Bendix (1974) has shown how economically self-interested strategies of worker control were expressed as management ideologies in industrializing nations. These ideologies were based on an economic rationale, but "ideologies of management can be explained only in part as rationalizations of self-interest; they also result from the legacy of institutions and ideas which is adopted by each generation" (p. 444).

Recent extensions of Weberian views are found in the works of Karl Weick, John Meyer and W. Richard Scott, and Charles Perrow.[20] Weick (1979) discusses how people in organizations enact role-based strategies of organizational control; the enactments contain ritual, and tradition (organizational culture) builds around ritualized enactments. Although enactments are certainly related to patterned behavior and the maintenance of predictable orders, they have no necessary connection with efficiency. Indeed, Meyer and Scott (1983) show that whole organizations adopt management practices for reasons of legitimacy; the organization enacts patterns understood and accepted by important constituents, not for reasons of economic rationality.[21] Perrow (1981, 1986) argues that firms are profitable not merely because they are efficient but because they are successful instruments of domination.

The market explanation concentrates on immediate factors and the culture explanation on distant ones. Both explanations are obviously important, but neither deals directly with organizations themselves; although both claim to account for organizations, they make organizations appear rather mysteriously out of a mix of economic variables or a brew of cultural beliefs. The authority explanation deals with organizations themselves and conceptualizes them broadly as patterned interactions among people—that is, as structures of authority. It aims at understanding how these structures came into being, how they are maintained, and to what consequence. As such, it attempts historically adequate explanations and therefore differs from both general cultural theories and specified, predictive economic models.

In applying this approach to account for business organization in East Asia, one must demonstrate decisive differences among the three societies in terms of the structures of authority and further demonstrate that these differences affect organizational practices. Two factors seem particularly important and in need of explanation. First, what are the relationships established between the state and the business sector in the three societies? And second, given that relationship between state and enterprise, what are the structures of authority in each type of business network? In each of the

three societies, the state has pursued similar policies promoting industrialization. Economists describe these policies in terms of a product-cycle industrialization pattern (Cumings, 1984) in which import substitution was gradually replaced by aggressive, export-led growth policies (Ranis, 1979). What
is apparent but left unanalyzed is that such state policies are administered in
very different political contexts.

In South Korea, government-business relations follow in the form of what
can be called the "strong state" model. In South Korea, the state actively
participates in the public and private spheres of the economy and is in fact
the leading actor (SaKong, 1980). The state achieves its central position
through centralized economic planning and through aggressive implementation procedures. The entire government is "geared toward economic policy-
making and growth" (Bunge, 1982, p. 115). "Economic decision making [is]
extremely centralized, and the executive branch dominate[s]" (Mason, Kim,
Perkins, Kim, & Cole, 1980, p. 257). Implementation procedures aim at
controlling the entire economy. For public enterprises, control is direct and
bureaucratic. This sector of the economy, which is relatively small, is run as
departmental agencies of the state, with civil servants as managers. Although
not in as direct a fashion as occurs in the public sector, the state controls the
private sector "primarily from its control of the banking system and credit
rationing" (Westphal et al., 1984, p. 510) and through other financial controls. The state, however, does not hesitate to use noneconomic means to
achieve compliance with policy directives.

> A firm that does not respond as expected to particular incentives may find that
> its tax returns are subject to careful examination, or that its application for bank
> credit is studiously ignored, or that its outstanding bank loans are not renewed.
> If incentive procedures do not work, government agencies show no hesitation
> in resorting to command backed by compulsion. In general, it does not take a
> Korean firm long to learn that it will "get along" best by "going along." (Mason
> et al., 1980, p. 265)

These procedures apply to all sizes of firms but especially to medium and
large firms, which are in fact favored by such planning and implementation
procedures (Koo, 1984, p. 1032). This is particularly the case for business
groups, the *chaebol*. State policies support business concentration, and
statistics indeed reveal a rapid change in this direction (Hankook Ilbo, 1985;
Jones & SaKong, 1980, p. 268; Koo, 1984). In addition, many medium-sized
and all large firms are tethered by government-controlled credit, by govern-

ment regulation of the purchase of raw materials and energy, and by government price-setting policies for selected commodities (Weiner, 1985, p. 20).

In Japan, the government has developed quite a different relationship with business. The state policy toward business is one of creating and promoting strong intermediate powers, each having considerable autonomy, with the state acting as coordinator of activity and mediator of conflicting interests (Johnson, 1982).[22] In business, the most important of these strong intermediate powers are the intermarket groups of large firms. The *zaibatsu* rose to great power in the pre-World War II era, and, because of their link to Japan's imperial past and because of their monopoly characteristics, American occupation authorities legally dissolved them and attempted to set up a new economic system based on the U.S. model. They promoted a union movement and encouraged small and medium-sized competitive enterprises (Bisson, 1954). After the American occupation ended, however, the Japanese government, through both action and strategic inaction, allowed a maze of large and powerful intermarket groups to reappear.

These business networks and member firms are independent of direct state control, although they may acquiesce to the state's "administrative guidance." This administrative guidance has no statutory or legal basis; rather, it "reflects above all a recognized common interest between MITI [the Ministry of International Trade and Industry] and the leading firms in certain oligopolistic industries, the latter recognizing that guidance may occasionally impair their profits but in the long run will promote joint net revenues in the industry" (Caves & Uekusa, 1976, p. 54). As Johnson (1982) points out, this political system has led "to genuine public-private cooperation" (p. 196).

The strong state model in South Korea and the strong intermediate power model in Japan contrast sharply with what might be called the strong society model of state-business relations in Taiwan. The state in Taiwan is by no means weak. It is omnipresent, and, ceremonially at least, it repeatedly exacts obeisance. But, in regard to the export business sector, the Taiwan government promotes what Little (1979) identifies as "virtually free trade conditions" (p. 475) and what Myers (1984) calls "planning within the context of a free economy" (p. 522). Such policies have allowed familial patterns to shape the course of Taiwan's industrialization; this has in turn led to decentralized patterns of industrialization, a low level of firm concentration, and a predominance of small and medium-sized firms.

Before we explain the strong society model further, three aspects of active state-business relations should be stressed. First, the state owns and manages a range of public enterprises that provide import-substituting commodities (e.g., petroleum, steel, and power) and services (e.g., railways and road and harbor construction) and that have been very important to Taiwan's economic development (Amsden, 1985; Gold, 1986). Unlike this sector in South Korea, public enterprises in Taiwan are relatively large and have maintained a steady importance during the entire period of industrialization (see Chapter 10, this volume). Second, the state imposes import controls on selected products and promotes industrial development in export products through special tax incentive programs and the establishment of export processing zones (Amsden, 1985; Gold, 1986). These incentives for export production, although they have certainly encouraged industrialization, have not favored industrial concentration, as has occurred in South Korea. Third, as in Japan and South Korea, the state in Taiwan exerts strong controls over the financial system, which includes the banking, insurance, and saving systems. Having one of the highest rates of savings in the world, Taiwan has also developed what Wade (1985) calls a "rigid" fiscal policy of high interest rates to control inflation, a preference for short-term loans, and an attitude of nonsupport for markets in equity capital (e.g., the stock market). Unlike Japan's and South Korea's, however, this financial system favored the development of a curb market, "an unregulated, semi-legal credit market in which loan suppliers and demanders can transact freely at uncontrolled interest rates" (Wade, 1985, p. 113). Because most small and medium-sized firms require only moderate to little investment capital, and because such firms have difficulty obtaining bank loans, the curb market has played an extremely important role in financing Taiwan's industrial development (Yang, 1981).

The difference in the role of the state between Taiwan and the other two societies is revealed in state planning. Like the South Korean state, Taiwan's government develops economic plans, but unlike in South Korea there are no implementation procedures. State planning is done in a "loose, noncommand style," is "unsupported by controls," has no credibility in its economic projections, and has "no importance" in determining economic behavior (Little, 1979, p. 487). This unimportance of planning, Little (1979, pp. 487-489) further believes, is true even in public sector enterprises. Moreover, of great importance in Taiwan's pattern of industrialization has been the absence, until recently, of spatial planning, including industrial zoning, at the municipal, provincial, and state levels. Considered together, these factors have led Little to argue that "Taiwan planning has not even been intended to be indicative [authoritative]. The mechanism usually associated with indicative planning is lacking. There are no standing consultative committees with private industry; any consultations are ad hoc. There are virtually no teeth either" (p. 488).

The lack of strong government intervention in the domestic economy, unlike that in South Korea, and the absence of active support for large firms, unlike that in Japan, has left the economy in Taiwan, especially the export sector, free to work out its own patterns. Using either Chandler's or Williamson's model, one would expect rapid concentration and the development of managerial capitalism. What has in fact emerged is something quite different, almost the opposite of what either theorist would predict: a low level of business concentration and a decentralized pattern of industrial development. And with this approach, Taiwan's sustained rate of economic growth during the past 30 years is one of the highest in the world.

Why did the state officials in each case choose one form of business relationship over other possible alternatives? For each society, it is clear that the choices were neither random nor inevitable. In each case, there was latitude. For instance, after the American occupation, the Japanese government could have supported and built on the system the Americans established, which was based on competition among small and medium-sized firms. But instead it opted for creating strong intermediate powers, in terms of both economic and social controls (Johnson, 1982, pp. 198-241). South Korea could have chosen the Japanese route, by building on the *zaibatsu* model it had inherited from the Japanese. Or it could have adopted the model found in Taiwan, by supporting the small to medium-sized private sector firms that had developed in Korea before World War II (Juhn, 1971) and still operate there to some extent. Instead, it opted for a strong state. Finally, Taiwan could have followed the other courses as well. In the early 1950s, in fact, Taiwan clearly was moving toward the strong state model: The state had incorporated the former *zaibatsu* into the state apparatus, had aggressively forced the landowning class to accept sweeping land reform policies, and, with a strong military presence, was making ready to return to the mainland. On the other hand, the state could have supported a strong business class, as the Chiang Kai-shek regime had done with the Shanghai industrialists in the early 1930s on the mainland. But, after some hesitation, the Nationalist government developed and since then has pursued a nonfavoritist policy of "letting the people prosper." In each case, the decisions about state-business relations were not inevitable, and certainly in the case of Taiwan it takes no imagination to envision a different course, because another outcome occurred across the Taiwan straits, in mainland China.

Therefore, what determined the choice? Many factors were important, but it seems likely that the most important were not economic factors at all. Rather, the key decisions about state-business relations should be seen in a much larger context, as flowing from the attempt on the part of political leaders to legitimate a system of rule. Each regime was at a crucial point in its survival after wars and occupations, and needed to establish a rationale for its existence. In fashioning such a rationale, each regime in the end resorted to time-tested, institutionally acceptable ways of fashioning a system of political power. In each case, the first independent regime of the postwar era attempted to legitimate state power by adopting a reformulated model of imperial power of the kind that had existed before industrialization began. Such a model built on the preexisting normative expectations of political subjects and contained an ideology of rulership. Moreover, some of the institutions to support these models were still in place.

In Japan, the decisive factor was the presence of the emperor, who continues to stand as a symbol of political unity (Bendix, 1977, p. 489). But the emperor was above politics and so was a weak center. The U.S.-installed legislature also was a weak center, a place of haggling as opposed to unity. Gradually, successive decisions allowed for the creation of a modern version of the decentralized structure of the Tokugawa and Meiji periods: The center (in Tokugawa, the shogun, and in Meiji, the emperor) coordinates strong and, in normative terms, fiercely loyal independent powers. In turn, the independent powers have normative responsibility for the people and groups who are subordinate to them. The symbolism of the past shaped the reality of the present.

The economic consequences of this type of legitimation strategy were to create large, autonomous enterprises. These enterprises needed to legitimate their own conduct and, accordingly, to develop distinctive "personalities." Such efforts to build corporate cultures traded heavily on established systems of loyalty—the family, community, and paternalism—but also added mythologies of their own. In addition, given their size and status, these business enterprises needed to secure oligarchic positions in the marketplace and did so through a variety of economic tactics with which we are now familiar (Abegglen & Stalk, 1985; Vogel, 1979). But the theoretically important point is that Japanese intermarket groups are not creations of market forces. In the middle 1950s, when they reappeared, they began large and they began prestigious, and their economic integration followed from those facts, rather than being simply the cause of them. They enacted and, in due course, institutionalized a managerial structure that, from the outside, looks like a corporation but, on the inside, acts like a fiefdom.

In South Korea, the present form of government arose in a time of crisis, during a brutal war in which more than 1 million Koreans died and 5.5 million more were dislocated (Cole & Lyman, 1971, p. 22). Social disruption on an extraordinary scale, destruction of rural society, and the historical absence of strong intermediary institutions placed great power in the hands of a state structure propped up by U.S. aid and occupying forces. The authoritarian postwar government of Syngman Rhee shaped the basic institutions that the Park government later gained control of and turned in the direction of economic development. The legitimating strategy for both governments, although articulated quite differently, centered on the imagery of the strong Confucian state: a central ruler, bureaucratic administration, weak intermediate powers, and a direct relationship between ruler and subjects based on the subjects' unconditional loyalty to the state. As Henderson (1968) writes: "The physics of Korean political dynamics appears to resemble a strong vortex tending to sweep all active elements of the society upward toward central power. . . . Vertical pressures cannot be countered because local or independent aggregations do not exist to impede their formation or to check the resulting vortex once formed" (p. 5).

South Korean firms draw their managerial culture from the same source, the state, and from state-promoted management policies; they do not have the local character of the corporate culture of Japanese firms. Instead, they have developed an ideology of administration, an updated counterpart to the traditional Confucian ideology of the scholar-official (Jones & SaKong, 1980, p. 291). For this reason, American business ideology has had an important effect in South Korea, far more than in either Japan or Taiwan. In the late 1950s, the South Korean government, with a grant from the U.S. State Department, instituted American management programs in South Korean universities (Zo, 1970, pp. 13-14). South Korea now has a generation of managers trained in American business practice, including persons at the top levels of the state. In 1981, South Korea's prime minister and deputy prime minister (who was chief of the Economic Planning Board) were U.S.-trained economists (Bunge, 1982, p. 115).

In Taiwan the state-business relationship also results from a basic legitimation strategy undertaken by the state. The Chiang Kai-shek government, after an initial attempt to create a military state in preparation for a return to the mainland, tried to secure the regime's legitimacy on a long-term basis. Composed largely of northern Chinese, Chiang Kai-shek's forces virtually conquered and totally subordinated the linguistically distinct Taiwanese. This created much resentment and some continuing attempts to create a Taiwanese independence movement. When a return to the mainland became unlikely, Chiang began creating a stable, long-term government. He actively promoted an updated Confucian state based on the model of the late imperial system. Unlike the more legalistic model of the Confucian state developed in Korea, Chiang attempted to make the state an exemplary institution and its leader a benevolent ruler: a state that upholds moral principles (*dedao*), that explicitly allows no corruption and unfair wealth, and that "leaves the people at rest." In this role, the state supervises internal moral order and takes care of foreign affairs. This policy militates against the emergence of favorite groups, which had been a weakness of the Nationalist regime in the 1930s and 1940s. This policy also limits participation of the state in what was seen in late imperial times as the private sector (*sishi*), an area that includes not only people's economic livelihood but also all aspects of family and religious life. Taiwan's state policy toward business operates within the limits established by Chiang's legitimation strategy (Peng, 1984).

The consequences of this state policy have been to allow society, unfettered by the state, to respond to the economic opportunities that existed in the world economy and for which the state offered incentives. The Chinese of Taiwan, using traditional commercial practices and customary norms, quickly adapted to modern economic conditions. This outcome should not be surprising, because Chinese business practices have for some time operated competitively in the world economy. In nineteenth-century China, there was a thriving commercial system that functioned well in the absence of a legal framework, even in the deteriorating political conditions of the time (Chen & Myers, 1976, 1978; Feuerwerker, 1984; Hamilton, 1985; Hao, 1970, 1986; Myers, 1980). The Chinese used the same patterns of business relations to gain industrial and commercial control of the economies in Southeast Asia (Hamilton, 1977; Omohundro, 1981; Wickberg, 1965) and, more recently, to develop highly industrial societies in Hong Kong and Singapore (Nyaw & Chan, 1982; Redding, 1980; Ward, 1972). Therefore, when we consider the similar free market conditions that exist in these other locations, the Chinese economic success in Taiwan is perhaps not surprising, but needs to be examined nonetheless.

The industrial patterns in Taiwan reflect the same invigoration of Chinese commercial practices found in late imperial China and in Southeast Asia. As analysts have noted, in all these locations Chinese businesses develop on the basis of small family-run firms and personalistic networks linking firms backward to sources of supply and forward to consumers (e.g., Chan, 1982; Omohundro, 1981; Wong, 1985). Two sets of factors account for the prevalence of these small family firms. The first concerns the nature of the Chinese family system.[23] The Japanese family system is based on a household unit and on primogeniture; younger sons must start households of their own. In contrast, the Chinese system is based on patrilineage and equal inheritance among all sons. The eldest son has seniority but no particular privileges in regard to property or authority over property. Because all males remain in the line of descent, the patrilineage expands quickly within just a few generations. Adoption of a son into any household is considered improper, and the only approved way is to adopt the son of a kinsman (see Watson, 1975a). Equally privileged sons connected to networks of relatives create a situation of bifurcated loyalties, with wealth itself becoming a measure of an individual's standing in the community of relatives. Accordingly, conflict between sons is ubiquitous, intralineage rivalries are common, and lineage segmentation is the rule (Baker, 1979, pp. 26-70). Hence, the argument goes, besides the lineage and the state, there is no central integrating unit in Chinese society, and the lineage itself breeds as much conflict as unity. Therefore, it is difficult in Chinese society to build a large cohesive group.

This leads to a closely related set of explanations of how Chinese businesses are run.[24] The Chinese firm duplicates family structure; the head of the household is the head of the firm, family members are the core employees, and sons are the ones who will inherit the firm.[25] If the firm prospers, the family will reinvest its profits in branch establishments or, more likely, in unrelated but commercially promising business ventures (see, e.g., Chen, 1985). Different family members run the different enterprises, and at the death of the head of household the family assets are divided (*fenjia*) by allocating separate enterprises to the surviving sons, each of whom attempts to expand his own firm as did the father. In this way, the assets of a Chinese family are always considered divisible, control of the assets is always considered family business, and decisions (in normative terms) should be made in light of long-term family interests. This pattern leads to what might be described as a "nesting box" system of Chinese management (see, e.g., Huang, 1984; Omohundro, 1981; Redding, 1980). In the small, innermost box are those core family members who own or will inherit the business; in the next box are more distant relatives and friends who owe their positions to their connection with the owners and who are in a position to influence and be influenced by them; in the outer boxes are ranks of unrelated people who work in the firm for money. Depending on the size of the firm, the outer boxes may contain ranks of professional managers, technicians, supervisors, and other craftspeople. The outermost box would include unskilled wage laborers. This pattern of business organization is most stable when the business is fairly small. Loyalty among unrelated employees is often low, which makes personalistic connections an essential part of management strategy (Huang, 1984). The preference is always to begin one's own small business if one has sufficient capital to do so; as the Chinese saying goes, "It is better to be a rooster's beak than a cow's tail!"

Because everyone works in small to medium-sized firms, the Chinese have historically developed techniques to aid forward and backward linkages. These techniques include putting-out systems, satellite factory systems, and a variety of distribution networks often based on personalistic ties (see, e.g., Hamilton, 1985; Willmott, 1972). In fact, so complex and all-encompassing are these various techniques, and seemingly so efficient (Y. M. Ho, 1980), that they contribute to keeping businesses fairly small and investment patterns directed toward conglomerate accumulations rather than vertical integration (see Chan, 1982).

In summary, as illustrated in Table 5.6, in each of the three societies, a different combination of present and past circumstances led to the selection of a strategy of political legitimation. This strategy, in turn, had direct consequences for the relations between state and business sectors and for the formation of economic institutions.

Finally, we should note that the three types of business networks that developed in these three countries are usually not in direct competition with one another, except in a few product areas (e.g., electronics). Each possesses different economic capabilities, and each seems to fill a different niche in the world economy. Much more research needs to be done on this topic, but it appears that the following division is occurring: Taiwan's system of small

Table 5.6 Firm Structure and Firm-State Relationships

	State-Business Relations	Principal Corporate Actors	Intrafirm Managerial Strategies	Extrafirm Market Strategies
Japan	cooperative partnership	intermarket groups	company ideologies; consensus building; peer group controls	high R&D; manufacture and marketing of new products
South Korea	political capitalism	*chaebol*	state Confucianism; impersonal management; strong, centralized control	high capital ventures in established markets
Taiwan	separation of spheres	family firms	"family-style" management; control through personal ties	low capital; low R&D; manufacture of consumer expendables

family firms, which can flexibly shift from producing one commodity to another, has become a dominant producer of an extensive range of medium- to high-quality consumer goods (e.g., clothes, small household items) of the kind that fill the modern home and office but that require very little research and development. Large Japanese corporations specialize in particular product areas and, through research, development, and marketing strategies, attempt to create new commodities and consumers for those commodities (Abegglen & Stalk, 1985). Exploiting their competitive advantage in technology and mass production, Japanese businesses operate on the frontiers of product development. With the entire economy orchestrated by the state, South Korean businesses are attempting to become important producers of commodities that require extensive capital investment but for which markets already exist (e.g., steel, major construction materials, automobiles). Such ventures require large amounts of capital and coordination but relatively little research and development. All of these three strategies of industrialization may well be, in the economist's terminology, "least-cost" strategies in their respective niches of the world economy. But that fact does not make these strategies any less the outcomes of noneconomic factors. Moreover, a strategy of efficiency can be calculated only in terms of an existing array of economic and social institutions.

Conclusion

The theoretical question underlying this chapter is, What level of analysis best explains organizational structure? We argue that, on the one hand, profit and efficiency arguments are too specific and too narrow to account for different organizational forms. Economic models predict organizational structure only at the most superficial level (e.g., successful businesses seek profit). On the other hand, cultural arguments seize on such general, omnipresent value patterns as to make it difficult to account for historical and societal variations occurring within the same cultural area. Culture pervades everything and therefore explains nothing. The authority explanation provides the most successful explanation because it aims at a middle level, at explanations having historical and structural adequacy. We argue that enterprise structure represents situational adaptations of preexisting organizational forms to specific political and economic conditions. Organizational structure is not inevitable; it results from neither cultural predispositions nor specific economic tasks and technology. Instead, organizational structure is situationally determined, and, therefore, the most appropriate form of analysis is one that taps the historical dimension.

Given this conclusion, then, this analysis suggests that the key factors in explaining economic organization may not be economic, at least in economists' usual meaning of that term. Economic and cultural factors are clearly critical in understanding the growth of markets and economic enterprise, but the form or structure of enterprise is better understood by patterns of authority relations in the society. This suggests, further, that the economic theory of the firm may in fact be a theory based on, and only well suited to, the American firm as it has developed historically in American society. Chandler's analysis of firm formation in the United States concentrates on how firm development permitted the lowering of costs under changing market conditions. It is important to note, however, that firm development also allowed the concentration of economic interests and market control by private parties. The American state (in both the nineteenth and twentieth centuries) exists to allow the market to function in the service of private interests; it intervenes only to prevent market breakdowns or overconcentration. This state role was not an inevitability dictated by the market, however; it emerged from a historically developed vision about the "correct" state-industry relation. The American vision has always been that of a weak state and powerful private institutions (Hamilton & Sutton, 1982). Industrialists of the nineteenth century, unfettered by transportation and communications impediments, realized that vision with the aid of a laissez-faire government. But the American firm, like the firms in Japan, South Korea, and Taiwan, had no inevitable developmental sequence to traverse.

Notes

1. Although this is true for all three societies, Japan is best known for these extrafirm networks. So prevalent and important are these networks in Japan that Clark (1979) suggests that they constitute a "society of industry": "No discussion of the Japanese company can disregard this context. The society of industry circumscribes, for example, the organization and administration of the company" (pp. 95-96).

2. Usually, overlapping networks founded on banks are the networks of firms linked by general trading companies (*sogo shosha*) (Kunio, 1982; Young, 1979). These trading companies market and distribute the products of the firms that are affiliated with them. Some companies

handle as many as 20,000 individual items and have offices in more than 100 locations outside Japan (Krause & Sueo, 1976, p. 389). Each bank-based network has its own trading company that supports its affiliate firms. Otherwise unaffiliated companies, usually small and medium-sized businesses, also form their own trading company cartels to market their products overseas as well as in Japan (Ozawa, 1979, pp. 30-32).

3. Many of these major firms are independent of the established *keiretsu.* According to Abegglen and Stalk (1985), these firms represent the fastest-growing sector of the Japanese economy. As these firms grow larger, however, they come to resemble the *keiretsu:* "Some have become so large and successful that through subsidiaries and affiliates they now control groups of their own" (pp. 189-190).

4. Public sector enterprises are important in South Korea, even in export manufacturing. This sector continues to grow in importance in tandem with the *chaebol,* at the same time that the public sectors in Japan and Taiwan are declining both in size and in their involvement in export manufacturing. As in Japan, in South Korea there also are large associations of firms: the Korean Federation of Small Business, the Korean Traders' Association, the Federation of Korean Industries. But these associations do not have the influence of their Japanese counterparts, and "they have been accused of meekly obeying government directives" (Bunge, 1982, p. 122).

5. In a personal comment, William G. Roy reminded us that Chandler's explanation is economic only in a narrow sense. Chandler considers mainly the flow of goods within and between firms. He does not include in his explanation the dynamics of money and finance. Inflation and deflation, busts and booms, credit and capital—none of these factors is part of his explanation for the rise of modern corporations.

6. This idea is a central thesis in the work of other economists as well: "Absent fiat, the form of organization that survives in an activity is the one that delivers the product demanded by customers at the lowest price while covering costs" (Fama & Jensen, 1983, p. 327).

7. Writing with Ouchi, Williamson acknowledges that different societies may have preferences for either a "hard" or a "soft" form of making contracts (Williamson & Ouchi, 1981). Chandler (1977, pp. 498-500) implicitly qualifies his theory by noting that in some other societies there were social factors blocking what would otherwise be the natural development of managerial capitalism.

8. Although state-business cooperation is greater in Japan and South Korea than in the United States, these countries do not protect enterprise from business failure.

9. There is now a considerable literature on the Gerschenkron (1962) thesis that, among developing societies, strong states are able to promote industrialization better than those having different state formations (for a survey of this literature, see Evans, Rueschemeyer, & Skocpol, 1985).

10. For another, related treatment of Taiwan as a deviant case, see Barrett and Whyte's (1982) insightful use of Taiwan data to criticize dependency theory.

11. This information is based on interview material.

12. The family enterprise was rocked by scandals in the early months of 1985. The scandal forced the family to open their books and to account for their economic success. For one of the better descriptions of the Cai family enterprise, see Chen (1985).

13. Very little research has been done on the business environment in which small and medium-sized firms in Taiwan operate. Some hints are found in Myers (1984), Peng (1984), Hu (1984), and DeGlopper (1972). In the popular press, however, the topic is discussed frequently, particularly in the very good business magazines, which are among the most widely read magazines in Taiwan. The following discussion draws particularly on Chen (1983).

14. See Dore (1983) for an excellent critique of Williamson's theory as it would be applied to Japan.

15. It is important to note the collaborative work of Williamson and Ouchi (1981), which is an attempt to introduce a cultural variable concerning trust into Williamson's transaction and Chandler's visible hand theories.

16. From a cultural perspective, organizations can be seen in two ways: first, as culture-producing entities and, second, as expressions of the larger culture of the society. Recent studies of corporate culture reflect the first approach, but the second holds more promise for an understanding of the development of organizational arrangements in a given society.

17. For a very persuasive argument, in line with the one we present here, assessing the contribution of culture to Japanese corporate practices, see Dore (1973, pp. 375-403); see also Johnson (1982, p. 307).

18. First published in 1956, Bendix's work has long been noted as one of the most important attempts to analyze management structure in modern industry. For this reason, it is more than surprising that Chandler seems totally to have ignored the one key work in which a clear alternative hypothesis to his own work could be found. For a recent expression of Bendix's thesis, see Bendix (1984, pp. 70-90).

19. For Weber's chief statements on a sociology of domination, see Weber (1958, pp. 77-128; 1978, pp. 941-1211). For general works commenting on Weber's sociology of domination, see Bendix and Roth (1971) and Schluchter (1981); on Weber's sociology of domination in regard to Asia, see Hamilton (1984).

20. After this article had been revised for publication, two articles appeared that independently call for the kind of institutional analysis of culture that we attempt to develop with the authority approach. Swidler (1986) calls for a "culture in action." "Cultural end values," she argues, do not "shape action in the long run. Indeed a culture has enduring effects on those who hold it, not by shaping the ends they pursue, but by providing the characteristic repertoire from which they build lines of action" (p. 284). Arguing for an institutional approach, Wuthnow (1985) applies a very similar line of reasoning in his critique of the "ideological" model of state structure.

21. It is, of course, true that, for purposes of legitimating authority in modern industry, concepts of profit and efficiency are extremely important, as important in political as in economic ways. On this point, see Bendix (1974) and particularly Zucker (1983) and Perrow (1986).

22. The best analysis of state-business relations is found in Johnson (1982, pp. 196-197, 310-311). He notes that, of the various types of state-business relationships occurring in the past 50 years, "that of public-private cooperation is by far the most important. . . . The chief mechanisms of the cooperative relationship are selective access to governmental or government-guaranteed financing, targeted tax breaks, government supervised investment coordination in order to keep all participants profitable, the equitable allocation by the state of burdens during times of adversity (something the private cartel finds very hard to do), governmental assistance in the commercialization and sale of products, and governmental assistance when an industry as a whole begins to decline."

23. The available material on Chinese kinship is extensive. The best general treatments are found in Baker (1979), Freedman (1966), Hsu (1971), Watson (1982), and Cohen (1970).

24. For treatments of the Chinese kinship system in relation to Taiwan's business development, see Lin (1984), Chen and Qiu (1984), Chen (1984), Hu (1984), and Huang (1984). For the role of an extended lineage in modern commercial ventures, see Cohen (1970), Watson (1975b), and Wong (1985).

25. The literature on large business enterprises in Japan often cites the family as having an important influence on how the firms are run. In comparison with the Chinese case, however, the Japanese family provides much more a metaphor for organization than an actual model. In Taiwan, the family structure and enterprise organization cannot be readily distinguished in many cases, so much so that the effect of the family on business in Taiwan is not metaphorical but actual and of great significance. Moreover, although the data are limited, the role of the family in modern business in Taiwan seems very similar to the role of the family in traditional agriculture (Baker, 1979).

6

Organizational Isomorphism in East Asia

MARCO ORRÙ
NICOLE WOOLSEY BIGGART
GARY G. HAMILTON

he new institutionalism has attracted attention as an alternative to, or significant modifier of, resource dependency and population ecology approaches to the study of organizational environments. Resource dependency theorists stress the environmental constraints generated by organizational interdependence as organiza-

AUTHORS' NOTE: This chapter is reprinted here by permission of The University of Chicago Press from "Organizational Isomorphism in East Asia," by Marco Orrù, Nicole Woolsey Biggart, and Gary G. Hamilton, in *The New Institutionalism in Organizational Analysis,* edited by Walter W. Powell and Paul J. DiMaggio. Copyright 1991 by The University of Chicago Press; all rights reserved.

tions attempt to secure resources necessary for survival (e.g., Pfeffer & Salancik, 1978). Population ecologists focus instead on the survival of organizational forms under given environmental conditions (e.g., Aldrich, 1979; Hannan & Freeman, 1977, 1981). Although these two approaches to the study of organizational environments have different units of analysis (focal organizations versus populations) and different assumptions about the efficacy of human agency in determining outcomes (the utility versus the futility of strategic action), they share a common concern with technical environments. Technical environments include production and control technologies, patterns of interorganizational exchange, regulatory processes, and other factors that lead to relatively more or less efficient or effective forms of organization.

The new institutionalism departs from these technically oriented approaches by turning our attention to *institutional* environments, the socially constructed normative worlds in which organizations exist. It is a theoretical perspective that focuses on organizational conformity with social rules and rituals rather than with the technically efficient processing of inputs and outputs. It is a perspective concerned more with legitimacy than with efficiency.

All of these different theoretical approaches share a common concern, however, with organizational structure or form. In different ways, each argues that environmental pressures shape organizations and, moreover, that organizations in the same environment will become structurally similar as they respond to like pressures; that is, they will demonstrate isomorphism (DiMaggio & Powell, 1983). Technical environments shape organizations through competitive isomorphism or competition over scarce resources. In the heat of competition, organizations adopt efficient structures and practices or risk defeat by relatively better-adapted rivals. Institutional environments shape organizations through social pressure and result in institutional isomorphism. Organizations in a common institutional environment begin to look like each other as they respond to similar regulatory and normative pressures, or as they copy structures adopted by successful organizations under conditions of uncertainty. They adopt organizational forms because they have been dictated by patron organizations such as funding agencies or because given forms become generally accepted practice in their sector. Institutional pressures have no direct concern with efficiency, although maverick organizations that fail to conform may risk survival as surely as inefficient firms.

Analytically, there is no reason any organization might not be as subject to competitive factors as to institutional factors. In fact, however, theorists have tended to see organizations as subject more to one sort of pressure than another (Perrow, 1985, p. 152). Although Aldrich (1979) suggests the influence of institutional factors in his overview of the ecological perspective, population ecologists have not taken these factors seriously (for exceptions, see Carroll & Huo, 1986; Hannan & Freeman, 1984). At the very least, most theorists have chosen to study one type of organizational environment rather than another, based on the presumption of dichotomous environmental pressures. In support of this view, DiMaggio and Powell (1983) claim that competitive isomorphism "is most relevant for those fields in which free and open competition exists," such as manufacturing firms in a market economy (p. 150), whereas institutional isomorphism is likely among organizations that seek "political power and institutional legitimacy," for example, schools and government agencies. Scott and Meyer (1983) agree that some organizational sectors, such as banking, may be subject to both technical and institutional factors, but argue that where that is the case there will be "higher levels of internal conflict" as organizations try to cope with the competing demands of legitimacy and efficiency (pp. 140-141). The possibility that technical and institutional environments might converge in an organizational setting has been contemplated theoretically, but it has not been seriously entertained in empirical analysis.

With this chapter we hope to broaden the horizons of the new institutionalism both empirically and theoretically by challenging the current presumption of the dichotomy or necessary antagonism of technical and institutional environments. Using data about East Asian businesses, we make two general theoretical claims. First, we claim that the institutional approach need not be limited in its application to organizational environments where institutionalization is most predictable; rather, institutional arrangements have a paramount role and can be observed at the very core of market-regulated, technically dominated environments. We argue that, in East Asia, private businesses operate according to substantively distinct institutional models that differentially shape organizational behavior and structure.

Our second, related claim is that the institutional and technical components of environments need not be at odds with each other, nor do they need to be mutually exclusive; to the contrary, they can converge harmoniously in shaping organizational forms. Institutional arrangements do not necessarily lead to loss of efficiency or effectiveness in organizational forms; our research shows, rather, that the institutional traits of different East Asian businesses constitute one of the ingredients (if not the key ingredient) to their economic success and organizational fitness. We challenge Scott and Meyer's (1983, p. 141) hypothesis that internal conflict is the result of simultaneous technical and institutional demands. On the contrary, we claim that institutional pressures can contribute to the emergence and maintenance of market order both within and between competitive organizations.

Our data suggest that large business groups in South Korea, Taiwan, and Japan operate according to different institutional principles and exhibit different organizational and interorganizational structures that manifest those principles. The business organizations found in each of these economies are not corruptions of technically ideal organizational forms, but represent qualitatively distinct conceptualizations of what constitutes appropriate economic activity. Each economy rests on institutional principles that provide a coherent logic for competitive economic action. Socially constructed, accepted models of correct market behavior shape interfirm relations, prompting firms to behave with and against each other in characteristically homogeneous ways. To be "technically efficient," firms must consider and comply with the institutional settings in which they are embedded.

Each of the three market economies we examine has a distinct pattern of firm relations that express themselves as characteristic firm structures and interfirm networks. The networks are strikingly uniform or isomorphic within each economy, but different from each of the others—each expresses the organizing principles of that economy's environment. The institutional principles that shape organizational forms in these three countries do not hamper organizational efficiency, but rather provide a basis for market order and for competitive relations.

We organize our chapter in four sections. In the first section, we highlight the significance of institutionalization theory in accounting for patterns of intrasocietal isomorphism and intersocietal variation of large business groups in Japan, South Korea, and Taiwan, comparing it with other theories that would predict intrasocietal variation and with competing explanations of intersocietal differences. In the second section, we deal with data sources, methodology, and definitional problems. In the third section, we analyze the interfirm network structure of the major enterprise groups in each society, showing the distinctive organizational forms that obtain in each and proposing the "institutional principles" that provide the organizing logic for macro-organizational relations in each instance. Finally, we elaborate on the significance of the institutional approach for the study of organizational forms, by showing its relevance in the analysis of East Asian enterprise groups and by arguing in favor of a broader interpretation and application of the new institutionalism to encompass not only the study of predictably institutionalized organizational environments, but also, and more important, to include those organizational environments where the institutional aspects might appear to be secondary or altogether irrelevant. It is only by entering into the latter arena, we believe, that the new institutionalism can realize its full potential.

Isomorphism and Variation in Organizational Forms

Our thesis is but one of several that attempt to account for organizational form. For example, its classical formulation—the population ecology model of organizations—embraces Hawley's (1968) notion that "the diversity of organizational forms is isomorphic to the diversity of environments" (cited in Hannan & Freeman, 1977, p. 939). Organizational variation is essential to this model, because such variation provides "the raw material from which selection is made" (Aldrich, 1979, p. 35). Summarizing the dominant views in the field, DiMaggio and Powell (1983) point out that "much of modern organizational theory posits a diverse and differentiated world of organizations and seeks to explain variation among organizations in structure and behavior" (p. 148). Arguments explaining organizational variation from a resource dependency perspective have appealed to the growing interdependence that accompanies the "increased specialization and division of labor among organizational entities" (Pfeffer & Salancik, 1978, p. 43); population ecologists, instead, have emphasized the existence of "multiple, dynamic environments" that impose conflicting constraints on populations of organizations (Hannan & Freeman, 1977, p. 939). In both scenarios, one would expect the variation of organizational forms to be a dominant feature.

A transaction cost perspective also predicts a diversity of organizational forms reflecting involvement in different industrial and nonindustrial sectors, varying accessibility to technologies, and differential access to financial resources and markets (Williamson, 1981). The variation in market factors and technological factors should translate into a variation in organizational forms.

Despite the predictions of variation postulated by these theories, we have found that business groups in East Asian countries show a remarkable degree of intrasocietal isomorphism; more to the point, such isomorphism does not seem to hamper the organizations' economic fitness, but to enhance it. To be sure, population ecologists identify an isomorphic stage of competition in which "competitors become more similar as standard conditions of competition bring forth a uniform response" (Hannan & Freeman, 1977, p. 940), but this stage is followed, in the population ecology model, by the elimination of weaker competitors and their subsequent differentiation "either territorially or functionally." The isomorphism we identify in East Asian business groups, on the contrary, is far from episodic and shows remarkable continuity over time. The explanation for East Asian isomorphism cannot be found in competitive mechanisms alone (although they are a key source of isomorphic organizational behavior), but must be justified by the larger social and political contexts in each of the three countries.

The intersocietal variation of organizational forms is also amenable to alternative theoretical predictions and competing explanations. From an anthropological perspective that identifies broad cultural traits across East Asian societies (e.g., a common Confucian work ethic, obedience to authority, high rates of literacy, desire to achieve), one would predict the homogeneity of organizational forms across societies. But as we have argued elsewhere when examining the anthropological arguments, cultural explanations at this broad level mislead us in focusing on "primordial constants that undergird everything" (Hamilton & Biggart, 1988). A similar prediction of homogeneity would obtain, for opposite reasons, if one postulated the automatic application of universal economic principles in the behavior of profit-seeking organizations. In this case, not the overwhelming emphasis on cultural factors but the upholding of a cross-cultural, undifferentiated economic ethic (which rests on the individuation of *homo economicus* as a universally applicable ideal type) would lead to prediction of nearly total homogeneity in organizational forms.

Both the cultural and the economic approaches err in adopting a unidimensional view of the environment (either as a culture or as a market) to explain organizational forms that are subject to more articulated and detailed environmental factors. The new institutionalism is more sensitive to the details of environments because it escapes reductionism in either direction; it provides, one could say, a middle-range theory of organizational environments.

But even if the existence of identifiably different organizational forms in Japan, South Korea, and Taiwan is acknowledged, it would be far from obvious that such difference should be attributed to varying institutional characteristics across the three societies. Alternative theoretical explanations have focused on the different stages of development reached by the three economies (Cumings, 1984), on the differing industrial structures in the three countries (Scitovsky, 1985), and on the political and historical factors shaping organizational forms (Hamilton & Biggart, 1988). These alternative explanations are not necessarily at odds with an institutional explanation of variation; on the contrary, the new institutionalism incorporates the roles of technological development, the state, and market factors in the study of organizational forms. Obviously, the level of economic development of Japan is far ahead of those of South Korea and Taiwan, but it is far from evident that either of the latter countries (especially Taiwan) will go on to develop organizational forms similar to Japan's. Moreover, the differential development argument would be less applicable in a comparison of South Korea and Taiwan; there, if anything, we identify not two different stages of development, but rather two different roads to development—two different institutional notions of development.

The roles of the state and of historical, political events in these three countries are also paramount in explaining the development of different organizational forms. In previous work we have amply illustrated such roles, but have argued against a one-way causal flow from state action to organizational forms (Hamilton & Biggart, 1988). Institutional arrangements influence political action as much as they are influenced by it; it would be misleading to see the state as an extrasocietal entity that is unaffected by the social institutions of which it is a part. Therefore, rather than positing state action as the prime mover, we are inclined to see the state in each society as interacting (in different degrees and with different strategies) with the other organizational forms in that society.

As for the variation in the industrial composition of the countries (where, for instance, South Korea concentrates on shipbuilding and steel, whereas Taiwan specializes in metal products and textiles), it is clear that such variation would accompany a variation in organizational forms, but it is less evident, again, that the relation between the two should be one of cause and effect—or at least that the causal relation should be unidirectional. In fact, we argue that an institutional environment that favors small, family-centered businesses, as found in Taiwan, would also favor the concentration of production in light metal industries and textiles. The affinity between organizational forms and types of production is obvious, but the causal pattern influencing each is far from self-evident. It is here that a broadening of the institutionalization perspective to encompass both technical and sociocultural arguments, without presuming a priori causal directions, can show its full potential.

Methodology, Sources of Data, and Definitional Problems

In Japan, South Korea, and Taiwan there are numerous clusters of interlinked firms, or what we call enterprise groups. Enterprise groups are relatively stable and identifiable aggregates of firms that are related by way of shared ownership or management, mutual financial and market transactions, and other identifiable, patterned interdependencies. In each of the three countries, we have focused on the dominant enterprise groups in the private sector, because their existence, historical formation, and organizational patterns have been systematically documented. Although firms in enterprise groups have stable relations over time, they might not have a legal status that externally sanctions such relations; however, the published literature available in each country on the exact configuration of these groups makes it possible to identify them fairly accurately. East Asian enterprise groups differ from the clusters of firms found in the United States, which are often short-term, episodic combinations of convenience (Pfeffer & Salancik, 1978). In each of the three East Asian societies, a substantial journalistic and professional literature speculates about the shifting configurations of enterprise groups; in Japan, substantial scholarly literature has also focused on the exact configuration and implications of the country's domestic enterprise groups.

For each society, we examined the complete set of organizational networks at the top of each economy, as they are identified in each setting, rather than a predetermined number of clusters (e.g., the top five). Instead of selecting equal numbers of enterprise groups across the border, we chose to analyze naturally occurring patterns within each economy. Our rationale is that the number of enterprise groups included in each society's set is itself a crucial variable in explaining the variation across societies; this approach helps provide institutional comparability. For each cluster of enterprise groups within each society, we wanted to know what sorts of firms come to be identified with which groups and according to what criteria, what kinds of linkages exist among member firms, and how business group firms differ from unaligned but similarly successful firms. In short, we wanted to know how the clusters were internally organized and how they related to the general economy. Our intent was to see if firms could be understood to align with each other in discernible patterns. To identify such patterns, we resorted to measures of isomorphism, that is, measures of uniformity of group configurations.[1]

A Comparison of Enterprise Groups

Although a firm-level analysis reveals distinctive organizational characteristics in each country (Fukuda, 1983; Redding & Tam, 1986), such an analysis is, by itself, insufficient. The wide availability of publications that identify groups of firms according to standardized patterns in each of the three countries is, in itself, an indication that group membership is a significant organizational phenomenon in East Asia. The aggregation of firm-level statistics according to indigenous enterprise groups dramatizes the organizational similarities within each country and the differences among them in a way that firm-level analysis cannot. The adoption of this unit of analysis led us to the identification of three distinct organizational sets. For Japan, we looked at the 6 major intermarket groups (*kigyo shudan*) and the 10 largest independent industrial and financial groups (*keiretsu*); for South Korea, we looked at the 50 largest enterprise groups, the so-called *chaebol;* for Taiwan, we examined the top 96 business groups, called *jituanqiye.*

As a preliminary indication of the significant variation across societies, we should emphasize selected general areas of difference among the business groups as a whole before we begin a detailed analysis of each organizational pattern. Table 6.1 provides a comparative statistical overview. First, the numbers and sizes of affiliated firms in these groups differ markedly. Japan's business groups (the fewest in absolute terms) embrace the largest number of individual firms, with an average of more than 112 firms for each of the 6 intermarket groups, and about 33 firms for each of the 10 independent *keiretsu*. South Korea's *chaebol*, in contrast, include only an average of about 11 firms each. The largest (and often oldest) *chaebol,* however, include 20 or more firms on average, suggesting that the smaller, younger *chaebol* will perhaps grow with time. Taiwan's business groups are smaller still, typically having fewer than 8 affiliated firms each.

Table 6.1 General Characteristics of Business Groups in Japan,
South Korea, and Taiwan

	Japan 1982 (16 groups)	Korea 1983 (50 groups)	Taiwan 1983 (96 groups)
Total sales in local currency	217,033 billion yen	54,663 billion won	633.7 billion NT$
In $U.S. billions	871.26	68.32	16.48
Total workers	2,841,000	795,000	333,000
Total firms	1,001	552	745
Firms per group	62.60	11.04	7.76
Workers per firm	2,838	1,440	444
Percentage of total workforce	9.5	5.5	4.7

SOURCES: Dodwell Marketing Consultants (1984), Hankook Ilbo (1985), and China Credit Information Service (1985).

Second, the sizes of business group firms also differ markedly from country to country. Firms in Japan's business groups are large, with an average of more than 2,800 workers. Korean *chaebol* firms are not as large, averaging fewer than 1,500 workers (although top *chaebol* firms can average up to 3,600 workers). Taiwan's groups, in contrast, comprise relatively small companies with only a few hundred workers.

Third, the economic impacts of enterprise groups differ among the three countries, even accounting for the economies' relative size differences (Japan's GNP is 22 times greater and South Korea's is 1.3 times greater than Taiwan's). Although our data set for Taiwan comprises more business groups than the other two countries combined, their collective economic importance is, by far, the smallest. The South Korean economy, only slightly larger than Taiwan's, is in contrast dominated by the *chaebol*. Japan's business groups are similarly important economic actors, representing an extraordinary $871 billion U.S. in sales in 1982. Their relative contribution to GNP, however, is smaller than that of the Korean *chaebol* (Hahn, Kim, & Kim, 1987, p. 128).

Japanese Enterprise Groups: A Community of Firms

Scholars agree that at the top of the Japanese economy there are a few well-defined clusters of firms (Futatsugi, 1986; Kobayashi, 1980; Okumura, 1982a, 1984, 1985; Sumiya, 1986). These groups of firms are not conglom-

Table 6.2 Intermarket Groups and Independent Groups in Japan

Intermarket Groups	Independent Groups
Mitsubishi	Tokai Bank
Mitsui	IBJ
Sumitomo	Nippon Steel
Fuyo	Hitachi
DKB	Nissan
Sanwa	Toyota
	Matsushita
	Toshiba-IHI
	Tokyu
	Seibu

erates in the American sense of that term; they are social rather than legal entities (although there is joint stock ownership, as we describe below). Nonetheless, these clusters of firms take their social relationship seriously and are organized for the mutual benefit of all affiliated firms. Enterprise group firms straightforwardly identify themselves as members of a community of corporations with a distinct identity; individual firms understand their relative ranking in the community and the economic role they are expected to play for the good of the whole group.

In recent years, analysts have identified two major types of enterprise groups in Japan—the intermarket groups and the independent groups (Dodwell Marketing Consultants, 1984; Toyo Keizai Shimposha, 1986a, 1986b). Each represents a distinct form of corporate community, although they share many features (see Orrù, Hamilton, & Suzuki, 1989). Table 6.2 lists the 6 intermarket groups and the 10 independent groups. Although each has a distinctive "community character" that sets it apart from the other groups, all intermarket groups share at least four isomorphic features. First, all 6 groups are structured around a horizontally bound web of large firms, most of which occupy leading positions in different economic sectors. As Table 6.3 shows, all intermarket groups contain a similar lineup of firms competing across sectors, but not within them. This is known as the one-set principle (Futatsugi, 1986). In this way, intermarket groups compete with each other for shares of the total economy. Accordingly, when new industrial areas appear, each intermarket group creates or attempts to include firms specializing in those areas. Second, all 6 groups have their own banking institutions, insurance companies, and trading firms that take care of the

Table 6.3 Presidents' Club Firms by Sector in Japan's Six Intermarket Groups, 1982

Sector	Mitsubishi	Mitsui	Sumitomo	Fuyo	DKB	Sanwa
Banking and insurance	4	4	4	4	7	4
Trading and commerce	1	2	1	1	5	4
Forestry and mining		1	2			
Construction	1	2	1	1	1	3
Food and beverages	1	1		3		2
Fibers and textiles	1	1		2	1	2
Pulp and paper	1	1		1	1	
Chemicals	5	2	2	3	6	7
Petroleum products	1			1	1	1
Rubber products					1	1
Glass and cement	2	1	2	1	1	1
Iron and steel	1	1	1	1	3	4
Nonferrous metals	2	1	4		3	1
Machinery—general	1		1	2	3	1
Electrical and electronics	1	1	1	3	5	
Transportation machinery	2	2		1	3	5
Precision instruments	1			1	1	3
Real estate	1	1	1	1		
Land transportation				2	1	
Marine transportation	1	1		1	1	2
Warehousing	1	1	1		1	1
Service industry					1	
Total number of firms	28	23	21	29	46	42

SOURCE: Dodwell Marketing Consultants (1984, pp. 53, 64-65, 74, 82, 91, 100).

financial and market transaction needs of the group. Third, all the intermarket groups have a "presidents' club": The president of each of the leading companies in the group belongs to a council that meets once a month to discuss the affairs of that group (Okumura, 1985, pp. 15-16). Fourth, each presidents' club member firm maintains vertically aligned affiliate and subsidiary firms. These vertical alignments are conventionally called *keiretsu.* Affiliate and subsidiary firms, in addition, maintain numerous, differentially ranked, long-term subcontract relationships with small and middle-sized firms that are not counted as part of the intermarket *keiretsu,* but are nonetheless vital to the overall system of production (Ishida, 1983; Okumura, 1982a, 1984; Shimokawa, 1985). Subcontract relationships are ranked as primary, secondary, and tertiary, depending on the roles they play in the production process. Although they usually are not formal members of the *keiretsu,* subcontractors identify readily with the *keiretsu* community.

In contrast to the intermarket groups, independent groups represent a network of vertically integrated firms in one industrial sector. Independent groups tend to be structurally similar to the *keiretsu* within intermarket groups, each consisting of a very large, highly successful parent company and vertically aligned subordinate companies (Dodwell Marketing Consultants, 1984). For example, Nissan Motor, the automotive giant and head of an important independent group, is often referred to as a *keiretsu* in its own right. It maintains long-term relations with parts subcontractors, many of which are located adjacent to or near Nissan plants, so that members of independent groups often form a geographic, as well as an economic and social, community.

Despite their label, the 10 large independent groups are not, in fact, independent of each other or of the 6 intermarket groups. Independent groups maintain linkages to other enterprise groups through mutual shareholding by financial institutions. As we have argued elsewhere, these interlinkages closely resemble the sort of ties found among presidents' club firms within intermarket groups (Orrù et al., 1989). Hence the independent groups collectively form a super-intermarket group whose presidential club would include the leading firms of the independent groups and the leading financial institutions of the intermarket groups.

In summary, two important types of configurations occur within Japanese enterprise groups. The first configuration consists of stable horizontal linkages across noncompeting industrial sectors that result in a community of equals or near equals; in these horizontally aligned communities, no one firm dominates, but rather all firms exercise collective mutual control. The second configuration is a vertical alignment characterized by hierarchical relationships among firms, in terms of both production links and status positions.

The isomorphic qualities of these two types of configurations in intermarket groups can be evinced by comparing rates of intra- and intergroup stockholding for the six groups, and rates of stockholding for *keiretsu* (including both the very large *keiretsu* formed by the independent groups and the smaller ones formed around the presidents' club firms in intermarket groups). Table 6.4 shows the rates of intra- and intergroup stockholding for the intermarket groups. Here we can distinguish two patterns. First, all six intermarket groups have a similar substantial level of intragroup shareholding. For example, Mitsui group firms collectively own, on average, more than 18% of all Mitsui firms' stock; likewise, members of the Sumitomo group own 28% of member companies' shares. Although individual firms typically own only between 2% and 7% of other member firms, the joint holdings of several members can be substantial, representing a controlling interest of 20-30%. In fact, as we show in Table 6.5, 65% of the shares owned by the top 10 shareholders of Mitsubishi firms belong to Mitsubishi firms. Second, firms in intermarket groups (especially financial firms) own small percentages of shares in other intermarket groups (between 1% and 2% on average). This pattern, like the first one, is remarkably stable across groups. Although there is some variation, the isomorphic pattern of mutual shareholding within and across enterprise groups is clear.

Table 6.5 gives additional evidence for a distinctive patterning of firm relations in Japan, providing measures of shareholding density for intermarket group members. A network with a value of 1.0 is one in which all members are individually connected to each other—in this case through ownership of shares. The first column in the table shows the relative density of shareholding among the top 5 members of each intermarket group. The second column measures saturation for all other presidents' club firms within each group. The third column shows the percentage of member firms' shares in the top 10 shareholders of each presidents' club firm in that group. This last figure measures the level of internal control of each intermarket group. In all instances, the three intermarket groups that predate World War II— Mitsubishi, Mitsui, and Sumitomo (still frequently referred to as *zaibatsu*) —show higher levels of internal cohesiveness. The postwar groups, instead, have relatively looser internal ties and more linkages outside the group,

Table 6.4 Percentage Cross-Holding of Stocks by Enterprise Groups, 1977

				Owned			
Owner	Mitsui	Mitsubishi	Sumitomo	Fuyo	DKB	Sanwa	Total
Mitsui	18.42	0.79	1.16	1.60	2.35	2.98	27.30
Mitsubishi	1.02	25.01	0.44	2.30	2.59	2.07	33.43
Sumitomo	1.06	0.17	28.24	1.24	0.98	1.03	32.72
Fuyo	0.96	1.02	1.00	16.59	2.92	8.36	30.85
DKB	1.47	1.96	0.68	2.27	13.73	10.21	30.32
Sanwa	0.72	0.63	1.06	1.39	2.10	17.35	23.25
Total	23.65	29.58	32.58	25.39	24.67	42.00	

SOURCE: Okumura (1982a, p. 70).

Table 6.5 Selected Measures of Isomorphism for Japan's Intermarket Groups, 1982

Group	Relative Density: Top Five Firms	Relative Density: Council Firms	Internal Control: Council Firms
Sumitomo	.88 (1)	.128 (1)	72.5 (1)
Mitsubishi	.86 (2)	.063 (2)	64.6 (2)
Mitsui	.79 (3)	.050 (3)	53.1 (3)
Fuyo	.64 (4)	.022 (4)	42.1 (4)
Sanwa	.53 (5)	.010 (6)	39.0 (5)
DKB	.48 (6)	.020 (5)	38.2 (6)

SOURCE: Dodwell Marketing Consultants (1984).
NOTE: Ranks are given in parentheses.

although the group density is still extraordinary when compared with U.S. firm clusters.

Not only do intermarket groups resemble each other in their level of intragroup and intergroup shareholdings, they are also isomorphic in the relative importance they attribute to the top shareholders in their group. Table 6.6 shows the top five firms in each intermarket group ranked according to the average shares they own in presidents' club firms and according to the number of presidents' club firms in which they own shares. For the former *zaibatsu* groups, Mitsui, Mitsubishi, and Sumitomo, the identity in rankings is startling. The top shareholder in all three groups is the mutual life insurance company of the group; in every instance, this company is privately owned (see Nishiyama, 1984). The second shareholder is the city bank, and the third shareholder is the trust and banking firm. In the fourth and fifth spots are the marine and fire insurance and the trading companies of each group. The post-World War II groups (also called the bank groups) show a slightly different pattern, with the city banks as top shareholders and the trust and banking and mutual life companies in either second or third ranking.

Tables 6.7 and 6.8 show vertical shareholding patterns within intermarket groups and within independent groups. In both instances, parent firms typically own 20-30% of stocks in their affiliate firms, but independent groups are characterized by a larger number of vertically aligned firms.

It is clear from these measures that Japan's large corporations, although legally independent of each other, are highly connected. Moreover, the nature of these connections is not idiosyncratic but forms distinctive patterns within each of two identifiable types of business groups. Our indicators of

Table 6.6 Top Five Stockholding Firms in Intermarket Groups, 1982

| | Former Zaibatsu Groups | | | | | | City Bank Groups | | | | | |
| | Mitsubishi | | Mitsui | | Sumitomo | | Fuyo | | DKB | | Sanwa | |
	A	B	A	B	A	B	A	B	A	B	A	B
First	MLI	MLI	MLI	MLI	MLI	MLI	CTB	CTB	CTB	FKE	CTB	CTB
Second	CTB	CTB	CTB	CTB	CTB	CTB	T&B	MLI	MLI	CTB	MLI	MLI
Third	T&B	T&B	T&B	T&B	T&B	T&B	MLI	MFI	FKE	MLI	T&B	GTC
Fourth	MFI	MFI	MFI	MFI	GTC	GTC	MFI	T&B	FKC	FKC	HZC	HZC
Fifth	GTC	GTC	GTC	GTC	MFI	MFI	GTC	GTC	GTC	GTC	GTC	T&B

SOURCE: Dodwell Marketing Consultants (1984).

NOTE: A = rank according to average shares held in presidents' club firms; B = rank according to number of presidents' club firms in which shares are held; CTB = city bank; T&B = trust and banking; MLI = mutual life insurance company; MFI = marine and fire insurance company; GTC = general trading company; FKE = Furukawa Electric; FKC = Furukawa Corporation; and HZC = Hitachi Zosen Corporation.

167

Table 6.7 Keiretsu Isomorphism in Intermarket Groups, 1982

Mitsubishi Chem. Industries		Mitsui & Co. (Trading Co.)		Sumitomo Metal Industries		Marubeni Corp. (Fuyo Group)		Fujitsu Ltd. (DKB Group)		Nisso Iwai Corp. (Sanwa Group)	
N. Kasei Ch.	37.4	N. Univac	34.2	Nippon Pipe	46.9	Marub Constr.	34.1	Fanuc Ltd.	44.6	Kanoh Steel	33.4
Taiyo Sanso	36.3	F-One Ltd.	34.2	N.S. Steel	37.5	Toyo Sugar	33.7	Takeda Riken	21.5	Fuji Seito	43.9
N. Carbide	17.7	Showa Min.	16.7	Chuo Denki	30.1	Nankai Spinn	15.7	Fuji El-Chem	51.8	Goto Drop	23.2
Teikoku Kako	25.0	Chuo Build	20.5	Kanto Steel	33.6	Katakura Chi	34.0	Takamisawa	37.1	Nihon Mining	35.4
M. Plastics	51.0	N Feed Mfg.	12.1	Osaka Titan.	28.2	Japan Carlit	10.0	Towa Electr.	36.8	Japan Bridge	7.1
N. Synthetic	49.1	M. Sugar	26.6	S Lig Met In	28.9	Okamoto Rik.	7.1	Fuji Electr.	9.4		
Kodama Chem.	10.3	Taito Co.	26.1	Sumikura Ind.	46.4	Amatei Inc.	32.7				
Nitto Kako	44.6	Mikuni CC	76.9	S Precision	50.1	Nippei Ind.	20.6				
Toyo Carbon	46.1	Hohnen Oil	9.3	Daikin Inds	16.9	Kaji Iron Wk	40.0				
		Daito Wool	9.5	S Spec Metal	52.1	Okano Valve	43.1				
		Takasaki P.	34.6								
		Honshu Chem	39.2								
		Kawakami Pt	6.0								
		Fuji Kisen	26.5								
		Utoku Expr	22.3								
		Tokai-Kanko	38.7								
		Asia Air s.	27.2								
Average shares	35.3		27.1		37.1		27.1		33.5		28.6

SOURCE: Dodwell Marketing Consultants (1984).

Table 6.8   *Keiretsu* Isomorphism in Independent Groups, 1982

	Average Shares	Number of Firms
Financial Groups		
Tokai Bank	6.46	22
IBJ	6.69	22
Industrial Groups		
Nippon Steel	21.00	33
Hitachi	44.17	35
Nissan	34.48	30
Toyota	26.12	34
Matsushita	44.95	24
Toshiba-IHI	37.94	39
Tokyu	23.18	17
Seibu	34.80	14

SOURCE: Dodwell Marketing Consultants (1984).

isomorphism are based on mutual shareholding, but other types of linkages exist that point to the same patterns (see Orrù et al., 1989). For example, business group firms have interlocking directorates, share logos and trademarks, exchange executives, participate in joint public relations activities, and in other ways act as corporate communities.

Having demonstrated the existence of isomorphic patterns in Japanese enterprise groups, we need to justify their occurrence. Japanese enterprise groups are clearly an economic success, and one might say that competitive isomorphism is the key to the striking homogeneity we have observed. We feel, however, that institutional factors are more relevant than competitive ones, although both are present. What is embodied in the isomorphism of Japanese enterprise groups is not simply organizational efficiency and effectiveness in the Western sense, but also a unique concern with group solidarity and cooperation. The economic philosophy of the groups is to merge the goals of profit maximization and risk sharing. In relations among equally ranked and unequally ranked firms, benevolence and good faith are not simply good economic policy; they are a duty (Dore, 1983). Power is not perceived to be located in individual firms, but in the group as a whole. In the Japanese organizational environment, competition and cooperation do not pull in opposite directions, but are integrated in the structure of the enterprise groups. The crucial factor here is what DiMaggio and Powell (1983) call coercive isomorphism, as it pertains particularly to "the cultural expectations in the society within which organizations function" (p. 150).

The Japanese state had a distinctive role in clearing the way for the establishment of the large intermarket groups, once the Allied forces had disbanded the old, family-centered *zaibatsu* groups. But even the relation between the Japanese state and large enterprise groups is fashioned according to cultural expectations and mirrors the relation within enterprise groups; it is not a one-way domination of the groups by the state, but rather a collaborative partnership. It "reflects above all a recognized common interest between MITI [the Ministry of International Trade and Industry] and the leading firms in certain oligopolistic industries" (Caves & Uekusa, 1976, p. 54).

The theoretical importance of this convergence between technical and institutional environments, between the requirements of competition and of cooperation and conformity, is that it questions the Western assumption of an irreconcilable divergence between them. It is not despite their institutional isomorphism that Japanese enterprise groups are economically fit, but because of the incorporation of institutional elements in their organizations that they are so successful.

South Korean Business Groups:
Corporate Patrimonialism

On the surface, South Korean and Japanese business groups seem to show similar interfirm configurations, and in fact they are often compared favorably with each other (e.g., Lee, 1986). A closer look, however, reveals substantial differences. South Korean enterprise groups are called *chaebol*, the Korean transliteration of the Japanese term *zaibatsu*. Like the prewar *zaibatsu*, most *chaebol* are usually owned and controlled by a single person or family and are organized through a central holding company. These similarities, however, are largely superficial. In fact, the *chaebol* have distinctive characteristics that set them apart from current intermarket groups in Japan.

First, the Japanese intermarket groups expanded through the pursuit of horizontal diversification as well as vertical integration; *chaebol* typically started their businesses in only a few related industrial sectors. As Table 6.9 shows, *chaebol* firms are involved in a narrower range of industrial and commercial pursuits than are the intermarket groups of Japan, and their resources are unevenly distributed across industrial sectors.

Chaebol resemble Japan's independent groups in their patterns of industrial sector concentration, but also differ from them in important ways. For instance, *chaebol* do not rely on stable subcontracting relations with small

Table 6.9 Sector Distribution of Selected Firms in Top Six Korean *Chaebol*

Sector	Hyundai	Samsung	Lucky-GS	Sunkyung	Daewoo	Ssangyong
Banking and insurance	3	2	4		3	2
Trading and commerce	1	2	1		2	1
Forestry and mining			1	1	1	
Construction	2	3	1	1	1	1
Food and beverages		2			4	
Fibers and textiles	1	3	1	3		
Pulp and paper	1	3	1			1
Chemicals	1	1	1	1	2	
Petroleum products						4
Rubber products	1					
Glass and cement	2					
Iron and steel	2					
Nonferrous metals	1					1
Metal products	1				3	1
Machinery—general	1		3	1		1
Electrical and electronics	6	5	7	1	3	1
Transportation machinery		1		1	3	
Precision instruments	1	1	2		1	
Real estate	1	1		1	1	1
Land transportation				2		
Marine transportation	1					
Warehousing				1		1
Service industry			1			
Total number of firms	26	24	23	13	23	15

SOURCES: Hankook Ilbo (1985) and Daily Economic News (1986).

171

firms, a distinctive feature of Japanese *keiretsu*. Instead, *chaebol* buy or start new firms to care for their own production needs, and to a large extent they rely on Japanese firms for the supply of production components. Consequently, the size of major member firms in the top *chaebol* is on average larger than those in Japanese intermarket groups. The tendency to internalize production within *chaebol* boundaries is particularly evident in the overall percentage contribution of the *chaebol* to the South Korean economy, a figure significantly higher than that of the Japanese business groups (Hahn et al., 1987).

The internalization of production sequences and of other transactions points to the major difference between Japanese and South Korean business groups: South Korean business groups, somewhat similar to U.S. corporations, represent an integrated set of economic activities under a unified, centralized management structure. Japanese business groups, instead, represent genuine associations of firms, some more tightly bound to the group than others. Control in Japanese business groups is, in principle, not centralized, but rather dispersed throughout the network of firms.

A number of indicators illustrate these differences. In Japan, interfirm relationships are signified by a number of different horizontal and vertical reciprocal ties. Joint stockholding is the most important of these and contributes to the fact that the Japanese stock markets are, by far, the largest and most important in all of Asia.

In South Korea, in contrast, the stock market has, until recently, played a very minor role; it is small, and 70-80% of firms within *chaebol* groups are not listed (compared with only 10% of Japanese business group firms). Unlisted firms are usually owned entirely by the individuals and families controlling the *chaebol*. The South Korean government has recently encouraged *chaebol* owners to put their firms on the stock market, thereby reducing the amount of debt financing that has gone into building South Korean capitalism. The emerging pattern, as joint stock firms are created, is not one of systematic reciprocal shareholding, as is the case in Japan, although it might come to resemble Japan's as more and more firms go public. For now *chaebol* are listing only a few key firms (on average 20-25% of their firms), and then appear to be using the equity funds, as they had used the loans before, to create and buy out other firms. The stock market does not reinforce community ownership, but rather hierarchical control by top corporations over smaller ones. The emphasis on control is reflected in the shareholding patterns of firms listed on the stock market. Major shareholders are (a) the *chaebol* leader (usually the founder or his son and his family); (b) the leading firm of the *chaebol,* typically the trading company or holding company; and (c) one or more financial institutions in which the *chaebol* owns significant shares. The founders' control over the *chaebol* may be substantially greater than the figures in Table 6.10 suggest, however, if the founders are significant partners in securities companies, many of which are privately owned.

Korean management structure reinforces the Korean isomorphic pattern of vertical domination. In Japanese *keiretsu,* the core firm is the major stockholder for affiliated and subsidiary firms; affiliated firms may in turn own some shares of the core firm and, more likely, of equally ranked affiliated and subsidiary firms. The core firm develops interlocking directorates with affiliated and subsidiary firms with much greater frequency than do presidents' club firms. In South Korea, however, the individual owner of the *chaebol,* a holding company, or a main firm usually owns most firms that are not joint stock firms, and owns or controls, through family and bank holdings, a very high percentage of all shares of those firms that are listed. In South Korea, there is little evidence of interlocking directorates among *chaebol* firms; instead, there is widespread use of family members as directors of key subordinate firms and use of professional managers for other firms. Significant interlocking directorates obtain only between the *chaebol* and the main, privately owned financial institutions with which the *chaebol* deal.

Chaebol do not own banks, but have minority shares in banks controlled by the government. This explains, in part, the reliance on vertical patterns of hierarchy in Korean *chaebol* and the reluctance to go public. The government, which historically supplied the *chaebol* with huge amounts of capital to stimulate their rapid growth, retains the right to appoint bank directors who are usually not *chaebol* executives. Japanese intermarket groups, in contrast, own their own banks. As Table 6.11 shows, individual *chaebol* own, usually, between 5% and 15% of major banks' shares. The Korean government is the majority shareholder in most commercial banks, and the *chaebol* own substantial shares only in regional and local banks (see Table 6.12). This pattern of bank ownership shows the strong influence of the Korean state on business concentration and on *chaebol* industrial policy and organizational structure. The centralized domination of the state over each *chaebol* is isomorphic with the centralized domination that obtains within each *chaebol*'s organizational structure; in both instances, the pattern is one of a strong vertical hierarchy of powers.

Table 6.10   Stockholding Structure of Major Firms in Top Six *Chaebol*

Hyundai Corporation		**Hyundai Construction**	
Korea Securities	21.4	Chung Ju-Yung (founder)	54.6
Chung Ju-Yung (founder)	19.2	Hyundai Heavy Industries	7.9
Korea Inv. & Finance Co.	6.9	Hyundai Pipe Company	5.6
Hyundai Cement	1.8	Hyundai Chung Jung-Gi	2.8
Gum Gang	0.6		
Samsung Corporation		**Samsung Electronics**	
Seoul Bank	15.2	Korea Securities	17.9
Lee Kun-Hee (son) & others	11.5	Seoul Bank	12.1
Shin Young Securities	8.1	Lee Kun-Hee (son)	9.9
Daewoo Securities	6.0	Daewoo Securities	6.6
Korea Fund	4.6	Dongbang Life Insurance	6.4
Lucky-Goldstar Corporation		**Goldstar Co. (home appliances)**	
Data not available		Seoul Bank	8.9
		Lucky Securities	8.0
		Kukje Gum Yung Gong Sha	7.6
		Lucky Ltd.	6.8
		Daewoo Securities	5.5
Sunkyong Ltd. (trading company)		**Yukong Ltd. (petrol. products)**	
Choi Jong-Hyun (chairman)	10.9	Sunkyong Ltd.	50.0
GongMoonWon KuanLi GongDan	3.9	Jae-Il Securities	6.1
KanRuk GoDeung KyoDeng KyoYuk	1.9	Hyundai Securities	4.0
		Daewoo Securities	3.6
		HanKuk SanUp Bank	3.5
Daewoo Corporation		**Daewoo Heavy Industries**	
Daewoo Jae Dan	19.2	Daewoo Corporation	17.4
Korea Investment and Finance	8.7	Daewoo Jae Dan	3.3
Daewoo Hak Won	3.3	Pung Guk Yung Yoo	2.8
Ssangyong Corporation		**Ssangyong Cement**	
Ssangyong Cement	29.0	Kim Suk-Won (founder)	17.9
Korea Securities	17.1	KumMin KakWon	3.2
Kim Suk-Won (founder)	9.2	SungYoo HakSul MunHwa	1.2
Seoul Bank	6.9		
Cho-Heung Bank	6.4		
Korea Invest. & Finance Co.	3.4		
Ssangyong Hau Un	0.4		

SOURCE: Daily Economic News (1986).

Although we restricted our statistical analysis to just the top 10 *chaebol,* we believe that similar patterns, except those related to size, continue through all *chaebol.* Size is an important factor, however, because the top 5 *chaebol* alone account for 50% of the total manufacturing sales of the top 50 *chaebol* combined.

Table 6.11   Percentage of *Chaebol* Stockholdings in Commercial Banks

Chaebol	Commercial Bank of Korea	Cho-Heung Bank	Korea First Bank	Bank of Seoul	Hanil Bank
Hyundai		2.4	10.3	12.0	11.7
Samsung	16.6	10.3	6.5		
Lucky-Goldstar		1.7	8.5		7.4
Daewoo			14.4		
Ssangyong		6.0			
Hankuk Hwayak					4.3
Han Jin					9.9
Shin Dong Ha		4.8	6.0	9.9	
Dong Ah				10.0	
Tae Kwang Sun Up		11.4		4.6	
Hanil Hap Sung					
Dae Han				5.7	
Dongkuk				3.9	
Total shares	16.6	36.6	45.7	46.1	50.1

SOURCE: Hankook Ilbo (1985).

If we discount the effects of size, the above analysis shows, for South Korean business groups, the predominance of one isomorphic network configuration: a centralized management and ownership structure controlled by a founding patriarch and his heirs. The uniformity is remarkable when one considers the rapid change that has taken place in the Korean economy in the past two decades.

Horizontal linkages are few, but perhaps important, given that they seem to be concentrated around regional and city banks. However, there seem to be no significant mutual webs among vertically integrated clusters of firms— a common practice of the Japanese business groups. Moreover, even within vertically integrated networks, there is little evidence of reciprocality (or "relational contracting," as Dore, 1986b, calls it) among hierarchically ranked firms—a characteristic of Japanese *keiretsu*.

Finally, the volatility of *chaebol* growth differs from Japanese business group stability. Table 6.13 shows that in Japan the market share of major enterprise groups, although not fixed, is relatively stable (both in size and over time), and there seems little likelihood of great change in the near future. In South Korea, however, the number of *chaebol* has grown rapidly as new economic sectors have opened. One of the most recent analyses of *chaebol* lists 50 such groups, which include a total of 552 firms. Unlike the mature

Table 6.12 Percentage of *Chaebol* Stockholdings in Regional Banks

Chaebol	Kangwon Bank	Daegu Bank	Kyungki Bank	Chung Buk Bank	Kwangju Bank	Gyeong Nam Bank	Bank of Pusan	Chung Chong Bank	Jeonbuk Bank
Hyundai	32.7								
Samsung									
Sun Kyung		14.7							
Daewoo			11.0						
Kukje				41.5	5.8	13.2	2.9		
Hankuk Hwa Yak								27.2	
Han Jin			23.0						
Hyo Sung						21.5			
Du San		11.8							
Lotte							31.0		
Kolon		7.7							
Kumho					24.4				
Shin Dong Ha			17.6						
Miwon									8.9
Dongkuk Jae Gang							17.4		
Sam Yung									23.5
Total shares	32.7	34.2	51.6	41.5	30.2	34.7	51.3	27.2	32.4

SOURCE: Hankook Ilbo (1985).

Table 6.13   Assets of Intermarket Groups, 1955-1984
(percentage of national figures)

	1955	*1965*	*1975*	*1984*
Mitsui	6.1	5.0	2.9	2.4
Mitsubishi	5.0	7.2	3.4	2.6
Sumitomo	3.2	5.4	1.8	1.5
Fuyo	2.9	3.8	3.4	2.8
DKB	3.1	3.2	2.7	4.4
Sanwa	1.4	2.6	3.3	3.2

SOURCES: Caves and Uekusa (1976, p. 64) and Toyo Keizai Shimposha (1986a).

Table 6.14   *Fortune* International 500 Ranking of Top Korean *Chaebol*

Rank in 1976	*Rank in 1980*	*Rank in 1984*
209 Korea Oil	72 Hyundai	38 Samsung
278 Hyundai	101 Lucky	39 Hyundai
459 Ssangyong	125 Samsung	43 Lucky
	139 Korea Oil	48 Daewoo
	237 Hyosung	61 Sunkyong
	275 Ssangyong	139 Ssangyong
	297 Pohang Steel	185 Korea Explosives
	322 Sunkyong	209 Pohang Steel
	338 Kukje	216 Hyosung
	376 Korea Explosives	413 Doosan

SOURCES: "500 Largest Industrial Corporations Outside U.S." (1976, 1980), "The International 500" (1984).

patterning that characterizes the Japanese case, the numbers of *chaebol*, their ranks, and the numbers of firms in each *chaebol* change constantly. Table 6.14 shows that *chaebol* positions are subject to rapid changes not only in terms of relative ranking among the *chaebol* themselves, but also in absolute terms, in relation to other international industrial corporations. The difference in organizational structure between Japan and South Korea could be dismissed as simply showing the different stages of development reached by the two countries; we claim, however, that significant institutional factors account for the observed differences.

One factor, as we have observed, is the presence of a strong Korean state, which is actively involved in the planning and enforcement of economic policies favoring industrial concentration and vertical lines of domination;

this is the coercive isomorphism generated by the political influence of a strong state. A second factor has been the cultural impact, in South Korea, of American managerial practices brought through the institution of management programs in South Korean universities (Zo, 1970). Third, and more broadly, we point to the persistence in South Korean society of what Norman Jacobs (1985) calls a "patrimonial social order." He explains: "The present situation is attributable to the desire of industrial decision-makers within and without the polity to use time-tested patrimonial techniques of controlling and prebendally exploiting an industrial economy" (p. 154). It is then far from self-evident that today's Japanese organizational forms are tomorrow's Korean ones; rather, we are inclined to think that the two are unlikely ever to resemble each other.

Taiwanese Business Groups: Familial Networks

A simple description of Taiwan's business groups (*jituanqiye* in Chinese) is enough to reveal sharp differences between the Taiwanese case and the other two. Two of the most obvious differences are the size and importance of Taiwanese groups in that country's economy. Japanese and South Korean business groups are central features of their respective economies, and include, as member firms in some cluster, most leading industrial firms. In Taiwan, however, the business groups do not occupy nearly so central a position. Of the largest 500 manufacturing firms in Taiwan, only about 40% belong to business groups; moreover, some of these firms are not leaders in their own sectors of production. Instead, in Taiwan, many large enterprises remain single-unit operations and are not included within any business group at all. The lack of centrality is reflected in the total sales figure for the 743 firms that belong to the top 96 business groups, which accounts for only a modest percentage of Taiwan's GNP.

The difference in the size of business groups in Taiwan also testifies to their lack of centrality. On average, Taiwanese groups have fewer and smaller member firms than do the business groups in Japan and Korea, and the total assets and sales figures of Taiwanese business groups are much lower than the figures for the other two countries.

The differences of size and centrality of the Taiwan business groups point to more fundamental organizational differences. First, Chinese business groups have none of the tightly coupled vertical ties (in terms of both production and ownership) that characterize, in different ways, Japanese

Table 6.15   Summary Statistics of Taiwan's 96 Business Groups, 1983

Average number of core persons per business group	2.90
Average number of firms per business group	7.76
Average number of positions in individual firms	7.18
Average number of industrial sectors per group	4.00
Mean number of workers per business group	3,456
Median number of workers per group	1,396
Mean number of workers per firm	459
Median number of workers per firm	90
Average year of firm establishment	1971
Average sales per business group (million NT$)	633.68
Average sales per firm (million NT$)	103.20

SOURCE: China Credit Information Service (1985).

keiretsu and Korean *chaebol*. Instead, although they have fewer firms per group and the firms themselves have a smaller percentage of total sales per industrial sector when compared with the other two cases, Taiwanese business groups typically diversify their holdings. As Table 6.15 shows, Taiwanese business groups have, on average, 7.76 firms; those few firms are spread among an average of four different industrial sectors. Moreover, none of the 96 business groups is based solely on vertical linkages among member firms within the same business sector. Instead of being vertically integrated, tightly controlled sets of firms, Taiwanese business groups are agglomerations of different size firms—mostly small—in different economic sectors.

Taiwanese groups have several isomorphic organizational features that set them off from South Korean and Japanese business groups. First, in contrast to Japan, where 90% of business group firms are publicly held, in Taiwan only 10% of all firms in the business groups are joint stock firms. Moreover, only 40% of the 96 business groups have one or more publicly listed firms. Instead, the prevailing ownership pattern is one of private family control. Taiwanese enterprise groups are owned either by a single family or by several individuals in limited partnership; in the Chinese context, partnerships amount to a form of family ownership (Wong, 1985).

Second, firm financing in Taiwan differs from that in both Japan and South Korea. Japanese business groups rely heavily on equity markets and bank loans to raise funds, hence Japan's extraordinarily large financial markets. South Korean business groups instead rely heavily on debt financing, most of which is controlled by the state; South Korea is Asia's largest debtor nation. Taiwanese business groups, in contrast, rely largely on curb market financing. Financial institutions, including banks and cooperative credit associations, supply 31.2% of firm funds, usually in the form of short-term operating loans. The capital and money markets supply only 8.4% of funds. By far the largest source of money, more than 60%, comes from privately arranged loans from family and friends, as well as from retained earnings. The state-owned financial institutions invest very little in private enterprises; partly for this reason, Taiwan has one of the largest foreign reserves of any country in the world.

Third, Taiwanese business group firms are typically only loosely integrated. For example, according to our data there are only limited capital transfers (an average of 0.66 capital links per firm) and equally limited market transactions among firms in a group. Even more significant, the business groups lack a unified command or management structure. What occurs, instead, is that every firm duplicates a command structure (see Table 6.16). The same set of people, usually the owners and their close relatives, holds multiple managerial, often identical positions in several firms within the group, and sometimes several positions within a single firm. Business groups are loosely coupled networks of firms owned by the same individual or related persons who join together in multiple enterprises. Although there are Taiwanese patriarchs, their control of enterprise groups is less certain, less centralized, and more circumscribed than is typical for heads of *chaebol*. South Korean *chaebol* owners, holding one position at the top, exercise their authority through all the firms in the group, all the way down to the last employee in the smallest firm. The duplication of positions in Taiwanese business groups suggests the weakness or boundedness of authority structures in that economy and the necessity for maintaining face-to-face relations in order to sustain control.

Finally, like Japan, but unlike South Korea, Taiwanese business groups rely extensively on subcontracting relations with nongroup firms. Unlike Japan, however, subcontract relations are neither exclusive nor necessarily long lasting. Small firms typically supply goods or services for more than one firm. In fact, it is not unusual for several small and middle-sized firms to create fairly short-lived production networks to provide components for assembly in a business group company.

The unstructured character of Taiwanese business groups has several institutional sources (see Chapter 12, this volume). First is the Chinese system of equal inheritance for all sons—a system that favors the fragmentation of family holdings from generation to generation (see Wong, 1985).

Table 6.16 Management Isomorphism for Top Six Taiwanese *Jituanqiye*, 1983

				Positions Held by Core Persons		
Group	Firms	Core Persons	Relationship	Director	Manager	Stockholder
Formosa	18	2	two brothers	10	5	14
Linden	12	1	—	5	0	1
Tainan	33	11	two families	28	7	59
Yue Loong	10	1	—	7	2	4
Far Eastern	17	4	family and one friend	9	8	10
Shin Kong	21	5	one family	21	12	18

SOURCE: China Credit Information Service (1985).

181

Second is the centrality of family relations in business activities, which allows new firms to be established overnight, thanks to the pooling of financial and human resources of the extended family. The business groups in Taiwan are, after all, selected family firms that succeeded best in their economic activities. Third is the state policy of noninterference in the private sector. As Scitovsky (1985) describes it, "In Taiwan, today, government does not have the strong ascendancy it still has in Korea, and economic controls tend to be moderate" (p. 223). The Taiwanese policy is that market forces should be left to their own devices; competition is enhanced by the presence of large numbers of small firms, not by the presence of a few giant corporations. Accordingly, the Taiwanese state has reinforced the role of family-centered business groups by refusing to influence through direct intervention the growth of selected firms in selected industrial sectors.

The picture emerging of the Taiwanese case, then, is again one of isomorphic organizational structures that are surrounded, in the cultural and political arena, by institutionalized practices that reinforce organizational homogeneity. Most relevant to this pattern of organizational forms is that it well served Taiwan's role in the international market. Through their flexible organizational structures, Taiwanese firms have been able to adjust readily to changing market demands in textiles, leather goods, electrical appliances, and small metal products. Again, meeting the demands of its institutional environment has favored, not hindered, Taiwan's organizational fitness in the technical environment.

Institutionalization and Isomorphism

Enterprise groups in Japan, South Korea, and Taiwan display distinctive organizational patterns of ownership, management, finance, and production. Measures of isomorphism confirm the uniformity of firm relations within each country and, equally, the differences among them. These distinctive characteristics are summarized in Table 6.17. The economies of these nations are not reducible to the business groups we have examined, of course, but these groups are significant economic actors in their respective economies, and their isomorphism demands explanation.

Why are business groups so uniform within each market economy, yet so different in comparison with the others? Multiple answers are necessary for a full account, but they are not reducible to purely economic variables—the

Table 6.17 Organizational Characteristics of Business Groups

	Japan	South Korea	Taiwan
Ownership patterns	shareholding of group firms	state-financed family groups	family ownership and partnership
Intragroup networks	cross-shareholding mutual dominance	strict hierarchical structure from top	multiple positions of core personnel
Intergroup networks	cross-shares, loans, and joint ventures	coordination through banks and government	cross-investment by individuals and firms
Subcontract relations	structured or semiformal	insignificant	informal and highly flexible
Investment patterns	vertical and horizontal integration	vertical and horizontal	vertical integration or diversification
Growth patterns	bank-financed group activities	state-financed sector growth	informal financing and reinvestment

pressures of technical environments or patterns of competitive isomorphism. Business groups might be explained as competitive collusions—the opportunistic response to technical environmental pressures in Northeast Asia. The organizational isomorphisms we have identified, however, cannot simply be explained as the attempt to achieve market fitness. Business groups are too widespread and too isomorphic to be viewed as idiosyncratic responses to market factors. Moreover, multiple social institutions in each society support the formation of patterned firm relations, as we have described, and do not press organizations toward the Western idea of autonomously competing firms. Technical requirements alone cannot explain East Asian isomorphism.

Following the arguments of institutional theorists, we assert that each society creates a context of fiscal, political, and social institutions that limit and direct the development of fit organizational forms. In all three economies we have discussed, but especially in South Korea and Japan, the important role of the state in economic affairs leads us to believe that institutional and normative factors are particularly important to organizational viability in those nations. Asian firms, like all firms, operate in an institutional environment that presents a structure of constraints and possibilities, but, most important, of normative forms of economic action. Each of these economies, our data suggest, fashions itself after a distinctive institutional environment, generating a characteristic pattern of business relationships. These relationships are not simply ones of convenience or efficiency, but represent enactments of socially acceptable, institutionalized forms of economic behavior— they are the manifestations of a normative structure that underlies economic activity and provides market order. Clearly, the firms in these economies are capitalist and profit seeking, but they seek profit not abstractly, but with a knowledge of legitimate strategies for gaining market advantage. This they accomplish by merging together the technical and institutional requirements of their environments.

Different fundamental principles of control, which are not solely economic in character but rather are drawn from other institutional sources such as the state, the community, and the family, are at work in each society. These principles inform predictable social relations in multiple arenas, including the economic, and are supported in various ways by state agencies.

Japanese enterprise groups enact a communitarian ideal. Like residential, intellectual, and other forms of community, Japanese business groups maintain clearly defined status relations among firms, some of which are egalitarian and others hierarchical. Although there are clearly more important and more influential firms within enterprise groups, the decision-making unit is the group, and command is exercised not by fiat but by consensus. Decisions are made considering what is best for the collectivity, not simply for individual firms, however powerful.

The South Korean *chaebol* are an expression of a patrimonial principle. The *chaebol* are, in a Weberian typology, "patrimonial households"— organizations dominated by a patriarch and his children, but extending beyond them to include professional managers from outside the family. Each of these industrial empires is the property of an authoritarian leader and his designees, who manage not by consensus, but by centralized command supported by the state.

Taiwanese business groups enact yet another principle, that of the familial network. Although they are based on family ties, as in South Korea, the Taiwanese business groups do not express the will of a single patriarch but rather the interests of an extended family in which division of financial holdings on the death of the patriarch is the rule (Cohen, 1976). There is patriarchalism in Taiwan, to be sure, but it is more contested and less unified than in South Korea. Unlike Korean patriarchs, who may direct their business empires even in the absence of corporate positions, Taiwanese business leaders assume multiple executive posts to reinforce their authority.

East Asian enterprise groups are both an expression and a product of these three organizing principles. None is a corruption of a mythical ideal of competitive market fitness; rather, each is an enactment of socially constructed technical and institutional requirements. Although these three principles are subject to variation in each economy, exceptions are variations on a common theme. For example, the relatively nonpatriarchal character of the Daewoo *chaebol* is frequently noted because it breaks the expected and understood patriarchal pattern of *chaebol* organization (e.g., Hahn et al., 1987).

The new institutionalism has been instrumental in calling attention to the cultural, political, and normative pressures present in the environment, and it has proven useful in the analysis of organizations that are particularly vulnerable to these pressures. Yet the new institutionalism seems to have shortchanged itself by claiming only partial relevance in the analysis of organizational environments. As we have shown in this study, the new institutionalism is just as fruitful (if not more fruitful) in the analysis of organizational environments with a strong technical component. Institutional features need not be limited to explaining the achievement of legitimacy in organizations; institutional features can be shown to be just as crucial to achieving the technical and competitive fitness of organizations. We have demonstrated that this is indeed the case in East Asian enterprise groups.

If one assumes, in a Western vein, that firm individuation is the natural state of an orderly market, then the organizational principles we have described can be understood only as institutional obstacles to a successful and competitive economy. Indeed, the U.S. officials' breakup of the Japanese *zaibatsu* after World War II was an expression of this presumption. Today's success of East Asian economies, including Japan's adoption of the *kigyo shudan* arrangement, challenges this fundamental assumption of Western economic analyses. From a perspective that integrates institutional and technical requirements, we argue that the patterns of institutional isomorphism observed in Japan, Taiwan, and South Korea not only aim at achieving legitimacy, but also serve the function of market order by providing norms that channel economic activity. Indeed, breaches of institutional patterns of economic behavior would be disruptive in the respective economies in which they are found. Japanese firms that act without regard for the business groups of which they are a part create chaos and impede successful economic planning and investment strategy. Taiwanese executives who do not consider the interests of the lineage likewise disrupt an orderly market. East Asian economies have prospered not because they have unilaterally adapted to technical environmental requirements, but because they have successfully institutionalized the principles of market activity suited to their sociocultural environment and to their strategies of economic development.

Note

1. Our sources of information differ for each society, but are roughly comparable. For Japan, we relied on annual reports of firms collected by private research institutes (Dodwell Marketing Consultants, 1984; Toyo Keizai Shimposha, 1986a, 1986b) and by the Japanese government (Kosei Torihiki Iinkai Jimukyoku, 1983). Besides identifying firm membership in enterprise groups, these reports contain information on joint shareholding, bank loans, and interlocking directorates as well as the standard information on firm size, sales, and assets. For additional data sources as well as for their interpretation, we have drawn on the excellent discussions in Aoki (1984a), Caves and Uekusa (1976), Futatsugi (1982, 1986), Hadley (1970), Kobayashi (1980), Nakatani (1982, 1984), Okumura (1982a, 1984, 1985), Sumiya (1986), and Ueda (1983, 1986).

For South Korea, we relied on the statistics on enterprise groups collected by the Hankook Ilbo (Korean Daily News) and on those compiled in Daily Economic News (1986). The first source contains the identification of firms in enterprise groups, statistics about each of the top

50 enterprise groups, and information about each individual firm. The second source lists owners, managers, and (when applicable) major shareholders and gives some information about product specialization as well as standard information on firm assets and liabilities. We supplemented these statistics with newspaper reports, other journalistic accounts, and the few recent scholarly examinations available (Hahn et al., 1987; Koo, 1984; Lee, 1986).

For Taiwan, we relied on the extensive surveys done by the China Credit Information Service (Zhonghua Zhengxinso). Published on a yearly basis since 1971, these surveys identify firms within business groups and provide data on assets, liabilities, product specialization, management structure and key personnel in business groups, and a list of principal owners and managers in individual firms. We supplemented these data with journalistic, anecdotal accounts of specific enterprise groups and a few scholarly examinations on related topics (Gold, 1986; Numazaki, 1986). To add to our interpretation of the Taiwan material, we also drew upon Wong Sui-lun's (1985, 1988) and Redding and Tam's (1986) discussions of the similarly organized Chinese family-based enterprises in Hong Kong.

7

Patterns of
Interfirm Control in
Japanese Business

MARCO ORRÙ
GARY G. HAMILTON
MARIKO SUZUKI

estern sociologists have recently resorted to network analysis to understand the structure of interfirm relations in the United States and in Western Europe (Allen, 1974; Burt, 1983; Mintz & Schwartz, 1985; Mizruchi, 1982; Roy, 1983; Scott, 1979; Scott & Griff, 1984; Stockman, Ziegler, & Scott, 1985) and to shed light on

AUTHORS' NOTE: This chapter is reprinted here by permission of Walter de Gruyter & Co. from "Patterns of Inter-Firm Control in Japanese Business," by Marco Orrù, Gary G. Hamilton, and Mariko Suzuki, *Organization Studies,* 1989, vol. 10, pp. 549-574. Copyright 1989 by Walter de Gruyter und Co.; all rights reserved.

the class orientations of owners and managers (Domhoff, 1978, 1980; Mills, 1956; Palmer, Friedland, & Singh, 1986; Soref, 1976; Useem, 1982, 1984). Most network analyses of capitalist enterprises emphasize the role of interlocking directorships—by far the most common form of intercorporate relations in the West. Interlocking directorships are said to indicate techniques of control among business firms and to reveal cohesiveness within the capitalist class. Although some writers have detected differences in the network patterns (Stockman et al., 1985), most researchers see interfirm relationships as significant indicators of the structural foundations of capitalism.

Interfirm relationships in the West are significant, but their precise meaning remains unclear. Palmer et al. (1986) show that interfirm networks often manifest either intraclass or interorganizational patterns that reflect, in turn, competing forms of control in capitalist business, where power is defined either in terms of hierarchies or in terms of resources. These approaches emphasize different aspects of control and often enrich the analysis of business networks in Western societies, yet neither one is well suited to the analysis of stable networks among similarly organized firms—a pattern typical of Northeast Asian economies such as those of Taiwan, South Korea, and especially Japan (Hamilton, Orrù, & Biggart, 1987; Leff, 1978). When studying stable networks of similarly organized firms, a more useful approach is to augment network analysis with a contextually more sensitive, neo-Weberian perspective developed by Meyer and Rowan (1977), Meyer and Scott (1983), DiMaggio and Powell (1983), Zucker (1983), and others, broadly known as the institutional perspective. This perspective still lacks an articulate, comprehensive formulation (W. R. Scott, 1987), but it allows us to look at domination in non-Western business not as an instance of an unchanging pattern of capitalist domination, but as originating in varying institutional environments that in turn shape modes of economic and political control. In this chapter, we offer an analysis of interfirm control in Japan and argue for a view of control as contextually defined by institutionalized rules, roles, and role relationships. Based upon distinctive sociocultural foundations, intercorporate relations in different societies are seen as being the outcome of different institutional principles and hence as exhibiting different characteristics (e.g., Ziegler, 1985).

An institutional view of power highlights the distinctive features of interfirm relations in the Japanese economy—an economy with structural characteristics different from those found in the West and especially the

United States. To be sure, interfirm coordinating mechanisms do exist in other capitalist societies and have been described in some detail (Francis, Turk, & Willman, 1983), but in Japan more than anywhere else, and unlike the situation in the United States, it is not the firm (corporation) but rather networks of firms (business groups) that are the key units organizing the economy. Accordingly, institutional strategies of interfirm collaboration are devised. Interlocking directorships are only one of several forms of interfirm control; equally important are joint shareholdings, commodity transactions, joint investments, common trademarks, and bank loans among firms. Through these collaborative means, Japanese firms provide themselves with mutual assurance and stability in an uncertain market environment.

Interfirm relationships in Japan do not create a stratification of firms—a system of inequalities and hierarchies of the type described in the West. Although inequalities certainly exist, interfirm relations must be understood in their institutionalized character. Japanese firms are embedded in culturally defined and explicitly organized networks; firm location within a network is established by means of recognized symbols marking organizational status; rank-conscious norms of conduct, which apply to all firms in the network, create a corporate etiquette that no member firm can readily circumvent. Control in Japanese business groups is based not solely on market principles, but also on culturally specific principles of hierarchy—an institutionalized decorum that sets up patterns of normative expectations. The enactment of these principles leads to what DiMaggio and Powell (1983) call "institutional isomorphism"—uniformity in the network structure and firm organization that constitute, coordinate, and direct economic activities (see Chapter 6, this volume). Within existing institutional parameters, market forces and organizational control combine, creating distinctive patterns.

We divide this chapter into four sections. First is a brief discussion of the three definitions of interfirm power relationships. Second, we describe the two major types of business groups (i.e., firm clusters) in Japan—intermarket groups and independent groups. Third, analyzing joint shareholding, we present two types of control strategies that operate within firm clusters: one aimed at controlling equally ranked firms (horizontal control) and the other aimed at controlling unequally ranked firms (vertical control). Drawing on existing Japanese research, we also outline other prominent forms of inter-firm relationships (interlocking directorships, commodity transactions, joint investments, common trademarks, bank loans, and business associations) that reinforce the patterns of horizontal and vertical control. In the concluding section, we contrast the structured patterns of control in Japanese business with the more loosely organized, hegemonic mode of domination in U.S. business. As capitalism becomes more thoroughly international in nature and subject to transnational institutions of control, more differentiated, institutionalized forms of intercorporate controls are likely to ensue.

Three Models of Interfirm Control

Interorganizational and intraclass accounts of corporate relationships rest, in part, on the opposing conceptions of power that each implies. Most network theorists favor interorganizational interpretations that draw on an exchange theory of power, sometimes identified as "resource dependency theory" (see, e.g., Aldrich, 1979; Burt, 1977, 1982; Pennings, 1980; Pfeffer & Salancik, 1978). Interfirm controls arise from environmental constraints created by independent actors (i.e., firms and corporate owners and managers) as they attempt to secure needed resources by linking themselves to other actors capable of supplying these resources. Interdependency is worked out for the benefit, as well as the mutual constraint, of the parties involved. Some exchanges are symmetrical, others are asymmetrical, depending on the balance of resources needed by one but controlled by others. Power is held by those controlling more resources.

The implications of an exchange theory of power have been indicated by Emerson (1962, 1972), Blau (1964), and Cook (1977, 1982). Applying this conception of power to interfirm relations, Aldrich (1979), Burt (1977, 1982), Pennings (1980), and Pfeffer and Salancik (1978) claim that interfirm structures emerge from exchange relationships—they result from coalitions built on interdependencies and are usually tenuous and episodic, rather than long-term and stable (Mintz & Schwartz, 1985, p. 26). Noting instability in interfirm controls, Mintz and Schwartz (1985) augment the resource dependency theory with their "bank control theory." Because the resource most needed by firms is money, banks are crucial in interfirm networks and thus have hegemony over other types of firms.

Intraclass explanations of interfirm relationships rely on structural theories of control that stand opposite to exchange theories (Hamilton & Biggart, 1985). Exchange theories emphasize a market-derived control, where network structures obtain from the rational calculations and decisions of independent actors. Structural theories of power, instead, draw upon a social stratification model, where patterns of inequality persist over time. In the clearest examples of this genre, Domhoff (1967, 1970, 1979, 1983) has evidenced the "processes of ruling-class domination in America" (1979). According to Domhoff, interfirm relationships are a means for elites to perpetuate class domination (see also Mills, 1956; Scott, 1979; Useem, 1979, 1984; Zeitlin, 1974, 1976). Firm owners and managers are not independent decision makers, but individuals who embody, and act on behalf of, their class interests.

A structural theory of power interprets interfirm relations as the means for the capitalist class to obtain and maintain profits, to increase class cohesiveness, and to reinforce domination over subordinate classes. Power relationships reflect the capitalists' hegemonic position in society; hence such relationships are mostly stable over time. Structural theories posit obdurate situations where inequality is endemic and maintained by strong, coercive powers.

The literature on power and authority from an institutional perspective is witnessing rapid growth, but with few attempts to apply such a view to interfirm relationships. This neglect signals the reluctance to view interfirm relations as being organized in their own right and shaped by factors other than the economic activities at hand. Most analysts view such networks as interorganizational: resulting from actions taken by the firms themselves and immune to exogenous factors (e.g., Cook, 1977; Mintz & Schwartz, 1985; Pfeffer & Salancik, 1978). That interfirm networks in the United States are relatively unstable and episodic reinforces these researchers' belief, but they fail to consider that instability could, in fact, demonstrate institutional isomorphism in the U.S. context—a hypothesis that gains support when we contrast it with the stability of interfirm networks in Japan. Ouchi's (1981, 1984) work is a notable exception in his attempt to expand economistic models to encompass the roles of organic solidarity and social integration in economic action.

Our institutional theory of power has three essential components. First, the formal structures of organizations "dramatically reflect the myths of their institutional environments" (Meyer & Rowan, 1977). These myths are principles of domination or logics of organizing people according to the ultimate validity of commands and the legitimacy of relationships (Weber, 1968b, pp. 952-954). Second, the enactment of institutionalized rules is not uniform, but differs depending upon the alignments and institutional arrangements in the society and according to what sector of activities is being organized

(Hamilton & Kao, 1987b; Imai & Itami, 1984; Meyer & Scott, 1983, pp. 129-153). "Organizations are embedded in larger systems of relations" (Meyer & Scott, 1983, p. 150), and this embeddedness influences the organization of firms (Granovetter, 1985; Hirsch, 1972, 1986). Third, the identification of organizing principles provides justification for those who act in the name of others or in the name of the group as a whole. Displaying institutionalized principles legitimates not only the goal-oriented activities of organizations, but, more important, the hierarchies, the role relationships, and the exercise of authority (Biggart & Hamilton, 1984; Hamilton & Biggart, 1984). Taken together, these three components of an institutional view of power suggest that interfirm relations should be directly influenced by the institutionalized principles of domination existing within a society, by the sector of activity, and by the institutional arrangement and alignments within that sector.

In a broader framework, and with reference to non-Western settings, we emphasize that principles of domination should be expected to differ among civilizational areas (e.g., Geertz, 1977, 1980). Bellah (1970), Hamilton (1984), and Needham (1956b), among others, have argued that the very principles of domination in East Asia and Western Europe have different ontological constructs and differ dramatically in their institutional patterns. In the West, domination rests on the ultimate right of command embodied in formalized command structures and jurisdictions. In contrast, domination in East Asia rests on the ultimate necessity of adhesion to one's role, which institutionally favors the development of status hierarchies and role relationships (Hamilton, 1984). We argue, then, that East Asian forms of control profoundly influence the formation and stability of network structure in Japanese business groups.

Business Groups in Japan

The literature on Japanese business groups encompasses scholarly studies as well as a wide array of government and journalistic reports. Such popular journals as *Ekonomisuto, Daiyamondo, Japan Economic Journal,* and *Tokyo Business Today* feature articles on business groups quite regularly. The academic literature is extensive (e.g., Futatsugi, 1986; Goto, 1982; Kobayashi, 1980; Okumura, 1982a, 1984, 1985; Sumiya, 1986). Individual business groups have been examined both in their historical and present standings

(Narushima, 1980; Nishikiori, 1975, 1977; Oishi, 1975; Okumura, 1982a, 1982b; Wada, 1977; Yuki, 1985). For all the business groups, voluminous statistics have been compiled in Japan by private research institutes and publishing houses (Dodwell Marketing Consultants, 1984; Toyo Keizai Shimposha, 1986a, 1986b) and by the Japanese government (Kosei Torihiki Iinkai Jimukyoku, 1983). Researchers have debated the exact identification of multitiered group membership while agreeing on the broad identification of two major types: intermarket groups and independent groups (Dodwell Marketing Consultants, 1984; Toyo Keizai Shimposha, 1986a). Writers have provided various rationales for Japanese business alliances: organizationally contrived mutual control (Okumura, 1985), risk and benefit sharing (Nakatani, 1984), boundary maintenance and self-containment (Futatsugi, 1986), hegemony of capitalist class (Sumiya, 1986), minimization of general transaction costs (Goto, 1982), and interfirm corporate culture (Kobayashi, 1979).

Independent groups and intermarket groups have been analyzed in terms of class domination within a hierarchy of firms (Sumiya, 1986), reciprocity among unequally ranked firms for reduction of aggregate risk costs (Aoki, 1984a), organizational and technological advantages for parent companies (Takamiya, 1982), and vertical control of production and distribution (Ishida, 1983; Miyazaki & Fujinami, 1980; Shimokawa, 1985). The available literature shows that the distinctive unit of Japanese capitalism is not the firm per se, but rather the business group. Depending on the criteria of selection, scholars have identified different numbers of business groups; in our study (based on data provided by Dodwell Marketing Consultants, 1984) we have included 16 groups: the top 6 intermarket groups and the top 10 independent industrial and financial groups. These are listed in Table 7.1. Together, these groups account for a high share of the financial and manufacturing capacity of the Japanese economy: 24% of the nation's 1982 sales figure, with their 1,001 firms accounting for 10% of Japan's workforce. Unlike in the United States, where memberships in business cliques are unclear (Mizruchi, 1982), in Japan, groups and member firms are known to the public and are frequently discussed in the press.

Specific traits define intermarket and independent groups in Japan. Each intermarket group consists of a horizontally bound web of large firms in different economic sectors, with an isomorphic lineup of firms competing across groups, but not within them (Hamilton et al., 1987). All intermarket groups have their own banks, insurance companies, and trading firms. The presidents of the largest firms are members of the presidents' council or club,

Table 7.1 Intermarket Groups and Independent Groups in Japan

Six Intermarket Groups	Top 10 Independent Groups
1. Mitsubishi	1. Tokai Bank
2. Mitsui	2. Industrial Bank of Japan
3. Sumitomo	3. Nippon Steel
4. Fuyo	4. Hitachi
5. DKB	5. Nissan
6. Sanwa	6. Toyota
	7. Matsushita
	8. Toshiba-IHI
	9. Tokyu
	10. Seibu

which meets once a month to discuss the affairs of the group (Okumura, 1985).

Each of these large firms has vertically aligned affiliate and subsidiary firms—a pattern called *keiretsu*. In addition, affiliates and subsidiaries maintain long-term subcontract relations with small and middle-sized firms that are not part of the *keiretsu* (Ishida, 1983; Okumura, 1982a, 1984; Shimokawa, 1985). Subcontract relationships are ranked as primary, secondary, or tertiary, depending on the roles they serve in the production process.

Three of the intermarket groups (Mitsubishi, Mitsui, and Sumitomo) grew directly out of the *zaibatsu* conglomerates that controlled Japanese industry before World War II. In the postwar period, the American occupational forces tried to dissolve these conglomerates into many independent firms (Bisson, 1954; Uekusa, 1977), but after the occupation ended, the firms rebuilt their network linkages, though in a less centralized fashion. The other three intermarket groups (Fuyo, DKB, and Sanwa) grew in the postwar period around prominent city banks; these new groups are sometimes known as the bank groups.

In contrast to intermarket groups, independent industrial and financial groups represent a network of vertically integrated firms in one or more industrial sectors (except for two financial groups: Tokai Bank and the Industrial Bank of Japan). Independent groups are organized as *keiretsu*, each consisting of a large, highly successful parent company and vertically aligned subordinate companies (Dodwell Marketing Consultants, 1984). Independent groups developed in the 1950s and 1960s, as Japan's economy grew rapidly. Some of the firms were and some still are associated with one or more of the intermarket groups, but their great success enabled them to gain autonomy from intermarket groups. Given this preliminary description, let us now examine the networking patterns of control that obtain.

Shareholding and Other
Means of Interfirm Control

Interlocking ties are the most common means of intercorporate control in American business, but not in Japan. Although interlocking directorates are present in Japan, their role is subordinate to the ownership of stocks (Okumura, 1985; Ueda, 1986). In Japan, shareholding is the key factor in the structure of economic control; every year, Toyo Keizai Shimposha publishes a list of all firms quoted in the Japanese stock markets, together with the major stockholders in each firm.

Japanese scholars have amply discussed the organizational manipulation of reciprocal shareholding in intermarket groups. Reciprocal shareholding is crucial to the horizontal control structure of these groups (Okumura, 1984, pp. 179-180; 1985, pp. 110-116) and it differs from the unilateral shareholding in independent groups and *keiretsu* (Okumura, 1984, p. 168; 1985, pp. 110-111). Researchers have examined the negative capital function of reciprocal shareholding (Futatsugi, 1986; Kobayashi, 1979; Okumura, 1985) and have treated such shareholdings as organizational means of maintaining group territory (Sumiya, 1986) and group solidarity (Kosei Torihiki Iinkai Jimukyoku, 1983; Sumiya, 1986). The analysis of stock ownership shows two major organizational patterns in Japanese groups: one of horizontal control and one of vertical control (Okumura, 1982a, 1984, 1985; Sato, 1986; Ueda, 1983). *Horizontal control* refers to patterns of power and influence exercised reciprocally among firms through shareholding, interlocking ties, trade links, bank loans, and business associations; *vertical control,* in contrast, refers to the unilateral flow of power and influence, through the ownership of shares and other means, from one firm to others.

Horizontal Control

Intragroup Horizontal Patterns

Horizontal and vertical patterns coexist in Japan's 6 major intermarket groups and in the 10 independent groups. At the highest organizational level,

Table 7.2 Matrix of Mutual Stockholdings of Four Mitsubishi Firms, 1982
(in percentages)

Owner	Owned			
	1	2	3	4
1. Mitsubishi Bank	—	5.1	5.6	4.9
2. Tokio M&F Insurance	4.7	—	6.5	2.8
3. Mitsubishi Corp.	2.2	2.5	—	2.2
4. Mitsubishi Heavy Industries	3.5	1.9	3.9	—

SOURCE: Compiled from Dodwell Marketing Consultants (1984, p. 8).

the intermarket group is structured around two or three leading companies—usually the main financial institution (called the city bank), the group's trading company, and the leading industrial firm. Beyond this nucleus, the intermarket group is organized around the presidential council, made up of presidents of leading firms in various industrial sectors. The number of firms included in the presidential councils varied in 1982 from 21 (for the Sumitomo group) to 46 (for the DKB group). The relationships among presidents' club firms are horizontal. Beyond the presidents' club, intermarket groups are organized around a larger committee that coordinates the public relations of the group. For instance, Mitsubishi has a committee that "consists of 44 group companies and is responsible for joint public relations activities in order to improve consumers' awareness of Mitsubishi group companies and the common brand name 'Mitsubishi' or 'Three Diamond' logo in Japan and abroad" (Dodwell Marketing Consultants, 1984, p. 51). But the main horizontal nucleus is the presidents' club. Reciprocal ownership of small amounts of stocks is typical in all intermarket groups. Table 7.2 shows the mutual shareholding pattern in four group firms that belong to the Mitsubishi Kinyo-Kai (Mitsubishi Friday Conference).

The cross-holding of shares illustrates the pattern of mutual control among presidents' club firms. Mutual shareholding strengthens the group's internal cohesion both symbolically and materially; through it, the group's financial and industrial leaders act in concert to maintain control of group firms. In fact, while stock ownership of an individual firm in another firm does not alone guarantee control, the combined effect of stock ownership by several group firms provides the group with ample means of control. Individual firms usually own between 2% and 7% of another firm's stocks, but the combined shareholding of several group firms is between 20% and 30% on average.

The influence of the group is even greater when we look at the top 10 shareholders in a firm; the relative power of group firms becomes, then, even stronger. For instance, if we look at the top 10 shareholders in the Mitsubishi presidents' club firms, the combined stockholdings of Mitsubishi firms are, on average, more than 64%, giving the Mitsubishi group an additional margin of control over presidents' club member firms.

This horizontal ownership of stocks shows a pattern that Western economists might find odd, if not altogether alien to their way of thinking. The control of Japanese intermarket groups does not reside in any single, individual firm or corporation, but in the collectivity of firms. No single firm can exercise total control over member firms, and collective control of club firms over each other is preferred. Because of the collective power of presidents' club firms, the monthly presidents' meeting has relevance beyond mere organizational matters. Futatsugi (1986) asserts that "in substance [it] has the character of a shareholders' general meeting" (p. 40).

The presidents' club firms bond togethr and provide collective support to the economic policy of the group and to the strategies of individual member firms. Nakatani (1984) sees this organizational design as meeting the need of member firms to share or spread the risks or contingencies that arise in the capital market; the goal is risk minimization rather than profit maximization.

Within this framework of mutual ownership, we must qualify our argument. If we look closely at the matrix of ownership among the presidents' club firms, we observe that the reciprocity is by no means symmetrical. Whereas financial institutions and industrial leaders hold substantial amounts of shares in almost every member firm, many industrial firms own very few or no shares in other firms. To wit, all firms are equal but some are more equal than others. This asymmetric pattern is typical for all intermarket groups, so that few companies (three to seven) have systematically significant ownership of other firms' stocks. Table 7.3 shows the top six Mitsubishi stockholders.

Financial institutions are the undisputed leaders of intermarket groups. Their prominence has been attributed to the changed economic and institutional structure of Japan since World War II (Miyazaki, 1976; Okumura, 1985; Shimura, 1976; Sumiya, 1986). The banks' leadership has been evaluated in terms of the banks' sizable holdings of group shares (Okumura, 1984), preferential loans for group members (Okumura, 1985), and general coordination of risk and profit sharing among members (Nakatani, 1984).

Table 7.3 Top Six Stockholding Firms in the Mitsubishi Club

	Number of Firms	Average Shares (%)	Range
Meiji Mutual Life Ins.	23	5.5	1.6 - 9.6
Mitsubishi Bank	22	4.8	1.6 - 7.7
Mitsubishi Trust & Banking	20	3.6	2.1 - 5.2
Tokio M&F Insurance	20	3.5	0.9 - 6.5
Mitsubishi Heavy Industries	11	3.5	1.9 - 6.9
Mitsubishi Corporation	10	3.1	1.4 - 5.4

SOURCE: Compiled from Dodwell Marketing Consultants (1984, pp. 152-187).

The banks' leadership would seem to support Mintz and Schwartz's "bank control theory" and to contradict our claim of horizontal relations within groups, but although financial institutions have a prominent position in intermarket groups, their position strengthens horizontal patterns. Financial institutions and insurance companies are in fact agents of control within the group, because they provide, through bank loans, the capital necessary for the firms' investments and growth; and yet no single firm in the group has sufficient power to claim hegemonic control over other firms or over the group. Financial institutions act as mediators rather than as autonomous firms capable of exercising control over other firms. This is clear when one realizes that a group's financial institution is, in turn, controlled by the group's other financial institutions and by a score of presidents' club firms. An extreme case is shown in Table 7.4, which lists the top shareholders of Mitsubishi Trust and Banking, a leading Mitsubishi financial institution. All the listed stockholding firms are members of the Mitsubishi group.

The combined stockholdings of these 9 firms account for 95% of the top 10 shareholders' total. Mitsubishi T&B exercises significant control over the presidents' club firms, but such control is exercised on behalf of the presidents' club firms (who are the majority stockholders of Mitsubishi T&B), not as an expression of the bank's own economic clout. The mutuality of stock ownership and the degree of mutual control vary from group to group, showing different levels of group cohesiveness. The figures in the table show that older groups (Mitsubishi, Mitsui, and Sumitomo) have higher group cohesiveness, whereas more recent groups show weaker links, both in absolute terms and in terms of relative influential power. This pattern, based on 1982 data, confirms the one pointed out with 1973 data by Futatsugi (1986),

Table 7.4 Top Stockholders of Mitsubishi Trust & Banking

Firm	Percentage Shares Held
Meiji Mutual Life	6.2
Mitsubishi Corporation	3.7
Mitsubishi Bank	3.1
Mitsubishi Heavy Industries	3.1
Asahi Glass	2.5
Tokio M&F Insurance	2.1
Mitsubishi Estate	2.0
Mitsubishi Electric	1.8
Nippon Yusen	1.4

SOURCE: Compiled from Dodwell Marketing Consultants (1984, p. 154).

showing not only the variation across groups in degree of control, but also that such variation is stable over time.

As a general trend, the degree of internal control over member firms has increased for all groups, and has been labeled the "corporationalization of stock ownership" (Futatsugi, 1986, p. 1) and a "shareholding stabilization strategy" (Dore, 1986b, p. 48). Various factors explain this trend. Most significant is the liberalization of capital in the 1960s, which accelerated the accumulation of stockholdings as a deterrent against foreign corporations' takeovers (Dore, 1986b; Sumiya, 1986). Also, the increased mutual control of shares allows firms in the groups to sell stocks and raise capital without fearing a loss of internal control. Basically, a strengthened mutual shareholding scheme allows group firms to maintain internal control with relatively little financial cost, because the mutuality of ownership of stocks, and the subsequent mutual transfer of capital funds, makes for a zero-sum game. For example, Futatsugi (1986) points out that, in 1973, Mitsubishi firms had acquired new shares worth 84 billion yen. However, he explains, "If we now correct for the direct reciprocal holdings within the Mitsubishi group, we see that . . . the increase in stocks corresponds to 39 billion yen" (pp. 84-85). The group thus strengthens its internal cohesion and its ability to keep out-group shareholders under ample margins of control with nominally high but effectively low financial cost.

Intergroup Horizontal Patterns

The pattern of horizontal control through reciprocal shareholding is present not only in the ownership of stocks within groups, but also among groups; each intermarket group owns a small percentage of stocks in other groups, so that a matrix of reciprocal intergroup stockholdings obtains, as shown in Table 7.5. Researchers have considered intergroup shareholding as having little significance, because it in no way undermines the hegemonic control of each group over its own member firms and because intergroup stockholding is usually carried out unilaterally by each group's financial institutions (Okumura, 1982a). This interpretation underestimates the relevance of intergroup stockholding on several grounds.

First, intergroup stockholding is not uniform across intermarket groups. Just as we saw a variation in levels of intragroup stockholding, so we can detect a variation in intergroup stockholding. Specifically, intragroup and intergroup patterns are inversely related: The higher the level of intragroup stockholding for a group, the lower the level of its outside stockholdings and the lower the level of that group's involvement in intergroup stockholding. Second, we detect different patterns for the three older groups and the three more recent ones (Fuyo, DKB, and Sanwa). Older groups are less prone to intergroup stockholding—the pattern for ex-*zaibatsu* groups is one of strong internal control and weak intergroup control. The postwar groups, in contrast, show weaker within-group and stronger intergroup links. Third, it is erroneous to interpret the role of financial institutions in intergroup shareholding as simply representing the banks' power. As we argued earlier, the role of financial institutions is chiefly to exercise control on behalf of the group itself—they represent the intermarket group as a whole, not only in intragroup but also in intergroup strategies.

Last, intergroup stockholding has strong symbolic value: It signals the reciprocal trust of all groups in each other's conduct of economic affairs. This is the *giri* constraint, which Japanese economists see as "merely symbolic." Yes, outside banks with their symbolic shares cannot have a voice in another group's economic policy—groups cherish their independence above all else. But we cannot conclude, from this premise, that only rivalry characterizes relations among intermarket groups. Although it is understood in Japan that executives could never quit Mitsubishi to work for Sumitomo, nevertheless, all intermarket groups are organized in very similar ways and abide by the same unwritten rules of economic conduct. Intermarket groups also engage in joint economic activities (as in the construction of the new international airport in Osaka). The pattern of relations among groups is not one of all-out competition, but one of competition within the boundaries of a shared economic philosophy (Nakatani, 1984) and a shared mode of or-

Table 7.5 Mutual Stock Ownership by Enterprise Groups, 1977 (in percentages)

Owner	Owned						
	Mitsui	Mitsubishi	Sumitomo	Fuyo	DKB	Sanwa	Total
Mitsui	—	0.79	1.16	1.60	2.35	2.98	8.88
Mitsubishi	1.02	—	0.44	2.30	2.59	2.07	8.42
Sumitomo	1.06	0.17	—	1.24	0.98	1.03	4.48
Fuyo	0.96	1.02	1.00	—	2.92	8.36	14.26
DKB	1.47	1.96	0.68	2.27	—	10.21	16.59
Sanwa	0.72	0.63	1.06	1.39	2.10	—	5.90
Total	5.23	4.57	4.34	8.80	10.94	24.65	—

SOURCE: Okumura (1982a, p. 70).

ganizing. The pattern of intergroup links, then, is not an insignificant phenomenon in Japanese business, but it reinforces through symbolic means the underlying pattern of reciprocal control we have outlined so far.

Horizontal Patterns in Independent Groups

Intragroup shareholding in independent groups points clearly toward a vertical pattern of control, but now we are concerned with the horizontal patterns that obtain for the independent groups' leading firms. We know that the top firm in independent groups exercises strict control over its subsidiaries and affiliates, but who controls the leading firm itself? Table 7.6 shows the pertinent data. The evidence is of a pattern of horizontal control. Table 7.6 shows that the six intermarket groups (mostly through financial firms) are major shareholders of the independent groups' leading firms. However, no single group has hegemonic control over any single firm; instead, two or more groups share control. This allows for different interpretations: Either the control of independent groups is exercised collectively by banks representing different intermarket groups or, given the spread of shareholders, the independent group's leading firm exercises a form of self-control. We favor a combination of these two hypotheses. Independent industrial groups usually make up the leading edge of Japanese manufacturing; there we find the largest automobile manufacturers (Toyota, Nissan), the largest steel firm (Nippon Steel), and the largest electronics firms (Hitachi, Matsushita, Toshiba). The industrial growth of these firms required and still requires a financial muscle that no intermarket group can exercise alone. Thus a cooperative financial effort is required, and multiple sources of capital are sought by independent group leaders. This prompts the creation of multiple partnerships, where Toyota Motor, for instance, is simultaneously linked to the Mitsui group, the Sanwa group, the Tokai Bank group, Dai-Ichi Mutual Life Insurance, and the Long-Term Credit Bank of Japan. Toyota Motor is thus able to exercise a measure of autonomous power over firms in the Toyota group, to the extent that no single source of capital stands out as a strong enough power broker (besides, Toyota as a group has enough liquidity to be nicknamed Toyota Bank). Still, financing groups are not altogether powerless; rather, they can exercise power only collectively, and in concert with the leading firm in the independent group.

Another significant pattern of horizontal control emerges in relation to the independent financial groups of Tokai Bank and IBJ. Here we have a mutual

Table 7.6 Stock Ownership in Independent Groups' Leading Firms (in percentages)

Owned	Owner													
	MTB	MUI	SMT	FUY	DKB	SNW	TOK	IBJ	SUI	TOY	NIP	NIS	DML	LTC
Tokai Bank	2.2									5.4				
IBJ	6.0										2.8	2.3		
Nippon Steel	3.6		3.2	1.8	1.6	4.7		3.1					1.9	
Hitachi	2.4			2.2	2.2	5.2		2.6	2.3				2.8	
Nissan			3.0	9.6	2.3	3.9		6.2	5.5				5.2	
Toyota		9.6				8.7	5.0						2.3	3.2
Matsushita	1.5		11.2			4.1			1.4					
Toshiba-IHI		9.6	2.3		2.8	10.7	1.7						8.0	1.9
Tokyu	3.3	3.3				8.2		2.3					8.2	
Seibu	0.8	2.7		2.9	0.8	0.8		1.1						
Average owned	2.83	5.04	4.93	4.13	2.16	4.85	3.35	3.06	3.07	5.4	2.8	2.3	4.73	2.55

SOURCE: Compiled from Dodwell Marketing Consultants (1984).
NOTE: MTB = Mitsubishi, MUI = Mitsui, SMT = Sumitomo, FUY = Fuyo, DKB = Dai-Ichi Kangyo Bank, SNW = Sanwa, TOK = Tokai Bank, IBJ = Industrial Bank of Japan, SUI = Credit Suisse, TOY = Toyota Motor, NIP = Nippon Steel, NIS = Nissan Motor, DML = Dai-Ichi Mutual Life, LTC = Long-Term Credit Bank of Japan. The ownership matrix is not saturated.

shareholding pattern between financial groups and industrial groups. For instance, Toyota Motor is Tokai Bank's number-one stockholder, with 5.4%; in turn, Tokai Bank owns 5% of Toyota. Similarly, Nippon Steel and Nissan Motor are IBJ's key shareholders with, respectively, 2.8 and 2.3%, and conversely IBJ owns significant amounts of shares in Nippon Steel (3.1%) and in Nissan Motor (6.2%). Both instances reinforce a pattern of horizontal control in independent groups.

If we look at the larger picture, independent industrial groups as a whole show another significant element of horizontal control. Leader firms, here, are the equivalent of presidents' club firms in the six intermarket groups. The horizontal control among presidents' club firms is paralleled in industrial groups by the horizontal web of financial enterprises that share the financing of industrial firms. Therefore, if we take the independent groups together and consider all major shareholders in these groups, we obtain a pattern similar to the one observed in each intermarket group. The independent groups form a "maxi-intermarket group," where financial institutions are provided by intermarket and independent banks, and where the leading firms in the industrial groups are the members of the presidents' club. These patterns are similar to the ones found for the intermarket groups, but on a much larger scale.

Vertical Control

Beyond the presidents' club, intermarket groups are organized around a clear, hierarchical structure of subsidiary and affiliate firms (Okumura, 1985). Leading firms in different industrial sectors control a number of the same or similar sector firms. Beyond the subsidiary and affiliate firms that officially belong to and are controlled by the intermarket group, the influence of each leader firm extends, through subcontracting relations, to small and medium-sized firms that provide group subsidiaries and affiliates with manufacturing parts and components (Okumura, 1982a, 1984).

In our data collection, we identified all firms whose top shareholding firm owned at least 15% as that firm's affiliates or subsidiaries. These affiliates are closely related to their mother firms' sectors of production—hinting at the notion that vertical control parallels a vertical integration of production within firms. Subsidiaries of trading companies are an exception; they spread across sectors, according to the need of trading companies as mediators in

Table 7.7   Average Shareholding of Leader Firms in Their Group Firms for 10 Independent Groups

	Average Shares	Number of Firms
Tokai Bank	6.46	22
IBJ	6.69	22
Nippon Steel	21.00	33
Hitachi	44.17	35
Nissan	33.48	30
Toyota	26.12	34
Matsushita	44.95	24
Toshiba-IHI	37.94	39
Tokyu	23.18	17
Seibu	34.80	14

SOURCE: Compiled from Dodwell Marketing Consultants (1984).

the exchange of goods between and among industrial firms. Patterns of vertical control are mostly related to integration of production, and they show a clear hierarchical economic structure.

Vertical control in intermarket groups is exercised by presidents' club firms; in independent industrial groups, instead, control is exercised by the group leader over all other firms in the group. Financial groups such as Tokai Bank, which owns on average 6.5% of its group firms, and IBJ, which owns 6.7% on average, are an exception to the pattern we show in Table 7.7. Vertical control in independent groups mirrors the presidents' club *keiretsu* alignments. In independent groups, however, the vertical pattern is magnified because, as we noted earlier, the independent leading firms are, on average, larger than most industrial firms that belong to the presidents' club of intermarket groups. Accordingly, independent groups' production is organized around a tighter, vertically integrated set of firms.

Vertical Control and Interfirm Relations

A vertical pattern of control through stockholding obtains in Japan in both intermarket groups and independent groups, but what kind of relations among firms does it yield? Intuitively, we contrast the relations among equals (such as those in the presidents' club) with the vertical patterns of *keiretsu* alignments within sectors of production. It seems obvious that if a corporation owns 30-40% of affiliate firms' stocks, it should exercise unilateral control—but things are more complicated than that. Okumura (1984) argues that vertical alignments of subsidiaries and affiliates have three major aims: (a) the profitable utilization of a "dual structure" of wages, in which workers in small and middle-sized enterprises are paid less than workers in large firms; (b) the "avoidance of risk which can be achieved by large corporations through the use of enterprises in their alignments"; and (c) "the prevention of hypertrophied expansion of large corporations" (pp. 170-171). Okumura looks at vertical integration from the leading firms' point of view; accordingly, he mostly sees benefits for the leading firms. We partially share Okumura's interpretation, but question his reasoning on two counts. In terms of the dual-wage structure, Okumura (1984, p. 170) argues that the wage differential between large and small firms was pronounced in the early 1950s but declined after 1955, and yet we know that the web of vertical alignments has increased sharply in recent decades (Futatsugi, 1986, pp. 12, 63). That leading corporations seek to avoid risk through vertical alignments is also questionable—it can be argued that corporations retain or even increase their risk by dealing with companies in which they have high stakes as majority stockholders. The rationale for vertical alignments should be extended to include other factors.

The main rationale for constructing a solid vertical structure of subsidiary firms in Japanese business is not the ability to exercise unrestrained control over them or the search for unilateral financial advantages; rather, it is aimed at guaranteeing a mutually beneficial, self-sufficient industrial structure to leading firms and to affiliates. In the literature, this is referred to as "one setist behavior." Futatsugi (1986) explains that "for an enterprise group this implies that all the raw materials needed for production can be procured within the group" (p. 57). The pattern of "one setist behavior" is most common in independent groups, which, as we have pointed out, show a higher level of vertical integration, but it is also found in the industrial sectors of intermarket groups. This rationale is in line with the economic philosophy framing the behavior of firms at all levels of business organization in Japan.

Self-containment of production and the group's ability to isolate itself from shifting market conditions characterize intermarket and independent groups at the higher level of presidential councils, at the intermediate levels of subsidiary alignments, and at the lower levels of subcontracting. Whether the relations are among equals (as in the case of presidential councils) or among unequals (as in the case of affiliates and subcontractors), the philosophy is still one of mutual economic support in a world of market uncertainties. In *keiretsu* alignments, such mutuality of roles among unequals is formalized through the official sponsorship (by means of stocks ownership) of affiliates and subsidiaries. The achievement of self-sufficiency in the production process is a crucial goal of vertical integration. The relations within vertically integrated firms aim at mutual sustenance and cooperation so as to minimize the need for outside firms to carry out the production process.

Ronald Dore aptly illustrates the philosophy of Japanese interfirm etiquette with the term "relational contracting." In presidents' councils, the cross-holding of shares points to "networks of preferential trading relations" among member firms (Dore, 1986b, p. 55); in *keiretsu* alignments, Dore argues, "such relations are at their densest" (1986b, p. 54). Describing subcontractual relations, Dore (1983) identifies three underlying principles: (a) "losses . . . and gains . . . should be shared," (b) in bad times the weaker party will suffer more, and (c) "the stronger . . . should not use his bargaining power in recession times" (p. 465). The philosophy common at all organizational levels is that mutual consideration of needs is the best policy in interfirm relations. Intermarket and independent groups show distinguishing patterns of horizontal and vertical interfirm relations, but the underlying philosophy for both kinds of relations is one and the same. In both instances, domination is not embedded in or legitimated by the right to command. Rather, control is most of all a matter of self-control, a matter of adhesion to one's own duties as prescribed by role positions. No single firm, however powerful, is exempt from duties; top financial institutions and industrial firms are bound by role expectations as much as the smallest subcontracting firm in the organizational hierarchy.

Additional Means of Horizontal Control

Next to stock ownership, there are other mechanisms that foster intragroup and intergroup cohesiveness: interlocking directorates, bank loans, intragroup and intergroup exchanges through trading companies, joint enterprises with domestic and foreign groups or firms, and involvement in business associations. Each of these plays a role in reinforcing intra- or intergroup alignments, or both.

Interlocking directorates. The literature on director appointments and exchanges is sparse, consisting mostly of statistical data (Kosei Torihiki Iinkai Jimukyoku, 1983; Toyo Keizai Shimposha, 1986a), sources of recruitment for directorships (Johnson, 1985; Sumiya, 1986), and network analyses influenced by American sociometry (Sato, 1986; Ueda, 1983, 1986). Interlocks in group firms reflect the existence of vertical alignments that prompt the mother company to put representatives on the boards of directors of its affiliates. Ueda (1986) shows that independent groups with strong vertical alignment have the highest rates of interlocks (the top three are Hitachi, Toyota, and Tokyu). Our data show that 157 directors in Hitachi's affiliates were sent from the mother company (Dodwell Marketing Consultants, 1984). In the Toyota group, 101 directors were sent by Toyota Motor. Beyond vertical control, Ueda (1986) identifies three functions of multiple directors: (a) to maintain and promote transactions between companies, (b) to keep the unity of the group, and (c) to create a communication network (p. 247). All three functions emphasize horizontal control, supporting our earlier contention about the Japanese business philosophy. The last function of the three is most important for public utilities firms, which are required to work in collaboration with government officials.

Bank loans. A distinguishing characteristic of Japanese business financing is its reliance on debt rather than equity, which explains the key role played by financial institutions. The financing of business groups reflects their cooperative philosophy. As in the case of stockholdings, bank loans show two distinct patterns: intragroup and intergroup financing. For each group, the group's city bank and other affiliated financial institutions provide the bulk of financing. Data for 1973 reported by Futatsugi (1986, pp. 52-54) show that firms associated with the Mitsui, Mitsubishi, and Sumitomo groups relied on their groups' financial institutions for, respectively, 23.7%, 27.1%, and 30.1% of their bank loans. These figures reiterate the finding of stockholding patterns, showing different levels of internal cohesiveness of intermarket groups. However, whereas the rates of intragroup stockholdings have increased over time, the rates of intragroup borrowing have declined steadily. Sumitomo's intragroup borrowings averaged 45% in 1962, but were down to less than 35% in 1972. Futatsugi (1986) interprets this trend as a symptom of the city banks' inability to sustain alone the growth of their own groups' industrial firms, but this is only a partial reason. Further decline of intragroup borrowing was prompted by the 1975 Japanese legislation regulating corporate financing. Such legislation established that loans provided to a firm by a trust bank or long-term credit bank could not exceed 30% of the total loans for that firm (for commercial banks the limit was 20%), thus reducing intragroup borrowing and increasing intergroup loans. Okumura (1985) provides an illustration of intergroup borrowing patterns triggered by the 1975 legislation. Sumitomo Bank and Mitsubishi Bank agreed in 1977 to cross-finance Sumitomo Metal Industries and Mitsubishi Heavy Industries. Although each group's city bank provided the bulk of loans to its member firms, other groups' banks provided supplementary loans beyond the limit that was put on intragroup banks.

Intergroup borrowings parallel the intergroup stockholding patterns we have outlined above—both point to the existence of networks beyond the existence of individual, isolated intermarket groups. The emerging picture is, in both cases, one of concerted effort on the part of the leading intermarket groups to provide necessary means for the harmonious growth of large Japanese business enterprises.

General trading companies. Japanese general trading companies (*sogo shosha*) have been acclaimed for their expertise and information on market opportunities around the world (Mori, 1980; Yoshihara, 1981) and for their ability to realize economies of scale (Tsurumi, 1984), organize joint ventures (Okumura, 1985), and provide financing through trade credits, direct loans, and loan guarantees (Miyazaki, 1981). The role played by trading companies within each intermarket group and outside it reiterates the networking features of large groups in Japan. Within intermarket groups, the trading company facilitates the reciprocal exchange of goods. In some cases, the trading firm acts only as intermediary in the reciprocal exchange of goods between two group firms; in other instances, however, such reciprocity is created by the trading company. Okumura (1985) observes that a trading firm can contrive a reciprocal deal where only a unilateral deal would otherwise be possible. For example, Mitsubishi Heavy Industries might sell ships to Nippon Yusen, but Nippon Yusen would have nothing to sell to Mitsubishi Heavy Industries. Mitsubishi Corporation, however, has a reciprocal relation with both firms: It sells steel to and purchases ships from Mitsubishi Heavy Industries and, in turn, sells these ships to Nippon Yusen and relies on its services for the transportation of goods. Hence double reciprocal deals are made possible by the trading firm. Beyond intragroup trade, trading companies also promote intergroup exchanges. Outside firms that sell their products to group firms are obliged to purchase goods from these companies. The reciprocity of the transaction is made possible by the mediation of the general trading company (Okumura, 1985).

Joint enterprises. Students of Japanese business groups make only cursory reference to joint advertising, common trademarks (Sumiya, 1986), and joint investments (Okumura, 1985). The Dodwell Marketing Consultants (1984) report states that the pattern of joint investments by intermarket groups and independent groups goes back several decades. In the 1950s, joint enterprises were established in the field of nuclear energy. "During the 1960s and 70s the six major industrial groups successively established joint ventures in the fields of leasing, computers and information processing services, urban development, ocean development, oil development, etc." (Dodwell Marketing Consultants, 1984, p. 13). In more recent years, the six intermarket groups have been involved in numerous projects related to the construction of a 24-hour international airport in Osaka waters. The exclusion of foreign firms from this project has been a source of friction between Japan and the United States and other Western countries. Close collaborative efforts among Japanese intermarket and independent groups have made it harder for foreign competitors to participate in such projects.

Business associations. One last instance of horizontal patterns is Japanese groups' involvement in business associations. The Dodwell Marketing Consultants (1984) report describes four major associations: Keidanren (Federation of Economic Organizations), Keizai Doyukai (Japan Committee for Economic Development), Nikkeiren (Japan Federation of Employers Association), and Nihon Shoko Kaigisho (Japan Chamber of Commerce and Industry). The first two groups provide business views regarding economic development to foreign countries, Japanese government and legislators, and political parties. The third group focuses on labor-management relations, and the fourth concentrates on the development of commerce and industry in Japan. Representatives of intermarket and independent groups hold key positions in these associations. In 1982 the chairman of Keidanren was from Nippon Steel; vice chairmen were related to Toshiba, Sumitomo, Mitsubishi, Mitsui, Hitachi, and Toyota. Similar affiliations obtained in the other three business associations (Dodwell Marketing Consultants, 1984, pp. 22-23). Additional evidence of cooperative interfirm relations in Japan could be provided (e.g., common trademarks, logos, and advertising), but the ones we have presented suffice to show that the guiding economic philosophy of Japanese business groups is strikingly different from the one of most Western firms. In our conclusion we bring these distinctions into sharper focus.

Conclusion

In this chapter, we have identified business groups as a basic organizing unit in the Japanese economy. In these groups, interfirm relationships are highly structured; they are stable over time and, in terms of organizational patterns, they are broadly uniform or isomorphic and are based upon clearly defined authority relationships. Two major patterns of control characterize interfirm relations in Japanese business groups: horizontal and vertical control. The former pattern applies to the top level of the organizational system, whereas the latter pattern is typical of organizational features within lines of production in individual industrial sectors. Taken in its entirety, the Japanese organizational pattern is characterized by a highly structured and cohesive network of firms going up and down and spanning across the hierarchy. In the organizational structure of Japanese business, vertical and horizontal patterns of control are informed by the same underlying institutional notion—that people (and firms and institutions) must fulfill the expectations attached to their roles and positions. Expectations are mutual: Both the more and the less powerful are equally bound by role prescriptions. The duties of "relational contracting" (Dore, 1983) bind both the supplier and the supplied; in interfirm relations, goodwill is not optional, but mandatory. Not only horizontal patterns but vertical patterns as well rest on a mutual understanding of role expectations and on a reciprocal show of goodwill.

These patterns are best understood against an institutional backdrop. Horizontal and vertical interfirm relations are not a postwar development, but go back to the beginnings of Japanese industrialization, to the early twentieth century, if not before (Hamilton & Biggart, 1988; Uekusa, 1977). In *The Development of Japanese Business,* Hirschmeier and Yui (1975) describe the "vertical order" and the "horizontal web" of the seventeenth- and eighteenth-century Japanese merchant world. Of the vertical order, they write:

> For the merchant the maximization of profits had nothing to do with utilitarian thinking, it was rather firmly based on the duty to serve the House and thus the

ancestors who had founded it. . . . Economic aspects *per se* were thus, even within the merchant class, subordinated to the vertical order of loyalty, filial piety, and subordination of the private to the public; in Japanese terms, the *ko* (public) ranked above the *shi* (private), the *gi* (virtue) over the *ri* (profit). (p. 46)

Similarly, in relation to the horizontal web, Hirschmeier and Yui write, "In decision making within the group each was supposed to restrain himself, and decisions would of course be made on the principle of solidarity, rather than majority decision" (p. 47). Business groups have developed over time and changed in many ways, yet the key organizational patterns remain much the same today. Japanese groups are not a product of maturing capitalism or an outcome of recent economic events. While modern business groups developed in Japan, the corporation was emerging as an organizational form in the United States. This development too should be seen against an institutional backdrop, but often is not. Despite his superb historical documentation, Chandler (1977) employs primarily economic variables to account for the development of the American corporation, arguing that the corporation is universal in developed capitalist environments. Recently, organizational theorists have questioned the adequacy of Chandler's explanation for the rise of the corporation in the United States (Fligstein, 1985; Perrow, 1981) as well as for its universality (Hamilton & Biggart, 1988), arguing instead for institutional causes (Imai & Itami, 1984). Whatever the emphasis, there is agreement that the institutional framework of the market, as it developed in the United States, assumed and built upon the autonomy and competitiveness of individual firms. Even during the crucial period of corporation building, interfirm relationships rested on contractually based capital or commodity transactions. Antimonopoly legislation made collusion illegal, but even without such legislation it was unlikely that cooperative business networks would emerge. Indeed, the legislation aimed not at preventing cooperation among businesses, but at slowing the rate of monopolization arising from the cutthroat competition of the era. The U.S. economy was never institutionally favorable to the sort of business groups found in Japan; instead, the enforced individuation of American interfirm relations rides on waves of mergers, takeovers, and forced bankruptcies—all rare phenomena in the Japanese context.

Once the institutional context is clear, differences in patterns of interfirm control come into focus. In the United States, the institutional individuation of firms favors episodic, resource-based cooperation (Palmer, 1983; Pfeffer

& Salancik, 1978) and informal, class-based collusion (Domhoff, 1980, 1983; Useem & Karabel, 1986). As Palmer (1983; Palmer et al., 1986) shows, interlocking directorates are unstable unless corporations have long-term contractual relationships.

In Japan, interfirm relationships have a very different character. Japanese firms are not autonomous but belong to various types of business groups, and thus the nature of interfirm ties is distinctly organizational. Ties are long-term and stable and represent reciprocal obligations. In Japan, joint shares and interlocks do not (and cannot) have the same meaning as in the United States. The patterns of vertical and horizontal control can be understood only meaningfully in their institutional context; these patterns embody cultural and normative prescriptions that inform the organizational strategies that have led to Japan's economic success. Our study of interfirm relations in Japanese business and our comparison with the evidence available on their counterparts in the United States lead us to believe that the search for a universally applicable theory of capitalist domination is misplaced. Our efforts will be more productive if we instead focus on the variants of capitalism in different geographic and cultural areas, emphasizing not their sterile sameness, but their rich, challenging diversity.

8

Institutionalized Patrimonialism in Korean Business

NICOLE WOOLSEY BIGGART

outh Korean industrial organization has frequently been
compared to that of Japan, and on the face of it, the comparison seems reasonable. Both economies are dominated
by large business groups, *zaibatsu*-descendant *keiretsu* and independent
groups in Japan, and *chaebol* in the case of South Korea. Indeed, the Chinese
characters for *zaibatsu* and *chaebol* are identical, similarly translating into
"money group" or "financial clique." In both nations the business groups are
large and diversified combinations of firms that dominate the export sectors

AUTHOR'S NOTE: This chapter is reprinted here by permission of JAI Press, Inc., from
"Institutionalized Patrimonialism in Korean Business," by Nicole Woolsey Biggart, *Comparative Social Research,* 1990, vol. 12, pp. 113-133. Copyright 1990 by JAI Press, Inc.; all
rights reserved.

of their respective economies. In both cases, the business groups have been the leading actors in bringing about postwar economic recovery and are the centerpieces of the Japanese and South Korean states' industrial plans (Hamilton & Biggart, 1988). The differences between them are important, however. Japanese business groups are composed of legally independent but socially affiliated companies. They are characterized by vertical relationships between firms of greater or lesser status in the group, who nonetheless recognize a common identity. Diffused ownership within the group via reciprocal shareholding forms horizontal bonds that give material substance to what is a normative ideal of communitarianism. A communitarian institutional logic predisposes individual firms to see their self-interest in terms of the group and is expressed in such practices as shared planning and mutual financial and technological assistance (Orrù, Biggart, & Hamilton, 1991).

Moreover, a communitarian logic is sustained by and penetrates other levels of the Japanese economy and society. For example, within the firm such practices as consensual decision making (*nemawashi* and *ringi*) and many labor practices similarly express a concern with the harmonious operation of the whole rather than the unilateral exercise of power by constituent individuals and groups.

Relations among individuals, groups, and firms within Korean *chaebol* could not be more different. Ownership is concentrated within a family and subject to the autocratic decision making of a patriarch and his heirs. Consensus is neither sought nor desired. *Chaebol* firms are under the centralized control of the patriarch and have no horizontal relations independent of him. Although there may be shareholding between firms, or family foundations may own shares in multiple *chaebol* companies, the intention is not to diffuse control throughout the group, but to provide alternative vehicles for family control in the face of government pressures to divest stock. Labor unions are regularly in violent confrontation with employers, in contrast to the gentility of postwar Japanese industrial relations. The symbolic shareholding that occurs across Japan's business groups is inconceivable in South Korea, where *chaebol* rivalries are deep and even acrimonious.

Harmony and communitarianism characterize neither the ideal nor the reality of Korean organization and management. Rather, as I will argue below, South Korea's industrial arrangements and practices are expressions of a patrimonial logic. In this chapter, I will define patrimonialism and trace its origins in Korean history, showing how patrimonialism came to be entwined with regionalism and factionalism in Korea. Second, I will discuss how Korean patrimonialism is institutionalized today in state-business group relations and in the structure and management practices of the *chaebol*. Finally, I will consider the strategic implications of institutionalized patrimonialism and show its distinctive advantages and limitations as a way to organize economic action.

This analysis is predicated on the belief that the best approach for understanding organizational structure and practice is an institutional perspective. Although institutional theories of organizations vary, for the most part they accept that social order, including organization, is socially constructed, as people interpret and give shared meaning to reality.[1] Over time, these shared meanings come to be understood as "institutionalized" structures of social action. Institutional analysis, therefore, presumes that organizations can be understood only within their historical contexts; analysis must consider how present-day organizational arrangements have been shaped by institutionalized beliefs and social arrangements.[2]

Patrimonialism in Korea

Patrimonialism is a form of rule in which power is held by a patriarch and administered through a personal staff; historically, it has often included a military force (Weber, 1978, p. 226). The subjects of rule are treated as, and may in fact be, members of the patriarch's household. The household, whether a manor or a principality, is run at the pleasure of the master, whose rule extends over the economic, moral, and personal affairs of the household and is limited only by tradition. Members of the household are obligated to the patriarch, who rewards them with stipends as he wills; he has no reciprocal obligation to his subjects.

Patrimonialism is distinguished from feudalism, the other important form of traditional authority, by its absence of defined rights and obligations. Feudal retainers are, like patrimonial subjects, required to submit dutifully to superiors, but their duties are defined and limited. Moreover, a feudal lord has stipulated obligations to his subjects, such as financial support and privileges associated with rank and inheritance. Feudal social orders are composed of status unequals connected by ties (such as fealty and homage) that mutually bind them.

Japan's communities of firms, bound by reciprocal rights and duties, seem a modern extension of that nation's feudal past. Korea, like China, never developed a feudal state. Instead, it has a patrimonial, dynastic heritage grounded in Confucianism. Jacobs (1985) argues persuasively that Korea's patrimonial past is the sociopolitical basis of modern South Korea and, as I will argue here, of its dominant economic structure, the *chaebol.*

The roots of patrimonialism are deep in Korea, but mixed with an aristo-cratic tradition and Chinese influences. From the first to fourth centuries, primitive Korea was populated by aristocratically organized tribal clans subject to periodic colonial exploitation by the Chinese, until the Chinese were driven into Manchuria by the Koguryo tribes of northeast Korea. In the sixth century, militarily successful tribes subdued rivals and unified the peninsula into three kingdoms. The kingdoms were organized into royal state structures largely copied from the neighboring Chinese bureaucratic system of government. Indeed, tribal unification brought greater contact with China, as representatives of the three kingdoms exchanged regular court visits with the Chinese. In the following centuries, Chinese Buddhism, dress, language, and education were embraced by Korean elites. According to Han (1974), "In particular, the Confucian system of ethics and government now began to have a similar effect upon Korea" (p. 52). The later United Kingdom of Silla, and the Korean Koryo and Yi Dynasties, which extended to the nineteenth century, were under periods of more or less influence by China.[3] Korea was always considered a tribute state by the Chinese empire, and court life was greatly influenced by Chinese culture, especially Confucianism.

At the heart of Confucianism is the belief that social order depends on hierarchy. The family is the fundamental social unit and is divided into hierarchically arranged roles, each with attendant duties and privileges. Likewise, society is ordered into distinct statuses, each with its own preroga-tives and obligations. Confucian ethics dictates the relationships between hereditary social statuses, such as artisans and farmers, and between family members, such as elder and younger brothers, and fathers and sons. Even nations have their place in the ordering of things; Korea was seen as subordinate to China and required to pay tribute as a dutiful inferior.

Confucian morality requires the subordination of the self to roles and relies heavily on the self-control of individuals. The proper functioning of the Confucian cosmos depends on the loyal obedience of inferiors to superiors in the social order and the carrying out of role-defined duties.

By the time of the Yi Dynasty (1392-1910), Koreans recognized four ranked classes roughly equivalent to those in China: the *yangban* ruling class; the small *chungin* middle class of technicians and clerks; the *sangmin,* or common people, composed of farmers, merchants, and craftsmen; and the despised *ch'onmin,* a low-born, degraded class that included slaves (Henderson, 1968, pp. 36-37). Each of these classes had subclasses with incrementally higher or lower status.

The role of the ruler atop a Confucian status hierarchy such as Korea's was foremost a moral one. The king was judged by the virtue of his rule and his benevolent and proper orientation to his subordinates. Although given deference as the supreme earthly power in the state, Korean kings were never fully hegemonic powers and were constantly challenged by organized *yangban* elites. In particular, the Censorate, a watchdog unit whose purpose was to rout out corruption and administrative incompetence in the bureaucracy, often became an independent power even while reporting to the king. Members of the Censorate were known to critique the king's performance of his role in the social order.

In the Confucian ideal, the king was a political patriarch required to articulate a personal vision of morality. Aristocrats attempted to keep him from wielding power against their interests, to see that, in practice, he reigned through moral example rather than through active participation in the polity. Nonetheless, duty was owed to the king as a status superior, and failure to obey was interpreted as nothing less than betrayal. Confucian politics has no concept of a loyal opposition.

The *yangban* were the equivalent of the Chinese literati. They served as the officials, both civil and military, in the royal bureaucracy and, like their Chinese counterparts, were schooled in Confucian classics. Similarly, too, they were appointed and promoted based on their successful performance in a meritorious examination system. Scholarly achievement gave them the right to an official status and income from a small landholding. Although the form of the system paralleled China's, in fact it was different in a crucial regard: The right to sit for the examination was limited to *yangban* descendants who were heirs of elite clans. The top officialdom surrounding the emperor was less a meritocracy as in China than a "clique of court 'aristocrats' [who encircled] the throne with a kind of presumptive right on higher position. . . . they appear to have been a tight, Seoul-residing, intermarried clique that did its best to sit astride the mobility struggle" (Henderson, 1968, p. 38). This small elite institutionalized its power by sitting on political councils, military boards, and the Censorate. *Yangban* clans outside this inner circle struggled for influence and had discontinuous access to power; they "competed with each other for more bureaucratic power in an atmosphere of bitterness that Korea's smallness did much to enhance" (Henderson, 1968, p. 38).

Historians paint a picture of the Korean dynastic court as an arena of competing elites. Regionally based *yangban* elites, acting as guardians of Confucian principles of virtue and privilege, were bold and barely restrained accusers. According to Henderson (1968), "Officials were daily reviewed and dropped. With legal boundaries lacking, few matters were free from contest. The dynasty prated of tranquillity, but it lived on agitation and controversy" (p. 31).

Stories of the lives of local elites are notable for the preoccupation with maintaining a position at court or for calculating a way to enter court life. Public office was the only acceptable route to wealth and status in a society where physical labor and commerce were considered degraded occupations. During the Yi Dynasty, competition for positions became increasingly fierce as the number of royal relations with presumptive right to office grew. Unlike feudal societies, where income and titles were sustained until challenged militarily, in Korea, typical of a patrimonial society, favors were regularly extended and withdrawn by the royal patriarch. The result was an environment of personalism and the idiosyncratic conferring of privilege that bred bitterness. According to Weems (1971),

> The factionalism and corruption observable increasingly since 1575 now became much worse and, by the nineteenth century, reached such depths of venality that money and intrigue, rather than *yangban* birth of membership in the right "party," became the main prerequisite for political success, although the official was still technically a *yangban* and still claimed pompously to understand Confucian principles. (p. 164)

Brandt (1987) further argues that tensions between an authoritarian patrimonialism and competition for power by regional pretenders to office gave rise to an unofficial ideology of individualism: "A pattern of unrestrained self-expression and cocky self-confidence on the part of many Koreans has been remarked on ever since foreign observers first reported their impressions in the mid-nineteenth century. . . . Respect for authority has coexisted with constant challenges to it" (pp. 212-213). The Confucian requirement to subordinate the self gave rise in Korea to egoistic outbursts when the morality of others was so clearly compromised. Even today, Koreans seem noisy and outspoken, and more frequently engage in massive protests compared with other Confucian peoples.

Factions, largely based in geographic regions, fought for the favor of the king. Unlike in China, local political elites were a hereditary aristocracy whose influence was based on membership in a patriarchal clan; even when elite individuals went to Seoul, they were able to maintain their local power base. "Although consequently the center was never a truly centralized enforcer of its will, the locals were never feudators legitimately able to exercise legally recognized rights in dealing with it. Rather, the locals strove to create groups—factions if you will—to represent their prebendary interests at the center court" (Jacobs, 1985, p. 28). Jacobs (1985) refers to this system as "multicentered patrimonialism"; Henderson (1968) calls it "oligarchic centrism." Both refer to the process whereby the court continually tried to assert control over regions through financial and status rewards, but where control was only tenuously maintained and often divided.

The social structure of Korea at the end of the imperial period was one of contested centrism, with the court imposing its will, during periods of greater or lesser success, on regional patriarchal clans. Observers have noted the inability of other social groupings in Korea to challenge the authoritarianism of a patrimonial system. Henderson (1968) attributes the fractionated, factionalized Korean society to its homogeneity and long period of isolation. Koreans had no language, ethnic, or religious differences around which to form intermediate institutions or to create pockets of solidarity larger than the clan. A long period of geographic and cultural isolation, wherein Korea earned the nickname of Hermit Kingdom, prevented contact through trade and cultural exchange throughout much of its dynastic history. The nation was a hothouse for the opportunistic struggles for power by a highly politicized elite with local patrimonial roots.

The annexation of a weakened and corrupted Korea by the Japanese in 1910 did little to change the political structure. Authoritarian dynastic rule was replaced by an authoritarian colonizer. Nor was the factionalism suppressed when the nation was faced by an alien conqueror. Korean independence organizations, largely based in religious groups, came together to declare opposition against the Japanese in 1919, but their unity was short-lived. They fell to arguing over goals, leadership, and ideology, and the coalition split apart within a few years. The period of Japanese colonial rule did stimulate Korean nationalism, but, ironically, without resulting in cohesive nationalist institutions. In sum, Korea's institutional heritage is Confucian and patrimonial. As in other Confucian nations, it is based on a belief in hierarchy—a conviction that social order can come about only if one dutifully performs the obligations appropriate to one's rank. It is also a patrimonial heritage that places the locus of political control in the hands of a patriarch who is responsible for articulating and defending the moral bases of society.

However, in Korea this Confucian and patrimonial heritage was expressed differently from the way it was in China. In particular, control by the king, while dutifully recognized as an ideal, was, in fact, frequently contested by patrimonial clans with regional roots. They asserted their interests against the center and in competition with one another. An important platform for this contest was criticism of the ruler's morality, articulated through the yangban-controlled Censorate. Moral obligations, including those of the emperor to rule correctly, were part of the daily discourse. Even today, according to Brandt (1987), "the duties that are required of individuals are contingent on the proper fulfillment of the right [to benevolent rule]" (p. 208). Although a Korean accepts the obligation to obey a superior, "he is also inclined to judge his superior's behavior on moral grounds, and he is highly sensitive to the issue of whether he himself is being treated fairly" (p. 208). Koreans, more than most Asians, can be outspoken critics of the morality of superiors and are apt to voice loudly any objections they have to a breach of their status rights.

State-Business Relations

Although patrimonialism was the dominant political model for Korea for millennia, there were important forces for breaking with the past and developing a new structure more apparently suited to economic modernization after World War II. Japan, especially, provided a ready model for Korean industrial organization.

When Japan lost the war, it lost its Korean and Taiwanese colonies, and Koreans, especially, were happy to be rid of a despised conqueror. Nonetheless, Japanese influence in economic matters had been substantial during the colonial period (1910-1945), and, indeed, Japanese occupation provided the only industrial model Koreans had ever experienced. Prior to Japan's annexation of the corrupt and decaying Yi dynastic state, there was no industry to speak of in Korea. Japan, enjoying economic expansion on the heels of the Meiji Restoration and an opening of cultural exchange and trade with the West, practiced economic imperialism by exporting technology and management to Korea's preindustrial colonial labor. Japan developed a substantial transportation and communications infrastructure during its occupation of Korea, as well as an industrial base. Although colonial enterprises were run by Japanese residents of Korea—200,000 in 1910, growing to nearly 700,000 by 1940—Koreans certainly gained industrial experience from Japan, however distasteful that experience may have been. And although all Japanese nationals were ousted from Korea at the end of the war, hundreds of thousands of Korean residents of Japan returned to their homeland, bringing with them experience in Japanese enterprise. Koreans had 35 years of direct experience with Japanese industrial organization, both in Korea and in Japan, to draw on in creating a new economic order.

The presence of the United States in Korea provided yet another organizational model after the war. Although American military administration of the former colony ceased with Korea's independence in 1948, American influence continued for years in economic and political matters because of the Korean War, and remains yet because of South Korea's strategic importance to the West as a buffer to China and the Soviet Union.

American ideas have entered South Korea largely through three routes: religion, education, and military experience. Western Christian missionaries were in Korea as early as the seventeenth century, and by 1886 gained the sanction of the Yi Dynasty, whence they "were spreading Western assumptions and Western approaches to problems" (Weems, 1971, p. 168). Protestant missionaries founded Western-style schools, hospitals, churches, and publishing houses. South Korea today remains a Christian stronghold.

Second, American aid contributed to universal primary education and near-universal adult literacy by 1960, and support for the growth of secondary and higher education after that. Clearly, an educated populace provided South Korea with trained human capital, an important industrial resource. More important, American ideas were carried back by Korean elites who received subsidized higher education in the United States. In 1956, the Graduate School of Public Administration was established at Seoul National University under a technical assistance contract with the University of Minnesota. In the next 2 years, 19 Korean scholars went to Minnesota to learn American public management philosophy and techniques (Lee & Kang, 1982). These South Korean academics, as well as American professors of management and public administration, set up Korean university programs based on American management curricula. Even today, South Koreans, unlike the Japanese, attend American universities in large numbers, and the highest-level economic planning officials in Seoul are apt to have Ph.D.s in economics from prestigious universities in the United States. Western neo-classical economic theories and democratic political principles are well understood in South Korea.

Perhaps more important than curricular development and abstract ideas has been the experience of American-influenced organization through military influence. When Japan lost the war and left behind a massive industrial structure, the United States brought in American managers and technicians to run the factories according to Western ideas (Juhn, 1971, p. 250). South Korea's army was established after the Japanese occupation by American military advisers and, as may be expected, was based on such American bureaucratic principles as unity of command and meritorious promotion. South Korea remains officially at war with North Korea and, to sustain military strength, practices universal conscription; every South Korean man of recent generations has spent at least 3 years in the military. Moreover, the American military presence and its heavy investment in defense installations has created support jobs for South Korean nationals in U.S. military organizations. South Koreans, first serving as labor and eventually as contractors, learned to work for and with defense contractors to the U.S. Army.

It is clear that South Koreans had familiarity with at least two organizational models, the group-based industrial organization of Japanese colonialism and the individualistic, meritocratic, and democratic ideas of American political and economic thought. Although South Koreans have clearly adopted aspects of both of these models, they have done so within a framework that is substantially different from both. Beginning with the military coup of Park Chung Hee in 1961, the first indigenous administration to organize the South Korean economy successfully, the country has fashioned an organizational model that reflects its own historical experience. Park's rule, according to Geel Yong Yang (1988), "was marked by consolidation, concentration, and cooperation of political, economic and administrative power. By so doing he was acting within the traditional concepts of the Korean court" (p. 23). Park created a state-business relationship that, although shaped in different ways by his successors, was in essence patrimonial. In addition, South Korean organization, at both the level of the state and within the business sector, continues to reflect the regionalism and factionalism that characterized Korean preindustrial society.

Control of the Economy

Park staged a military coup in May 1961 in response to widespread frustration with the regime of strongman Syngman Rhee, noted for its corruption and inability to develop the economy, and the brief and ineffective 3-month regime of Jang Myeon. Rhee's economic policy in the 1950s had five elements: the disposal of Japanese property to Korean nationals, distribution of foreign aid income and goods, allocation of import licenses and imposition of quotas, the award of government contracts for construction projects, and preferential treatment on bank loans and taxes to favored projects (Hahn, Kim, & Kim, 1987). These economic activities were carried out by Rhee in a centralized and personalistic, even idiosyncratic, fashion. Rhee's private acquaintances and political favorites were given preferential financing and monopolistic access to markets. The corruption of the regime even led the United States to give aid in the form of agricultural products, not money, for fear that the funds would go into the pockets of Rhee's supporters.

Founders of state-supported businesses from after the Korean War in 1953 to 1961 established the first *chaebol,* not through the working out of market forces, but through a process of "political capitalism":

> [They] accumulated capital mainly through such "nonrational" processes as speculation, price-fixing, tax evasion, and taking advantage of cumulative inflation. More crucial to this process, however, was that they played on political connections to gain economic favors in exchange for political contributions. (Kim, 1976, p. 469)

The industrial empires of Samsung, Hyundai, Lucky, and Kia began during this era. Their founders received state favors, including the noncompetitive and below-market purchase of Japanese colonial businesses, in exchange for large contributions to Rhee and other politicians.

In April 1960, student revolts erupted, protesting, among other issues, the concentration of wealth by the few elite families who enjoyed the favor of the president and the contrasting poverty of the mass of Korean workers. The moral outrage of a populace confronted with Rhee's abuse of position led to his ouster the next year. Park assumed the presidency not because of popular support, but as the result of a successful military coup; he then faced a legitimation crisis.

A few days after the coup took place, Park formed the Committee for Investigation and Execution of the Illicit Wealth Accumulation Act, a piece of legislation enacted but unenforced after Rhee's fall. Park used the act to round up the heads of all the major *chaebol* and, not incidentally, to seek the support of public opinion (Kim, 1988). The business leaders were arrested, jailed, and threatened with confiscation of their assets.

Byung Chul Lee, founder of the Samsung *chaebol,* was a leading target of the act. Official calculations placed Lee's illicit wealth at 800 million won, 19% of the nation's wealth. With Rhee's approval, he had purchased almost half of all commercial bank shares in the country: he owned 85% of Hanil Bank, nearly 50% of Cho-Heung Bank, and 30% of the Commercial Bank of Korea. Lee was also accused of funneling 64 million won to politicians and of evading 451 million won in taxes.

Lee was in Japan at the time of Park's coup and subsequent roundup of the *chaebol* founders, and so initially avoided arrest. When he returned to Korea, he announced that he would donate his entire fortune to the government but requested a meeting with Park. Park granted the meeting, and accounts suggest he was convinced by Lee that the nation needed to utilize the business acumen of the only Koreans who had run substantial enterprises. Park summoned 10 *chaebol* leaders to a meeting in which a three-point agreement between the state and business was hammered out:

1. The government would exempt most businessmen from criminal prosecution.
2. With the exception of bank shares, which would be turned over to the government, assets would not be confiscated.
3. Businessmen would pay off their assessed obligations by establishing new businesses in basic industries and donating them to the government.

Under this agreement, the state had control of finances and could effectively direct the development of the economy while keeping existing industries intact. The state also assumed control over a substantial portion of the industrial capacity of the nation through new business formation by *chaebol* owners, as well as by its own ventures with foreign capital. Park established the Economic Development Board, which remains the central planning organ of the state, to direct state intervention in the economy. He also controlled agriculture through state consolidation of agricultural cooperatives and through the appointment of administrators down to the township level. This last effort to control rural regions was extended further, to the village level, and more effectively centralized through the Saemaul or New Community program of regional industrial planning in 1971.

Park rationalized economic development through his use of professional economists and by establishing controls on favored enterprises. In addition, the *chaebol* were made to compete with each other for contracts, the chance to develop crucial industries, and other economic opportunities. The state managed the *chaebol* through personal ties, the placement of military generals on *chaebol* boards of directors, and other social means. Banking, however, was the most effective control, because other sources of funds were unavailable or uneconomical. The equity markets were undeveloped and unattractive to empire-building founders, the curb market (still important to small businesses) charged usurious rates, and access to foreign capital was controlled by the state. The opportunity to develop the South Korean economy—in the 1960s and 1970s moving aggressively into export production under Park's direction—and to profit from it remained to the *chaebol,* but only if they worked according to state rules. "A pattern was established whereby substantial assistance was given to established businessmen who proved themselves capable of initiating new manufacturing and export activity" (Jones & SaKong, 1980, p. 282).

The concentration of political and economic power by the state with regional economic elites took on a traditionally Korean quality, despite familiarity with the less centralized partnership model of Japan and the laissez-faire market model espoused by American advisers. Although economic performance became critical to continued state support for *chaebol* in South Korea, personal ties, especially those based on common regional origins and graduation from the same school or military class, remained important. Nor was state support guaranteed to last. Typical of patrimonial regimes, Park and his successor, Chun Doo Hwan, extended and withdrew favors to manipulate their subordinates. Bank loans were called when businessmen became independent, and lavish political contributions remained a requirement of continuing support. Business group competition for state favors still keeps the business community from unifying against the state, segmenting rather than integrating the economy as in Japan (Yang, 1988, p. 38).

Despite, and to some extent because of, state control over the *chaebol,* the business groups grew enormously and dominated the economy by 1980. Chun attempted to break their strength by pushing through the Fair Trade and Anti-Monopoly Act in 1981, but it was largely ignored by the *chaebol,* an indication of their strength. South Korea is still a strong state by any measure, but the balance of power between business and the state tipped back toward the *chaebol* in the 1980s, recollecting the periodic movement of power from the center to the regions and back again in dynastic Korea.

Structure and Management of the *Chaebol*

State-business relations in South Korea are reminiscent of the dynamics of a preindustrial political and economic elite, and the structure and management of *chaebol* are clearly patrimonial. *Chaebol* integrate crucial aspects of modern enterprise, such as professional management and rational financial techniques, but they do so within a patrimonial framework. All *chaebol* were founded by entrepreneurial men who built personal business empires that they regard as their own politico-economic spheres. The position of *haejang,* or conglomerate chairman, is more than that of a business executive. The *haejang* are overlords of their holdings and, like premodern patrimonial officials, articulate moral ideologies as well as rational economic strategies. For example, the ideology of Choong-Hoon Cho, founder of Hanjin *chaebol* (Korea Airlines), is summarized in the statement, "Business is an art. To make a good work of art, there should be harmony, just as an orchestra's" (Yoo & Lee, 1987, p. 101). The motto reflects a deep faith in Confucian principles of order and obedience to status and role prescriptions. Cho runs one of the most patrimonial of all the *chaebol,* eschewing professional managers almost entirely in favor of management by members of his family. Hanjin, unlike most *chaebol,* has a policy of lifetime employment and attempts to keep the "household" of workers together.

In contrast to Cho's philosophy of harmony and order, Daewoo's *haejang,* Woo-Choong Kim, has a philosophy of aggressiveness and hard work, and, unlike many Korean firms, Daewoo offers performance-based pay. Kim is noted as one of the only *haejang* to use professional managers in lieu of family members in top positions. Daewoo, nonetheless, uses the particularistic recruitment criteria of regional origins and alumni ties, and Kim favors hiring alumni from his high school (Yoo & Lee, 1987, p. 101).

Similarly, Chey Jong Hyon, *haejang* of Sunkyong *chaebol,* fourth largest after Samsung, Daewoo, and Hyundai in 1985, is noted for his less patrimonial approach to management. According to Ensor's (1986) profile in the *Far Eastern Economic Review,* "Chey is an unusual *chaebol* chairman, highly respected for his scholarly background and self-effacement in this Confucian country. Unlike other chairmen, who seem to thrive on patriarchal personality cults within their business empires, Chey reportedly dislikes seeing too many pictures of himself, and avoids the press" (p. 66). Chey has a more professional approach to management and is noted for allowing some decentralized decision making within the Sunkyong group. But the relative professionalism of Chey must be seen against an essentially patrimonial structure: Chey took over as chairman at the death of his elder brother, and another brother is a senior executive in the group. Indeed, Chey's entry into the oil industry—taking over a Gulf Oil joint venture with the government—came about through his political connections with the newly installed regime of Chun Doo Hwan. As one observer put it, "This was a time when the new government were thanking their friends for support" (Ensor, 1986, p. 66).

In varying degrees, personalism, through family connections, common regional origins, and alumni ties, is important in all the *chaebol.* Family members control the stock of the enterprises, and despite government pressure to list shares on the stock exchange, control is still closely held by the *haejang* and his heirs and in-laws. The ownership structures vary, however, among three types, according to Yoo and Lee (1987). The first type of business group—for example, Hanjin—is in the sole possession of the founder and his heirs through ownership of stock in each member company. The second type is characterized by the domination of the conglomerate by a core company, which in turn owns shares in affiliated subsidiaries. The family owns and controls the stock of the core company. Daewoo is an example of this type. Finally, there is the "mutual possession" type, where the family owns the core company and/or a foundation, which in turn owns the stock of affiliated companies; in some instances member companies own each other's stock. Samsung is an example of this type. Although ownership structures vary formally, in fact they are all characterized by family ownership and control.

Families not only own the *chaebol,* they typically run them (Daewoo being the notable exception). Again, although management structures vary, with family playing a greater or lesser role in management depending on the *haejang*'s philosophy and the size of the family, the common pattern is for the *haejang* to appoint his sons, and sometimes brothers and sons-in-law, to top positions in business group firms. For example, the power structure of the Hyundai group, the largest *chaebol* in South Korea, with 32 operating companies and 1983 sales of $8.6 billion U.S., is firmly controlled by the three brothers and seven sons—known in Korea as the "seven princes"—of *haejang* Jung Ju Yung:

- Brothers

  Second brother, Hyundai Cement
  Third brother, Hyundai Automobile
  Fourth brother, Korea Chemical, Hyundai Gum Gang

(In Young, another brother, became an independent entrepreneur in 1977 and formed Hanra Group; the youngest brother died in an automobile accident while studying in Germany.)

- Sons

  First son, died in an automobile accident in 1982
  Second son, Hyundai Refinery, Hyundai Gang Gwan, Hyundai Auto Service
  Third son, Gum Gang Ghebal
  Fourth son, Han Guk Pojang Construction
  Fifth son, Hyundai Construction Company
  Sixth son, Hyundai Heavy Industry, Hyundai Engines
  Seventh son, in the South Korean Army

Samsung's founding *haejang,* Byung Chul Lee, passed over his first two sons and named his third son heir apparent to the *haejang* position. In 1966, Lee's eldest son had been found to have illegally profited from smuggling saccharin while importing other raw materials from Japan. A major scandal ensued, and the son spent a year in jail. On his release, he reported Samsung company tax evasion to the government, initiating a major investigation of a Samsung firm. The incident concluded with Lee "donating" 51% of the company's shares to the government. The father concluded that his two eldest sons conspired against him to destroy Samsung and passed over them in the line of succession. The third son in fact assumed the *haejang* post on his father's death in 1987.

Founder Lee's family is involved in business in the following ways:

Third son, *haejang* (conglomerate president)
First son's wife, Anguk Wha-Jae (insurance)

Second son, JaiIl Hap Sung (textiles) (also founded independent firms Media Korea and Shahan JunJa, which are very successful and are included as Samsung subsidiary firms)

First daughter and husband, Korea Hospital, Shilla Hotel, Jun Ju Jai Ji (lumber)

Fourth daughter and husband, Shin She Ge Department Store, Jo Sun Hotel, Samsung Electronics

Father-in-law of third son, Samsung Heavy Industry, Samsung Shipping, Samsung Construction

Lee has three wives, two in Korea and one in Japan. In addition to the Korean children listed above, he has two children by his Japanese wife, a daughter and a son. The son works as a director in a Samsung firm; the daughter remains in Japan.

Regional and Clan Rivalries

The familism of modern South Korea often entwines with regionalism and clan rivalries between the *chaebol;* indeed, it is difficult to separate rivalries on these two dimensions because each clan is associated with a region and, within a region, with a town or city. Koreans have a widespread belief that one's place of origin imprints a personality or character traits, and discussions of *kohyang* or "native place" are embedded in the popular culture. "Anyone who has spent some time in Korea is familiar with the gross characterizations that are used to describe people from different provinces: Cholla people are lazy, Kyonggi people are miserly." But the characterization extends "downward from province into county, from village to village, and then into the neighborhoods that make up a single village" (Goldberg, 1977, p. 91). Social action of all types—from courtship to hiring decisions—is influenced by regional considerations.

One of the most publicized clan rivalries occurred between Samsung's Lee and Lucky-Goldstar *haejang* Gu In Hae (sometimes anglicized as Koo or Ku). Lee's second daughter is married to Gu's third son, but the marital tie did not prevent in-law rivalry. The feud began in 1968, when Lee wrote an essay titled "Why Korea Must Promote Electronic Enterprise" in the *Jungang Il Bo,* a widely read newspaper owned by Samsung. The essay was recognized as an announcement that Samsung would enter the electronics market, a sector in which Lucky-Goldstar was a pioneer. Lucky-Goldstar's Gu construed this as a declaration of war from Samsung. Gu responded to the challenge by writing a counterdeclaration in *Guk Jae Sinbo,* a paper owned by Lucky-Goldstar.

After writing the essay, Lee established Samsung Electronic Company and Samsung Electrical Company, both in 1969, and Samsung Electron Devices in 1970. "Tta Do Gum Sung" (Down with Lucky-Goldstar) became the battle cry of Samsung electronics workers as Lee challenged them to become number one in electronics.

The competition created a victim in Lee's second daughter because of her marriage to Gu's third son. Lee disinherited her, citing that when a daughter marries she belongs to her husband's family. All of his other daughters are Samsung owners and hold directorships with their husbands in Samsung subsidiary firms.

There are other rivalries among the *chaebol,* and as the above example suggests, they are personal and clan rivalries that go beyond business competition. Daewoo and Hyundai are archcompetitors known to have antagonistic relations. The senior manager of a Hyundai group firm explained that both groups make cars and ships and compete directly in those markets. Of the two, only Hyundai, however, makes rubber that Daewoo needs for tires and other products. According to this Hyundai official, Daewoo refuses to buy Hyundai rubber even if it is the cheapest available (personal communication, April 1988).

An executive with the American electronics manufacturer Hewlett-Packard confirmed the intense rivalries among *chaebol* managements. When H-P wanted to form a joint venture with a South Korean firm, it was extremely careful in its choice of partners; the Americans realized that if they aligned with one *chaebol* they were then excluded from doing business with any of the others. According to the executive, "Hewlett-Packard competes very strongly with IBM and DEC, but at times we work with competitors when it is in our mutual interest; for example, we buy parts from them. But not in South Korea. The *chaebol* won't buy from each other even if it is the only place to get an item, or if it's cheaper" (personal communication, March 1988). The social relations of competitive patrimonialism push economic decision making away from the impersonal and rational Western model.

Controls on Management and Workers

The *chaebol* are structured like patrimonial households in a number of respects. Although they vary in structure, typically a *chaebol* has a centralized personal staff that helps the *haejang* maintain control of the collection of enterprises in the group. In some instances, such as the case of Samsung, the staff forms a separate secretariat. In others, such as Hyundai, there is a "mother" company that in effect controls the other subsidiaries. Hyundai Engineering and Construction was the first enterprise in the Hyundai group and is its mother company. It originally nurtured other businesses as divisions and over time spun them off as independent companies while retaining a tight hold on top management. According to a top Hyundai executive in a subordinate company, "At first they met with us once a week; now it's about once a month" (personal communication, April 1988).

The Samsung secretariat, which reportedly functions similarly to the *haejang*'s staffs at Hyundai and Lucky-Goldstar, maintains tight control over strategic planning, finance, and investment decisions. Although group companies are given operating autonomy, supervision is close. Each Samsung company has a "management team" at the secretariat that advises the company and is a go-between for the *haejang*. The team, the company's top management, and frequently the *haejang* meet one or two times a month. Unlike the "presidents' clubs" of Japanese business groups, where all the member-firm chief executives meet together monthly as a community, in the *chaebol* meetings are one-on-one, between the *haejang* and his subordinate executive.

Although group companies develop their own business projections, they are subject to the approval and monitoring of the secretariat. An annual performance review subjects the group firms to a rigorous inspection. If a company achieves 95% or better of its target, or if there are extenuating circumstances for poor business performance, such as an upward revaluation of the currency, then the performance is considered acceptable. Otherwise, there are penalties to top management, including dismissal. Lifetime employment is not an ideal or practice in most Korean firms.

Although the Samsung secretariat has no legal ties to group firms except through family ownership, it clearly acts like a U.S. conglomerate headquarters in its planning and financial oversight functions. But control goes beyond what is typical in U.S. conglomerates. For example, the secretariat is in charge of management personnel selection and development. It hires university graduates for employment in group firms and then trains them for 2 months before sending them to positions in affiliate firms. An important part of the training develops loyalty to the group as a whole and to the ideology of the *haejang;* training is not intended to provide job-specific knowledge. In addition to selection, the secretariat maintains control of the career paths of middle and top management, reinforcing management's orientation toward the patrimonial center of the *chaebol,* not to the company in which they are employed. *Chaebol* management is increasingly professionalized, to be sure, but the framework remains patrimonial.

For example, compensation systems in South Korea are personalistic. Employees are not paid primarily on the type of work they do or on their performance in the job, as in the West. Rather, as in many patrimonial systems, compensation is based on particularistic criteria and on how well their superiors choose to reward them. According to Se-Il Park (1988), "Among the major pay-determining characteristics of workers are educational background, age (or length of service) and sex. The other characteristic is that various kinds of 'allowances' comprise a large portion of total monthly remuneration. Whether the allowances are offered as compensation for work done or as a 'benevolent gift' is not clear." The allowances often range from 400% to 700% of monthly base pay.

Although the *haejang*'s staff typically oversees the hiring of university graduates, the approval of supervisors along the career path is crucial to advancement as well as to compensation. Supervisors assume personalistic mentoring roles for their juniors, with shared regionalism assuming a subtle importance in chances for advancement (Chan, 1987). "Employees in Korean companies are promoted largely based on seniority, dedication, and relationship with top management rather than on contribution and achievement" (Yoo & Lee, 1987, pp. 105-106). Although recruitment for managers is influenced by considerations of ability, the top ranks of the *chaebol* are disproportionately filled with executives from the *haejang*'s region of origin.

Selecting people from a home region certainly reflects Koreans' historic belief that a region stamps a personality on its residents. More important, it assures a density of social networks that act as a control on the individual. Individuals must demonstrate their loyalty to the company or risk shame for themselves and their families at home. This form of personalistic network control is formalized in hiring practices, too. Workers are encouraged to recommend friends and relatives for employment, and frequently must name three "guarantors" inside the company and three outside who will vouch for the worker. Nepotism and regionalism provide continuing guarantees of loyalty, if not competence.

Conclusion: Patrimonialism
and Industrial Strategy

To a Western observer, South Korea's patrimonial approach to industrialization would not seem an obvious route to development. Personalistic ties, family-based decision making, selection for particularism rather than competence—all appear mired in inefficient premodern patterns ill suited to competition in the modern world economy. That these practices are rooted in Korea's past is clear, but it is equally clear that they have worked spectacularly well in bringing South Korea from the devastation of the Korean War to rapid economic growth. Patrimonialism has worked in modern South Korea at least in part because it was a widely understood pattern of authority; although it conflicted with other strains of Korean culture—individualism, and more recently democracy—patrimonialism in the 1950s had the force of experience and perhaps some level of acceptance in a populace dealing with the effects of a brutal civil war and a destroyed economy. Patrimonialism was a familiar, institutionalized means for political and economic organization. Moreover, it was indigenous, not a model supplied by Japanese colonial experience or the American occupation.

Although not "efficient" in the sense suggested by neoclassical economics, patrimonialism served economic development. It subordinated individualism to the needs of society and egalitarianism to the discipline of hierarchy. Centralized control by a patrimonial state structure concentrated limited resources into strategically selected capital-intensive industries such as steelmaking and shipbuilding.

The limits of patrimonialism as a development strategy have become obvious with the success of the South Korean economy, however. The enormous wealth of the *chaebol*-owning families contrasts with the modest fortunes of workers. Although income inequality decreased in the 1960s, it increased during the export boom of the next two decades (Koo, 1984). Rising expectations, a new generation untouched by the experience of war, and the historic Korean propensity to protest moral wrongs on the part of superiors has led in recent years to political uprisings and violent labor strikes. In 1986 there were 200 labor disputes; there were as many in 2 months in 1987 (Clifford, 1987, p. 53). In the first 6 months of 1988, there were 1,000 strikes (Magnanini, 1988, p. D1).

Patrimonialism is limited by more than political unrest in South Korea; it is proving to have economic limitations as well. South Korean hierarchy is poorly suited to the development of technology and other forms of innovation; Korea has had to pay for technology, usually from Japan or the United States, or has had to enter joint ventures with technological superiors.[4]

Centralization and personal obedience do not suit the new sectors into which the economy is moving, most notably electronics. Clan rivalries limit the ability of domestic joint ventures and distort the development of the internal economy.

Although some have proclaimed South Korea the "next Japan," it is doubtful that Korean industrial patterns will emulate the Japanese. If institutional history is a guide, the future will develop out of Korea's patrimonial experience, changed, no doubt, to serve changing situations.

Notes

1. For good reviews of institutional theories, see W. R. Scott (1987) and Zucker (1987).

2. Institutional analysis is distinguished from the variable analysis of economics and other forms of statistical methodology. Variable analysis explains organization in the correlation of variables such as size, industry characteristics, factor endowments, and product diversity. These variables are conceived transhistorically: Anywhere the same variables are present, the same or like outcomes will occur. Variable analysis seeks to find universal laws of social phenomena, whereas institutional analysis explains social outcomes as embedded in context and history. See Ragin and Zaret (1983).

3. The Koryo Dynasty, which unified much of Korea, is today being invoked as a model for the reunification of North and South Korea.

4. The continuing economic dependence of South Korea on Japan is the subject of much scholarship. The "neo-imperialists" argue that the economic interests of Japan's powerful capitalist class are causal in shaping relations between the two economies; "neo-mercantilists" emphasize relations between states that direct economic processes as part of an economic foreign policy. Chang (1985) reviews these and other explanations for Japanese involvement in South Korea.

Organization and Market Processes in Taiwan's Capitalist Economy

GARY G. HAMILTON

The State and Economic Organization

Most attempts to explain capitalist development in Taiwan follow the political economy, or what might be called the strong state, perspective. The theorists who argue from this point of view typically apply the same general theories with equal fervor to explain the industrialization of all East Asian capitalist countries. If their theses were correct, however, one would predict

AUTHOR'S NOTE: Portions of this chapter are reprinted here from The Organization of Business in Taiwan, AJS 96:4, pp. 999-1006 by permission from the University of Chicago Press. © 1996 by the University of Chicago. All rights reserved.

a similar range of organizational outcomes throughout Asia, and, in fact, many observers of Taiwan's industrialization have jumped to this conclusion. Proceeding from the known fact of Taiwan's rapid industrialization, a considerable number of analysts have argued, ex post, that Taiwan's development has been a result of state policy.

Alice Amsden (1985), Thomas Gold (1986, 1988), Chien-Kuo Pang (1992), Robert Wade (1990), and Joel Aberbach, David Dollar, and Kenneth Sokoloff (1994) have been among the best of those to reach this conclusion.[1] In similar ways, Gold and Pang both draw on Cardoso and Faletto's (1979) theory of dependent development in Latin American and on Peter Evans's (1979) systematization of that theory in his study of Brazil to argue that "in Taiwan the state played a much greater role than in the commonly analyzed Latin American cases" (Gold, 1988, p. 175). Also in equally similar ways, Wade and Amsden argue strenuously against a neoclassical thesis that Taiwan's development arises from the workings of free markets and just as strenuously for the position that the Taiwan state effectively "governs the market" (Wade, 1990), thereby creating the conditions for economic development. All four authors would likely concur with Pang's (1992) conclusions:

> In sum, facilitated by a number of advantages, the strong capacities of the KMT state in economic policy-making largely derived from its internal structuring. This consisted of an impregnable leadership who recruited competent officials to take charge of economic development and maintained internal coherence of the state apparatus; a group of clean, honest, and capable economic policy makers who played a pivotal role in synthesizing the various opinions and demands of the different parties within or outside the state apparatus; and a company of skilled and loyal economic bureaucrats who offered required expertise and worked hard. Surrounded by the various favorable or unfavorable conditions in the Taiwanese society and the international political-economic environment, they played the major role in formulating [and] executing various development policies for regulating Taiwan's economic transformation. (p. 273)

Despite their persistence in claiming that Taiwan's development resulted from state policy, all of these writers acknowledge a weakness in the thesis when it is used to account for the organization of the economy. In Japan (Johnson, 1982), the state encouraged and, as in the case of South Korea (Amsden, 1989a; Kim, 1991), often actively promoted the formation of a networked industrial structure made up of large business groups. These analysts would like to make exactly the same case for Taiwan, and would be successful except for two points: First, although there are some large business conglomerates and although they are important in the overall economy, the most influential segment of the Taiwan economy is made up of small and medium-sized businesses; second, the state has little direct influence on those who own the large businesses and next to none on those who own the smaller businesses. Accordingly, the state has little influence on those who actually organize Taiwan's economy.

Pang's (1992) commentary is again to the point: "For most times and cases, . . . the local capitalists did not play a decisive role in the KMT state's economic policy-making. . . . Different from the situation in Japan and Korea, the state-business relations were relatively 'distant' and 'cool' in Taiwan" (p. 263). Pang concurs with Gold's assessment: "The problem in Taiwan," says Gold (1986), "has not been a dearth of entrepreneurship, but rather a structure to let it prosper" (p. 126). Gold concludes that the state provided that structure, that good "investment climate," but "maintained an aloofness" from the "bourgeoisie" (p. 128).

None of the strong state theorists has actually examined the organization of Taiwan's economy. Instead, drawing on extensive interviews with government elites and a few top industrialists and on government archives, they essentially give a view from the center, from Taipei, from the seat of government in its most sophisticated posture. What they provide, in a finely framed analysis, are the elite's own views of their roles in promoting industrialization. State leaders and the elite businessmen would like to see themselves cast as the prime movers, *deus ex machina,* creating Taiwan's economic prosperity. This is a view that legitimates their own position of power and status in Taiwan's society, and, it just so happens, this is a view that marries nicely with current thinking on the political economy of development.[2] But this is also a view that ignores much of what has actually occurred in the economy, a great deal of which cannot be laid to government policy. In his masterful argument for a strong state explanation of Taiwan's industrialization, Robert Wade's (1990) disarmingly honest assessment of his approach makes this exact point, thus providing a segue to an explanatory emphasis on economic organization:

> Taiwan's dualistic industrial structure is densely interconnected, and the export success of the smaller firms cannot be understood independently of the productive performance of the big firms. This being said, I should stress that the organization of firms—their size, the way they grow, their methods of doing business, and the relationships between them—is a major gap in the argument

of this book. Any discussion of an economy's development should give a central place to the organization of firms and industries. But since little evidence is available on this subject for Taiwan, and since my primary interest is the uses of public power, I say little more about it. (p. 70)

Disclaimers aside, Wade's generally excellent study of the state's role in Taiwan's industrialization is a little like the sound of one hand clapping: On the one hand, there is the government's effort to shape the economy, and on the other, there is the actual shape of the economy. Not knowing the latter, how can we assess the former?

What is the organizational shape of Taiwan's economy? As Wade indicates, with rare exceptions until very recently, very few scholars have tried, or even thought it worthwhile, to examine Taiwan's industrial structure. Looking at this structure by using the government's official statistics, which are collected, as they are in most countries, through a firm-by-firm census, one would find nothing peculiar, only the usual lineup of large, medium, and small firms. Moreover, comparing this lineup with the same set of statistics for Japan and South Korea, one finds that both Japan and South Korea have, as a percentage of all firms, as many small firms as Taiwan, and Taiwan has as many large firms as either Japan or South Korea.[3] Unlike Japan and South Korea, however, Taiwan is not known for having large business groups, and therefore, because Taiwan's large firms are not as large as those in Japan or South Korea, and as they do not appear to be interconnected with many other large firms, there appears to be nothing terribly distinctive about Taiwan's industrial structure, at least at first glance.

In fact, more than a few observers who have just looked at these statistics have written that Taiwan is one of the best examples of a free market economy in Asia (e.g., Galenson, 1979). It is exactly these kinds of comments that Robert Wade has so forcefully and correctly criticized; Taiwan's economy does not conform to a neoclassical ideal of what a free market should look like in terms of either state action or market organization. But Wade looks only at state intervention in market processes, and not at the macro-organizational features of the economy.

The few researchers who have looked at these features have gotten out in the field to do the necessary observation, interviews, and historical work to interpret how the economy actually works. All of these researchers have observed that Taiwan's economy is densely networked, and that these networks themselves have significant independent effects upon the economy.

One of the first and clearest statements of these effects comes from Susan Greenhalgh (1988).[4] In a conference volume devoted primarily to debates concerning the "contending approaches to the political economy of Taiwan," she argues for an alternative approach, which she calls the "network paradigm." The structure of Taiwan's economy, Greenhalgh states, may be "distorted," but the distortion does not come from state intervention; rather, "it is distorted, or at least shaped, by the excessive influence of family enterprises and network strategies" (p. 243).

> This conclusion challenges a basic assumption of both radical and liberal theories [of political economy] about the balance of power among constituent elements of the world system. These theories assume that microsocial institutions are weak entities, passive elements in processes that are dominated largely by macroeconomic and macropolitical forces. A close look at Taiwan suggests a very different balance of power, one in which microsocial forces not only shape larger outcomes, but also constrain the actions of the state and multinationals. (p. 241)

This is my conclusion in this chapter as well. The existing social and economic organizations within Taiwan influence the state's economic planners as much as, and likely more than, the state's planners shape that society's economic organizations.

Taiwan's Economic Organization: Demand-Responsive, Buyer-Driven Networks

Taiwan business groups are quite different from those found in South Korea. Taiwan's interfirm networks do not have the characteristics of vertical control that are so obvious in South Korea (see Chapter 3, this volume); quite the contrary, interfirm networks in Taiwan tend to link people and firms together on a horizontal basis. Such vertical networks as exist in Taiwan are found in relatively modest groups of small and medium-sized firms that are controlled through family ties. Moreover, unlike the control manifest in the family-owned *chaebol* in South Korea, the span of effective control achieved through such family groups in Taiwan is quite narrow and fragmented. However, despite the narrowness of control and the fragmentation of group holdings, the Taiwan economy is among the most densely networked and highly productive economies in the world. In fact, Taiwan, a country of 21 million people, has accumulated, at various points in the past decade, the world's largest economic surplus and, among all world economies, has one of the highest ratios of manufactured goods to total output and one of the highest ratios of exported goods to total manufacturing. Taiwan has achieved this position of industrial preeminence with an economic organization based on flexible horizontally based interfirm relationships that respond to, rather than create, external demand. The main economic characteristic of this type of network is that it is what I call *demand responsive*. The responsiveness of these networks is facilitated and even enhanced by the flexibilities within the horizontal networks, but the productiveness and rapid growth of these networks result from their being linked into what Gary Gereffi (1993) calls "buyer-driven" commodities chains.

In the following sections, I will demonstrate that Taiwan's economy is organized through horizontally controlled networks that facilitate economic development in response to external economic demand. The first step in this argument is to demonstrate the relative lack of vertical linkages in the Taiwan economy. The second step is to discuss the characteristics of intra- and interfamily business networks, which show the weakness of vertical controls but the strength of horizontal connections.

Macro-Organizational Features of the Taiwan Economy

In contrast with the industrial structure of Japan and South Korea, several features of Taiwan's industrial structure stand out: Although the actual number of firms in each size category is roughly consistent with the other two countries, the relative value-added contribution of each size category to the total GNP differs: Taiwan has the largest state-owned sector, the smallest big business sector, and much the largest small and medium-sized business sector. As we look at each of these sectors in turn, the distinctive qualities of this economy become more apparent.

State-Owned Enterprises

In Japan and South Korea, where political assistance and at times intervention are significant features of the economies, the state-owned sectors have steadily declined over many years; by the 1990s in both societies the state-owned sector constituted less than 5%. Paradoxically, in Taiwan, the society in which, as I will show, the overall economic role of the state is less significant than in the other two, a substantial state-owned sector has for the past two decades (1970-1990) constituted between 10% and 15% of the total valued added in manufacturing. In the 1950s, state-owned enterprises accounted for nearly 50% of the valued added in the manufacturing sectors, but this proportion declined quickly until 1971, when it leveled out at an average for the next 15 years of 14% (Council for Economic Planning and Development, 1987, p. 89). Because a great portion of Taiwan's industrialization has occurred since 1970, it stands to reason that during this period the public sector has grown at about the same rate as the private sector. It should be noted that this is just the first of a number of relatively "steady-state" ratios in an economy that is in all other respects burgeoning.

It is apparent that the state-owned sector has come to occupy a very special role in the overall economy since the 1970s. During the colonial period (1895-1945), the Japanese government owned large segments of Taiwan's agricultural economy, as well as the financial and transportation infrastructure (Myers & Peattie, 1984).[5] In the years immediately after World War II, the Kuomintang government moved quickly to claim the enterprises owned by the Japanese government, including the railway system, banks, and a number of agricultural and industrial firms. Acting on the advice of the Sino-American Joint Commission on Rural Reconstruction, Kuomintang officials stabilized Taiwan's agricultural economy by embarking on comprehensive land reforms (Yager, 1988). These land reforms led to the redistribution of nearly one-fourth of Taiwan's cultivated land to Taiwan's tenant farmers and small landowners. As a partial inducement to give up their land, the former landlords received from the Taiwan government shares in four government enterprises (including Taiwan Cement and Taiwan Paper and Pulp) (Gold, 1986, p. 66). After this dispersal, however, the government did not again privatize any of its enterprises until the 1980s. Instead, in an effort to add an industrial wing to its agricultural holdings, the state established a number of import-substituting firms in such heavy industries as iron and steel manufacturing, shipbuilding, and petroleum production. The postwar state firms grew in importance relative to those established earlier and became the principal value-added component in the early industrializing period in the late 1950s and the 1960s, and a reduced but relatively steady component since then.

From 1970 on, most of the state's economic assets, production, and value added have come from only a dozen state-owned enterprises, including Taiwan Power, China Petroleum, China Steel, and China Petrochemical Development.[6] From this list, it is easy to see that Taiwan's state-owned enterprises occupy a position furthermost upstream, a position supplying the basic raw materials (i.e., the steel and the petroleum products) and the electrical power that runs most of the factories. Moreover, it is obvious from the categories of Taiwan's exports that the state-owned enterprises do not export their products; rather, these early state ventures in import substitution produce commodities and services for the domestic economy. As Taiwan's economy has grown, the demand for these upstream products has increased roughly in proportion to overall growth, so that, for example, Taiwan Power has had to build more nuclear power generators and China Petroleum has become involved in extensive offshore oil exploration. To an important extent, state-owned enterprises subsidize the economy by maintaining low prices on upstream goods and services.

In addition to supplying basic commodities and infrastructural services, the state has tried to stimulate specific sectors of the economy by subsidizing upstream manufacturing as well as research and development firms to help establish private firms in targeted sectors (Wade, 1990, pp. 90-108). These efforts began in the early years of the KMT government with direct support for plastic and textile industries and continue today with support for food processing, biotechnology, and semiconductor industries. As in the overall economy, in these targeted sectors, the state supports upstream components of industries; state-owned enterprises serve the private sector by undertaking those research and development tasks and those capital-intensive, economy-of-scale activities that are beyond the capabilities of private firms. For instance, the charter for the 48.3% state-owned Taiwan Semiconductor Manufacturing Company states that the company is "forbidden to make any products of its own." Instead, "partly to prevent it from becoming a rival to the small firms it was set up to serve," the company was created to supply local firms with the semiconductors they need to make their products (Johnstone, 1988, p. 84).

Interviews with the directors of the Development Center for Biotechnology and the Food Industry Research and Development Institute reveal a similar rationale: Such research institutes see themselves as partly private and partly public. They are private in the sense that they need partially to support themselves from the sale of goods and services to domestic users, who are typically the main producing firms in their respective industries; they are public in the sense that they are mainly funded by the government, are charged with servicing the research and technology needs of their respective industries, and are forbidden to compete with private sector firms.

State-owned enterprises primarily supply infrastructure and basic initial goods and services, such as electricity, gasoline, steel, and even technology transfers, that all other companies might use, regardless of size. In these roles, state-owned businesses fill a position in a societal division of labor by supplying commodities that are essential for the prosperity of the people. "Allowing the people to prosper" is, in fact, a formula that the Taiwan government has taken from Chinese statecraft and has elevated to a point of principle. Therefore, removing the production of essential goods and services from private greed and manipulation in order to preserve them as a public good is consistent with the way the Taiwan state legitimates itself. Because most of these enterprises involve huge economies of scale, state ownership has indeed prevented these sectors from being monopolized by the richest, the most powerful, or the best-connected people. In effect, the Taiwan state has blocked the development of Japanese- and South Korean-style business groups in the very areas where some form of monopolization is most likely necessary to achieve the scale and scope of service required by users.

As public accounts show, however, state-owned enterprises are neither efficient nor profit oriented. Instead, they are reputedly bureaucratic and distant from their customers. This aloof public role of state-owned enterprises in the midst of a surging and ever-changing private sector, composed primarily of modest-sized firms owned by wealthy and very speculative "deal makers," helps to explain the continuity of the state-owned sector. Unlike state officials in Japan and South Korea, state officials in Taiwan have shown a great reluctance to privatize state-owned enterprises by turning them into public corporations, thus making shares of them available to the public through local equity markets.

Does this reluctance reveal, to use state theory jargon, the state's considerable "autonomy" and "capacity"? Or does it reveal that the lines of state power and control do not penetrate very deeply into society? Does it reveal that, once privatized, the corporations would move beyond state control and come into the orbit of prominent families or powerful political factions of the KMT? I believe that this reluctance shows that to remove them from direct state control, even by creating public corporations, obscures the lines of authority. Being neither state nor family owned (the two clear nodes of authority in Chinese society), a privatized public corporation, in the Chinese context, would have unclear responsibility to anyone, thus making it open to the possibility of corruption and the undermining of public welfare for private gain. Such an outcome would clearly discredit state and party leaders at a time when their legitimacy is already being challenged by new reformist factions.

Large Business Groups

To those in the private sector, state-owned enterprises are large and far away, as is the government itself. They are there to preserve economic order by providing infrastructure and essential goods, not to interfere or compete with the livelihood of those in the private sector. Within the private sector, there is, of course, considerable competition and mutual interference in pursuit of profit and economic success. But, unlike the strong and sometimes cutthroat competition among business groups in South Korea and to a somewhat lesser extent in Japan, the most intense competition exists not among big business groups, but among networks of small firms competing in the same commodity chains for export markets. In the midst of this competition, another sort of division of labor emerges, one that divides the big and the little business networks.

As my colleagues and I have shown in earlier work, in contrast with business groups in Japan and South Korea, Taiwan's business groups contain fewer firms on average and those firms are much smaller, both in absolute terms and in their percentage of contribution to the total economy (Hamilton, Zeile, & Kim, 1990). Taiwan's business groups are also more tightly clustered in the manufacturing sectors of the economy, with lesser concentrations in construction, financial services, and commercial sectors. And within the manufacturing sector, on an aggregate basis, they have far less influence within specific subsectors than is true in either Japan or South Korea. Taiwan's top 96 business groups have major concentrations (that is, aggregated group sales in excess of 40% of the total sales in a sector) only in textiles (e.g., synthetic fabrics and cotton spinning), chemical materials, and nonmetallic mineral products (e.g., plastic). They have lesser concentration in food products, transportation equipment, and electrical and electronic products (see Tables 9.1 and 9.2).

From an examination of these aggregate statistics it is apparent that Taiwan's business groups are considerably less significant than are business groups in South Korea. That surface appearance now needs to be qualified with a more in-depth look at Taiwan's industrial structure. My general argument is that the organization of Taiwan's private sector differs from the

Table 9.1 Business Group Shares by Broad Economic Sector

Sector	Korea (1983 sales share of top 50 chaebol)	Taiwan (1983 sales share of top 96 largest groups)
Mining	10.6	0.0
Manufacturing	45.4	19.0
Construction	66.0	5.6
Transport and storage	23.1	1.8
Banking and financial services	—	5.8
Trading and commerce	—	4.1

SOURCES: Data for Korea are from Management Efficiency Research Institute (1986) and Bank of Korea (1987). For construction and transport and storage, the figures for Korea are the percentage rate of *chaebol* sales to industry gross output. Data for Taiwan are from China Credit Information Service (1983), Directorate-General of Budget, Accounting and Statistics (1983, 1985), and Council for Economic Planning and Development (1987). For construction, the 1983 total sales figure used to calculate the ratio for Taiwan was estimated using reported index numbers for building construction and the transaction figures in the 1984 input-output tables for Taiwan. Total sales figures for the other sectors come from the 1983 Taiwan industrial census. For the transport and storage and banking and financial services sectors, revenue figures are used.

other two cases not only in degree, but, more important, in kind. In specific terms, the large business groups do not organize the economy; rather, they are themselves driven by the demand created by the export-oriented sector of the economy, which is, in turn, dominated by more small firms and less extensive business networks.

The first clue to this qualitative difference between Taiwan and the other two cases is the location of business groups in commodity chains that lead to the production and distribution of export products. With the exception of producing a little more than 20% of Taiwan's electrical and electronics products, the top business groups predominate in sectors producing intermediate products, goods that are not in final form and are not made for export. This is significant because Taiwan's economy is one of the world's most export-oriented economies (World Bank, 1988). In 1985, Taiwan's exports accounted for 51% of the GNP, compared with South Korea's 37.5% and Japan's 16.4% for the same calculation. South Korea's and Japan's biggest business groups control the production and distribution of final export products; they dominate the export sectors of these economies. Yet in Taiwan, the country with the one of the world's highest ratios of export goods to total output, the biggest businesses produce intermediate goods sold domestically.

Table 9.2 Business Group Shares by Manufacturing Sector (percentages)

	Korea (top 50 chaebol)	Taiwan (96 largest enterprise groups)
Food products	33.7	40.9
Beverage and tobacco	27.6	3.8
Textiles	38.4	50.7
Garments and apparel	12.6	12.0
Leather products	15.2	9.1
Lumber and wood products	31.5	4.0
Pulp and paper products; printing and publishing	6.7	20.1
Chemical materials	54.3	42.4
Chemical products	24.0	8.4
Petroleum and coal products	91.9	0.0
Rubber products	76.8	13.0
Plastic products	0.1	5.4
Nonmetallic mineral products	44.6	47.6
Basic metal	28.0	7.8
Metal products	26.7	6.0
Machinery	34.9	3.6
Electrical and electronic products	50.9	22.7
Transportation equipment	79.0	23.6
Precision machinery	14.0	0.0
Miscellaneous industrial products	5.2	10.7

SOURCES: Figures for Korea are calculated from 1983 sales data for each *chaebol* member firm and 1983 industrial census data (Daily Economic News, 1986; Economic Planning Board, 1985; Management Efficiency Research Institute, 1985). Figures for Taiwan are calculated from 1983 sales data for each group member firm and 1983 industrial census data (China Credit Information Service, 1983; Directorate-General of Budget, Accounting and Statistics, 1983).

How can this paradox be explained? It is easy enough to explain for the large business groups, but the ease of explanation here only adds to the complexity of explaining how the third sector of the economy, the small and medium-sized businesses, actually works. The private businesses in Taiwan that have been able to grow large relative to other businesses are upstream producers for the tens of thousands of small and medium-sized firms that are downstream consumers of these intermediate goods. The Taiwan government calculates that firms having fewer than 300 employees account for nearly 50% of Taiwan's total manufacturing output and 65% of all exports, a fact that has been true for more than two decades (Wu, 1988; see also Biggs, 1988b, pp. 3-4). By contrast, large firms of more than 500 employees represent a steady, if not slightly declining, share of total production. Since the mid-1960s, the share of net value added for these large firms has gone from 46% to 37%, a figure that would be much lower if we were counting only exports (Biggs, 1988b, pp. 3-4).

Groups of modest-sized firms have sprung up around every easily assembled consumer fashion that has appeared in the past 20 years, everything from trail bikes to computers. Big businesses supply small businesses with what they need to produce. Accordingly, the largest privately owned businesses have a similar position in Taiwan's economy as state-owned enterprises: They are the major producers of intermediate goods sold domestically and the major suppliers of local services. So marked is this tendency that one Taiwanese economist, Chou Tein-Chen (1985), has argued that Taiwan has a dichotomous market structure in the private sector. The smallest firms are those that produce for export, and the largest are those that produce for local use.

My own data substantiate Chou's findings. The correlation between business groups' participation in a manufacturing sector and the characteristics of that sector shows a strong positive relation to the production of intermediate products and a strong negative relation to export intensity (Hamilton et al., 1990). Chou's findings and my independent correlations make abundant sense as one examines the sales of each of the largest business groups, as shown in Table 9.3. Among the top 10 business groups in 1983, which account for nearly 50% of the total sales and assets for the top 96 groups, only Yue Loong Motors and Tatung Electronics manufacture final products. Tatung produces for both export and domestic markets, and Yue Loong produces automobiles exclusively for local use. Of the 10 largest business groups in Taiwan, only 1 produces much for export markets. The other groups supply services and intermediate goods for the local market.

A second clue to Taiwan's unique industrial structure is that it is not based on a logic of "one setism," as is the case in Japan and South Korea (see Chapter 3, this volume). Taiwan's top business groups have distinct areas of specialization, but also with smaller sets of diversified holdings outside those areas. A close examination of the top business groups shows that most of the groups have well-established principal lines of business, and that these lines are represented by relatively small sets of vertically integrated firms. In the same groups, however, there are also other firms that are outside the vertically integrated sets, often in completely unrelated business areas.

Using several standard measures of diversification, measures that assess the relative strength of the main business activity in relation to the entire group of firms, I have found that Taiwanese business groups are considerably

Table 9.3 Sales Among the Top 10 Taiwanese Business Groups, 1983

	Cathay Trust	Far Eastern	Formosa Plastics	Linden International	Sampo	San Yang	Shin Kong	Tainan Spinning	Tatung Electronics	Yue Loong Motors
Total number of firms in group	25	22	27	18	11	8	26	36	32	12
Number of manufacturing firms	9	7	15	0	5	2	9	24	17	9
Intermediate manufacturing	4	5	14	0	3	0	8	19	13	7
Total group sales (A)	15,680,224	27,073,736	82,026,471	33,083,069	12,149,757	15,504,037	26,670,577	30,665,126		28,836,735
Total manufacturing sales (B)	2,531,510	21,471,884	81,788,176	0	12,096,250	9,749,723	9,443,224	25,079,372		28,835,382
Total intermediate manufacturing sales (C)	1,270,138	21,050,215	81,216,657	0	854,157	0	9,443,224	11,922,389		8,086,371
% C/A	8.10025418	77.751423	99.01274066	0	7.0302394	0	35.4069	38.8793087		28.041909
% C/B	50.17313777	98.0361807	99.30122051	0	7.0613372	0	100	47.53862657		28.043225

less diversified than their counterparts in South Korea and Japan. Whereas South Korean and Japanese business groups attempt to control all links in the commodity chains of the products they produce, from far upstream to far downstream, Taiwanese business groups tend to control only one upstream link. But for that specific link, they may constitute nearly a monopoly in the domestic market.

Alice Amsden's (1989b) conclusion about Taiwan's big business groups and state-owned enterprises is probably correct: "The groups, together with state monopolies on the one hand and foreign investors on the other, may account for a higher degree of market concentration in 'upstream' industries in Taiwan than exists even in South Korea" (p. 8). This conclusion, however, also needs an important qualification. The small-firm customers for the basic and intermediate products and services produced by Taiwan's business groups and state-owned enterprises are not in the same network and are not controlled by the state or the big firms, as they are in Japan and South Korea. State enterprises and big firms monopolize short links in upstream manufacturing and services sectors, but do not control downstream production.

The pattern of business group ownership—near monopoly in one sector and unrelated holdings in other sectors—can be further specified with a temporal dimension. By tracing the growth of groups through their surviving firms, one can get a fairly clear impression of their emerging patterns of diversification. Groups that have been included in the top 100 business groups for more than 15 years are, unsurprisingly, the most diversified. The main sectors of specialization, however, continue to be the areas of their initial success. The following pattern is typical: Once a group has established an area of economic importance as an upstream supplier or a provider of services and has enlarged its core firms to keep pace with increasing domestic demand, it subsequently diversifies its assets by creating new firms in unrelated business areas. Large business groups can be very large indeed, with network structures and assets that rival any other business groups located elsewhere. They seem content, however, with being upstream suppliers of narrowly defined sets of commodities and services; they seldom attempt to go downstream to incorporate export production on a mass scale, and, of course, the state-owned enterprises stand in the way of most attempts to integrate further upstream. Instead, big business groups invest their profits opportunistically, in unrelated business areas. They gradually take on a conglomerate structure, and seem to disappear as a group at the margins of their business activities (Hamilton & Kao, 1990). This same developmental pattern is also evident among those groups that have been prominent for fewer than 15 years but more than 5 years. Only in those groups that have appeared in the top 100 list for fewer than 5 years is diversification minimal.

This finding that big business groups in Taiwan do most of their business through providing a very limited range of upstream products and services is also paradoxical. Taiwan's exports are extraordinarily diverse. Based on an examination of imports into the United States, Taiwan exports many more kinds of products than does South Korea, but the biggest business groups provide vastly fewer products and services than those provided by business groups in Japan and South Korea (Feenstra, Yang, & Hamilton, 1993).

The third indication of Taiwan's unusual business structure is the relative continuity of this tripartite division of labor since 1970 despite a changing composition of groups at the top. The relative percentage of the total output for the state, big business, and small and medium-sized firm sectors has remained fairly constant during the most recent two decades, a time when Taiwan's output and per capita income have soared. The large business portion of this output has remained fairly constant, with perhaps a slight decline in recent years, despite considerable variation in the internal mix in the groups listed among the top 100 (Chou, 1985, p. 46).

One of the key points about the big-firm sector is that these firms are not the creation of the government alone; they are the product of market forces, of the demand created by other firms. In other words, big firms are generated from the bottom up, rather than from the top down as creations of the government, either directly through mandate or indirectly through loan policies, or as spin-offs from other firms. This conclusion is further substantiated by Y. M. Ho's (1980) finding that Taiwan's big and little firms coexist spatially and are evenly distributed throughout the island. By comparison, Japanese and South Korean big firms are highly concentrated in major industrial cities.

The continuity of the overall division of labor suggests that the export sector of Taiwan's economy, consisting primarily of small and medium-sized firms, creates demands for intermediate goods and services that allow the large business groups and state-owned enterprises to grow at roughly the same rate as the export sector. The changes in the mix of the big business groups on top, however, reflect changes in the demands for intermediate goods as the composition of Taiwan's exports themselves change over time. As the demand for specific intermediate goods declines, the group or groups supplying those goods decline in importance as well. As one group falls, however, its position among the biggest groups is given over to another group supplying a good for which demand has risen. Business groups of all sizes rise and decline for other reasons as well, but in terms of creating market institutions and controlling economic forces, the data are clear that the largest business groups are not the main organizational force propelling the Taiwanese economy, as is the case in both the Japanese and South Korean economies. Instead, Taiwan's business groups are themselves the creation of other market forces, in particular the export sector. In short, the small-firm tail of Taiwan's industrial structure wags the entire economy.

Small and Medium-Sized Firms

How can an economy be propelled into industrialization by the smallest, least vertically integrated segment of its industrial structure? To answer this question, let me start with an analogy. The industrial structure in Taiwan reflects what might be called a *gold rush effect*. In a gold rush, a great many people get caught up in the stampede to find gold, and although a few people do indeed strike it rich in the mines, those who make the most money are the ones who supply the miners with the goods and services they need to search for gold. This analogy applies rather directly to Taiwan.

The export segment of the Taiwan economy, composed primarily of a mix of small and medium-sized firms, represents those who want to strike it rich by manufacturing products for global markets. Entrepreneurs search for products that will hit it big in the export arena, and when one person finds such a product and it becomes known, many others rush into the same area of production.

One of the clearest demonstrations of this gold rush effect can be found in textiles. Fabric making is the only manufacturing sector in which business groups produce more than 50% of total sales. But business groups account for only 12% of the total sales in the garment and apparel sector. Business groups produce the fabrics, not the clothes; the next step is done by countless small factories working on consignments from medium-sized clothing firms, who in turn produce batch orders for major retail outlets located in the United States, Europe, and Southeast Asia. This same process is repeated in almost every other sector, and for almost every large business group.

By far the biggest business group in Taiwan is Formosa Plastics, one of the world's largest producers of PVC (polyvinyl chloride) plastics. Founded by Y. C. Wang in the mid-1950s with government assistance, this group first became important in the 1960s, when Taiwan's small factories began pouring inexpensive plastic products of every type into the world market. "Between 1957 and 1971," notes Ramon Myers (1984), "plastic production grew 45% annually. In 1957 only 100 small firms fabricated products from plastic supplied by Wang's company, but in 1970 more than 1,300 small firms bought from plastic suppliers" (p. 516). By the mid-1980s, more intermediate suppliers of raw plastic had entered the domestic market, so that the top business groups, including Formosa Plastics, accounted for only 42.4% of the total sales of the chemical material sector and a measly 5.4% of the plastic products sector.

The explosion of small firms has also occurred around the manufacture of bicycles and such electronic items as televisions and, most recently, laptop computers. So common is this rush into the same area of production that Taiwanese call this sort of competition "a swarm of bees" (*i wo feng*) (Mark, 1972, p. 28). The swarming effect immediately drives down profits, shortens product cycles, and limits high returns to the first arrivals. This process—the entrepreneurial discovery of new products to sell in global markets and then the headlong rush into the same area of export production—fuels constant but shifting demands for domestic intermediate inputs and for necessary services to make and deliver those products. Taiwan's economic structure rests upon these entrepreneurs, upon their search for and their manufacture of new products that will sell well, and the industrial structure itself shifts as these entrepreneurs shift into new areas of production.

The gold rush analogy works well to explain Taiwan's industrialization because capitalist expansion there rests so heavily upon relatively small-scale entrepreneurs and the way they create export products for and obtain access to world markets. It is the entrepreneur, the analogue of the gold miner, who drives the system. This is individual entrepreneurship that characterizes Taiwan, as opposed to corporate entrepreneurship that characterizes Japan and South Korea. For social structural reasons that I will describe in the next section, the Chinese prefer to be their own bosses, to be entrepreneurs themselves and *laoban* (persons in charge). Moreover, in Taiwan's densely networked economy, entrepreneurship is relatively easy; start-up costs are quite low, capital is comparatively easy to raise, barriers to entry are low, and information about what to do with one's money is ubiquitous.

The omnipresent entrepreneurialism of Taiwan society is not a fiction. The desire to be an independent businessperson and to earn one's living and possibly get rich that way is based in reality. In Taiwan, with a population of 21 million, there are 700,000 registered businesses, all of which have their *laoban*. This works out to be 1 *laoban* for every 15 persons, and if we count only adults, then the figure is 1 *laoban* for every 8 persons (Chang, 1988, p. 10).[7] The Taipei businessman that Tyler Biggs (1988b) quotes, therefore, is exaggerating only slightly when he says, "If you stood in the middle of this city and tossed a stone in any direction, you'd probably hit a boss" (p. 3).

Individuals' desire to be their own bosses creates an extremely high turnover of personnel in most businesses, especially the largest businesses, a fact that is also in direct contrast with the long-term employment practices of Japanese and South Korean businesses. In fact, most Taiwanese believe that if one is really capable, one can own one's own business. As the conventional Chinese saying has it, "It is better to be a rooster's beak than a cow's tail."

This entrepreneurialism can be put into motion with a contrast with South Korea. According to the calculations of Tyler S. Biggs (1988a), who expanded earlier findings by Scitovsky (1986, p. 146), in Taiwan between 1966 and 1986, "the *number* of reported firms increased by 315 percent . . . and the average firm size expanded 15 percent"; in the same time, the exact reverse process occurred in South Korea, where "average *firm* size jumped by 300 percent and its firms grew in number by only 10 percent" (pp. 3-4; emphases added). One can make sense of these diametrically opposed developmental trajectories through Brian Levy's (1988) case studies contrasting the export production of footwear and computer keyboards in Taiwan and South Korea. Levy concludes:

> The comparative field research revealed that Korean producers of footwear tended to be vertically integrated, stitching in-house the uppers for footwear, and manufacturing in-house rubber soles, as well assembling complete shoes; by contrast, Taiwanese producers specialized in footwear assembly, and sub-contracted the task of upper stitching and sole manufacture to independent vendors. Similarly whereas Korean producers of keyboards for personal computers manufactured in-house both plastic key parts and mechanical key-switches, Taiwanese producers tended to procure these components from arms-length suppliers. (p. 44)

Therefore, as economic development in both locations accelerated, South Korean export production grew as the largest businesses further increased the size of their firms. In contrast, Taiwan's export production grew through starting new firms and linking these firms to the output of other small and medium-sized firms. In other words, South Korea grew through management, whereas Taiwan grew through entrepreneurship.

We can specify this distinction between management and entrepreneurship with Howard Pack's (1992) careful econometric study of Taiwan's industrial growth. In trying to explain the high rates of growth in Taiwan's overall productivity, as measured by total factor productivity (TFP) or the value-added component of goods and services, Pack shows that much of Taiwan's growth in productivity can be traced to a rapid increase in exports. But he argues that in most countries, the "major gains" in creating the sources for rapid productivity gains come very early in the industrializing process, with the development of "scale economies" and with "greater utilization of capacity." "Why then," he ponders, "does the supply in Taiwan continue to grow at such rapid rates—is there some characteristic of exports themselves that helps to increase TFP growth?" (p. 86).

Answering his question, Pack goes through a number of theories of export trade that have been offered to explain growth in total factor productivity. Most such theories argue that growth is caused either by the reduction in structural obstacles to efficient markets; by an increase in technology transfers from foreign buyers, returning nationals, and multinational corporations; or by effective state economic policies. Pack finds some contribution from each of these sources, but even together they are insufficient to explain Taiwan's high rates of growth in TFP. For instance, Pack finds "Wade's case that wide [state] intervention was employed to be persuasive," even though "his evidence is anecdotal." Nonetheless, using the state's economic policy to explain the long-term continuity in total factor productivity growth, says Pack, is unconvincing: "While it is possible that the government's attention to a sector accelerated its introduction, to have an impact on measured TFP growth rates requires not an occasional success but a continuing stream of them. The existing evidence . . . does not support this view" (p. 100).

Pack concludes that three features of Taiwan's economy most contribute to rapid TFP growth: rapid shifts in sectoral structure that create new investments, high levels of education, and the importance of small enterprises in the industrial structure. First, Pack finds that the products that Taiwan exports are constantly and quickly changing, with some sectors rapidly rising in importance and some just as rapidly falling. This finding fits with the gold rush effect described above. Pack reasons that these abrupt shifts in products being produced for export require rapid deployment of new capital investments and, even more important, require high levels of education that enable entrepreneurs to be flexible in their orientation. "My own sense of the evidence," states Pack, "is that if any one factor allowed the rapid changes in sectoral structure . . . it is likely to have been the dramatic rise in education" (p. 101).

Both factors—swift investments in rising sectors and high levels of education—Pack continues, are located in and are shaped by an export economy in which small and medium-sized firms dominate. Although Pack (1992) does not explain the exact relationship between an industrial structure dominated by small firms on the one hand and investment and education on the other, he does conclude:

> The ability to maintain a small firm structure surely contributed to productivity growth over the first three decades of industrialization. . . . The smaller firm structure permitted more detailed supervision and the avoidance of principal-agent problems, flexibility in product niches, subcontracting and the exploitation of economies of scope, and the tapping of the ability of many innovative skillful entrepreneurs who would have been consigned to employee status in the larger industrial structure. (p. 106)

Pack points in the right direction. Entrepreneurship in a small-firm economy rather than management in a large-firm economy is the source of Taiwan's dynamic form of capitalism. But his analysis raises more questions than it answers. It does not explain how modest-sized firms in such an economy can be so flexible and still produce great quantities of a vast array of high-quality products that are consumed around the world. That is indeed the question that must be answered if we are to understand Taiwan's economy. It is somehow understandable that huge business groups in Japan or South Korea, linking sometimes thousands of firms of different sizes together and exploiting their internal synergies, can concentrate their research and development efforts and their production expertise to manufacture some of the world's finest products. It is much more difficult to understand—as one walks down dusty streets in central Taiwan and sees family after family working around tables in their storefront homes that are open to everyone's view, or as one drives in the countryside and sees small concrete boxes located in the midst of rice fields that are factories employing only handfuls of people—how someone here, in these locations, could be producing a piece of a part that will go into a component that is in 50% of all the computers worldwide. Taiwan's business organizations achieve both economies of scale and economies of scope, and they do so because they utilize the resources contained in Taiwan's densely networked society.

Embedded Networks in Taiwan's Economy: Vertical and Horizontal Controls

The reason Taiwan has been so successful as a small-firm economy—and, I might add, relatively unsuccessful as a large-firm economy—is found in its distinctive pattern of organizing economic networks. Networks within Asian societies should be seen as institutionalized frameworks of control, and in Taiwan these frameworks center on the family. Every person who has studied Taiwan's business organizations has reached a similar conclusion: Overwhelmingly, Taiwan's privately owned businesses, large and small, are family-owned and family-controlled enterprises. Although certainly correct, this conclusion obscures another related and equally important aspect of Taiwan's economic organization. The networks that exist between family-owned enterprise groups are as crucial to Taiwan's economy as are the business networks that exist within families. In fact, these two types of networks, the intra- and interfamily networks, represent two distinct types of control structures that I will analyze in this section.

When one sets out to analyze family ownership and control, it is essential that one begin with a precise definition of *family*. Here, *family* refers to the unit of procreation; in Chinese this unit is called the *jia*. A family-owned firm, then, is a business owned by persons of the same *jia*. The important point of analysis is how, in different societies, the unit of procreation is embedded in larger kinship and community institutions. Unlike for the Japanese and Koreans, for the Chinese, the *jia* is the foundational building block of a patrilineal, patrilocal kinship system. The patrilineage itself constitutes a network composed of normative, hierarchically structured relationships.

As I have argued in the preceding section, firms in Taiwan are not created in top-down fashion, as a part of a command economy, but rather grow large from the bottom up because of domestic or export demand. As a consequence, the organizational dynamics are very similar in all family-based networks in Taiwan, regardless of whether firms are large or small. All firm owners must contend with intrafamily organizational controls and extrafamily connections. These concerns generate two types of networks. The first type, which I term family networks, occurs within spheres of family control;

like family networks in Korea, these networks are strongly hierarchical, but unlike those in Korea, Taiwan family networks have relatively short vertical spans of control. The second type of network, which I term *guanxi* networks, occurs outside spheres of direct family control; these networks are based on norms of reciprocity, are situationally based, and have broad horizontal spans of control. In this section, I will first describe how these two types of networks are organized and distributed in the Chinese economy, and then explain how both types are embedded features of Chinese society.

Family Ownership and Vertical Controls

As in Japan and South Korea, ownership networks provide a first indication of the patterns of interfirm control. All the researchers who have studied ownership patterns among large firms in Taiwan have emphasized the importance of family (*jia*) ownership and family control (Greenhalgh, 1988; Hamilton & Biggart, 1988; Mark, 1972). An analysis of the 1983 and 1986 data on Taiwan business groups, as well as interviews with core people in some of the business groups, substantiates this finding. Majority ownership and control of business group firms are in the hands of core family members and heads of households. The Tunghai team in Taiwan have determined, on a group-by-group basis, that 84 of the top 97 business groups in 1983 can be strictly classified as family-owned business groups (Peng, 1989, p. 277). Of these, 23 are owned primarily by a single head of household; the remaining 61 business groups have multiple family members classified among the core people in the group, and most of those family members (54 out of the 61) are of three types: fathers and sons, brothers, and brothers and their sons (Peng, 1989, p. 278).

The preponderance of family ownership, however, does not explain the success of Taiwan firms. Quite the reverse is true. As Wong Siu-lun (1985) has so ably described, the Chinese family firm is inherently short-term and unstable. Redding (1991) refers to the Chinese family firm as a "weak organization." A large part of this instability arises from institutional sources, from the kinship system in particular.

The Chinese family, the household (*jia*), or what Fei Xiaotong (1992, p. 81) calls the "small lineage," is the basic unit of the patrilineal patrilocal kinship system. In principle, a patrilineage traces descent through the male line and, accordingly, joins all males in the same line of descent into an organized network of mutual obligation. It is also patrilocal in that the normative residential pattern enjoins married sons and their wives to live in or near their father's house.

Because the number of males included in a patrilineage grows geometrically across generations and rapidly fills whatever space exists, patrilineages always segment into smaller units that correspond not only to differences in age and generation but also to differences in wealth, power, and residential location. This quality of segmentation means that every male simultaneously is linked to all other males in his line of descent and is the potential founder of a new lineage segment. In normative terms, males are obligated to their kinsmen, particularly those kinsmen closest to them—to uncles, grandfathers, and especially fathers. Males are also obligated to extend their lineage into the future by establishing their own small lineages, their own households with lines of male descendants. This dual obligation—to other people in the lineage on one hand and to oneself as a propagator of the lineage in the future on the other—institutionalizes a conflict over the control of resources within households and between households that reverberates through the entire society and creates institutional patterns that shape the economy.

The first of these institutional patterns is that of ownership and inheritance. In theory as well as in practice, Chinese family firms are the property of the household, "small lineages," and not individuals. In the West, unincorporated firms are the property of an individual owner and can be passed on to the owner's legal heirs as specified in a will. In the case of corporations, property rights are split among a set of owners, each of whom has a specifiable number of shares, and inheritance rules apply to the shares held and not to the whole firm. In Chinese societies such as Taiwan, however, firms are specifically household property, but also are considered to belong, at a more abstract level, to a general pool of resources that lineage members can utilize if the need arises. Therefore, when viewed in the short term, a head of household has authoritative control over household property. In the long term, however, the head of household is merely the custodian of a past inheritance that will be passed on to future holders, his sons and his sons' sons. At the same time, the current head of household is also obligated to the members of his lineage outside of his household. Depending upon their distance from him, these relatives have a legitimate moral claim to lineage assets, because they are in principle shared assets; the closer the relationship, the stronger the claim on the resources. Conceptually, then, assets, like the lineage itself, are produced and reproduced across time. Individuals may die, property may be sold, but the lineage and its collective assets, though divided and controlled by the many households in the lineage, continue into the future.

Inheritance in this system is necessarily partible: Each having an obligation to start his own household and each being potentially the head of a lineage segment in the future, all sons receive equal shares of their father's estate. Established inheritance rules specify that, at some point after the father dies, the sons will *fen jia,* will divide the household and all its assets on a formal basis. Taking their own shares from the past and being the heads of their own small lineages, the sons will start building their own estates, which will be divided after they die. After *fen jia,* the brothers may jointly cooperate in mutual business activities, but even if they do, no brother has the authoritative claim to exclusive control over what the father once controlled. Each brother has become the father and the head of his own household. Subsequently, brothers might cooperate as close colleagues, formally ranked according to seniority, but it is unlikely that this cooperation will produce a unified, authoritatively controlled organization, as is the case in Korea.

Based upon his studies of Chinese businesses in Hong Kong and Southeast Asia, Wong (1985) has developed a theoretical model of the Chinese family firm that incorporates the institutional dynamics of the patrilineal kinship system. He suggests that firms typically go through a cycle of four stages. In the first, the "emergent stage," early in the household's existence, the family, led by the father, accumulates capital through loans from family and friends and sometimes through the establishment of a partnership with a friend or trusted business acquaintance. In this stage, the head of household has absolute control over the enterprise, and if a system of shareholding is established, the head of household will claim the "founder's shares," which are equivalent in voting power to all other shares combined.

In the second stage, which Wong calls the "centralization stage," the father will heavily reinvest the firm's profits and centralize the control of decision making over money and strategy. If the business began as a partnership in the first stage, in the second the founding and dominant family will occupy all the positions of power and responsibility in the firm. Also in this stage, the sons are gradually brought into the business and groomed for the various business roles they will later assume.

In the third stage, the "segmentation stage," the founder retires or dies, and the sons assume control of the firm. If the business is good and sufficient to support the heirs, the surviving sons may decide not to divide the estate at the time of the father's death. If that is the case, the sons involved in the business will typically divide the business into spheres of influence over which individual sons will have control. Having served in the firm the longest and having the most managerial experience, the eldest son may take a key managerial role in the overall business. But as this situation continues over time, each son will gradually operate more independently of the others and will begin to bring his own sons into his area as well.

The fourth stage is the "disintegration stage." The surviving sons of the original founder, or their sons, decide finally to *fen jia*. By this stage, the points of disagreement and conflict among the heirs inevitably will have become insurmountable. The sons' sons will be dealing with their uncles and with their cousins. Inheritance is further complicated as the sons of the original founder will have unequal numbers of sons themselves. In the end, it becomes easier to divide the assets of the firm formally and for each of the surviving households to go its own way, which in turn starts the process of accumulation over again.

My own analysis of the largest business groups in Taiwan suggests that Wong's model needs to be amended to reflect the fact that successful accumulation results in the creation of a group of independent firms, rather than in the enlargement of a single firm. But given that addition, Wong's model is substantially correct. My revision, however, is an important one. Corresponding to what would be the early part of the centralization stage in Wong's model, the founders of successful firms will begin to reinvest their profits. At this point, do they expand the size of their successful firm, thereby capturing a greater share of the market in which they are operating, or do they diversify? At this crucial moment of decision, the data show that, in case after case, the founders of firms elect to diversify by establishing new independent firms, often in unrelated areas.

Intragroup Diversification

In examining these diversification strategies, however, one quickly recognizes that the strategies themselves are directly shaped by the same kinship dynamics that Wong identifies in his model of the Chinese firm. Within business groups, one finds two closely related types of diversification. First, firms in business groups are frequently spread across diverse product lines. As described above, there is often a core of vertically integrated firms reflecting the product line of the founding firms, but typically there are also additional sets of firms within business groups in areas completely unrelated to the core product lines. For instance, in the case of one business group of 13 firms, the first and still most successful firm is in textiles, but the second and third firms are in chemicals. The group subsequently started other firms related to textile production, but also started a hog farm and a magnet factory. The rationale for starting these factories differed case by case, but always revolved around the personal decisions of the owners. In one instance, an old friend asked one of the owners to help him out by investing money in the firm. Later the friend asked him to buy the firm.

Opportunistic diversification seems to be the rule. Business groups usually start with some core firms begun by the founders; these firms are then followed by opportunistic expansion into the same or other lines of endeavor. The strategy of expansion is to start new firms, even within the same product line, rather than to enlarge greatly the size of the original firm. This investment pattern leads to an unusually wide spread of product lines within groups and results in business groups' being largely composed of a series of medium-sized firms. This pattern is particularly relevant when compared with the investment patterns of Korean and Japanese business groups, where strong pressure toward vertical integration exists. By comparison, Taiwan's business groups resemble conglomerates.

According to a survey of the owners of the top business groups in Taiwan in the 1970s (Liu, Kuo, Huang, & Situ, 1981), the eventuality of *fen jia* is one of the main reasons business leaders choose to diversify. This trend shows up in the analysis of my data and in the interviews conducted by Kao Cheng-shu and his research team. Knowing that all household assets will eventually be divided among their sons, founders have an affinity for spreading household assets among independent firms. Sons assume top management in these firms while the father is still alive, and at the point of *fen jia* there is no need to take apart a vertically integrated firm, which would destroy an established business and greatly erode long-term lineage assets. By starting independent firms, the founder has, in effect, already divided the assets. The sons can simply continue as they have in the past, but now without their father's supervision.

Duplicating Hierarchies

Underlying this diversification among firms is another type of diversification, that of the management structure itself, which illustrates the weak, short spans of control achieved in family firms. Firms in a group tend to be

organizationally separate from other firms, each having a distinct management structure. Until recently, business groups had no formal unified management organization linking all the firms together, although in some groups
there has recently been a move in this direction (China Credit Information
Service, 1985). Instead, each firm has a person who formally occupies the
position of manager (*jingli*). This person may or may not be a family member
and, in fact, often is not. The person is usually a "professional" manager, in
terms of either education or experience. These firm managers, in turn, are
seldom linked into a larger formal management structure beyond the firms.
In this way, day-to-day management of firms is separated from the actual
control of the group. Management is defined, by comparison, as a lower-level
activity; it remains distinct from all long-term decisions affecting individual
firms as well as the group itself. Control of all these types of decisions
remains, as I will describe below, in the hands of the owners and those in the
inner circle. Therefore, management tends to be formal and localized to each
firm, whereas control tends to be informal and spans the group of family-
owned firms.

In theory, this separation of management and control is manifest in the
two separate types of positions found in most firms. One type identifies the
hierarchy assigned the responsibilities of operational management (*jingli*);
the other type identifies the hierarchy associated with control (*dongshi*). In
fact, it often occurs that an owner will assume both positions simultaneously,
and will be known formally as *dongshijang jien zhongjingli* (director of the
board and general manager). This split between control and management in
family enterprises parallels the split between control and management of
household and lineage assets that Myron Cohen (1976) has documented in
traditional Taiwanese families: "The general management of family enterprises may be distinguished from the fiscal management and control. The
first involves the disposition of family workers and the operation of the
family farm or other enterprises, while the second concerns family funds"
(pp. 90-91). Cohen shows that control over money is tightly held by the head
of household (*chia-chang*), but management responsibilities can be dispersed among family members. It should not be surprising that large-scale
family-owned business groups follow the same organizational patterns associated with practices in traditional Chinese families. My own research and
that of others (e.g., Tong, 1991) shows that this organizational split between
control and management has become an institutionalized feature of large,

modern Chinese-owned business groups in Hong Kong and Southeast Asia as well.

This duplication of hierarchies in firms and the managerial separation of firms in a business group lead to the multiplication of positions that key people in a business group hold. As shown in Tables 9.4 and 9.5, the same people hold a range of positions in different firms. It is not unusual for the same person simultaneously to hold multiple positions in the same firm as well as the same positions in several different firms in the business group. This pattern described for the top six firms in Table 9.4 holds throughout all the business groups. Moreover, this management pattern further sets Taiwan firms off from their counterparts in Japan and South Korea, where most key personnel have only one position in the business group. In fact, the duplication of an individual's positions commonly results in business cards requiring a full page and sometimes an additional page simply to list all the positions the person holds.

The Inner Circle

These overlapping hierarchies that form around a handful of key persons in the business groups coalesce into an inner circle. The inner circle consists of those few key people toward whom the principal owner feels the greatest degree of trust and confidence. This inner circle cannot necessarily be identified by outsiders, because it may not contain some individuals, such as an elder son, whom most would expect to be included. However, all informants interviewed by Kao and his team spoke about and felt they could accurately identify the inner circles of their own organizations. Ordinarily, the inner circles of business groups consist of the owners and a few close family members, but also often include longtime business associates and sometimes other sorts of confidants, such as a mistress. In fact, the China Credit Information Service survey lists the core persons in every business group that the business groups themselves identify. This listing can be seen as the core of the inner circle.

The closeness of this core group and the segmentation of firms and managerial positions in the business groups strengthen the control of owners and their confidants and lessen the possibility that their centrality can be challenged successfully. This exclusiveness and concern with control have several practical consequences. In many business groups, each member firm

Table 9.4 Isomorphism in the Management of the Top Six Taiwanese *Jituanqiye*, 1983 Data

Group	Firms	Core Persons	Relationship	Positions Held by Core Persons		
				Director	Manager	Stockholder
Formosa	18	2	two brothers	10	5	14
Linden	12	1	—	5	0	1
Tainan	33	11	two families	28	7	59
Yue Loong	10	1	—	7	2	4
Far Eastern	17	4	family and one friend	9	8	10
Shin Kong	21	5	one family	21	12	18

SOURCE: China Credit Information Service (1985).

Table 9.5 Numbers of Positions and Numbers of Persons in Positions in Taiwan Business Groups

		Chair/ Vice Chair		Manager/ Vice Manager	
Group	Number of Firms	Total Positions	Total Persons	Total Positions	Total Persons
Associated	N/A	N/A	N/A	N/A	N/A
Bow Chao Yun	9	9	4	7	5
Cathay Formost	7	6	1	5	4
Cathay Plastic	8	10	2	6	4
Cathay Trust	25	25	11	20	13
Chang Chun Petrochemical	4	4	2	4	4
Chao Tin Cheng	12	12	2	9	8
Chen Hong Chemical	14	14	10	3	3
Cheng Loong	6	6	3	6	6
Chi Mei Industrial	11	12	10	10	10
Chia Fha Industries	7	7	5	2	1
Chia Hsin Cement	4	4	3	4	3
Chien Hsin	4	4	3	3	3
Chih Lien Industrial	5	5	2	3	2
Chin Ho Fa Steel & Iron	3	3	2	3	2
China Chemical	3	3	2	3	3
China Investment & Trust	19	16	6	15	14
China Rebar	3	4	3	3	2
Chu Chen	3	3	1	3	1
Chun Yu Works	4	4	3	4	3
Chun Yuan Steel	7	7	6	6	2
Cosmos	10	10	5	10	8
E-Hsin International	6	6	5	6	6
Eternal Chemical	4	4	2	4	2
Ever Glory	13	5	6	15	11
Far Eastern	18	15	7	14	8
Fong Kuo Fishery	3	3	2	3	1
Formosa Plastics	18	18	9	16	12
Formosan Rubber	4	4	3	4	3
Fu I Industrial	3	3	1	3	1
Fu Tai Umbrella Works	7	7	1	7	1
Great Electronics	4	4	1	4	3
Ho Cheng	7	7	3	5	4
Hsu Chin Te	8	8	1	8	7
Hui Shung	6	6	5	3	2
Hua Eng Copper & Iron	4	4	2	4	1
International Auto	5	5	2	4	4
Kou Fong Industrial	14	14	10	12	10
Kung Hsue She	6	6	4	6	5
Kuo Chan Development	7	8	4	7	7
Kwong Fong Industries	3	3	2	2	1
Lea Lea	3	3	2	3	1

(continued)

Table 9.5 Continued

Group	Number of Firms	Chair/ Vice Chair		Manager/ Vice Manager	
		Total Positions	Total Persons	Total Positions	Total Persons
Lien Fu Garment	6	6	5	3	2
Lien Fu Flour	3	3	1	3	1
Lien Hwa Industrial	5	5	2	5	4
Lien-I Textiles	6	6	4	6	5
Linden International	12	12	7	9	9
Lio Ho Cotton Weaving	6	6	3	6	4
Lucky Cement	11	11	8	5	5
Men Yi Textile	4	4	4	4	4
Nan Chow Chemical	6	6	2	5	5
National Electric	6	6	2	6	5
Ocean Plastics	4	4	3	2	2
Oemec	7	7	3	7	6
Overseas Trust	12	12	6	9	8
Pacific Electric Wire	8	8	6	8	7
Prince Motors	4	4	2	3	2
Ruentex Industries	6	6	3	6	3
Sampo	10	10	6	8	8
Sam Shin Trading	7	7	2	7	2
San Wu Textile	3	3	3	3	3
San Yang Industry	8	8	3	8	7
Shin Kong	21	22	5	21	11
Shin Yen Textile	4	4	1	4	3
Shinung	4	4	2	4	2
Shung Ye Trading	5	6	5	3	2
Sino-Japan Feed	5	5	1	3	2
South East Cement	5	5	1	4	4
Sun-Lai	9	9	3	7	4
Ta Ya Electric Wire	3	3	1	3	2
Tah Hsin Industrial	5	5	1	4	4
Tai Hsin	4	4	1	4	3
Tai Hwa Oil	4	4	1	3	3
Tai Roun	8	8	5	8	6
Tai Shing Factory Oil	3	3	2	3	3
Taigene Electric	6	6	1	6	4
Tainan Spinning	35	35	15	31	27
Taiwan Cement	7	6	3	6	6
Taiwan Glass	7	6	2	7	2
Taiwan Pineapple	3	3	2	1	1
Tatung	29	29	10	30	26
Teco Elec. & Machinery	10	10	8	7	7
Tong Fong Trading	8	9	8	1	1
Tong Hsing Enterprise	4	4	1	3	1
Transworld	4	4	4	4	3
Tung Ho Steel	3	3	2	3	3
Tuntex	11	11	7	11	11
U-Lead	8	8	5	6	3

Table 9.5 Continued

Group	Number of Firms	Chair/ Vice Chair		Manager/ Vice Manager	
		Total Positions	Total Persons	Total Positions	Total Persons
Universal	10	10	3	9	8
Ve Dan	5	5	3	5	2
Wan Hsiang Tannery	3	3	2	0	0
Wei Chuan	14	15	11	13	13
Wintide Enterprises	6	6	1	5	1
Yeh Shan Mu	7	8	5	6	4
Yue Loong Motor	10	10	4	10	9
Yuen Foong	23	23	8	21	16
Total	738	741	367	628	480

keeps a separate account book. These separate accounts themselves are not integrated into a central accounting system, but rather remain separate; their contents are known only to the members of the inner circle, sometimes only to the key owner himself.[8] Another consequence, according to Kao's informants, is that owners are very reluctant to list their companies on the stock exchange for fear of losing exclusive control and of having to divulge financial information about the business group.[9]

Although control of assets is centralized, the management of people is decentralized, in large part because management involves identifiable personal relationships between the manager (*laoban*) and the employees. Many ethnographies of Chinese family firms stress the importance of personal relationships in maintaining the labor force. Managers try to employ friends and friends of friends, relatives and relatives of relatives, thereby overlapping the employer-employee relationship with a more personal bond. One of the key aspects of management, then, is the maintenance of a double bond created by the joining of firm and family. As most ethnographies show, this double bond often leads to managers' exploitation of their employees. In Taiwan's highly competitive economy, the needs of business often overwhelm the decorum in families. In the end, the tension between family management and worker exploitation encourages those who are not close family members and those who do not share in the control of assets to escape from the direct control of management.

Not all firms, of course, are managed this way. A few of the larger firms have attempted to "professionalize" their management by utilizing Western management techniques. A few other firms have offered their employees shares of the firms in exchange for their loyalty and continued employment. In all of these firms, however, employee turnover remains high, because the desire to start one's own family firm and the opportunities in owning a family firm seem always to be greater than one would have as an employee in someone else's firm.

With these additions, Wong's model shows that Chinese kinship institutions foster a small-firm economy. Even when businesses are very successful, assets, property, even managerial controls are still continually being subdivided. The process of asset accumulation leads to the establishment of new firms and to the formation of diversified business groups instead of large vertically integrated firms or even large vertically integrated networks of firms as occurs in Japan or South Korea. Firms are primarily asset holders for lineage interests, and when firms are not profitable, the assets are shifted to other sites. Subdividing, diversifying, and reallocating assets occurs within, and is accelerated by, an institutional environment that makes allowances for the diversification strategies of family ownership. These diversification strategies build upon the entrepreneurial ability to create horizontal linkages, to create interfamily networks that are based upon shared resources, or what I call *guanxi* ownership.

Guanxi Ownership and Horizontal Controls

Besides family ownership, most businesses also include a second type of ownership, *guanxi* ownership. *Guanxi* is a Chinese term meaning "relationship," but the Chinese do not classify all possible relationships as *guanxi*. Instead, *guanxi* is a term conventionally reserved for certain sets of ties that are bound by norms of reciprocity (*huibao*) or by what is more commonly referred to in Chinese as human emotion (*renqing* or *ganqing*). Very close familial ties, such as those between parents and children or husband and wife, are not based on reciprocity but rather on obedience (*xiao*), with the subordinate in the hierarchical relationship necessarily obligated to obey the superior (Hamilton, 1984, 1990; Hwang, 1987). Although parents and husbands have moral obligations to children and wives, children are morally and normatively required to obey their parents and wives their husbands, regardless of what the other party in the relationship demands. Within the household, therefore, norms of reciprocity do not provide a basis for action.

Likewise, many relationships, such as those that occur between people who are formally strangers, as between a clerk and customer in a store, are also not bound by norms of reciprocity. But between the familial and the distant, there are categories of relationships, should individuals choose to activate them, that are bound by norms of reciprocity. These categories include relationships between distant kinsmen, between neighbors, between class-mates, between coworkers, between people of the same surname, and be-tween people from the same region.

Most sociologists of Chinese society argue that *guanxi,* which includes relations and relation building, lies at the heart of Chinese society. Ambrose King (1991) writes:

> *Guanxi* building is based on shared "attributes" such as kinship, locality, surname, and so on, which are the building blocks the individual employs to establish "pluralistic" identifications with multiple individuals and groups. Indeed, network building is used (consciously or unconsciously) by Chinese adults as a cultural strategy in mobilizing social resources for goal attainment in various spheres of social life. To a significant degree the cultural dynamic of *guanxi* building is a source of vitality in Chinese society. (p. 79)

Probably better than anyone, Fei Xiaotong (1992) has worked out a theory of Chinese society showing that the very structure of society consists of networks built up from differentially categorized social relationships and *guanxi* building. Chinese society is not created from the top down through encompassing organizations and vertical chains of command, but rather, says Fei (1992), from the bottom up, from "webs woven out of countless personal relationships" (p. 78). These webs have only small degrees of hierarchy. As Mayfair Yang (1989) puts it: "In the art of *guanxi,* this transformation (from the unfamiliar to the familiar) occurs in the process of appealing to shared identities between persons—hence the emphasis on 'shared' (*tong*) qualities and experiences. . . . Familiarity, then, is born of the fusion of personal identities. And shared identities establish the basis for the obligation and compulsion to share one's wealth and to help with one's labor" (pp. 40-41). As these and other writers show, *guanxi* is not merely a cultural practice; it is one of the main organizational principles of Chinese society.

It is, therefore, not surprising to discover that Taiwan's economic organi-zations are often the products of *guanxi* networks and *guanxi* building. For Taiwan's largest business groups, *guanxi* networks are a primary source of investment capital and constitute an important type of ownership. In addition to family ownership, all firms within all the top 100 business groups are also limited partnerships. Of the 97 business groups in the 1983 data set, 12 are actually owned and managed by two or more unrelated individuals. Such partnerships are typically short-term arrangements, for sooner or later one partner or the other will assume control of the group (Wong, 1985; Yong, 1992). In this sense, limited partnerships in the Chinese context are not equivalent to those found in the West. By long convention, "every Chinese partnership is represented by one individual, who is solely responsible to the outside world for the solvency of his firm" (Anonymous, 1887, p. 41). In many cases, the Chinese practice of creating partnerships is similar to having "silent partners," people who do not participate actively in making business decisions, but who earn profits on their capital investments and who may represent the firm or firms to outsiders on behalf of the real owners.

More important in the Chinese context, these silent partners are usually either more distant kinsmen or, just as likely, members of the owner's personal network of acquaintances, his *guanxi* network.[10] In our 1983 sample of Taiwan's largest 96 business groups, which consists of 743 firms, every firm lists a number of such co-owners. Not counting duplications, which are numerous, there are nearly 2,500 names of co-owners listed for the 743 firms, some of whom are close family members and others of whom are friends, coworkers, and distant relatives.

How are the two types of ownership—family and *guanxi*—distributed? The data on the top business group enumerate only the shareholders and not the actual distribution of shares. Therefore, we cannot quantify the distribution of ownership or, on the basis of names alone, distinguish clearly between the two types of owners. However, based on interviews, on analyzing the few groups and firms whose ownership is known, and upon previous studies, it is a general rule of thumb that majority ownership is closely held within the family circle. In the two cases studied by Mark (1972), the family retained more than 50% of the shares, and among the business group owners interviewed by Kao Cheng-shu and his research team, family members normally retained majority control (Lin, 1991; Peng, 1989). In one case, however, the founder of a firm who became involved in a joint venture controlled only 25% of the shares; later, after a dispute among the other owners, he lost his position entirely. He subsequently started a new firm, proclaiming that he would "never control less than 70% of the shares" of his new firm (Lin, 1991, p. 97). As a rule, family control requires majority ownership.

Guanxi investors, however, remain an important feature of ownership. In her survey of firms in Taiwan, Mark (1972) concludes, "Almost all family firms have a large number of non-kin shareholders, while most non-kin enterprises tend to be dominated by several family blocks" (p. xv). "The Taiwan family enterprise," Greenhalgh (1988) notes, "relies extensively on networks of kin and friends for strategic resources such as labor, capital, and information" (p. 234). Neither Mark nor Greenhalgh makes a distinction between family and nonfamily networks, but Ichiro Numazaki (1986, 1991a, 1991b) clearly does (see this distinction also in Hamilton, 1990, 1991; Yong, 1992).

Numazaki argues that partnerships and other types of personal relationships among people from different families constitute a distinctive feature of Taiwan's economy. In an early article titled "Networks of Taiwanese Big Business: A Preliminary Analysis" (1986), he argues that the relationships among the top business groups are extensively interlocked, and hence Taiwan possesses a cohesive business elite. "The inner circle of the Taiwanese business elite is a distinct and dominant 'class segment' in contemporary Taiwan" (p. 520). His more recent works would qualify that conclusion somewhat. My own data demonstrate, however, that Taiwan's business elite, unlike the Japanese case, is by no means a unified one in terms of mutual shareholding. Nonetheless, Numazaki's main point that *guanxi* partners and family owners should be distinguished is very important. On the one hand, he notes, "What these diverse *guanxi* networks share . . . is that all are horizontal networks which allow individuals to expand their contacts beyond the narrow confines of immediate family. This type of personal network enables entrepreneurs to mobilize a wide range of people for investment and political purposes" (1991a, p. 90). On the other hand, he argues that family networks "are vertical ones. Father-son relationship stands out as the basic principle of inheritance. . . . In the case of inheritance at least, these vertical networks function as a mechanism for drawing group boundaries" (1991a, p. 90). This distinction between the verticality of family networks and the horizontal nature of *guanxi* networks goes to the heart of Chinese economic organization.

An analysis of ownership networks within Taiwan's business groups offers a first glimpse of the nature of the two kinds of networks. The data indicate that the ownership of firms is concentrated within business groups and not shared across business groups. Essentially, this ownership concentration means that each major business family has a distinctive set of trusted associates with whom they jointly own all firms in a business group. This joining of a family and its close business associates leads to tightly interlocked clusters of owners within business groups.

Circles characterized by high degrees of trust and strict rules of reciprocation among participants can, by definition, include only so many people. Accordingly, if a *guanxi* tie is the primary linkage between family and nonfamily owners, then one would expect very little overlap among clusters of owners. This outcome is exactly what we find. In fact, in comparison with patterns of interlocks in other countries, we find extraordinarily low levels of interlocking among business groups. My data, therefore, give evidence neither for the patterns of mutual shareholding so common in Japan nor for the formally interconnected unified business elite, the "web of partnerships," that Numazaki (1986) finds.

I used two procedures to reach these conclusions. First, to assess the density of intragroup interlocks, I constructed an index of ownership concentration within business groups (Table 9.6). An index reading of one would indicate that each firm in a group is owned and managed by the same set of people. This is a condition of 100% interlock, and would also indicate very high levels of family ownership and very low levels of *guanxi* ownership. An index reading of zero would indicate that each firm in a group is owned and managed by a discrete set of people, a condition of no interlocks whatsoever. This situation would indicate low levels of both shared family ownership and overlapping ties. For instance, take as an example a business group owned by three brothers. An index reading of one for this group would indicate that each brother holds an ownership or a management position in each of the three firms. An index reading of zero would indicate that each brother exclusively owns and manages his own firm and has nothing to do with the other firms. Because there is a kinship linkage among brothers, both types of groups would be listed in the China Credit Information Service survey, the source of my data.

A comparison of this measure of ownership concentration across business groups shows that only a very few groups are tightly interlocked, but that most groups still have a substantial amount of intragroup interlocking. On a case-by-case basis, this interlocking indicates that similar sets of family members and *guanxi* owners combine assets for each firm in the group. As might be expected, the fewer the firms and the fewer the owners (both of which correlate directly), the higher the level of ownership concentration (see Figures 9.1 and 9.2). Accordingly, the largest business groups, such as

Table 9.6 Index of Ownership Concentration in Taiwan Business Groups, 1983 (sorted by index)

Group	Number of Firms	Number of Major Owners	Index
Chu Chen	3	8	0.8750
Tai Shing Factory Oil	3	7	0.8571
Lea Lea	3	10	0.7500
Lien Fu Flour	3	6	0.7500
Prince Motors	4	10	0.6333
China Rebar	3	17	0.5000
Wintide Enterprises	6	14	0.4714
Shung Ye Trading	5	13	0.4615
Tung Ho Steel	3	12	0.4583
Chin Ho Fa Steel & Iron	3	10	0.4500
Ve Dan	5	15	0.4500
Hui Shung	6	13	0.4462
Transworld	4	9	0.4444
Fong Kuo Fishery	3	9	0.3889
Tong Hsing Enterprise	4	12	0.3889
Sam Shin Trading	7	16	0.3854
Chia Fha Industries	7	16	0.3333
Chien Hsin	4	12	0.3333
Hua Eng Copper & Iron	4	12	0.3333
Wan Hsiang Tannery	3	11	0.3182
Great Electronics	4	17	0.3137
Chih Lien Industrial	5	12	0.3125
San Wu Textile	3	15	0.3000
Ocean Plastics	4	15	0.2889
Formosan Rubber	4	11	0.2727
E-Hsin International	6	21	0.2667
Ruentex Industries	6	20	0.2600
Chun Yu Works	4	14	0.2381
Shinung	4	17	0.2353
Cathay Formost	7	18	0.2222
Tai Hsin	4	18	0.2222
Shin Yen Textile	4	16	0.2083
Taiwan Glass	7	16	0.2083
Chia Hsin Cement	4	18	0.2037
Lio Ho Cotton Weaving	6	18	0.2000
Sino-Japan Feed	4	20	0.2000
Associated	12	18	0.1970
Chang Chun Petrochemical	4	12	0.1944
Fu Tai Umbrella Works	7	26	0.1859
Tai Hwa Oil	4	22	0.1818
Taigene Electric	6	20	0.1800
Kwong Fong Industries	3	14	0.1786
Ta Ya Electric Wire	3	14	0.1786

(continued)

Table 9.6 Continued

Group	Number of Firms	Number of Major Owners	Index
Ho Cheng	7	16	0.1667
National Electric	6	11	0.1636
Chun Yuan Steel	7	27	0.1605
Lien Fu Garment	6	20	0.1600
San Yang Industry	8	20	0.1571
Ever Glory	13	30	0.1528
Men Yi Textile	4	18	0.1481
Kung Hsue She	6	19	0.1474
China Chemical	3	17	0.1471
Oemec	7	25	0.1467
Lucky Cement	11	34	0.1412
Universal	10	23	0.1401
Bow Chao Yun	9	18	0.1389
Tah Hsin Industrial	5	18	0.1389
U-Lead	8	23	0.1366
Fu I Industrial	3	15	0.1333
Lien-I Textiles	6	26	0.1308
Sun-Lai	9	25	0.1300
Tai Roun	8	33	0.1212
Nan Chow Chemical	6	17	0.1176
Cathay Plastic	8	23	0.1118
Tong Fong Trading	8	32	0.1116
South East Cement	5	23	0.1087
Sampo	10	27	0.1029
Cosmos	10	36	0.1019
Chi Mei Industrial	11	42	0.0952
Eternal Chemical	4	22	0.0909
Kuo Chan Development	7	26	0.0897
Pacific Electric Wire	8	31	0.0876
International Auto	5	20	0.0875
Cheng Loong	6	28	0.0857
Tuntex	11	42	0.0857
Far Eastern	18	32	0.0790
Overseas Trust	12	47	0.0735
Lien Hwa Industrial	5	24	0.0729
Yue Loong Motor	10	43	0.0724
Hsu Chin Te	8	43	0.0698
Taiwan Cement	7	22	0.0682
Taiwan Pineapple	3	16	0.0625
Kou Fong Industrial	14	53	0.0610
Cathay Trust	25	57	0.0585
Yeh Shan Mu	7	41	0.0569
Yuen Foong	23	61	0.0559
Shin Kong	21	63	0.0556
Teco Elec. & Machinery	10	26	0.0513

Table 9.6 Continued

Group	Number of Firms	Number of Major Owners	Index
Chao Tin Cheng	12	44	0.0455
Linden International	12	40	0.0455
Wei Chuan	14	68	0.0362
Formosa Plastics	18	57	0.0330
China Investment & Trust	19	50	0.0311
Tatung	29	55	0.0305
Chen Hong Chemical	14	64	0.0276
Tainan Spinning	35	123	0.0249
Total	749	2,440	0.2128 Average

NOTE: Firms for which no data are available on owners are excluded ($N = 58$). The number of firms used here is lower than the real total (807). The index figures are arrived at as follows: Index = (TIE − MIN)/RANGE($0 \leq$ Index ≤ 1), where FIRM = the number of firms in a group; OWNER = the number of major owners in a group; TIE = total positions occupied by owners, with all positions held by a person in one single firm, counted once (e.g., if a person was listed as the chair of the board, general manager, and one of the major shareholders of a firm, he was counted as having 1 tie in that firm, not 3); MAX = the maximum possible ties, or FIRM * OWNER; MIN = the minimum possible ties (equal to the number of owners); and RANGE = MAX − MIN.

Formosa Plastics and Tainan Spinning, have the lowest readings on the index. These groups have wide sets of nonfamily owners for the firms within the groups, but even so they remain tightly held by core families.[11] The smaller business groups, those with three to seven member firms, are more likely to be owned and managed by tightly interlocked sets of people, usually family members and a few close friends.

The second assessment of ownership, and a sharp contrast to the degrees of intragroup interlocking, is the very, very low level of interlocking among business groups. Of the 2,440 people listed as owners, directors, or managers, only 37 appear in two or more groups. Of these 37 people, only 5 appear in three or more groups. Figure 9.3 diagrams the intergroup interlocks in 1983. This diagram shows the centrality of two investment and trust companies, but at levels far below what one would find in Japanese, German, or even American bank-centered business networks.

The low level of interlocking among groups but the fairly high levels of interlocking within groups show that ownership of Taiwan's largest firms is clustered within groups of key families and their *guanxi* networks. This finding takes on further meaning when one examines two additional patterns

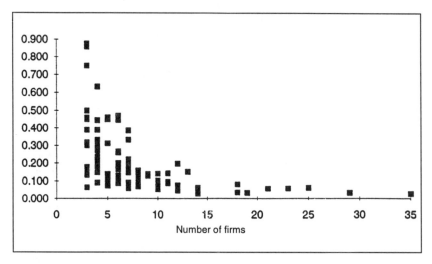

Figure 9.1.   Number of Firms in Business Group Versus Concentration Index, Taiwan, 1983

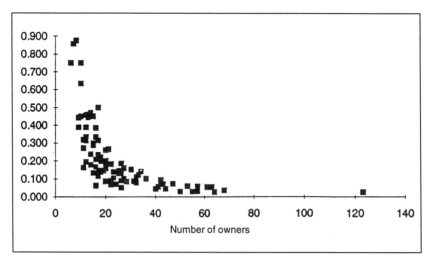

Figure 9.2.   Number of Owners in Business Group Versus Concentration Index, Taiwan, 1983

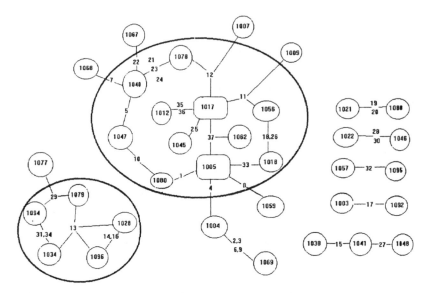

Figure 9.3. Intergroup Ownership in Taiwan's Business Groups, 1983

Investment Networks

As in South Korea, in Taiwan, until quite recently, the stock market was not used as a source of investment capital for business group firms. Only a few of the 97 business groups have even one listed firm. Unlike in South Korea, however, firms in Taiwan are not heavily financed through loans from government-owned banks or from international sources, such as the World Bank or multinational corporations. Instead, according to Tyler Biggs (1988b, pp. 26-29), capital investments for the manufacturing firms in the private sector come from two main sources. First, the largest portion, about 45-55%, comes from accumulated profits that were then reinvested to expand existing firms and to start new firms. The smaller the firm, the more likely it is that the owners supplied the capital themselves. Second, the next-largest portion, about 30% of the total investment capital, comes from the unregulated curb market, that is from family, friends, and personal associates. Again, the smaller the firm, the more likely it is that the owners obtained their investment capital from informal money markets.[12]

portion, about 30% of the total investment capital, comes from the unregulated curb market, that is from family, friends, and personal associates. Again, the smaller the firm, the more likely it is that the owners obtained their investment capital from informal money markets.[12]

Small and medium-sized firms, as we have seen, constitute the vast majority of Taiwan's firms and the leading segment of export manufacturing. By all accounts, a very large portion of these firms obtain their capital outside of formal channels, and it has been this way throughout the industrializing period. "In theory," notes Lee Sheng-Yi (1990), "as the money and capital markets become more developed, the informal money market should lose its significance. However, in spite of the falling interest rates [in the formal money markets in 1986 and 1987], the share of the informal money market was no lower" (p. 36). Taiwan's informal money market is, in fact, so large that in 1986 it accounted, according to Lee's (1990, p. 36-37) analysis of Taiwan's financial system, for about 20% of the money flow for the entire country. And it is also large enough that over time it has become a well-institutionalized source of investment and operating capital. The Central Bank of Taiwan even compiles and publishes the prevailing interest rates, including regional differences, for three categories of informal money markets: loans against postdated checks, unsecured loans, and deposits with firms (Lee, 1990, p. 34).

The major proportion of investment capital obtained in the informal market comes through unsecured loans. These loans are made through various types of savings clubs and mutual aid associations (*hui*), some of which are organized on a temporary basis and others of which are more permanent. "The basic condition for each of these associations," says Lin Pao-an (1991), "is its constituted base—a group of people joined by personal trust. The members may be one's relatives, friends, neighbors, or colleagues. For strangers to be included is rather rare. The rights and duties of *hui* members are based on personal trust. There are no formal laws and no administrative agencies to enforce the obligations of *hui* members" (p. 106).

Large businesses use bank loans much more frequently than do small businesses, especially for operating expenses. But even the large business groups, notes Kao Cheng-shu (1991), "rely heavily upon the private sector, which includes family members, friends, and business partners. . . . The private sector is the most important source of funds for businesses . . . in capital formation or in investment, businessmen always have to build a back-up system that can support them at the right time and in the right place. In

[Taiwan] a personal network based upon 'personal trust' is the foundation of this back-up system" (p. 71).

This backup system based on trust relationships in a personal *guanxi* network is what shows up in the data analysis described above. This *guanxi* network enables entrepreneurs to accomplish two things: It allows them to achieve flexibility in their use of capital, and it allows them to retain personal control of their majority-owned enterprises. In terms of flexibility, ready access to investment capital allows entrepreneurs rapid entrance into new lines of business. Pack's (1992) observation that one of the reasons for Taiwan's rising productivity lies in the ability of entrepreneurs to make quick investments in new sectors can best be explained by the fact that entrepreneurs can obtain capital quickly from established investment networks rooted in trusted personal relationships. The conservatively oriented, state-owned banks do not make loans quickly or without full collateral, and very few businesses use the equity markets at all. Therefore, except in the case of the largest firms in the largest business groups, which sometimes enter into joint ventures with multinational corporations, most investment capital for new projects comes either from reinvested profits or from the entrepreneur's personal network of family and friends. In most cases, the personal network is probably the more important source.

The interviews conducted by Kao and his team show how these investment networks normally work. Based upon interviews with the owners and managers of some of the top business groups, Kao (1991) describes the process of locating partners as follows:

> When a firm or enterprise group seeks a partnership with other people or businesses, the same principle applies. Usually, there will be no cooperation without intimate *guanxi*. If they want to make a linkage, it is necessary to find the "right" person first. The cooperative interbusiness relationship is primarily based upon the personal trust between the two major *laoban*. If this kind of trust exists, the deal is rather easy to make. . . . Even in those large business groups, the core group is usually constituted by family members, good friends, and old colleagues. . . . From this perspective, it is "personal trust" which makes the network of partnerships actually work. We do not want to overstate the role of "personal trust," but our analysis clearly shows that it is a necessary condition for doing business. Both within and between business organizations, "personal trust" is a basic organizational principle. (p. 68)

One does not normally think of personal trust as an organizational principle, but in Chinese businesses it is one. "In Chinese society," Kao continues, "trust is inseparable from 'personal intimacy.' Although intimacy is not equivalent to 'trust,' it is a prerequisite" (p. 69). In this context, "personal intimacy" and "intimate *guanxi*" refer to a *guanxi* relationship that two people have activated and in which an intimacy in the form of *renqing* (a quality of interpersonal warmth and the willingness to comply with the norms of reciprocity) has been achieved. "Relying upon personal relationships," Kao reminds us, is, however, "not merely a matter of emotionality but of rational calculations" (p. 72).

The rational calculations rest upon whether or not the people involved will follow social norms. Through their actions, two people show they are willing to enter into a *guanxi* relationship. This willingness provides a foundation for trust. One's trust in the other arises out of recognition that the other has both the power and resources to act and the personal desire to follow norms of the specific *guanxi* relationship that binds the two people together. In this context, trust (*xinyong*) means one's integrity and credibility as a person in relation not only to the other person, but also to all potential observers. A relationship based upon trust requires that the two people involved will act predictably and in accordance with the appropriate norms of reciprocity.

Embedded in a system of interpersonal relationships, trust in Chinese society has a sociological but not a legalistic foundation. Trust binds people together by obliging them to act according to set rules of social relationships (Fei, 1992). "In order to obtain 'trust,' " says Kao (1991), "persons have to demonstrate certain qualities according to intersubjective rules. These rules are not objectified, but are usually well recognized by the people involved. Because such informal, rather than formal, rules are used predominantly to regulate business activities, Western contractual relationships do not prevail" (p. 69).

Therefore, to have trust in another is to believe that the other is willing to obey a system of social rules. In the Chinese context, assessments of trustworthiness involve assessments of people. Trust, therefore, is highly personalized even though it is also bound by clear-cut rules of action. To judge another's trustworthiness is to judge, given the rules of interaction, how a specific person will act in relation to another in a specified context.

This sort of personal trust rooted in *guanxi* networks is a very different type of trust than that prevailing in Western businesses, where the participants have ultimate faith in the legal system and much less faith in the word of those with whom they do business. The distinction between Chinese and Western trust is not one, as some have argued (e.g., Menkhoff, 1990; Wong,

1991; Yong, 1992), between personal trust and system trust. Rather, it is a distinction between two different types of system trust: In Chinese society, system trust is based on normative, intersubjective rules that link people who are classified according to relational categories into networks and that specify their modes of interaction. In Western society, system trust rests on codified rules that define the jurisdictions of interacting units (e.g., an individual or a firm) and specify the terms and conditions of that interaction. In Chinese society, system trust is highly personalized; in the West, system trust is more abstract and impersonal. Put more concretely, the backup system for a Chinese businessperson is a *guanxi* network; the backup system for an American businessperson consists of the courts and lawyers.

Production and Marketing Networks

When used in the context of business, this system of trust can be activated among people linked in horizontally based *guanxi* networks to generate economic organizations.[13] Such *guanxi* networks may have several economic functions; for example, they may be a source of investment capital or a means to organize the production and distribution of commodities. Whatever the economic purpose, the typical organization is the same. People who own, or who at some time may own, their own firms are linked into a network in which the norms of reciprocity take a concrete form of mutual indebtedness. In other words, doing business is a process of reciprocation, with *guanxi* ties being an essential element of that process.

Many previous studies of Chinese businesses, particularly long-distance trading, have documented these horizontal networks. Eddie Kuo (1991), for example, has documented a case in which the Southeast Asian distribution network for mandarin oranges, which began in South China and through numerous exchanges ended in Malaysia, was able to resist the direct actions of the Malaysian government to intervene in the trade. In this case, the horizontal linkages of trust undermined attempts to create a vertically controlled, government-sponsored distribution system. The economic power of such horizontal ties is nicely illustrated in a comment by one informant in Yong's (1992) study of Chinese rubber businesses in Southeast Asia:

We Chinese are always financially tight. We depend a lot on giving credit. For example, rubber from Thailand may be sent here first and then we pay later, or my buyer will give me money first to buy the rubber. Either way, this sort of credit giving, you can basically take and run. So *xinyong* is important. With *xinyong,* I can do business up to a few hundred thousand dollars, even though I have, maybe, only ten thousand dollars. (p. 94)

In Taiwan as well, horizontal *guanxi* networks form the organizational backbone of the manufacturing sectors of the economy. My own data and particularly the interview material collected by Kao Cheng-shu's team in Taiwan show that *guanxi* networks provide small and medium-sized businesses with the resources by which to organize export-oriented commodity chains. When used to raise investment capital for manufacturing, personal networks of *guanxi* owners give entrepreneurs many advantages that a formal banking system would not. Such networks give them a ready source of capital that can be used as they wish. Should an area of manufacturing prove successful, the network gives the entrepreneur a potential set of partners in manufacturing and distributing products that can be rapidly increased to the level of the demand. Equally important, the *guanxi* network provides a low-cost source of information about what to produce, how to improve production, and where and how to sell the products. The data suggest that the denser and more extensive the *guanxi* network, the more production information, including research and development and product innovations, actually becomes a function of the network itself. Without the *guanxi* networks, small and medium-sized networks could not shift product lines and could not produce the array of products they do. But with the assistance of their *guanxi* "backup system," entrepreneurs can rationally calculate their speculative investments and, as Kao states, be "in the right place at the right time."

Satellite Assembly Systems

To explain the numerous ways that *guanxi* ties serve as a medium to create economic organizations, it is analytically useful to make a distinction between how entrepreneurs use *guanxi* ties to establish horizontally integrated commodity chains and how they use such ties to diversify their assets. In regard to commodity chains, interviews with large and medium-sized manufacturers of export products reveal that production is often organized through what is called a "satellite assembly system" (*weixing gongchang*) (also see Shieh, 1992). Satellite assembly systems vary in terms of the relative size of the firms directly involved. In general, a group of small, medium, and sometimes large independently owned firms join together to produce a product that has been ordered by an overseas buyer. Each firm will produce one part or one set of parts of the final product. Depending upon the size of the order and the complexity of the part, that firm might organize a secondary satellite assembly system to make the part. All the parts are then delivered to an assembly firm, which assembles, paints, packages, and ships the final product.

In some satellite assembly systems, the assembly firm is the largest firm in the group and is basically an end producer that subcontracts a portion, sometimes a very large portion, of the final product to small independent firms. For example, a hydraulic jack plant that I visited with Kao and his team employed about 200 people and subcontracted as much as two-thirds of the component parts for the jacks to smaller firms in the region. These smaller firms also worked for other local manufacturers. One of the principal owners and general manager of the firm told us that the company, which sold about $15 million U.S. worth of jacks in 1987, did not sell their products under their own brand name, but rather sold exclusively to such Western wholesale and retail companies as Price Club, Wells, Kmart, and Grand Auto. The company made the jacks to the specifications required by their buyers, and painted, labeled, and packaged the product accordingly. The general manager personally arranged for most of the orders by traveling to trade shows and by visiting distributors all over the world. When orders were plentiful, the final assembly plant and the subcontractors worked at full speed, but when the orders slackened, he would reduce his reliance on subcontractors and try to do more production in-house.

In other assembly systems, some of the component parts may be manufactured by firms much larger than the final assembly firm. For example, a large metalworking firm that I also visited with Kao and his team produced metal bicycle wheels as one among a number of component parts they produced. The firm, employing nearly 300 people, also subcontracted with other smaller firms for a portion of the component parts they made. The bicycle wheels that they manufactured, however, went to a number of different satellite assembly systems, all producing different bicycles. The firms in these satellite assembly systems were smaller than the metalworking firm.

This size differential was most pronounced in the case of an automobile parts maker that I interviewed in the United States. His firm produced custom-made parts for supply houses and mail-order distributors located primarily in the United States and Europe. He employed four people in his firm, two for quality control and two for processing orders. He, the owner and fifth person in the firm, traveled to the United States and Europe to arrange for orders from his buyers. His overseas buyers would give him the detailed specifications and sometimes sample parts. He would then take the specifications and samples to what he called "his manufacturing group," which consisted of 10 to 15 independently owned metalworking firms. These firms were all small, about 30 employees each, and 75% of his orders, he said, were made by these firms. The team, led by a mechanical engineer, divided each order into a manufacturing process consisting of smaller component parts and necessary steps. They would select the lineup of metalworking shops that would do each component part or step in the manufacturing process, and then would instruct the owners of the shops how to do the assigned tasks. Sometimes, for a large and expensive order, the person I interviewed would lend money for necessary machinery and supplies to the independent owners in the assembly system. Once the process started and the necessary level of quality had been reached, the manufacturing process would proceed without managerial supervision. Each firm would do its own part of the process and then would pass the unfinished part on to the next firm in the manufacturing sequence. When the product was finished and delivered to an exporting firm, the two quality control people would inspect each part and arrange for its export.

Like the others we interviewed, the owner of the automobile parts firm said that to make the manufacturing process work smoothly, human relationships in the group and the personalities of the independent owners were very important. "Business is business" he said, and for business you need people who "you can trust to do the job." To find these people, often he would ask his friends for recommendations. Sometimes he would drive around and just talk to the owners of small metal shops. When the "feeling" was right, when the "personality" matched, then he felt he could do business with the person. Once he located the right person, however, he would not use a contract to seal the deal. Rather, the parties reached an "understanding" that was in turn sealed by reciprocating gifts and banquets. The same lack of contracts, the same equality among independent entrepreneurs, and the same celebratory reciprocation of food and drink and small gifts reoccur in every satellite assembly system I visited.

One other theme found in all cases of establishing subcontracting networks and satellite assembly systems was that some, and often the majority, of the subcontracting firms were initially started by employees in one firm who created their own independent firms and established subcontracting relations with their former bosses (also see Shieh, 1992). Employers would often encourage such departures and even invest in firms started by their best and most capable employees in order to develop the subcontracting network. Although it is counterintuitive, such encouragement of and investment in potentially competing firms creates a satellite assembly system capable of achieving economies of scale on a temporary basis without enlarging the size of existing firms and without making large capital investments in labor and machines that might not produce at capacity or may not produce for very long. Investment capital is put into people who will repay at a premium, and who will likely remain morally bound to their former bosses and economically anchored in their satellite assembly systems, at least as long as the business orders hold out.

Diversifying Assets

Guanxi ties are used not only to develop and refine networks of firms to produce export commodities, but also to establish entirely new lines of business. Although more research is needed on this topic, it is my conclusion that *guanxi* networks provide an information-rich environment that facilitates rapid shifts in capital investment from one sector to another. The analysis of the business group data, as discussed above, shows that many of the large family-owned business groups in Taiwan develop diversification strategies that are "opportunistic." Entrepreneurial opportunities are nurtured in a highly speculative investment climate that takes very low overhead to establish a reliable production network. Ideas for how to get rich—the gold rush mentality—come from many sources: from the owners of small firms who travel around the world looking for orders, from big Western merchandisers who come to Asia to find firms that can manufacture the products they want to market, from local entrepreneurs who hit upon new ways to make existing products. Wherever the ideas come from, the success of a group of manufacturers stimulates the rapid entry of others into the same product areas.

This ability to diversify rapidly across product lines is nicely illustrated by an owner and manager of an import/export business whom I interviewed with Professor Kao and his team. This entrepreneur used the product ideas that he obtained from sales trips to organize and supervise many satellite assembly systems for the commodities he exported. He estimated that these commodities, ranging from kitchenware to computers, have a "product life" of around 3 months. His general strategy was to produce only those products from which he would recoup his full investment in one profit cycle. For the high-end products, primarily computers, he wanted to recover all expenses and gain some profits in the first 3 months, because, he said, a successful product would be mass-produced by firms in other competing countries, such as South Korea or the People's Republic of China. He did not mass-produce products himself. He asserted that the key to his own success in creating a group of firms employing a total of about 110 people, having assets of less than $2 million U.S., and having annual sales of around $60 million U.S., was the speed with which he could change his product lines to match market demand. He wanted always to enter the market in the early part of a product cycle. What allowed the speed, he said, was the flexible manufacturing system. He owned no factories, he did not directly manage production, his overhead was kept to a minimum, and he never produced a product without having existing orders in hand for that product.

This export trader is typical. As Brian Levy (1988) shows, the number of export traders in Taiwan grew more than sevenfold from 1973 to 1984, from 2,777 traders to 20,597. By contrast, at the same time, the number of South Korean export traders grew from 1,200 in 1973 to 5,300 in 1984. Levy concludes that "in Taiwan—but not in Korea—the expansion in the number of traders kept pace with the overall expansion of manufacturers" (p. 45). It is likely that most of export traders are linked to satellite assembly systems that rapidly and consistently change their product lines. Indeed, as Gary Gereffi and Pan Mei-lin (1994) have shown for Taiwan's garment industry, the ability to change production lines has grown easier over the past several decades: Flexibility becomes an expectation that is institutionalized into the production system through the introduction of specialized firms (such as automated machine retoolers) and specialized services (such as rotating credit banks) that allow for ever more speedy transformations of production lines and ever more rapid transfers of capital to areas of opportunity.

The institutionalization of flexibility is having several consequences. First, few manufacturers of export commodities would attempt to develop, and fewer yet would actually succeed in developing, a vertically integrated production facility that would aim for a large market share for the exported product. Indeed, for this reason, Taiwan's large firms are mostly upstream suppliers of intermediate parts or have carved out service niches for themselves in the domestic economy. In this kind of a climate, entrepreneurs will not normally choose to reinvest their profits by enlarging their production capacity to raise their market share, as is the case in Japan and South Korea.

Instead, investors typically choose to put their money into areas of expansion, and in recent years that has meant making investments in overseas markets, in production facilities in the People's Republic of China, in property in Hong Kong, or in the equity markets in Thailand. Capital rapidly flows where speculators believe the next boom will be. Some capital is, of course, retained, and is reinvested in existing firms to upgrade production capabilities. But this reinvestment in automation and equipment purchases will likely enhance the flexibility of small and medium-sized factory owners in participating in a range of satellite assembly systems.

Conclusion: Political Controls on Network Patterns

What is the state's role in Taiwan's industrialization? I can now answer this question in a way that differs somewhat from the way most students of Asian economic development might respond. As described earlier in this report, many theorists argue that the strong Asian states—the bureaucratic, authoritarian regimes that have autonomy from society and administrative capacity to act—create the conditions for rapid economic development.

My analysis differs from this line of reasoning. Although state policies and programs certainly enhance an economy's ability to grow and change, the effects of state actions are more limited than most theorists argue. Politicians know their countries. When they act, they act upon known subjects of which they themselves are products and participants. As Max Weber once said, "Politics is the art of the possible," and in this context doing what is possible means to refine what is already present, to cultivate what is already growing. Politicians and state officials build upon existing social patterns, and although they may work to restructure society, they do not start with a clean slate. Political actors tacitly accept and take for granted most of the organizational features of the societies in which they are a part, including economic organizations.

It was the purpose of the joint research project undertaken by my colleagues and me to explain the organizational patterns of Asian business and not the reasons for East Asian economic success. This distinction between organizational structure and economic growth is neither obscure nor insignificant. In social science terms, the organizational structure of East Asian economies is our dependent variable; it is a configurational variable reducible to neither a growth rate nor a policy choice. Focusing only on economic growth and on the proximate cause for that growth, most analysts neglect to examine the economic patterning and trajectories of growth. In most developing economies, state policies are proximate causes, the last acts at the end of a long sequence of events that leads to development. For this reason, most analysts maintain that there are no important differences among Japan, South Korea, and Taiwan in the strength of their states or the adaptability of their societies. In essence, they argue that all three states are strong, otherwise development would not have occurred. State structures become black boxes, economic organizations slip in theoretical insignificance, and rates of growth serve as the only important focus for explanation.

During the years of rapid economic growth, the Taiwan state played a role in the economy very different from that played by the states in South Korea and in Japan. The state seldom sponsored big businesses in the export sector, but continued to control many upstream, largely import-substitution industries, most of which require large economies of scale and upon which small and medium-sized businesses in the export sectors depend. With these actions, the state established a "public interest" economic sphere for itself, separate in both character and principle from that occupied by private businesses. Moreover, the state's monopolization of such industries as steel, petroleum, and electrical power prevented the growth of huge private businesses that occurred in South Korea and Japan.

This separation of spheres, however, should not lead to the conclusion that the Taiwan state has more concentrated economic power than the Korean or Japanese states, both of which have much smaller state-owned sectors. Quite the contrary is true. Taiwan state enterprises are organizationally decoupled from the rest of the economy, and they primarily (though not exclusively) respond to the market demand generated by private economy. They respond to economic development, rather than push it forward. Taiwan's huge economic growth has occurred in the export manufacturing sector, and that sector is dominated by small and medium-sized businesses. This economic pattern has accelerated and not declined over time, whereas in South Korea the reverse process has happened.

The capitalist states in Asia, along with most states elsewhere, try to control financial institutions, but here again the "strong state" policies of Taiwan have been quite unlike those in Japan and in Korea. The state-owned banking system in Taiwan strongly limited the amount of investment capital it was putting into Taiwan's businesses. At the same time, Japanese city banks and the banks run by the Korean state channeled huge amounts of domestic and foreign capital, in the form of cheap loans, into economic sectors selected for development.[14] In Taiwan, the large business groups and particularly the small and medium-sized firms got their investment capital from the curb market—from family and friends and informal money markets. In Korea and Japan, the banking system encouraged large, heavily leveraged firms. For instance, Korea's leverage, expressed as debt/equity ratios, is almost three times Taiwan's ratio in the manufacturing sector (Zeile, 1993, p. 78a). This fiscal leverage in Korea also gave the state political leverage, and it assumed virtually hegemonic control over the *chaebol* until the early 1980s. The active curb market in Taiwan shows that entrepreneurs could take care of their own financial needs and that the Taiwan state had very little leverage, fiscal or otherwise, over the export sector of the economy.

Robert Wade (1990) shows that the Taiwanese government had an active role in creating and implementing economic policies that led to rapid growth. But like the banking policy, most of the government's measures built on existing strengths already in the economy, and thereby encouraged the aggressiveness of the export sector. But, forever worrying about the small size and obscure brands of most firms, Taiwan's economic planners also tried occasionally to "upgrade" some aspects of the economy. For instance, they tried to create large trading companies by emulating the Japanese model, but these attempts were unsuccessful because most production networks grew from orders from overseas buyers that originated with or were handled by brokers in Taiwan who have their own very small trading firms. Accordingly, while these small trading firms proliferated, the government-sponsored trading firms languished (Fields, 1989). The state planners also supported the formation of integrated, more or less permanent subcontracting systems, again based upon the Japanese model, but these have also failed (Lorch & Biggs, 1989). The state also started special banks to increase the size of small and medium-sized firms through special financing, but the results have been disappointing, because businessmen do not want to take loans from state sources. Finally, state planners have tried to build an export-oriented transportation industry so that Taiwan could begin exporting automobiles and trucks. But to date Taiwan, the country that leads the world in the ratio of manufactured exports to total output, and a country that has 27 automobile firms (all for the domestic market), makes no automobile for export. All this indicates that state policy does not lead to accomplished fact. The Taiwan state has to contend with and ultimately accept the established patterns and economic momentum that exist within the society, the very patterns that arise out of Taiwan's horizontal economic networks. Taiwan's capitalism is not state-led capitalism; instead, it is *guanxi* capitalism, a capitalism built up and extended out from the networks embedded in Chinese society.

Notes

1. Also see Winckler and Greenhalgh (1988) for extended discussion of the various types of state interpretation used to explain the political economy of Taiwan.

2. These two views come together most clearly in *The Evolution of Policy Behind Taiwan's Development Success,* by K. T. Li (1988). Li, who is known as the chief architect of Taiwan's economic policies, describes the role of the state in laudatory terms. Li's comments are preceded by introductory essays by Gustav Ranis and John Fei, both developmental economists, who use Taiwan as a leading example in the case for a strong state thesis. See also Li (1976).

3. For such a comparative analysis of firm size that incorporates business networks, see Hamilton and Orrù (1989).

4. Numazaki (1991b) also makes a similar comment: "The configuration of larger networks in which [Taiwan's] business groups are 'embedded'—to borrow the expression of Mark Granovetter (1985)—has at least as much determining effect on the structure and behavior of business groups as cultural norms and values (e.g., Confucianism)" (pp. 90-91).

5. In their efforts to make Taiwan a productive, colonial economy, the Japanese developed a comprehensive system of transportation around the island and created an export-producing agricultural economy. In particular, the Japanese promoted a huge, state-owned sugar company, which the Chinese government took over in 1945 and still runs, albeit on a much reduced level. For good discussions of the transportation system and the Japanese sugar industry in Taiwan, see Hsu, Pannell, and Wheeler (1980) and Williams (1980).

6. Ranked by the value of their assets in 1986, the most important state-owned enterprises are Taiwan Power Company, China Petroleum Company, China Steel Company, Taiwan Sugar Company, China Shipbuilding Company, Chunghwa Machinery and Engineering Company, China Petrochemical Development Company, Taiwan Machinery Manufacturing Company, Taiwan Fertilizer Company, Taiwan Aluminum Company, Taiwan Metal Mining Company, and Taiwan Salt Works.

7. This figure is, however, an overstatement because our research shows that many successful entrepreneurs own more than one business.

8. See Tong (1991) for a similar conclusion regarding a Chinese business group in Singapore.

9. This reluctance to open their firms to outside scrutiny does not seem to reduce their willingness to accept investment capital from outsiders, especially from foreign corporations who want to enter into joint ventures. My preliminary analysis has shown that the most tightly held groups, other things being equal, are those most likely to undertake joint ventures.

10. For a more complete discussion of the network structure of Chinese society, see Fei (1992). Also see Hamilton and Wang's introduction to Fei's book.

11. For an analysis of the network structure of both groups, see Numazaki (1991b).

12. According to Lee (1990), "Some small enterprises, which do not yet have a properly audited account and cannot offer adequate collateral to banks, cannot borrow effectively from banks, and therefore have to borrow from the informal money market at a high rate of interest. There are about 70,000 exporting and importing firms, big and small, competing in the market. Moreover, there is a considerable number of small trading and manufacturing firms which are not registered at all, with the convenience of tax-evasion and freedom from all sorts of government regulations with respect to pollution control, fire precaution and other considerations. Naturally, an unregistered firm has to resort to the informal money market" (p. 36).

13. This is also true in a political context as well, when factional networks are generated. See Jacobs (1979).

14. William Zeile (1989) calculates that the ratio of debt to assets for member firms of the top 50 *chaebol* in 1983 was 453%, compared with 158% for Taiwan manufacturing firms. This figure overstates the Taiwan case, because it is biased toward larger Taiwan firms that report such financial matters.

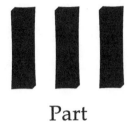

Part

Comparative Analysis
of Business Networks

10

The Institutional Analysis of Capitalist Economies

MARCO ORRÙ

This chapter highlights the relevance of the institutional framework for the analysis of the emergence and reproduction of distinct economic structures. Studies of economic organizations, especially at the level of national economies, traditionally have been conducted within the isolated confines of separate social science disciplines. The single-minded attention to distinct and specialized concerns has often turned potentially helpful angles of investigation into distorted views of economic structures' emergence and persistence. Political scientists have tended to focus exclusively on the roles of the state and of government agencies in directing and shaping economic structures (see, e.g., Evans, Rueschemeyer, & Skocpol, 1985; Weiss, 1988); economists have looked

298 COMPARATIVE ANALYSIS OF BUSINESS NETWORKS

almost always at domestic and international markets and competitive advantages to explain the emergence of national economies (see Porter, 1990); anthropologists have been inclined to identify the sets of values or cultural practices that influence economic development (see Redding, 1990). The partial perspective of a distinct disciplinary concern has had some initial usefulness that has often turned into an impediment to understanding economic structures by becoming the one and only relevant perspective.

Almost simultaneously in recent years, different social sciences have turned their attention away from a search for the prime movers of economic structures and toward the middle-level analysis of multiple interacting institutions—the battleground where economic and political structures are routinely created and maintained. Current elaborations in institutional economics (e.g., Williamson, 1985), economic sociology (e.g., Dore, 1986a; Hamilton & Biggart, 1988), organizational analysis (e.g., Powell & DiMaggio, 1991; Gerlach, 1992; March & Olson, 1984), and political sciences (e.g., Katzenstein, 1989; Samuels, 1987; Zysman, 1983) have similarly sought to overcome the problems of earlier sectoral analyses of economic and political structures in favor of a new approach that incorporates several organizational dimensions and their interrelations.

The institutional approach has emerged, often independently, as the way for different social science disciplines to advance the understanding of ever more complex economic, political, and social structures. The common argument supporting the new focus on institutions is that markets, cultures, state policies, and formal organizational features in isolation cannot satisfactorily account for the emergence and persistence of observed types of capitalist economies. Instead, researchers advocate the need to integrate multiple levels of analysis to show how different institutional spheres are interconnected and have a cumulative interactive effect in shaping economic structures. Correspondingly, the emerging institutional approach also abandons the traditional emphasis on unidirectional causal explanations of economic structures to emphasize the contextual, interactive production and reproduction of complex economic systems. Succinctly put, adopting an institutional approach to the analysis of economic structures means abandoning distorting unidimensional perspectives (whether political, economic, or cultural) in favor of a focus on the multidimensional, intersecting aspects of economic life; it also means, in parallel fashion, abandoning a unicausal model of explanation of economic structures, and privileging instead the contextual understanding of different economies and their institutional foundations.

Institutional analyses of capitalist economies are reasonably characterized as multidimensional and multicausal, but beyond this minimal description we need to articulate some of the analytic dimensions of the institutional framework. Four questions are most pertinent here. First, how does the institutional approach frame its general analysis of economic action? Second, how does it specify the identification of distinctive economic structures? Third, how does the same institutional approach encompass the analysis of noneconomic, especially political, institutions? And fourth, what kind of typologies of capitalism can be developed from the institutional framework? The first question demands that we identify "rationality contexts" that frame the distinctive conduct of economic affairs in different societies; the second requires that we augment these rationality contexts with a typology of equally distinctive economic organizational forms; the third forces us to broaden the description of key institutional features to encompass political and other pertinent societal sectors; and the fourth compels us to describe, schematically but holistically, what differing types of capitalist societies would look like within the institutional framework we have adopted. The next four sections of this chapter will address, in turn, each of these four issues.

Rationality Contexts of Economic Action

From the institutional perspective, economic action is understood as a historically emerging, socially constructed and patterned behavior of individuals and groups. Such economic behavior is routinely objectified in social institutions, simultaneously allowing for continuity and change in economic behavior; thus patterns of economic action are a prerogative of both individuals and organizations within a society, and social change is obtained through the interaction of individuals and institutions. Sven-Erik Sjöstrand (1993) describes the dynamics of patterned economic action as follows: "An individual, when interacting and exchanging, faces the institutions of a society, in both its physical and its artificial manifestations. Institutions are embedded in the emergent organizations in a society and in those ideas and concepts that the individual uses to sort out her or his view of reality" (p. 61).

A social context underlies the economic interactions of individuals and of social institutions alike, providing a meaningful framework for the emergence and reproduction of distinct types of economic structures.

At its broadest level, economic action takes place within the rationality context of social action in general. Max Weber's typologies of social action and of domination provide us with a preliminary classificatory scheme of distinct rationality contexts of economic action. Weber identifies instrumental rationality and its accompanying bureaucratic-legal form of domination as distinguishing characteristics of modern capitalism, but Weber's typology does not rule out alternative formulations of rationality contexts of economic action. Modern capitalism is not uniformly and completely driven by means-and-ends rationality; it is also affected by moral claims, traditional social arrangements, and affective ties among individuals. Although all economic structures are socially constructed from a combination of rationality contexts, one dimension or another is likely to emerge as its distinguishing feature.

Social action, and economic action as a subtype of it, tends toward one of three gravitational poles, depending upon the emphasis placed on impersonal rules, traditional authority structures, or the reasonableness of the individual. In the first instance, rationality is a property of the social system, and individuals become more rational as they submerge themselves within the system. Whereas individuals are at the center of personalistic and tradition-based contexts of social action, the system occupies the center of the means-and-ends rationality context. Here, the reasonable behavior of individuals is to become one with the institutions that embody the collective rationality of their society. In the second instance, social action is framed by the traditional authority structure of a society and its long-standing hierarchical organization. In this social context, the reasonable behavior of individuals requires that they endorse and maximize authority systems and the complementary command and obedience roles, subsuming their individual views to the views of their public leaders. In the third instance, the social frame of reference is one where reasonable individuals interact in an often irrational social system; thus their efforts are aimed at maximizing interpersonal networking while minimizing the pernicious effects of an irrational society.

The system-based, tradition-based, and individual-based contexts of rationality can be related to several dimensions of social action. Table 10.1 lists some of these dimensions systematically, thus articulating the coherent institutional logic that accompanies distinct patterns of economic action.

System-centered rationality is embodied by the rule of the office above the officeholder, and is supported by the official and self-regulating juris-

Table 10.1   Rationality Contexts of Economic Action

Modes of social action	means and ends	traditional	affective
Authority systems	bureaucratic	patrimonial	interpersonal
Forms of legitimation	juridical	political	personal
Regulatory systems	self-regulation	administrative governance	spontaneous regulation
Modes of transaction	reciprocity	distribution	exchange
Sources of integration	professional norms	public authority	local community

prudence of the system. Professional norms and the reciprocal acknowledgment of subsystems' legitimacy characterize the interaction among social institutions and the individuals who represent them in this context.

Tradition-based social action requires an authority system that is founded on the robust rule of the patrimonial leader and the virtuous obedience of the followers; the organizational structure of such a society is characterized by hierarchical administrative governance supported by the legitimacy of public authority figures. Authority relations frame the interactions among individuals and institutions within the tradition-based rationality context and fashion a social system that structures itself hierarchically from the top down.

The personalistic type of social action rests on the authority of interpersonal rationality that emerges from the multiple affective ties among individuals, and is legitimated and spontaneously regulated through the informal standards of local communities. In this context, the interactive rationality of individuals is pitted against the irrationality of the larger social system and of its representative institutions; thus social organization in this rationality context arises from the bottom up and expands horizontally through the social system.

These three typologies of rationality contexts are neither exhaustive nor prescriptive. They are simply schemes that can help prepare the ground for the comprehension of distinct economic structures. The advantage of this scheme is that it is pitched at a general enough level of analysis to allow for the inclusion of several empirical cases under a single typology, but it is also specific enough to allow for the theoretical identification of distinctive but equally coherent logics of economic action. Preventing our getting trapped in the detailed analysis of multiple, differing social institutions, the elaboration of types of rationality contexts still helps us capture the similar, diffuse pattern of social action that permeates the behavior of interacting individuals

Table 10.2   Organizational Patterns of Economic Action

Dominant economic units	small and large firms	large corporations	small firms
Modal economic interactons	alliances	hierarchies	networks
Modal means of organization	cartels and associations	autonomous conglomerates	flexible partnerships
Interfirm relations	horizontal and vertical cooperation	vertical integration	horizontal linkages
Formalization of transactions	medium	high	low
Noncontractual enforcement	medium	low	high

and institutions alike. But next we need to take these three typologies of rationality contexts beyond their general formulation to identify, in a parallel fashion, distinct organizational forms that prosper within each type of logic of economic action.

Organizational Patterns of Economic Action

Economic organizations, like their counterparts in other areas of social life, are collectively constructed through the interaction of individuals who apply their shared rationality to the identification of appropriate organizational forms and to efforts that guarantee the endurance of these forms over time. Horizontal and vertical organizational structures emerge and overlap with each other in all economic action, as attempts are made to coordinate multiple social agents involved in business transactions. The extent to which some forms of economic coordination are privileged over others helps identify the distinctiveness of one economic structure over another.

Any given rationality context is pliable and dynamic enough to allow for the emergence of a range of differing organizational forms; thus, for instance, vertically integrated large corporations are found alongside horizontally networked small and medium-sized business firms in most modern economies. And yet the kinds of business organizations that are central in any one economy vary considerably and reflect, somewhat homogeneously, the rationality context of a given society. Table 10.2 lists some features of economic organizations that relate to the distinct rationality contexts discussed earlier.

The organizational context of means-and-ends rationality, bound by professional norms and subsystem reciprocity, tends to include a balanced mix of small, medium, and large firms linked together through both horizontal and vertical cooperative ties. Economic transactions are only partly formalized, and noncontractual enforcements of transactions are moderately enacted. In this context, alliances among economic and noneconomic social institutions are diffuse and persistent, and cartels and business associations are often established to strengthen the institutional reciprocity of the economic system.

The rationality context of tradition translates, in the economic arena, into the dominance of large, autonomous conglomerates that vertically integrate most aspects of production and are organized in a strictly hierarchical fashion. Within this rationality context, administrative governance of hierarchies replaces the professional alliance of economic agents; open competition and the formalization of economic transactions is high, and cooperation and the noncontractual enforcement of transactions is low.

The rationality context of personalistic systems favors the emergence of small independent firms and their flexible networks. Horizontal-level linkages are prevalent, and partnerships are constantly enacted on the basis of personalistic ties among individuals. The authority system of business firms and networks follows a family-based organizational pattern; the formalization of transactions among firms is low, whereas the noncontractual enforcement of business activities is high. The local community, based on families and familylike networks, provides the fertile ground for multiple and persistent linkages among individual actors within this type of economic structure.

The three distinctive organizational patterns of economic life just outlined are neither exhaustive nor prescriptive; they are not meant to describe the way empirically observed economies are actually organized, but rather are intended as an orienting framework through which apparently homogeneous capitalist economies can be usefully differentiated and better comprehended. Thus actual economic structures consist in most cases of a combination of the typologies sketched above, but for each economic structure one can detect the dominance of one organizational type over the others. Next, we need to expand the typology to incorporate the characterization of organizational patterns that emerge in other social institutions, especially political ones.

Organizational Isomorphism
and Polity Structures

The institutional framework cannot conceive of rationality contexts that affect only economic transactions and organizations. A rationality context applies to multiple institutions and establishes homogeneity across societal sectors, creating isomorphic organizational features throughout the social structure. The political sphere is one institutional area that is significantly affected by distinct rationality contexts and modes of economic action, but it is also an institutional area that significantly affects, in turn, the emergence and persistence of distinct economic structures. The organizational isomorphism created by rationality contexts could be demonstrated in a number of institutions in a society (such as education, workers' training, and labor-management relations). Much of it will be covered in the next three chapters of this book. Here, however, I discuss in broad lines the significant patterns of political action that emerge from distinct rationality contexts—to exemplify how the pressure toward homogeneity translates into parallel organizational characteristics in the economic and political arenas as well as in other societal sectors.

Modern industrial economies do not exist apart from the political systems that support them. Political systems provide legitimacy to economic systems, and economic systems legitimate the political institutions of a society. Patterns of legitimation and the features of political structures are better understood through the rationality context of each society. But the ways political institutions are organized are hardly homogeneous from society to society; instead, they mirror isomorphically, in distinct ways, the larger rationality contexts of their own societies. Economic and political agents and organizations are privileged actors in the creation of economic structures; thus a description of patterns of political action is central to capturing the characteristics of this key institution that shapes economic structures.

Among the three types of rationality contexts and of patterns of economic action we can evince three major types of political structures. First, within means-and-ends rationality emerges a corporatist political structure that privileges federated societal concerns and the coalescence of civil society and political society in a collaborative framework. Second, within tradition-based social action arises a statist political structure that rests on the leadership of central governments and the subordination of private interests in the

Table 10.3 Political Institutions and Economic Action

Political structure	corporatist	statist	segmental
Forms of legitimation	societal concerns	national sovereignty	aggregate interests
Systematic relations	state with society	state above society	state outside society
Position of individuals	collectivity functionaries	political subjects	carriers of interests
Organizational structure	federated	centralized	fragmented
State leadership	medium	high	low
Separation of state and economy	medium	low	high

organization of economic life. Third, the interpersonal rationality context leads to a segmental political structure that promotes the separation of civil society and political society and pursues arm's-length relations with private business. Table 10.3 sketches some key characteristics of these three types of political structures and their pertinence to economic action. The corporatist type of polity is characterized by the partnership of the state and of economic actors in the enactment of a modern civic society. Ronald Jepperson and John Meyer (1991) provide an adept characterization of this corporatist polity:

> Here modernity arises through collective rationalization and institutionalization, not of subunit actors but of social functions and specialized activities, and the corporate groupings performing them—various occupations, classes, strata, regions, communities, professions. Individuals gain standing not as actors with autonomous interests, but as functionaries—as members of groups with legitimated functional needs and responsibilities. (p. 217)

In the corporatist polity, civil society and political society become indistinguishable because their legitimacy source is shared horizontally across the institutional sectors; thus the federation of interests, rather than their particularistic fragmentation, is the modal organizational type of the corporatist polity.

The statist political structure differs significantly from the corporatist polity in that it enacts a hierarchy of spheres whereby civil society is brought under the leadership and guidance of the political structure. Only through the blessing of the state do economic actors become legitimate bearers of societal authority. Jepperson and Meyer argue:

> Here we have the polity as unified rational organization of both legitimated social actors and functions. . . . The state exists as both the model of organizing rationality and the location for the articulation of the general will of society's actors (the Jacobin vision). . . . The state organizes both aspects of rationalization: persons and interests, activities and functions. (p. 216)

Within the statist typology the central government orchestrates and directs social and economic life, instead of acting as an equal partner with other social institutions. The state commands, and private business can itself command to the extent that it follows state directives. A clear hierarchical social order is thus enacted throughout this type of political and economic structure, as state leaders and business leaders become the captains and moral guides of their own society.

The segmented polity type does not advocate the supremacy of the state or the state's partnership with the civil society. Instead, it proclaims the clear separation, and often the opposition, of political action and economic action. The political system is seen as external to the local community and antagonistic to that community's interests; the particularistic goals of individuals and of localized networks are segmentally disconnected from, and often in conflict with, the self-reproducing and self-preservation interests of the state. Thus the political system and the economic system develop endogenously apart from each other, while following similarly sectoral interests that secure institutional survivability over time.

It is important to emphasize that this scheme of three polity types is ideal-typical, not empirical. It is simply meant to show the isomorphic features of political and economic structures and their variability across societies within distinct rationality contexts. Economic efficiency can be obtained through a variety of routes that emphasize horizontal, vertical, or horizontal-and-vertical organizational patterns; what is common to the economy and polity typologies described above is the homogeneous maximization of a distinct type of economic action through the isomorphic structuring of economic and political institutions. When the three levels of analysis (context rationalities, economic structures, and political structures) are combined, we can begin to evince the three distinct typologies of capitalism that are the focus of this book. In the next section I seek to provide a preliminary elaboration of these typologies, before moving to the detailed illustration of each of them in three separate chapters.

Three Capitalist Typologies

Social action, whether pertaining to economic transactions, political life, or everyday interpersonal encounters, embodies a coherent logic that cuts across different institutional realms and allows for the meaningful comprehension of interactions among the individuals and the institutions of a society. The distinct rationality context of any given society can provide a general framework that encompasses different societal sectors and institutions and helps us to understand them as a coherent, meaningful totality. Institutions and individuals share a similar rationality context, and thus display strongly isomorphic patterns of organization and interaction across societal sectors. The three typologies of capitalist economies presented here can be understood as three distinct combinations of organizational logics that frame institutional areas and the interactions of individuals.

At the most basic level, social organizations are structured along either horizontal or vertical lines, or both. The horizontal pattern is characterized by flexible networking among individuals and institutions; the organizational units tend to operate at the same hierarchical level, and little or no vertical integration is sought to organize economic transactions or other societal exchanges. The vertical pattern, in contrast, is characterized by rigid hierarchies that structure the relations among individuals and institutions that are unequally located in the social structure. Hierarchical structuring can be enacted either through vertical integration within autonomous social units or through interorganizational hierarchies that formalize power relations among societal sectors. The vertical-and-horizontal patterns of organization mix hierarchies with same-level relations among individuals and institutions, keeping simultaneously the unequal structuring among hierarchies and the horizontal linkages among equals in the social structure. Typically, the horizontal framework intersects various hierarchical levels, thus endowing the organizational structure with multiple flexibility points, and the vertical framework preserves clearly identifiable hierarchies.

Alliance Capitalism

Alliance capitalism combines horizontal organizational traits of institutional cooperation among organizations in political, economic, and other societal sectors, together with vertical arrangements that structure the work-

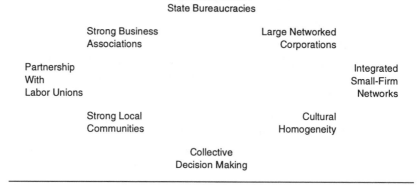

Figure 10.1. Alliance Capitalism

ings of groups of organizations involved in related activities. Institutional cooperation obtains at the highest organizational levels of a society, but also at intermediate and lower levels of the social hierarchies. Strong horizontal linkages are fashioned among social institutions within geographically defined communities, but also among regional-level and national-level economic and political institutions. Figure 10.1 represents alliance capitalism graphically as a circle of collaborative horizontal linkages, encompassing political, economic, and cultural factors that facilitate cooperative arrangements. Horizontal linkages are the dominant organizational dimension of alliance capitalism, but their cooperative strength is reinforced by multiple vertical ties (not shown in the figure) that connect one horizontal cooperation level to another. Thus both horizontal flexibility and vertical efficiency are maximized in this type of organizational structure.

Dirigiste Capitalism

Dirigiste capitalism can be envisioned as a giant pyramid that incorporates within itself multiple institutional levels connected hierarchically to each other through a clear subordination of the private economy to the leadership of the nation-state. This hierarchical arrangement is represented graphically in Figure 10.2. At the very top of the pyramid is the orchestrating role of the nation-state, which guides social life not only in political matters but in economic matters as well. Immediately below the central state are located the large industrial groups or corporations that act as economic leaders of

Strong
Leadership
of the Nation-State
Centralized Industrial Planning
by Government Bureaucracies
Targeted Flow of Financial Capital
Selection of Industrial Leaders by Sector
Privileged Economic Role of Large Corporations
Vertical Integration of Large-Firm Production Processes
Weak Presence of Small and Medium-Sized Firms and Firm Networks
Commanding Managerial Leadership and Strong Respect for Authority
Hierarchically Set Individual Roles—Traditional Rules of Conduct

Figure 10.2.   Dirigiste Capitalism

their society. The centralized management and vertical integration of business firms parallels the hierarchical structuring between the central state and the private economy. Horizontal networking among large firms, or among medium and small firms, is nearly absent, as the process of industrial production is accomplished mostly through internalized vertical structures that strive to achieve maximum self-sufficiency within the autonomous confines of large corporations or groups of corporations. The management style of dirigiste capitalism is fashioned through strict hierarchies, with strong managerial leadership throughout diverse political and business organizations. Tradition becomes a central feature of dirigiste capitalism, because social hierarchies are justified, by and large, by the centuries-old efficacy of a stratified social world that demands unquestioned allegiance to its organizational structure.

Familial Capitalism

Familial capitalism presents a strongly horizontal, segmented society where economic and political structures develop apart from each other, although along similar organizational patterns. The core of political and economic networks is constituted by personalistic ties among individuals related to each other through kinship or other ascriptive characteristics. Figure 10.3 illustrates familial capitalism as consisting of separate economic and political dimensions that develop in autonomous but similar ways. Strong central coordination is not a feature of either economic or political life under familial capitalism. Instead, fragmented economic interests trigger the creation of

E	Small-Firm Entrepreneurship
C	Family-Based Work Relations
O	Horizontal Interfirm Networks
N	Paternalistic Authority System
O	Personalistic Trust Relations
M	Distrust of Political System
Y	Strong Local Communities
P	Comparatively Weak Nation-State
O	Fragmented National Interests
L	Weak Industrial Planning
I	Strong Corporative Interests
T	High-Profile Local Government
Y	Clientelistic Power Relations

Figure 10.3. Familial Capitalism

independent entrepreneurial firms and their networking activities, just as fragmented and corporative interests characterize the activities within the political domain of the state. A wide gap between the social system and individuals' lives typically obtains within familial capitalism, thus leading to the chronic weakness of the state's role and the general disaffection of individuals from the social system in general. But the bottom-up quality of familial capitalism favors the flexible creation and re-creation of business networks geared toward specific business goals that can be shifted rapidly as the demands from the economic environment change.

From Theory To Practice

The institutional framework adopted in this chapter theoretically identifies and abstracts the distinctive features that characterize different capitalist economies; it articulates, theoretically, the general logic that guides social and economic action within different contexts. But the theoretical identification of typologies is not particularly useful unless it can help to clarify the standing of actual capitalist structures. How is the analysis of economic structures in Japan and Germany, South Korea and France, and Italy and Taiwan enhanced by the adoption of the three institutional typologies elaborated above? Can we identify better the distinctiveness of each economy's organizational structure by relating it to one of the three ideal types?

11

Institutional Cooperation in Japanese and German Capitalism

MARCO ORRÙ

n recent decades, the capitalist economies of Japan and Germany have shown unmatched strength and resilience in the face of international economic downturns that have prompted the decline of other major industrial nations, such as the United States and the United Kingdom.[1] Economists, business experts, political

AUTHOR'S NOTE: This chapter is reprinted here by permission of M. E. Sharpe, Inc., from "Institutional Cooperation in Japanese and German Capitalism," by Marco Orrù, in *Institutional Change: Theory and Empirical Findings,* edited by Sven-Erik Sjöstrand. Copyright 1993 by M. E. Sharpe, Inc.; all rights reserved.

scientists, students of organizations, and economic sociologists have in various ways sought to identify the distinguishing features that make some economies more successful than others in the international arena, and the German and Japanese economies have received a good share of attention in their own right,[2] but a direct, detailed comparison between these two leading world economies has been nearly absent.[3] This neglect is particularly puzzling because the capitalist structures of the two countries show a remarkable number of similarities when observed side by side.

Both Japan and Germany are poor in natural resources and have relatively small agricultural sectors. Their industrial activities are concentrated mostly in similar manufacturing areas, such as electrical products and electronics, automobile manufacturing, mechanical engineering, and steel, and in each area a number of large corporations stand out as sector leaders. Both countries have highly educated, highly skilled, well-paid, and disciplined labor forces. Also, in both Japan and Germany a significant share of economic activity is devoted to the export of goods that are valued around the world for their high quality. The roles of the two countries within their own economic regions also display similarities: Japan dominates the East Asian and Southeast Asian regions and is making significant inroads into mainland China, and Germany dominates the Western European economy and is poised to broaden its influence toward Eastern Europe and the countries of the former Soviet Union. Similar relations of regional interdependence can also be observed, for instance, between Japan and Taiwan on the one hand, and between Germany and Italy on the other. And yet no study has sought to explain systematically the remarkable affinity between the economic structures of these two countries that are geographically and culturally so far apart.

The neglect of a Japan-Germany comparison is easy to explain. In the past 20 years, especially in the United States, researchers have been fascinated by the East Asian economic miracle and have sought to identify broad cultural features, such as the Confucian work ethic, to account for East Asia's success story (see Nakane, 1970; Silin, 1976). In the process, the distinctive variations of economic structures in different East Asian countries, such as South Korea, Taiwan, and Japan, were often left by the wayside.[4] In a parallel fashion, less attention was devoted to the success stories of European economies such as those of Germany, France, and Italy, and the variations in Western capitalist economies were likewise downplayed. The emphasis fell, instead, on a sharp contrast between capitalism in East Asia and capitalism in the West, especially in the United States (see, e.g., Berger, 1984).

In this chapter I seek to identify the overarching logic of German and Japanese capitalist structures by emphasizing the pervasive organizational logic of mutual adjustment that characterizes the economic and social structures of both countries. Mutual adjustment pervades German and Japanese economies with regard to a broad range of institutional actors: industrial organizations, educational institutions, labor unions, financial institutions, federal and state bureaucracies, and political bodies. What is striking in both societies is the extent to which different institutional actors are able to develop shared communities of intents that are translated into widely supported national economic policies. In the economic structures of both Japan and Germany, institutional cooperation appears within institutions (e.g., work organization within firms, internal structure of labor unions, business groups' arrangements) and between institutions (e.g., between labor unions and large corporations, between educational institutions and industrial firms, among subcontracting firms, and between political bodies and business associations). Institutional cooperation can be identified as a key feature of the overarching organizational logic of both economies.

To show how institutional cooperation is a major feature in the capitalist structures of Japan and Germany, I present my argument in four parts. First, I provide national statistics for both countries to assess how the two economies compare in general terms. Second, I analyze each country's industrial structure to highlight its organizational distinctiveness. Third, I compare Japan's and Germany's capitalist structures in terms of contributing societal sectors and highlight the patterns of close interaction and collaboration within and among these sectors. Fourth, I summarize the comparative overview of the Japanese and German economies by presenting the concept of alliance capitalism as a key framework for understanding the institutional foundations of both economies.

The Economies of Japan and Germany

Germany's unification is today a political reality, but the 45 years of division into East Germany and West Germany following World War II created two very different economies. It would be misleading to treat the German economic structure as a unified whole; instead, West Germany will be the comparative case used here. As unification becomes an economic

Table 11.1   Summary Statistics on Germany and Japan, 1986

Category	West Germany	Japan
Area (square kilometers)	248,667	371,857
Population (1986)	61,080,000	121,490,000
Population density	246	327
Total civilian employees	25,267,000	58,530,000
Percentage in agriculture	5.3	8.5
Percentage in industry	40.9	34.5
Percentage in services	53.7	57.1
GDP ($U.S. billions)	892	1,956
GDP per capita ($U.S.)	14,611	16,109
Exports as percentage of GDP	27.2	10.8
Imports as percentage of GDP	21.3	6.5
Literacy rate (percentage)	99	99
Population per physician (1982)	431	735
Television sets per 1,000	373	580

SOURCES: OECD (1988b), *Japan Statistical Yearbook* (1988), *Statistisches Jahrbuch 1988 für die Bundesrepublik Deutschland* (1988), and *Information Please Almanac, 1990* (1990).

reality, the traits of West Germany's economic structure will likely come to characterize Germany in its entirety. My analysis of Germany therefore is based on West Germany's economic structure.

Japan and Germany are, respectively, the second- and third-ranking capitalist economies in the world. Both countries, having suffered total devastation during World War II, proceeded vigorously in the postwar decades to rebuild their shattered economies. Today, their economic and financial strengths challenge, and sometime surpass, those of the United States. For example, a 1989 ranking of the world's 50 largest commercial banks shows that 23 of them are based in Japan and 5 in Germany, whereas just 4 are based in the United States ("The International 500," 1989). Table 11.1 shows major comparative statistics for Japan and Germany.

Japan's population is twice the size of Germany's, and its gross domestic product (GDP) is more than twice as large; but overall size aside, the two countries show similar aggregate statistics. Both economies have high civilian employment (41% in Germany, 48% in Japan) compared with other industrialized countries such as France (38%) or the Netherlands (35%). Moreover, as Table 11.2 shows, Japan and Germany display the highest share of workers employed in industry among industrialized countries (41% for Germany, 35% for Japan). This compares with 31% in the United Kingdom, 28% in the United States, and 25% in Canada.

Table 11.2   Share of Civilian Employment in Industry for Selected
Industrialized Countries, 1986

Country	Percentage
Germany	40.9
Japan	34.5
Italy	33.1
France	31.3
United Kingdom	30.9
United States	27.7
Canada	25.3

SOURCE: OECD labor force statistics for 1986.

The economies of Japan and Germany rest indisputably on a very strong
industrial manufacturing base, and this fact is all the more significant when
one considers that the same two countries pay some of the highest wages for
industrial workers around the world. Both countries boast highly educated
labor forces, with Japan having the highest number of scientists and engi-
neers (around 70 per 10,000 workers), ahead of the United States and
Germany (Port, 1990, p. 35). Data on 1987 nonmilitary research and development activities also show a larger share of the gross national product
invested in Japan (2.8%) and Germany (2.6%) compared with the United
States (1.8%).

Not only do Japan and Germany lead industrialized nations in their share
of manufacturing activities, they also lead industrialized economies in the
absolute size of export activities. In 1986, Germany exported goods worth
$242 billion U.S., and Japan's exports amounted to $211 billion U.S.,
compared with France's $119 billion U.S. and the United Kingdom's $107
billion U.S. Exports for the United States in 1986 added up to slightly more
than Japan's in absolute terms, but amounted to only 5% of the U.S. total
GDP, compared with Germany's whopping 27% and Japan's 11% (Organization for Economic Cooperation and Development [OECD], 1988b). The
destinations of exports from the two countries differ geographically, according to regional market structures. Most German exports (75%) go to other
European countries, almost 10% go to the United States, and only 2% go to
Japan. Japanese exports are more widely distributed: 37% of Japanese
exports go to the United States, 30% to the rest of Asia, and 22% to European
countries. Despite their geographic diversity, the contents of Japanese and
German exports are remarkably similar. The largest shares of Germany's

exports are in machinery (23%), automobiles (19%), chemical products (13%), and electronics (6%). Japan's largest exports are in automobiles (28%), machinery (23%), and electronics (18%).[5] The similarity is not accidental; Japanese industrial policy has sought to emulate Germany's industrial structure for several decades. Magaziner and Hout (1981) report, "By 1985, the Japanese Economic Planning Agency hopes that Japan will have a structure similar to the structure of Germany's exports of manufactured goods in the mid-1970s" (p. 8).

The industrial structures of Japan and Germany are similar in yet another respect. In both countries, large industrial corporations are the leaders of their national economies in both domestic and international markets. Brand names like Toyota, Toshiba, and NEC are household words in Japan and abroad, just as Volkswagen, Siemens, and BASF are well-known in Germany and throughout the world. Table 11.3 lists the top 20 industrial businesses in Japan and Germany in 1988 to illustrate how the top corporations in the two countries compare. Except for the presence of large German chemical companies (BASF, Hoechst, and Bayer), the makeup of the two lists is remarkably similar. The top 20 corporations in both countries span six major industrial sectors: motor vehicles and parts, electronics, metal industries, computers, industrial and farm equipment, and oil refining. Automobile manufacturing constitutes a large share of top corporations in both countries (five for Germany, six for Japan), illustrating an additional similarity of industrial strategies in the two economies.

Research and development activities are given high priority in both Japan and Germany (see Porter, 1990, pp. 370-371). Research and development investments by private corporations are heavily emphasized, especially within large industrial firms. Table 11.4 shows top-ranking corporate research and development spenders in both countries; all firms listed rank within the top 20 corporations included in Table 11.3.

Although large manufacturing corporations dominate the economic activities in both countries, state ownership of manufacturing firms is nearly absent. Of Japan's 159 corporations listed in *Fortune's* International 500 in 1988, only one (Japan Tobacco) was government owned. Of Germany's 53 top corporations, only 2 (Salzgitter and Saarbergwerke) belonged to the government. This compares with 14 government-owned industrial corporations from France, 7 from India, and 5 from Finland in the same International 500 list. A similar absence of state ownership in Japan and Germany can be observed with regard to financial institutions. Of the largest 100 banks

Table 11.3 Top Twenty German and Japanese Corporations in "Fortune's International 500" 1988

	West Germany				Japan		
Name	Sector	Sales	Employees	Name	Sector	Sales	Employees
Daimler-Benz	40	41,818	338,749	Toyota	40	50,790	86,082
Siemens	36	34,129	353,000	Hitachi	36	41,331	263,996
Volkswagen	40	33,696	252,066	Matsushita	36	33,922	134,186
BASF	28	24,960	234,834	Nissan	40	29,097	108,716
Hoechst	28	23,308	164,527	Toshiba	36	25,441	122,000
Bayer	28	23,026	165,700	Honda	40	22,236	58,320
Thyssen	33	16,796	127,778	NEC	36	19,626	102,452
Bosch	40	15,747	167,780	Nippon Steel	33	17,109	67,766
BMW	40	11,762	58,000	Mitsubishi Elec.	36	16,857	75,795
Ruhrkohle	10	11,750	120,341	Mazda	40	15,151	28,027
Mannesmann	45	11,620	151,782	Fujitsu	44	14,797	94,825
Ford Werke	40	10,951	49,530	Mitsubishi Motor	40	14,183	25,600
Adam Opel	40	9,936	52,675	Mitsubishi H.I.	45	13,398	56,100
Metall G.	33	8,757	25,132	Nippon Oil	29	12,773	10,178
Man	45	8,639	61,901	Sony	36	10,134	60,500
Krupp	33	8,385	63,391	Sanyo	36	9,376	39,179
Veba Oel	29	6,788	171,546	Bridgestone	30	9,296	88,148
Bertellsmann	27	6,539	41,961	IBM Japan	44	9,270	21,061
IBM Deutsch	44	6,471	30,712	Isuzu	40	9,268	24,443
Henkel	28	5,833	35,943	Nippondenso	40	8,962	47,359
Total sales		320,911				383,017	
Total employees			2,382,958				1,514,733
Average sales per firm		16,046				19,151	
Average employees per firm			119,148				75,737
Average sales per employee		134,669				252,861	

SOURCE: "The International 500" (1989, pp. 291-294).
NOTE: Sector codes are as follows: 10 = mining; 27 = publishing and printing; 28 = chemicals; 29 = petroleum refining; 30 = rubber products; 33 = metals; 36 = electronics; 40 = motor vehicles and parts; 44 = computers; 45 = industrial/farm equipment. Sales are in $U.S. millions.

Table 11.4   Top Corporate Spenders in Japan and Germany in 1989

	Japan			Germany	
Firm	$U.S. Millions	Sales (%)	Firm	$U.S. Millions	Sales %
Hitachi	2,190	9.9	Siemens	3,684	11.2
Matsushita	2,140	7.9	Daimler-Benz	2,927	8.2
Toyota	1,190	3.9	Bayer	1,404	6.1
NEC	1,780	10.2	Hoechst	1,379	5.9
Fujitsu	1,740	12.8	Volkswagen	1,198	3.5

SOURCES: Gross (1990, p. 75) and Peterson (1990, p. 122).

outside the United States in 1988, 31 are Japanese, but only 1 of these is government owned; Germany lists 11 banks, of which only 2 are owned by the state. This compares with 7 government-owned banks in Italy and 4 in France in the same top 100 list. Overall, with respect to both industrial and financial activities, the Japanese and German governments seem, comparatively speaking, to keep their direct involvement in their national economies to a minimum.

Indisputably, both Japanese and German large corporations play a major role in the international economy as well as in their respective domestic economies. But it would be misleading to think that they alone account for these economies' industrial prowess. As Michael Porter (1990) remarks, "While there is a mixture of large and small firms, German international success is built to a surprising extent on small- and medium-sized firms, something often not well understood by observers of the German economy" (p. 374). Data on the distribution of manufacturing enterprises by number of employees from 1986 (see Table 11.5) show that even excluding manufacturing firms with fewer than 20 employees, large German firms (with 200 or more workers) account for less than 17% of the total number of enterprises. Large Japanese firms, then, make up an even smaller share of the total (a little more than 6%). Table 11.5 shows significant differences in the two countries' structure of manufacturing enterprises. Overall, Japan has stronger industrial muscle than Germany, but it has relatively fewer large corporations, and their average size is smaller than that of their German counterparts. Later in this chapter I will focus on the organizational features that account for differences between the two countries. For now it should suffice to point out that industrial collaboration among firms of different

Table 11.5 Manufacturing Enterprises by Number of Employees in Germany and Japan, 1986

	West Germany					Japan				
Size	*Firms*	*%*	*Employees*	*%*	*Average*	*Firms*	*%*	*Employees*	*%*	*Average*
20-49	16,634	43.5	545,682	7.5	32.8	16,634	43.5	545,682	24.3	30.1
50-199	15,183	39.7	1,466,708	21.3	96.6	33,494	28.6	2,999,000	31.7	89.5
200+	6,436	16.8	4,869,853	70.8	756.7	7,226	6.2	4,154,000	44.0	574.9
Total	38,254	100.0	6,882,253	100.0	179.9	117,135	100.0	9,450,000	100.0	80.7

SOURCES: *Japan Statistical Yearbook* (1988) and *Statistisches Jahrbuch 1988 für die Bundesrepublik Deutschland* (1988).

sizes is a distinctive feature of both the German and Japanese economies—although a much stronger feature in Japan than in Germany.

Collaborative arrangements among large industrial corporations and top financial institutions have been described by the business press as characteristic features of both German and Japanese capitalism. The casual reader is well acquainted with the notion of "Japan Inc."—the dense web among large banks, industrial corporations, national bureaucracies, and business associations that make the Japanese economy behave as one integrated conglomerate. But a similar metaphor can also be extended to Germany, as in this journalistic report: "In West Germany, major industrial groups are interlocked in a web of big banks and government ministries, sharing board members and shareholders. They are often called on to help bolster Germany Inc." (Templeman, 1990, p. 55). A recent *Business Week* cover story on Mitsubishi, the giant Japanese conglomerate, compared the interdependence of Mitsubishi member firms with "Deutsche Bank's large industrial holdings in Germany" (Neff, 1990, p. 100). What is most intriguing about the similarity in the industrial structures of the two countries is that collaboration between giant Japanese and German business groups is soon going to be an economic reality. Talks between Daimler-Benz and Mitsubishi top executives, reports *Business Week,* "could lead Germany and Japan's two largest business groups into joint ventures ranging from building a car plant in the [former] Soviet Union to designing hypersonic planes able to fly in space" (Neff, 1990, p. 98).

It is clear that Japan and Germany are among the most successful industrialized countries in the world, and it should be equally clear from the preceding overview that there are many similarities in the characteristics of these two economies. Yet it would be erroneous to assume that if the two countries have achieved similar results they must have utilized similar strategies throughout. In fact, if we look closely at the organizational patterns of business in the two countries, we will detect, along with numerous similarities, clear and remarkable differences.

The Structures of
Japanese and German Business

Studies of Japanese and other successful Asian and non-Asian economies have often been offered as examples of economic structures that disprove the superior efficiency of vertically integrated business activities based on the reduction of transaction costs (Dore, 1986a; Hamilton & Biggart, 1988: Lorenzoni & Ornati, 1988). The attempt to show how subcontractual arrangements can display a reduction of transaction costs equal or even superior to vertically integrated, in-house production arrangements has been worthwhile, but such an attempt might have gone overboard by assuming that the deep structures of the two production models would have to be as different from each other as the variations in their surface structure. On the one hand, Mark Granovetter (1985) has endeavored to show that opportunism and deceit are in no away absent from economic transactions among vertically integrated businesses; on the other hand, Ronald Dore (1983) has demonstrated that subcontractual relations among manufacturing firms in Japan can be nearly free of any opportunistic and deceitful economic behavior. However, it would be unwarranted to use these authors' evidence to turn transaction cost theory on its head and claim that subcontractual relations are necessarily more cost-efficient than vertically integrated relations. Simply put, matters of economic efficiency cannot be settled either way in theoretical, abstract terms.

The organizational structures of industrial sectors in Japan and Germany provide empirical evidence that subcontractual arrangements are not necessarily superior to vertical integration, or vice versa. One needs to go beyond the external structure of firms to gain a meaningful understanding of the economic logic that drives them. Table 11.6 illustrates external organizational differences by comparing paired sets of German and Japanese industrial and financial corporations.

Across a variety of sectors, from banking to motor vehicles and parts manufacturing to electronics to steel, Japanese corporations with sales figures equal to or higher than those of a paired German corporation employ, on average, one-third to one-half the number of workers. Automation of production is one significant factor in reducing the size of the workforce in large Japanese firms, but the main reason for the variation in firm size between Japan and Germany is to be found in the extensive subcontracting arrangements that characterize the entire Japanese production system, compared with the vertically integrated and internalized manufacturing system of most German firms. The automobile industries of the two countries provide a good comparative illustration.

In a study of Japan's automobile industry, Koichi Shimokawa (1985) describes the production system as "based primarily on a powerful *keiretsu* relationship between automobile manufacturers and technologically ad-

Table 11.6   Paired German and Japanese Corporations by Sector, 1988

Sector	Japanese Firm	Employees	German Firm	Employees
Autos	Toyota	86,082	Daimler-Benz	338,749
Auto Parts	Nippondenso	47,359	Bosch	167,780
Banking	Dai-Ichi Kangyo	18,663	Deutsche Bank	54,769
Computers	IBM Japan	21,061	IBM Deutschland	30,712
Electronics	Matsushita	134,186	Siemens	353,000
Ind. Equip.	Mitsubishi H.I.	56,100	Mannesmann	121,782
Oil	Nippon Oil	10,178	Veba Oël	17,156

SOURCE: "The International 500" (1989, pp. 291-294, 320-321).

vanced primary parts manufacturers and secondarily on numerous small and medium-sized parts producers" (p. 6). Thus Shimokawa assesses one large automobile manufacturer in Japan as having 168 primary subcontractors, 4,000 secondary subcontractors, and 31,600 tertiary subcontractors (p. 7, Table 1). This contrasts sharply with the German automobile manufacturing patterns described by Wolfgang Streeck (1989):

> West German auto assemblers are highly vertically integrated, and this is one major difference from their Japanese competitors. . . . The apparent preference for making rather than buying parts seems in part to be accounted for by pressures from the works councils for high and stable employment. . . . There is also a preference for large, integrated plants; the biggest German plant, VW Wolfsburg, employs no less than sixty-five thousand people. (p. 121)

To be sure, there is variation within the German organizational landscape; for instance, manufacturers in Germany's southern region are more likely to operate on the basis of interfirm networks than are their counterparts in the Ruhr Valley in the north. But when they are compared with the extensive Japanese subcontract patterns, even southern Germany's production networks of Daimler-Benz, BMW, Bosch, and others in the Baden Württemberg region appear as internalized production systems. BMW, with 58,000 employees, is a relatively small automobile manufacturer by German standards, but Japan's Mazda, with only 28,000 workers, posted nearly 30% higher sales figures than BMW in 1988 (see Table 11.3).

The organizational differences between German and Japanese manufacturing have already been suggested by the figures in Table 11.5. Germany has almost as many firms with 200 or more workers as Japan, but half as many firms with 50 to 199 workers, and only one-fifth the number of small firms with 20 to 49 workers. In this last category, Japan counts more than 76,000 manufacturing firms employing close to 3.3 million workers, whereas Germany counts fewer than 17,000 firms employing a little more than half a million workers. Small entrepreneurship is much more widespread in Japan than in Germany; 1983 data on the percentage of salaried employees in industry show Japan, Italy, and Belgium at the low end with 71-74%, whereas Germany, Canada, and the United States rank at the high end with 87-90% salaried employees (see Nanetti, 1988, p. 12). The difference between German and Japanese organizational patterns is emphatically underlined by these statistics.[6]

The surface differences between Japan and Germany are obvious, but one would be mistaken in equating the internalization of production by large German manufacturers with the mass production style of U.S. manufacturers who also tend to internalize production processes. Gary Herrigel (1989) describes the organizational pattern of German industrial corporations, especially in northern areas, as one of "autarkic-firm-based industrial order." Herrigel explains that in Germany, "firms grew very large very rapidly because the lack of surrounding infrastructure forced them to incorporate most of the stages of manufacture under their control" (p. 193). But with regard to these autarkic firms, Herrigel argues:

> The logic behind production organization was the opposite of that in large series and mass production processes: instead of building rigidity into process organization in the plant to produce a large series standard product efficiently, these firms sought to create structures—workshops—that enhanced the firm's ability to reorganize production quickly. (p. 194)

Herrigel characterizes these large industrial firms as "a collection of specialized workshops." Thus, despite the differences in the external structures of German and Japanese manufacturing, they are internally much closer to each other organizationally than either of them is to large firms in the United States. Both German and Japanese firms appear to emphasize flexible production and specialization of tasks. Piore and Sabel (1984) detected the similarities between the two economies despite different external patterns of organization, remarking:

> In West Germany the changes [toward craft production] are often centered in the large firms, rather than in the network of their suppliers. West German firms

are decentralizing internally, instead of dissolving into their supplier networks (the limiting case in Italy) or functioning as assemblers of customized components (the limiting case in Japan). (pp. 229-230)

If both German and Japanese manufacturers are able to achieve high levels of flexible specialization through the different avenues of extensive subcontracting (in Japan) and of large autarkic firms (in Germany), then the reasons for their similar economic efficiency must be sought below the surface, in the deeper institutional features that characterize the organization of each economy.

Institutional Cooperation in Japan and Germany

It should be apparent by now that the economic organizations observed in Germany and Japan are by no means identical; instead, they differ substantially in how they set the boundaries of individual corporations and to what extent they rely on subcontracting with external firms. Japan's manufacturing structure is often depicted as a giant production pyramid. The Ministry for International Trade and Industry (MITI) estimates that more than 50% of manufacturing firms with 300 or fewer workers are subcontractors for larger Japanese manufacturing firms. "One of Japan's top electronics makers has well over 6,000 subcontractors in that pyramid" (*Business Tokyo,* April 1990, p. 24).

The picture in German manufacturing is quite different. The 10 largest manufacturing enterprises in Germany literally dominate the industrial landscape, and their dominance has increased substantially in recent decades. In 1965, the top 10 industrial firms accounted for 15.6% of Germany's total industrial turnover and for 13.4% of total employment in industry. In 1980, the same top 10 firms accounted for 20.7% of turnover and 22.7% of industrial employment (Leaman, 1988, p. 66). In comparison, the 1,001 firms belonging to Japan's largest business groups employed, in 1985, only 9.4% of the industrial workforce (Dodwell Marketing Consultants, 1986, p. 41).

The striking differences in the industrial structures of Germany and Japan are too obvious to be overlooked, and yet these differences are not as significant as the similarities that underlie, in both economies, the internal structures of industrial firms and the relationships among the various institutional actors in the economies. I call the similar overarching characteristic of both countries' economic structure *institutional cooperation*—that is, a formulation of economic strategies and a practice of production based on the emergence of collectively shared responsibilities. This phenomenon of institutional cooperation can be shown at three distinct analytic levels: It characterizes (a) industrial relations within firms, (b) relations across institutional realms pertinent to economic action, and (c) relations between the private sector and the state in the two societies. Let us compare the Japanese and German economic structures in each of these areas in turn.

Internal Cooperation of Business Firms

Japan's labor relations have often been considered culturally unique for their emphasis on lifetime employment, seniority-based advancement, consensus-building decision making, and the structuring of manufacturing activities around responsible production teams. These organizational traits have often been contrasted with industrial relations in Western economies (especially in the United States and the United Kingdom), which emphasize elasticity in hiring and firing workers, performance-based job classifications for career advancement, highly stratified hierarchies for decision making, and narrow interpretation of job-related tasks and responsibilities. Such divergence in labor relations models, however, is neither universal nor unchanging.

In a 1984 article, Wolfgang Streeck identifies a convergence trend between German and Japanese models of industrial relations, noting that German firm relations have increasingly come to resemble those of the Japanese. Streeck lists four evolving features of German industrial relations:

> (1) [There is an] emergence of a system of stable and secure (guaranteed) employment for workers in large companies. . . . (2) The adoption of a "human resources" approach to manpower management by large companies aims at increased flexibility of manpower use in spite of employment stability. . . . (3) The works council has been incorporated into the management of the manpower function of large companies. . . . (4) There is a growing identification of the interests of workers in large firms with the interests of their employing organization as a production unit competing in the market. (pp. 112-113)

These four characteristics of industrial relations lead Streeck to argue that German firms are moving toward a cooperative model of firm management approaching that of the Japanese—although Streeck is quick to qualify:

"Clearly, the large enterprise as an interest community between capital and labour is much more apparent in Japan than it is in Germany" (p. 113).

Recent empirical studies have shown that organizational features of German manufacturing firms differ significantly from those of other European economies. Maurice, Sorge, and Warner (1980) highlight German firms' distinctive organization of manufacturing, compared with British and French firms. They observe, "The flexibility and cooperation between different production jobs was greater in Germany than in the other countries" (p. 70). Hartmann, Nicholas, Sorge, and Warner (1983) compare British and German manufacturing firms' skill utilization in introducing computerized machine tools and argue, "In Germany C.N.C. was more visibly used to reduce training differentials between technical staff and the shop-floor personnel, to increase the tradesman's status, to encourage even greater flexibility in production, and to reduce the 'decision-making overload' on top management" (p. 229).

With a similar thrust, Michael Schumann (1990) studied the trends emerging in Germany's automobile, machine building, and chemical industries; he identifies an increasing reliance of German firms on "teams of workers collectively responsible for a whole system of automated machinery" (p. 4). Schumann writes: "Nowhere in our empirical research did we come across an intensifying division of labor. Actually, the contrary is predominant. . . . Current attempts at gaining efficiency rely on the integration of functions and more complex responsibilities" (p. 24). As it pertains to their internal organization, it seems evident that both Japanese and German firms similarly emphasize the diffusion of responsibilities throughout the production process, the flexibility and interchangeability of tasks, the substantial reduction of managerial hierarchies, and consensus-based decision making.

Historically, different factors accounted for the development of similar organizational features in Japan and Germany. The German model is greatly indebted to the emergence of distinctive labor-management relations in German industry after World War II, sanctioned by the Co-Determination Act of 1951 and the Works Constitution Act of 1952. Streeck (1984) describes these two pieces of legislation as follows:

> Two different channels of employee representation in German industrial organizations: co-determination at the workplace . . . , which is exercised through work councils, and co-determination in the enterprise, which is exercised

through work force representatives on the supervisory board and, to an extent, the management board. (p. 95)

Streeck's assessment of codetermination is that on the one hand it narrowed the organizational control of management over hiring and firing, but on the other hand it broadened the potential utilization of a firm's stable workforce. "Co-determination has contributed to growing organizational rigidities and at the same time has provided the organizational instruments to cope with such rigidities without major losses in efficiency" (p. 105).

S. J. Park (1984) describes Japan's distinctive firm relations as having emerged historically to address the need for democratization of the economy, increased productivity, elimination of management/workers imbalances, and strengthening of the labor movement. The result was a labor-management consultation system that first emerged in the 1920s but did not see extensive adoption or implementation until the 1950s. The Japanese participatory system borrowed from the German Works Council and from the British Whitley Committee. But Park remarks: "Even though this system originated in Western Europe, there is no doubt that it has absorbed some typical Japanese traits" (p. 154). Whereas the German system co-opted workers into high-level managerial decision making, the Japanese system keeps worker participation from entering top- or even middle-level managerial decision making. Park argues, "The Japanese type of participation is a priori embedded into a management-centered economic system, while the West European concept of participation is directed towards expanding the strength of labour unions representing workers' and employees' interests" (p. 165).

Significantly, some German managers look with envy at industrial relations in Japan, wishing German workers would emulate their Japanese counterparts in being loyal to their firm, ready to sacrifice, and prone to consensus; yet, comparatively speaking, industrial relations in Germany are much closer to the harmonious Japanese model than to the belligerent industrial relations found in other European countries. Wolfgang Streeck (1990) argues:

West German unions . . . have mastered the crises of the 1970s and 1980s far better than their counterparts in countries like Italy or the United Kingdom. . . . Their less flamboyant approach helped West German unions build a foundation for union power strong enough to outlast the institutional dislocations and structural breaks in Western political economies after the first "oil shock." (p. 2)

Industrial relations in Japan and Germany display some differences, but overall they are similar to each other in the clear emphasis they give to consensus seeking and cooperation in their industrial organizations. However, the cooperation within firms is significantly amplified and strengthened by the larger framework of cooperation among the major institutional actors in the capitalist economies of both Japan and Germany.

Institutional Cooperation of Economic Actors

Researchers, especially in the United States, have been bewildered by the economic miracle that is Japan. The more closely they look at the structure of Japan's economy, however, the less willing they are to see it as in any way comparable to Western economies. The title of a business column by Alan Blinder (1990) captures the feeling: "There Are Capitalists, Then There Are the Japanese." Blinder explains:

> According to American doctrine, monopolies and cartels are economic pathologies. We are also wary of vertical integration, because captive suppliers or retailers may serve the interests of the dominant company rather than those of consumers. We worry that cozy relationships between upstream and downstream companies may lead to inefficiencies, so we favor arm's-length deals in which buyers seek the lowest prices. (p. 21)

But the Japanese, Blinder argues, do business differently. When they need parts supplied in their production process, or capital for business expansion, or a network of retail outlets, the Japanese do not search in the market for the best deal, but turn to the firms in their own business groups. "To their way of thinking, long-term, reliable relationships cut costs as business partners learn from and help one another." The Japanese government reinforces the cooperative thrust of the private sector by allowing cross-holding of stocks among grouped businesses to keep out foreign competition, by favoring domestic companies for significant national projects, and by cooperating in research and development activities.

Blinder's and other writers' descriptions of Japanese business practices are accurate, but researchers are mistaken in considering Japan's economic structure to be unique and eminently non-Western. Too often, capitalism is equated with U.S. capitalism, disregarding a wide variation in the economic structures of such countries as France, Italy, and Germany. If we compare

Germany's economic structure to that of the United States, it is apparent that it differs from U.S. capitalism as much as Japan's does, and that in fact it more closely resembles the latter than the former. In Germany, as in Japan, close ties and intensive collaboration obtain among industrial firms, financial institutions, local and central government, business associations, and labor unions. John Zysman (1983) describes the cooperative quality of the German economic structure: "The distinctive character of the German system of 'organized private enterprise' depends on the combination of four elements: concentration, tolerated cartel-like arrangements, centralized semiofficial trade associations, and a tutelary banking system" (p. 252). It is significant that the same four features Zysman attributes to the German economic structure also characterize Japan's economy. Let us examine each one in both countries.

Industrial concentration was already apparent when we assessed the extent to which large industrial firms dominate Germany's economic landscape.[7] More than 70% of industrial workers in Germany are employed by firms with 200 or more workers. But Japan also displays industrial concentration obtained through dense subcontracting; although small industrial firms are numerous, most of them do subcontracting work for large industrial firms. One insider reports: "Most people don't realize how extensive this system is. Many products are made entirely by smaller companies and simply labeled and packaged to look as if they were manufactured by one of Japan's 'giants' " (*Business Tokyo,* April 1990, p. 24).

Historically, *cartel-like arrangements* have also been a feature of German capitalism. German business historian Jürgen Kocka (1978) provides a detailed account of the emergence of cartels:

> Cartels were mostly voluntary agreements between concerns which remained independent . . . and they had the aim of establishing a common policy in the market. . . . They served to limit competition, to stabilize prices and profits, and they tended toward a monopoly control of the market. In 1897 the legality of cartels was confirmed by the highest court of the Reich. (p. I:563)

According to Kocka, the number of cartels rose dramatically, from only 4 in 1875, to 385 in 1905, to about 2,100 in 1930. Collusion among business enterprises was seen favorably by the Germans. Karl Hardach (1980), for instance, points out that "labor unions usually expected better job security from cartels than from unrestricted competition. . . . [They] regarded [them] as an intermediate stage in the industrial evolution toward socialism" (p. 148). Hardach reasons as follows: "Quite in contrast to the Anglo-American view, which connected competitive markets with equilibrium and monopolistic situations with indeterminacy and disorder, it was held [in Germany] that unrestricted competition was 'destructive' and that cartels were an 'element of order' " (p. 148).

Japan followed a different road to cartelization by organizing its financial and industrial structure around a limited number of large business groups to which most large corporations in Japan belong. The six largest groups are Mitsubishi, Mitsui, Sumitomo, Fuyo, Dai-Ichi Kangyo Bank (DKB), and Sanwa. The historical roots of some of these business groups go back a long way: The House of Sumitomo was founded in 1590; the House of Mitsui goes back to 1615. But the emergence of the modern industrial groups occurred during the Meiji era, in the last third of the nineteenth century (see Gerlach, 1992). Preferential financial, production, and trade operations obtain among members of each business group (see Orrù, Hamilton, & Suzuki, 1989; reprinted as Chapter 7, this volume). Ronald Dore (1986a) describes the business group philosophy: "It is a bit like an extended family grouping, where business is kept as much as possible within the family, and a certain degree of give and take is expected to modify the adversarial pursuit of market advantage" (p. 178).

Business associations are major partners in shaping industrial policies in both Japan and Germany. Germany lists three powerful institutions: the Federation of German Industry (BDI), the Federation of German Employers' Association (BDA), and the Diet of German Industry and Commerce (DIHT).[8] As Zysman (1983) describes them, "These organizations link German business to the government in an elaborate and centralized fashion. The federal constitution gives these associations consultative or semiofficial status that draws them into policymaking" (p. 253). Japan lists four major business associations (the so-called *zaikai*): Keidanren (the Federation of Economic Organizations), Keizai Doyukai (Japan's Committee for Economic Development), Nikkeiren (the Federation of Employers' Association), and Nihon Shoko Kaigisho (Japan Chamber of Commerce and Industry). These four business associations interact closely with the Japanese government and the business bureaucracies, especially MITI and the Ministry of Finance, in the development of national industrial policies.[9] Traditionally, these business associations have been headed by leaders of Japan's largest industrial and financial corporations (see Johnson, 1982; Samuels, 1987; Yamamura & Yasuba, 1987).

The *banking system* plays a "tutelary role" in the economic structures of both Japan and Germany. Schmiegelow and Schmiegelow (1990) point out the similarity between the two economies:

> The prevalence of indirect financing (of debt over equity financing), which characterized Japan's "overborrowed" corporate sector until the mid-1970s, may have seemed vertiginous from the point of view of the Anglo-Saxon countries, but basically similar conditions prevail in West Germany even today. Both in Japan and in West Germany, this system has been the cornerstone of the formation of long-term corporatist relationships in which management performance of participating enterprises is controlled by banks rather than by the capital market. (p. 568)

As Zysman (1983) notes, "The German 'universal' banks, preeminent players in all financial markets, contrast sharply with the more specialized banks of the Anglo-American system. For 'universal' banks equity investments and loans are alternative means of providing corporate finance" (p. 64). The automobile sector provides a good illustration of Germany's tutelary banking system. Wolfgang Streeck (1989) explains: "Bank representatives sit on all supervisory boards, either as shareholders or representing the proxy votes for shares they have in deposit. Each manufacturer has a long-standing relationship with one bank, which serves as *Hausbank*" (p. 120). Deutsche Bank is the main bank for Volkswagen and for Daimler-Benz; Dresdner Bank for BMW; Bayerische Vereinsbank for Audi; Landesgirokasse for Porsche. The *Hausbank* often evaluates the financial and managerial soundness of industrial companies and takes decisive action when problems arise. Streeck reports, "In the VW crisis of 1974 the Deutsche Bank was crucial in stimulating reorganization by threatening, in a supervisory board meeting, to withhold further credit and let the company go to the receiver" (p. 120).

Large Japanese industrial firms are also under the tutelage of major financial institutions. The three largest shareholders of Toyota Motor are Mitsui Bank, Sanwa Bank, and Tokai Bank; Nissan Motor's largest shareholder is the Industrial Bank of Japan. Mazda Motors's main bank, Sumitomo Bank, was instrumental in rescuing Mazda from bankruptcy in the mid-1970s, when the bank absorbed Mazda's huge default risks (Sheard,

1984). But beyond the one-on-one relations between individual banks and individual industrial firms, both German and Japanese banks have a privileged role in orchestrating their national economies.

As Ziegler, Bender, and Biehler (1985) report, "The efficiency of the German banking system and its close links with industry have often been cited as partial explanations for periods of rapid growth in German economic development" (p. 91). Historically, the authors explain, banks have been actively involved in shaping Germany's industrial structure:

> The banks took an active part in founding new firms, issued shares and bonds on behalf of industrial enterprises, held financial participations, provided long- and short-term loans and kept close personal connections, especially through representation on supervisory boards of the joint stock companies which were the dominant legal form among large industrials. (p. 92)

Three banks dominate the financial landscape in today's Germany: Deutsche Bank, Dresdner Bank, and Commerzbank. Germany's Ministry of Finance estimated in 1979 that these three banks "held 17 per cent of all participations and 38 per cent of the total stock value" (cited in Ziegler et al., 1985, p. 106). In their analysis of interlocks in the boards of financial and industrial companies, Ziegler et al. (1985) argue:

> There seems to be a hierarchical structure: executives of the three big banks sat on the supervisory boards of production companies, while the reverse occurred much less frequently. . . . [However,] this structure may well be the result of co-optive efforts from the side of production companies rather than the banks' attempts at control. (pp. 106-107)

Compared with other industrialized countries, both Japanese and German industrial corporations (especially the largest firms) rely more heavily on banks' long-term credit than on equity to raise capital. The largest three banks in Germany exert influence over about one-third of nonisolated industrial firms; thus they have strong direct links with industrial corporations. However, Ziegler et al. interpret the overall picture as follows:

> This does not seem to indicate one-sided bank control but more likely a coalescence of major interests from both the financial and the non-financial sectors. Banks act more like integrators cross-connecting industrials from various economic sectors and other fractional interests. They even seem to avoid too close a relationship with any particular group of enterprises. (p. 110)

Japanese banks also play a central role in their economy. As in Germany, Japanese firms rely more heavily on bank loans than on equity. Each Japanese business group has its own main bank that provides the bulk of loans for industrial firms belonging to the group and that dispatches directors to group firms. In 1985, Mitsubishi Petrochemical, a member of the Mitsubishi group, borrowed 32% of its capital from Mitsubishi financial institutions that held 20% of the firm's stocks. Three directors of Mitsubishi Petrochemicals were dispatched by the banks. Similarly, Sumitomo Cement borrowed 39% of its capital from Sumitomo financial institutions that held 19% of the firm's stocks and had two directors dispatched to it by Sumitomo Bank (Dodwell Marketing Consultants, 1986). The web spun by major Japanese banks is not restricted to the influence over members of their own business groups. For instance, Nippon Steel, the largest steel manufacturer that constitutes an independent industrial group, received financial loans from Mitsubishi (9.6%), Mitsui (5.6%), Sumitomo (8.5%), Fuyo (8.9%), Dai-Ichi Kangyo Bank (2.3%), Sanwa (8.2%), Tokai (3.2%), and the Industrial Bank of Japan (9.6%). Accordingly, most lending financial institutions held somewhere between 1.6% and 3.4% of Nippon Steel's stocks (Dodwell Marketing Consultants, 1986, p. 341). The coordinating core of the Japanese economic structure, in the end, is constituted by Japan's largest financial institutions—which include life insurance companies, city banks, trust and banking institutions, and marine and fire insurance companies (see Orrù, 1991b).

When considered together, the four structural features just outlined (concentration, cartels, business associations, and tutelary banking) all point to cooperative arrangements as characteristic of both Japan's and Germany's economic structures—especially when these are compared with the economic structures in most other industrialized countries. The uniqueness of Japanese and German capitalism resides in the close collaboration among large industrial firms, financial institutions, labor unions, business associations, and the government. Such collaboration rests on a view of national economic goals and priorities that is shared by all parties involved.

Cooperation of State and Private Sector

Political institutions in both Japan and Germany act as facilitators in the formulation and implementation of national industrial policies. On the one hand, they avoid direct involvement in industrial activities (as in France's dirigiste state) or in massively financing private industrial conglomerates (as in South Korea's powerful state banks); on the other hand, they avoid taking a minimalist stance of "governs best who governs least" typical of Anglo-Saxon economies (especially the conservative regimes of the United Kingdom and the United States in the 1980s). Instead, the role played by both the German and the Japanese governments is typically to facilitate the merging of interests among economic actors, rather than to impose unilateral decisions from the top down or to keep out of private business's way altogether.

The major political theme guiding the German economy since the end of World War II has been the principle of *Soziale Marktwirtschaft* (social market economy). Müller-Armack (1965) provides its classic definition:

> The Social Market Economy is a social and economic order. . . . The co-ordinated functions of the Social Market Economy do not conform exclusively to the mechanical rules of competition. Its principles of organization relate to the State and to society, both of which impress their notions of value and responsibilities on the whole system. . . . [It is] a co-ordination . . . between . . . the market, the State and the social groups. (pp. 90-91)

The cooperation of institutional economic actors in Germany rests on the *Soziale Marktwirtschaft* principle that the conflict of unrestrained competition should be mitigated by coordination and mutual adjustment. Müller-Armack argues that economic goals such as currency stability, full employment, growth, and equilibrium in the balance of payments require that "the institutional co-operation within the Government be organized on a permanent basis" (p. 101). With a slightly different vocabulary, but referring to the same principle, Keiko Körner (1971) speaks of "co-operative co-ordination . . . embracing the relevant State executive organs and representatives of several industries, sectors and groups" (p. 204). For example, Germany's policy of concerted action, Hardach (1980) explains, "sought to bring labor and management representatives together under the chairmanship of the minister of economics" (p. 202). As Katzenstein (1987) describes it, "Government by coalition, a system of cooperative federalism, and parapublic institutions are the three institutional nodes around which the politics of economic policy has unfolded in the Federal Republic" (p. 84). Katzenstein provides an example of the government's cooperation with the private sector during the 1960s coal mining crisis:

> The West German approach . . . amounted to concentration through coopera-
> tion. . . . The federal government bought out on favorable terms virtually all
> private owned mines and consolidated the industry under a holding company
> in which it owned substantial equity. . . . Significantly, both business and
> unions were centrally involved in the development of energy policy. The
> government neither imposed its preferred solution on the industry nor permitted
> market forces simply to dictate outcomes. (p. 102)

The same attempt to strike a balance between competition and coordination found in German economic policy characterizes Japanese industrial
policy. Chalmers Johnson (1985) labels the dynamics of Japanese business
"collusive rivalry"—a hybrid of competitive and cooperative forces. The
organization of Japan's industrial structure around a few very large business
groups makes it possible to promote competition among large corporations
in the same industrial sector while simultaneously favoring close cooperation
among firms that span industrial sectors. The role of the government and of
the national bureaucracy is not to impose its legislative fiat on private
business, but rather to provide "administrative guidance." As Johnson describes it, "The Japanese government is extremely intrusive into the privately
owned and managed economy, but it does this through market-conforming
methods and in cooperation rather than confrontation with the private sector"
(p. 61). In a similar vein, Richard Samuels (1987) characterizes the relation
between private business and the Japanese state as a "reciprocal consent"
where the market and the state come to mutual accommodation. Reciprocal
consent implies the mutual co-optation of private business in political economy issues and of the national government in the supervision of the industrial
structure in the service of national interests.

The Japanese pattern of interaction between political institutions and the
private sector is one of orchestrated consent and reciprocal support. For
example, when Texaco took over Getty Oil in 1984, it sought to dispose of
Getty's 50% shares of Mitsubishi Oil. The Mitsubishi group decided to
negotiate with Texaco for the purchase of Getty's shares. MITI supported
Mitsubishi's move by announcing that it would use Section 27 of Japan's
Foreign Exchange Law to block the sale of Mitsubishi Oil's shares to foreign
buyers (Sheard, 1984, p. 23). This and many other examples of reciprocal
support between the state and private business in Japan reflect "the explicit
recognition of the indivisibility of economy and politics" (Johnson, 1985,
p. 64). The Japanese government considers it its own business to facilitate

private business's pursuit of economic goals. Similarly, the German state's policy has been chiefly to promote economic growth and stability by providing the appropriate climate for a thriving and internationally competitive private business.

It should by now be apparent that if researchers are willing to abandon the preconceived notion that a unique "Asiatic" group-centeredness characterizes Japan's economic structure, it then becomes possible to see how much of what we observe in Japanese business can be also observed in German business. Thus it becomes possible to speak of typologies of capitalism, rather than resorting to culturally idiosyncratic models that vary endlessly from country to country. In relation to the German and Japanese economies' reliance on a centralized private sector and on an ideology of social partnership, Schmiegelow and Schmiegelow (1990) rightly observe that "analysts could speak of 'Germany Inc.' at least as easily as of 'Japan Inc.' " (p. 570).

Conclusion

Neoclassical economic theory assumes that economic actors (whether individuals, firms, or other social groups) compete in the marketplace as isolated entities in their rational pursuit of self-interested, utilitarian goals. Adam Smith (1976) has identified the principles underlying modern capitalism's ideal type of economic action. Economic action is motivated by self-interest: "It is not from the benevolence of the butcher, the brewer, or the baker, that we expect our dinner, but from their regard to their own interest" (p. 18). Economic order, accordingly, emerges from individualistic competition: "The individual intends only his own gain, and he is in this, as in many other cases, led by an invisible hand to promote an end which was no part of his intention" (p. 477).

The neoclassical paradigm dominates economic theory and is embodied (to some extent) in the economic structures of countries such as the United Kingdom and the United States. But it is doubtful that the same paradigm could be said to apply to the economic structures we have just examined in Germany and Japan. H. G. Peter Wallach (1985) argues the German case:

Adam Smith's "invisible hand" and the support for the ultimate "laissez-faire" idea that government should not be involved in economic affairs has hardly had strong support in Germany, for early artisans felt they were protected by the government, and later corporations found government backing advantageous. (p. 236)

Ronald Dore (1983) makes the case for Japan:

> The Japanese, in spite of what their political leaders say at summit conferences about the glories of free enterprise in the Free World . . . have never caught up with Adam Smith. They have never managed actually to bring themselves to *believe* in the invisible hand. (p. 470)

One cannot easily dismiss the Japanese and German economies (the second and third largest in the capitalist world, respectively) as simple aberrations from the ideal type of fully competitive free markets. Much less so given that most other capitalist economies around the world are just as removed (although in different ways) from such an ideal type. The institutional cooperation characterizing Japan and Germany needs to be studied and understood in its own right, as a distinctive pattern of economic action with status equal to that of other typologies of modern capitalism, like the laissez-faire economies of the United Kingdom and the United States, the family entrepreneurship economies of Italy and Taiwan, and the state-orchestrated economies of France and South Korea. Table 11.7 shows synoptically how cooperation is a significant component across a variety of organizational dimensions—within firms and across institutional sectors of the economy—in both Japanese and German capitalism. Cooperation is not a secondary feature, but a structural constant of both economies; it is not a behavioral afterthought of individuals, but an institutionalized principle that guides economic action at different structural and organizational levels.

The institutional cooperation characterizing the Japanese and the German economies demonstrates that their economic success does not come from competition alone, but also from a planned and balanced integration of individual and institutional actors, of private and public policies, of different social classes and political groups, in both the economic and the social arenas. Katzenstein (1989) describes the historically resilient consensus of Germany's political economy: "Social welfare and economic efficiency are not antithetical but mutually reinforcing" (p. 353). Accordingly, cooperation among labor unions, industrial corporations, financial institutions, governmental agencies, and other institutional actors is taken to be the obvious way of doing business. In Japan, Ronald Dore (1983) comments, economic action is pervasively accompanied by the *"need* to be benevolent as well as self-

Table 11.7   Typology of Capitalist Cooperation

	Japan	Germany
Intrafirm organization	team responsibility; quality training	flexibility of tasks; highly skilled workers
Labor-management relations	consultation system	codetermination
Production networks	extensive subcontracting	autarkic internal workshop or regional subcontracting
Interfirm relations	collusive rivalry	cartelization
Ownership networks	corporate cross-holdings	multiple-bank stockholding
Corporate networks	intermarket business groups	oligopolies and cartels
Capital sources	extensive bank loans and corporate profits	extensive bank loans and corporate profits
State-business relations	administrative guidance and reciprocal consent	cooperative coordination and concerted action

interested." Dore explains: "It is not just that benevolence is the best policy . . . the best way to material success. . . . But that . . . benevolence is a duty" (p. 470). Individuals and institutions in economic and noneconomic action alike are required to display mutual consideration, to think of collective goals and benefits rather than individual ones. Thus the inclination in economic action is to seek success through cooperation and mutual reinforcement, through the merging of interests, rather than to seek success through all-out competition.

The institutional analysis of economic structures relies on the inclusion of significant institutional factors without univocally assigning causal primacy to any single dimension (whether political, cultural, or economic). The combination of factors is here given priority over their analytic separation. The advantage of the institutional approach is that it makes it possible to identify the organizational logic that characterizes two economies with vastly different cultural and political histories without getting caught in the search for the ultimate causal factor (whether it be the culture, the state, or the market). Cooperation as a distinctive feature of Japanese and German capitalist structures has been shown here to be not the outcome of cultural or political or economic factors alone; rather, it has been shown to constitute an identifiable working logic of economic action that is empirically observed throughout the economic structure of the two societies. The identification of a pattern of capitalist cooperation and of other distinctive forms of capitalism around the world will advance in new directions our understanding of economic structures as socially constructed institutions—beyond the pointless search for one, undifferentiated model of world capitalism.

Notes

1. For basic economic statistics, see OECD (1988a, 1988b).

2. For recent studies on the German case, see Katzenstein (1987, 1989) and Leaman (1988). For studies on Japan, see Dore (1987), Sato and Hoshino (1984), and Caves and Uekusa (1976).

3. A rare exception is found in Shigeyoshi and Bergmann (1984). For a parallel comparison of family-based entrepreneurship in Italy and Taiwan, see Orrù (1991a; reprinted as Chapter 12, this volume).

4. A notable exception is found in Hamilton and Biggart (1988).

5. These data are from *Japan Statistical Yearbook* (1988) and *Statistisches Jahrbuch 1988 für die Bundesrepublik Deutschland* (1988).

6. Leaman (1988, p. 70) presents the following statistics on suppliers of large German firms: AEG, 30,000; Siemens, 30,000; Krupp, 23,000; Daimler-Benz, 18,000; BASF, 10,000; and Opel, 7,800. These data are from the 1960s, and I find the figures unbelievably high, but I have not been able to check Leaman's sources. Still, if one considers that 1986 figures show a total of 38,254 manufacturing firms with 20 or more employees in the entire Federal Republic, it becomes apparent how unlikely Leaman's suppliers' figures appear.

7. For a historical overview, see Tilly (1974). For a comparative perspective, see Chandler and Daems (1980).

8. For a description of these business associations, see Katzenstein (1989, pp. 10-12).

9. On the business associations' and government agencies' ties, see Taira and Wada (1987).

12

The Institutional Logic of Small-Firm Economies in Italy and Taiwan

MARCO ORRÙ

Recent research in institutional economics and in economic sociology has focused on the study of business organizations outside the United States—especially the successful economies of East Asia—to unveil the reasons for their outstanding performance and to verify whether and how patterns of business organization

AUTHOR'S NOTE: This chapter is reprinted here by permission of Transaction Publishers from "The Institutional Logic of Small-Firm Economies in Italy and Taiwan," by Marco Orrù, *Studies in Comparative International Development,* 1991, vol. 26, pp. 3-28. Copyright 1991 by Transaction Publishers; all rights reserved. Versions of this chapter were presented at the observed in these economies differ from the ones found in the United States (e.g., Dore, 1987; Hamilton & Biggart, 1988; Ouchi, 1982). The close scrutiny of East Asian and other economies outside the United States has helped overcome the limitations of existing theories of business organizations that see the vertical integration of business firms as the inevitable answer to problems of transaction costs. In one instance, the notion of "clans" was provided as an organizational principle exemplified in Japanese business. William Ouchi (1981) describes it as follows: "Industrial organizations can, in some instances, rely to a greater extent on socialization as the principal mechanism of mediation or control, and this 'clan' form . . . can be very efficient in mediating transactions between independent individuals" (p. 132). In another instance, drawing on studies of interfirm relations in Western Europe, East Asia, and the United States, researchers developed the notion of "networks" as yet another organizing principle of economic action between the extremes of free-floating markets on the one hand and tightly integrated hierarchies of firms on the other. Thorelli (1986) offers a characterization of networks: "The inter-organizational network may be conceived as a political economy concerned with the distribution of two scarce resources, money and authority. For the understanding of the configuration of any particular network, the flows of power and information may actually be more important than those of money and utilities" (p. 39).

The network principle of business organizations has emerged as a significant common denominator in cross-national studies of East Asian economies (see Hamilton & Biggart, 1988), but network configurations vary in different economies, such as in Japan, South Korea, and Taiwan—each economy displays distinctive organizational features, and it would be erroneous to lump them together as variations on one identical theme. Yet researchers have been eager to emphasize some uniformity in East Asian economies by contrasting a Western economic logic that rests on the individuality of the business firm with the different logic in the Far East emphasizing group-oriented economic action.

Recent theories of business organizations emphasize that economic action is socially specified and that it is never simply a matter of cost-benefit

XII World Congress of Sociology, Madrid, Spain, July 1990, and at the annual meetings of the American Sociological Association, Washington, D.C., August 1990. I am grateful to Gary G. Hamilton, William Zeile, Nicole Woolsey Biggart, Mark Ameo, Nancy A. Hewitt, Robert P. Ingalls, Pat Ruffin, and Candace Hinson for helpful comments and suggestions.

calculations made in an abstract way—rather, it is important to understand that economic action is also a matter of specified cultural values and beliefs, of socially shaped interpersonal and institutional routines and expectations, and of identifiable authority claims and legitimation principles. Institutional theories of organizations have touched most directly on the relevance of noneconomic factors in economic organizations by speaking of isomorphism in organizational fields (DiMaggio & Powell, 1983), of myths and ceremonies that provide organizational legitimation (Meyer & Rowan, 1977), and of the social embeddedness of economic action (Granovetter, 1985). For the institutional school, an adequate study of business organizations must incorporate both the material and the ideal interests that shape economic action, and must pay particular attention to the institutional traits that distinguish a given economic structure.

Recent research on East Asian business has shown that distinctive organizational patterns obtain in each society (Alston, 1989; Hamilton & Biggart, 1988) and that isomorphic organizational pressures prevail within each economy (Orrù, Biggart, & Hamilton, 1991). However, the identification of a group-oriented East Asian economic logic against the backdrop of an individual-oriented Western economic logic strains credulity and exaggerates the available evidence by advocating a mild version of cultural determinism. While showing that East Asian economies are not all of one kind, the researchers have forgotten that Western economies are not all of one kind either. The organizational logic that upholds the individuality of the firm as key economic actor might be applicable to one variant in the West (the Anglo-American variant, perhaps), but it is in no way (and should not be expected to be) representative of all other Western economies—especially in continental Europe. The economic routines and organizational patterns emerging from the interaction between material and ideal interests are not predetermined according to cultural uniformities any more than they are predetermined according to universal economic laws. Empirically, one should be able to observe different patterns of business in a given cultural area and similar patterns of business in different cultural areas. In this chapter I will provide evidence for the latter claim—that similar economic structures can be observed in different cultural areas—by comparing the organizational structures of business in the economies of Italy and Taiwan.

In broad economic terms, both Italy and Taiwan are characterized by the near absence of large-scale industrial corporations, by a strong state presence in heavy industry sectors, and by reliance on myriad small and medium-sized private firms that concentrate in similar lineups of manufacturing sectors. The structures of the two economies appear to be remarkably similar in many respects. A cultural or political explanation would fail to account for the similarities between Italian and Taiwanese business patterns because the two countries have very different cultural bases and sociopolitical histories. A market explanation would similarly be hard-pressed to show why the domestic and international markets would prompt similar responses in Taiwan and Italy but not, for example, in Great Britain or South Korea. In this chapter, I will argue that similar sets of institutional factors are present in the two societies that can help us understand the remarkable similarity in their business organizations. These institutional factors include cultural, political, and economic elements, to the extent that these elements are specified and observable in the patterns of business organization of the two countries. They also include elements that do not fall under market, political, or cultural headings, but relate more to the institutionalized routines and the logic of economic action that crucially affect and shape the economic structures of both countries.

The chapter is divided into three main sections. First, I will present the main features of the Italian and Taiwanese economies to sketch their distinctive similarities. Second, I will identify a set of institutional factors that help us understand the similarities observed in the two economies and classify them according to two analytic headings as they pertain to individual action and to the social structure. Third, I will explore the significance of my cross-national comparison of small-firm economies for improving the status of an institutional theory of business organizations. By emphasizing the role of institutional factors and the social embeddedness of economic activities in Italy and Taiwan, I hope to provide a corrective to the unilateral emphasis on an East-versus-West model of business organizations, and to show the obvious inadequacies of restrictively cultural, political, or economic interpretations of economic structures.

The Small-Firm Economies
of Italy and of Taiwan

In many respects, Italy and Taiwan are very different in their geographic, cultural, political, and economic characteristics. As Table 12.1 shows, Italy covers an area of 301,225 square kilometers (more than eight times the size

Table 12.1 Summary Statistics on Italy and Taiwan

	Italy	Taiwan
Area (square kilometers)	301,225	36,000
Population (1983)	56,300,000	18,596,000
Population density	187	517
Economically active population (%)	40.3	39.1
% in agriculture (1985)	11.8	17.5
GNP ($U.S. billions, 1985)	366.4	62.2
GNP per capita (1985)	6,216	3,127
Primary school enrollment rate	102	100
Secondary school enrollment rate	73	80
College enrollment rate	27	10
Telephones (per 100; 1986)	46.9	31.1
Energy consumption per capita (kg coal equivalent; 1986)	3,211	2,550

SOURCES: Economic Planning Council, Executive Yuan (1984), *Annuario Statistico Italiano* (1987), U.S. Bureau of the Census (1989), and Scitovsky (1985, Table 13.4).

of Taiwan), and its population is three times that of Taiwan. The two societies are steeped in vastly different cultures—the Western Greek and Judeo-Christian traditions in the case of Italy, Asian civilization and the religious traditions of Confucianism and Buddhism in the case of Taiwan. The two countries also have remarkably different sociopolitical and economic histories: Italy was unified as a country a little more than a century ago and was on its way to industrialization in the last decades of the nineteenth century; Taiwan's geopolitical identity and the country did not begin to emerge as an industrializing nation until the 1950s. Democratic change has become part of Taiwan's political life only in the past few years.

One would not expect to find similarities between the two countries' economic structures, and yet, when they are located in the larger international context and in their regional economic environments, Italy and Taiwan reveal many parallel features. For instance, although Taiwan has a larger share of population employed in agriculture (17.5% versus 11.8%), relatively speaking, Italy's share is larger than the share of most other Western European economies (West Germany's 3.5%, Great Britain's 1.9%, France's 7.9%), and therefore occupies within its region a position similar to the one occupied by Taiwan's 17.5% vis-à-vis Japan's 8%, Australia's 6%, and New Zealand's 10%. The economically active population is around 40% in both Italy and Taiwan—well below the average of other industrialized countries

(Japan, 48.7%; United States, 48.5%; West Germany, 46%; Great Britain, 47.1%).

In recent years, both Italy and Taiwan have emerged as success stories on the international economic scene. From 1978 to 1987, Italy's gross domestic product grew faster than that of most European economies, and in 1987 Italy's GDP surpassed Great Britain's, making Italy the fifth-largest economy in the Western world. Taiwan's economic performance in recent years has been even more outstanding. Thanks to the recent and long overdue revaluation of the Taiwan dollar, Taiwan's GNP has doubled since 1986 to a whopping $150 billion, adding up to a GNP per capita estimated at $7,300 for 1989 (from a little over $3,000 in 1985). In 1989, Taiwan ranked as the world's thirteenth-largest trading partner and the second richest (after Japan) in terms of foreign exchange reserves. Looking more closely at the economic structures of Italy and Taiwan, it becomes evident that the prosperity of both economies is not characterized by the development of huge, vertically integrated corporations, but rather is the product of myriad small and medium-sized firms that enact flexible subcontractual relations with each other to meet the expanding demand for consumer goods. A 1989 report on the Italian economy issued by the Organization for Economic Cooperation and Development states:

> Small and medium-sized enterprises (SMEs) bulk large in many sectors of the Italian economy and have played an active role in structural adjustment. . . . Gross profit margins are greater in firms with fewer than 200 employees than in larger ones. . . . Another aspect of the SMEs' dynamism is the particularly rapid growth of investment and, in particular, the relatively large share devoted to expanding productive capacity. (pp. 39-40)

Describing the Taiwanese economic system, Y. M. Ho (1980) has similarly shown that small firms have played a crucial role in the development of Taiwan's manufacturing sector since the 1960s and have proved themselves to be technically more efficient than large firms in most industrial sectors. Recent evidence on Taiwan's role in the semiconductor industry confirms the emphasis on small firms typical of that country's economy: Instead of concentrating on the production of powerful D-RAM chips (the battleground of Japanese and South Korean electronics giants), Taiwanese firms have focused on the development of custom chips for domestic and foreign markets, interacting individually with a large number of small firms instead of seeking to dominate the market through mass production.

An article in *The Economist* describes the typical success story of small firms in the Italian economic renaissance of the 1980s: "Benetton is a classic example of the decentralized structure of industry: firms subcontract to smaller firms, which subcontract to others. Benetton has fewer than 2,000 employees on its books. Most of its garments are made by 150 small firms, who employ 8,000 workers between them" ("The Flawed Renaissance," 1988, p. 21). The 150 firms that are part of the Benetton network contribute to the success of Italian textile exports and average a little more than 50 workers per firm—they exemplify the myriad successful small and medium-sized firms that populate the central and northeastern regions of Italy.

In the international markets, Italian and Taiwanese manufacturers often compete in the same industrial sectors (wood products, metal products, textiles, apparel and shoes, electronics, household appliances), and increasingly they compete for the same export niches, as Taiwan's products move toward the high-quality end already occupied by Italian goods. In an interview in Taiwan with the owners of a medium-sized firm that manufactures patio furniture, I was told that the firm competes directly with Italian firms for the same U.S. market. Unpublished quantitative research by William Zeile shows that Italy is the advanced industrial economy with an export structure that most closely correlates with that of Taiwan at the one-digit level; also, Italy is the only advanced industrial economy that ranks among the 10 most closely correlated with Taiwan's manufacturing export structure at the two-digit level. Perhaps Taiwan has not yet achieved the level of industrial sophistication found in the Italian economy, but the structures of the two economies have become increasingly similar in recent years.

Similarities between Italy and Taiwan can also be observed if one looks at the relatively small number of large corporations in both settings and at the role they play in their respective economies. The similar relative position occupied by large corporations in Italy and in Taiwan is shown in *Fortune*'s International 500 (1988 data), which lists only six corporations from Italy (compared with 74 from Great Britain, 53 from West Germany, and 39 from France). In that same list, we find only four corporations from Taiwan (compared with 159 from Japan, 13 from Australia, and 11 from South Korea) ("The International 500," 1989). What characterizes the industrial structures of Italy and Taiwan is, clearly, not the large conglomerates of countries such as the United States, Japan, and West Germany; instead, small

Table 12.2 Italian and Taiwanese Corporations in *Fortune*'s International 500 (1988 data)

Name	Owner	Sector	Sales	Employees
Italy				
IRI	state	metals	45,521	417,826
Fiat	private	motor vehicles	34,039	277,353
ENI	state	petroleum refining	25,227	116,364
Perruzzi Finanz.	private	chemicals	18,311	75,811
Olivetti	private	computers	6,459	57,560
Esso Italiana	private	petroleum refining	2,405	2,318
Taiwan				
China Petroleum	state	petroleum refining	6,706	23,328
Nan Ya Plastics	private	chemicals	1,840	13,679
Tatung	private	electronics	1,551	21,108
China Steel	state	metal products	1,538	9,662

SOURCE: "The International 500" (1989, 291-308).

and medium-sized manufacturing firms seem to dominate the economic landscape of the Italian and Taiwanese economies.

Not only is the number of large industrial corporations comparatively small in both economies, but, in such a short list, state-owned enterprises loom large—the state owns some of the largest industrial firms in both Italy and Taiwan. As Table 12.2 shows, state-owned corporations and business groups play a key role in providing their respective countries with industrial infrastructure and basic industrial products (as in Italy's Instituto per la Ricostruzione Industriale [IRI] and Taiwan's China Steel), and with exploration and production of energy sources, refining and distribution, and other energy-related activities (Ente Nazionale Idrocarburi [ENI] in Italy, China Petroleum in Taiwan). Interestingly, a parallel (but independent) literature has emerged regarding the role of large enterprises—both public and private —in Italy and Taiwan. Some researchers claim that large corporations were (and are) crucial in the development and sustenance of small-firm economies (for Taiwan, see Amsden, 1989b; for Italy, see King, 1985); other researchers argue that large corporations have been marginal or irrelevant to the development of the small-firm economies (for Taiwan, see S. P. Ho, 1980; for Italy, see Nanetti, 1988). Regardless of diverging evaluations on the role of large corporations, researchers agree that small to medium-sized firms hold center stage in the two economies.

Table 12.3   Enterprise Units in Manufacturing by Number of Workers in Italy and in Taiwan (1981 data)

	Italy		Taiwan		
Size	N	%	N	%	Ratio Italy/Taiwan
< 20 workers	555,551	93.4	75,860	82.0	7.3
20-99	32,753	5.5	12,843	13.9	2.6
100-499	5,735	1.0	3,304	3.6	1.7
500+	849	0.1	499	0.5	1.7
Total	594,888	100.0	92,506	100.0	6.4

SOURCES: 6' censimento generale dell'industria, del commercio, dei servizi e dell'artigianato (October 26, 1981) and Directorate-General of Budget, Accounting and Statistics (1981).

A direct measure of the relative roles played by small and medium-sized firms in Italy and in Taiwan is provided by the comparison of industrial firms by size presented in Table 12.3 for both countries. Data from the 1981 Census of Industry and Commerce in the two countries show that firms with fewer than 100 workers account for 98.9% of all manufacturing firms in Italy, and for 95.9% of firms in Taiwan. Italian firms are, on average, smaller than Taiwanese firms, with an overall figure of 10 workers per firm in Italy versus more than 20 workers per firm in Taiwan's industry. This variation is due to the much larger percentage of firms with fewer than 20 workers in Italy compared with Taiwan (93.4% versus 82.0%). I will address later in this chapter some of the factors contributing to the smallness of Italian industrial firms.

Despite the variation in average size of firms overall, the largest concentration of small firms occurs in Italy and in Taiwan in the same sectors of food industries, textiles, apparel and shoes, wood products, metal products, and machinery. With the exception of food industries, these constitute the largest export sectors in both countries. Data for 1983 show that metal products, machinery, and electrical products accounted for 28.5% of Taiwan's exports and 31.4% of Italy's exports; similarly, textiles, leather, wood, and paper products accounted for 28.7% of Taiwan's and 28.9% of Italy's exports. The destination of exports, of course, varies in the two countries according to their regional economic environments. Taiwan's top three export markets in 1983 were the United States with 45.1%, Japan with 9.9%, and Hong Kong (which includes mediated export to mainland China) with 6.5%. Italy's figures for 1985 show its top three export markets to be the

European Economic Community with 48.2%, the United States with 12.3%, and Switzerland with 4.1%.

The economies of Italy and Taiwan have received renewed attention in the 1980s because they illustrate an alternative route to industrialization that focuses not on mass production, but on what Piore and Sabel (1984) call "flexible specialization"—"a strategy of permanent innovation: accommodation to ceaseless change, rather than an effort to control it" (p. 17). Structural economic conditions that in earlier decades had been understood to be instances of economic backwardness (see Fuà, 1976; Gerschenkron, 1962) have been reassessed in recent years, highlighting the advantages of small-firm flexibility in periods of economic downturn as well as the ability of small firms to respond quickly to opportunities for economic expansion in the upturns of domestic and international markets. It is not my aim in this chapter to demonstrate the validity of claims regarding the desirability of small-firm economies, but rather to highlight the institutional factors on which these economies rest. Let us, then, look at the institutional characteristics of the Italian and Taiwanese economies that appear to have favored the emergence of their small-firm economic structure.

The Institutional Traits of Small-Firm Economies

As noted earlier, Italy and Taiwan display remarkable similarities in the structures of their small-firm economies. What factors can help us understand the emergence of these similarities? The answer, I believe, cannot be found in one single variable; rather, we must focus on a set of institutional factors characteristic of both societies. The institutional factors result from a combination of sociocultural, financial, political, and economic traits that are often linked with each other at multiple levels, and are, therefore, hard to isolate in a clear fashion. For analytic purposes I will, however, identify the institutional factors along two key dimensions: a first dimension that identifies some shared key values in the two societies as they are reflected in the behavior of individuals who engage in economic action, and a sociostructural dimension that identifies incentives and constraints that the environment creates for small business firms. My distinction is obviously artificial—in reality, most institutional factors display a combination of elements from the various levels (cultural, structural, economic, political), but it is useful to streamline the analysis of the numerous factors that contribute to the emergence and growth of small-firm economies.

Individual Values and Small-Firm Economies

In his discussion of the organization of exchange, Yoram Ben-Porath (1980) remarks that "the identity of people engaged in a transaction is a major determinant of the institutional mode of transaction" (p. 1). Emphasizing what he labels the "F-connection"—family, friends, and firms—Ben-Porath claims that social relations that are not seen as obviously economic in nature can significantly affect the patterns of economic organization in a society. Such an observation is pertinent to the study of the economies of Taiwan and Italy, which depart significantly from the extreme typology of unfettered individualistic competition envisioned by classical political economists. Although patterns of social relations and values do not by themselves explain the structure of small-firm economies, they go a long way toward clarifying the overall logic of economic action leading to that structural outcome. Here, under the heading of social relations and values relevant to small-firm economies, I list four factors: familism, entrepreneurship and independence, personal ties in business networks, and patterns of household savings.

Familism

At the sociocultural end of institutional features, the centrality of the family structure in business activities in both Italy and Taiwan is a key factor. A large majority of firms in both economies are characterized by family ownership and management. Of the 100 largest business enterprises in Taiwan, two-thirds are family owned and managed (China Credit Information Service, 1985; see also Greenhalgh, 1988). In the Italian context, Piore and Sabel (1984) point to the Italian extended family as one of the key factors leading to the development of flexible specialization of production in recent decades: "The tradition of familialism—the use of kinship relations as the structuring principle of industrial organization— . . . facilitated the accumulation of capital in the early stages of decentralization. A great many of the new firms were family operations" (pp. 227-228).

The description of how family structures relate to economic activities has led to the development of a similar vocabulary of motives for both Taiwan and Italy. In a study of family entrepreneurship in Hong Kong (which displays a socioeconomic context very similar to Taiwan's), Siu-lun Wong (1986) assesses the positive effects of familism on the conduct of business:

A much stronger measure of trust exists among family members than among unrelated business partners. Consensus is easier to attain. The need for mutual accountability is reduced. This enables family firms to be more adaptable in their operations. They can make rapid decisions during rapidly changing circumstance, and maintain greater secrecy by committing less to written records. As a result, they are well-suited to survive and flourish in situations where a high level of risk is involved, such as an unstable political environment, a fluctuating industrial sector, or a newly created line of business. (p. 318)

Similarly, identifying the new flexible entrepreneurship in the Italian economy of the late 1980s, Nanetti (1988) is quick to identify three major characteristics, of which "the first is the use of family members in various stages of the production and management process as the need arises" (p. 23).

The family-centeredness of business activities in Italy and in Taiwan does not appear to hinder the efficacy of their economic action; rather, familial values seem to foster a set of alternative values to the individualistic pursuit of profit. Siu-Kai Lau (1982) has developed the notion of "utilitarianistic familism" to characterize the socioeconomic context of Hong Kong entrepreneurship:

Utilitarianistic familism can be defined as the nonnative and behavioral tendency of an individual to place his familial interests above the interests of society and of other individuals and groups, and to structure his relationships with other individuals and groups in such a manner that the furtherance of his familial interests is the overriding concern. Moreover, among the familial interests, material interests take priority over non-material interests. (p. 72)

In parallel fashion for the Italian case, although with a stronger emphasis on the negative aspects of the phenomenon, Banfield (1958) has developed the concept of "amoral familism" to describe the philosophy that in Italian society privileges the maximization of profits for one's own family and that structures larger social relations within the instrumental framework of accruing family benefits. Banfield states, "In a society of amoral familists, no one will further the interest of the group or community except as it is to his [family's] private advantage to do so" (p. 85). The centrality of the family structure in both Taiwanese and Italian economic structures does not dimin-

Table 12.4   Percentage Salaried Employees in Industry, Selected Countries (1983 data)

Italy	70.9
Japan	71.0
Belgium	73.9
France	76.8
Netherlands	80.7
Denmark	84.5
Great Britain	85.4
West Germany	86.7
Canada	89.6
United States	90.2

SOURCE: Nanetti (1988, p. 12).

ish competition or effective economic action; rather, it shifts their emphasis from the individual level to the family level.

The family-centeredness of small business firms in Chinese culture has a significant impact on the pattern of small-firm development and growth. Because of a family's desire to provide male offspring with inheritance in the family business, the head of the family will expand business activities not by increasing the size of the existing firm, but by starting up new firms in related or unrelated industrial sectors. This strategy avoids inheritance problems in the transition of business activities to the younger generation in the family. Wong (1985, 1986) describes in detail the dynamics of family business growth for Hong Kong, but a similar dynamic is observed in the Taiwanese case as well. Hamilton and Kao (1990) describe how, in Taiwan, opportunistic diversification of business activities is the typical pattern for the growth of family business: "The strategy of expansion is to start new firms, even if it is in the same product line, rather than greatly enlarging the size of the original firm" (p. 144). The centrality of inheritance concerns observed for Taiwanese family firms is absent in the Italian case, but, as I will show later, other structural economic factors contribute significantly to keeping Italian family firms small.

Entrepreneurship and Independence

Another sociocultural characteristic of business activities in both Italy and Taiwan is the value attached to independent entrepreneurship. Statistics for 1983 (see Table 12.4) show that Italy has the lowest percentage of salaried employees of all industrialized countries; data for the early 1980s also show a marked increase in self-employment in the industrial sector and in services. In her research on small business in Italy, Weiss (1984) has identified "an extremely important aspect of the Italian context; the existence of a culturally pervasive 'demand' for economic independence," where the decision to start up one's own business is "clearly connected with the desire for independence and a firm rejection of the factory alternative" (p. 230). Weiss argues that the small entrepreneurship ideology was echoed historically by the Italian Christian Democrats, with their motto, "Non tutti proletari ma tutti praprietari" (Everyone property owners, not proletarians).

The Taiwanese also favor independent entrepreneurship over salaried work, showing high rates of job mobility and new business start-ups. As Hamilton (1989) reports, in Taiwan "everyone wants to be an entrepreneur; everyone wants to be a *laoban* (a boss)" (p. 19). The *Free China Review* reports that in Taiwan there are about 700,000 businesses (Wu, 1988). That is an average of one business (with its own boss) for every eight adults. Individuals often begin their careers by working in larger manufacturing firms, but they see this as a stepping-stone toward independent entrepreneurship. As Silin (1976) points out:

> Almost all Taiwanese managers at one time or another seriously consider leaving, usually with the intention of opening their own firm. The ideal of independent entrepreneurship . . . continues to exert considerable influence. . . . Managers whose abilities cannot be fully utilized will leave and begin independent businesses which serve as subcontractors to the parent firm. (p. 78)

A similar pattern of transition from dependent work to entrepreneurship is observed in Italy's small firms. Brusco (1982) comments: "The number of artisans or even major entrepreneurs previously employed as workers is very high. . . . Their knowledge of some part of the productive process facilitates their passage to independent work. . . . The system therefore operates as a 'forcing' ground for entrepreneurship" (p. 178).

The yearning for independent entrepreneurship is reflected in the Italians' dream of *mettersi in proprio* (to have a business of one's own). As *The Economist* reports, "The typical [Italian] entrepreneur would always prefer to own 100% of a small firm than a third of one three times as big" ("The Flawed Renaissance," 1988, p. 22). The Taiwanese feel just as strongly about business independence, as reflected in the popular Chinese proverb that claims it is better to be a rooster's beak than a cow's tail. As Sutter (1988) describes it, "To become the owner of a family business is a nearly universal goal within the working class in Taiwan" (p. 21). In this respect, Italian and Taiwanese businesspeople seem to be driven by a similar set of socioeconomic goals.

Personal Ties and Business Networks

Familism and independent entrepreneurship are key factors in prompting the emergence of large numbers of small firms, but the continued survival and growth of small firms—in both Italy and Taiwan—rely also on wider networks of personalistic relations. In Taiwan, these personalistic relations are called *guanxi,* which can be defined as "a friendship with overtones of unlimited exchange of favors" (Pye, 1982, p. 88). Jon Alston (1989) describes the *guanxi* dynamics in Chinese business:

> Two persons sharing a *guanxi* relationship assume that each is fully committed to the other. They have agreed to exchange favors in spite of official commands to act neutrally. . . . The moral dimension operating here is that a person who does not follow a rule of equity and refuses to return favor for favor loses face and becomes defined as untrustworthy. (p. 28)

Personal relationships through *guanxi* are the building blocks of the socioeconomic network to which one resorts for most business needs: hiring of workers, mobilization of financial resources, creation of subcontracting relations, procurement of production materials, the meeting of bureaucratic and political demands, and location of markets (see Hamilton & Kao, 1990). In interviews with directors and managers of large business firms in Taiwan, Cheng-shu Kao (1989) found that in recruiting people and in selecting business partners, "personal trust is the first principle." "It seems to be unfeasible for an employer to hire a top manager whom he is not familiar with. . . . This person must be either personally known by the boss (*Laoban*) or he/she must be introduced by a person whom the boss trusts" (p. 2). Kao concludes that in Taiwan "personal trust is a fundamental mechanism which makes personal relationships work" (p. 5). Having the right personal connections eases and lubricates social relations in the conduct of business activities: "The right connections can bring cheap and reliable material supplies, tax concessions, approval to sell goods domestically or for export, and provision of assistance when problems arise" (Tai, 1988, p. 8).

Researchers of Italian economic life have also highlighted the importance of personal ties in the conduct of business. Lazerson (1988) describes the tendency of small firms to hire "people recommended by other firms and friends." Trust is an important dimension in interpersonal business affairs, so that in times of economic expansion, "the selection of new [business] partners was always problematic because of the question of trust" (p. 338).

To describe the use of special interpersonal connections in the conduct of business activities, Italians speak of a *rapporto clientelare* (patron-client relation) in which personal favors are exchanged for the mutual benefit of the parties involved. Luigi Barzini (1964), an acute observer of Italian social life and morals, writes that in order to ensure one's own success in Italian society, one must observe two crucial rules: "Rule one: choose the right companions. . . . Rule two (perhaps the most important of all): choose the right protector" (p. 228). Whether one refers to hierarchical relations among unequals or horizontal relations among equals, one must be able to count unreservedly on a personal network of protectors and companions to ensure the successful achievement of set goals.

The economic benefit of relying on personalistic relations in the conduct of business in Italian small firms has been described by Lazerson (1988): "Only a minority of firms used time clocks. . . . Employees were often permitted some flexibility in working hours. Nor were piece rates or any work-incentive pay systems used, reflecting . . . the employer's preference for self-motivated employees" (p. 388). Although it is not directly pertinent to the analysis of small-firm economies, it must be pointed out that the flexible specialization described by Piore and Sabel (1984) is frequently achieved through the exploitation of one's own family and friends beyond the limits usually imposed by the labor regulations that govern work activities in large corporations. In the small family firm, it is taken for granted that members will often work overtime to meet temporary needs without receiving additional financial rewards—but people seem to accept more readily this form of self-exploitation.

Patterns of Personal Savings and Investment

Another shared trait of individual economic action in Italy and Taiwan is displayed in the high rate of personal savings in both societies. Data on selected OECD countries (Table 12.5) show that household savings in Italy add up to almost one-fourth of that country's gross domestic product—a rate

Table 12.5   Household Savings as Percentage of GDP, Selected Countries
(1987 data)

Italy	23
Japan	18
France	14
Belgium	13
West Germany	13
Canada	10
Great Britain	9
United States	4
Holland	3

SOURCE: "The Flawed Renaissance" (1988, p. 10).

higher than Japan's 18%, and way above West Germany's 13%, not to
mention the meager 4% figure in the United States. In its analysis of Italy's
prosperity in the 1980s, *The Economist* observes:

> Italian households are among the thriftiest in the world. . . . Unlike Americans
> and Britons who happily mortgage themselves up to the hilt to buy a house, the
> two thirds of Italians who own their homes save up much of the money first. . . .
> In Italy . . . there is a strong tradition against getting into debt. Household debt
> was equivalent to only 10% of disposable income at the end of 1986, compared
> with around 90% in America and Britain. ("The Flawed Renaissance," 1988,
> p. 10)

The Taiwanese have been even thriftier than the Italians. In his paper
"Social Sources of Capital Investment in Taiwan's Industrialization," Pao-an
Lin (1989) describes the logic of domestic savings in Taiwan: "Chinese
families normally provide for their children's education, marriage, and even
housing. . . . Wishing to provide a more secure environment for their family
members, families need to save most of the money left after taking care of
routine necessities. . . . It is a social attitude that money needs to be saved
and managed" (pp. 7-8). Data on domestic savings as percentage of national
income in Taiwan show a 1985 figure of 30.7% (versus 27.6% in South
Korea); the percentage of household savings over disposable income in
Taiwan was 17.6% (versus 7.6% in South Korea). Comparing the patterns
in the two societies, Tibor Scitovsky (1985) remarks:

> Growth Taiwanese-style kept business firms small and encouraged personal
> savings by the newly entering or about-to-enter small businessmen; growth

Korean-style discouraged new entrants and their saving, and made it easy for established firms to grow without generating their own savings. . . . Taiwanese firms are half as heavily indebted as Koreans because more than half of their new industrial capacity consists of small firms newly established by individual proprietors and financed out of their and their family's personal savings. (p. 248)

In the Taiwanese social context we observe a virtuous (as opposed to vicious) circle where a small-firm economy encourages personal savings with the realistic possibility of business independence, and patterns of personal savings in turn reinforce the small-firm economy by making small entrepreneurship a reality. The culturally ingrained attitudes that value thrifty management of financial resources, then, reinforce the sociostructural pattern in turn. The institutional factor of savings patterns illustrates clearly the close interrelation between individual values and social structure in economic life; one can easily move back and forth between the two levels and observe how they reciprocally reinforce each other.

Small-Firm Economies and Social Structure

In considering familism, entrepreneurship, independence, personalistic relations, and thrifty attitudes in Italy and Taiwan, I have emphasized the culturally shared desirability of a set of individual value traits in both societies. Clearly this is a key set of components of small-firm economies, but next to it we must consider the larger social contexts and identify extra-individual factors that purposefully or unwittingly contribute to the development and maintenance of small-firm economies. In his "Entrepreneurship and Development," McCullagh (1984) observes:

> The key to understanding entrepreneurial activity lies not in the personalities of individual entrepreneurs but in the nature of uncertainties encountered in the investment process. . . .
> The emergence of entrepreneurial behavior must be considered as a function of the surrounding social structure, a structure which has been shaped by the economic and political history of the particular society under examination. (pp. 111, 117)

For both Italy and Taiwan, we can identify social structural factors that directly enhance small-firm economies, as well as factors that, by inhibiting the emergence of large corporations, reinforce the existing business patterns. Here I will examine two factors that enhance the proliferation of small firms (economic legal incentives and state ideology) and three factors that inhibit the growth of small firms into large corporations (system distrust, lack of centralized planning, and rigidity of the financial system).

Economic and Legal Incentives for Small Firms

I have already observed how a virtuous circle can be created through the interaction of family savings and small-firm entrepreneurship. There are, however, more direct external incentives that favor the proliferation of small firms in Italy and Taiwan. In the Italian context, firm size has been a major criterion for economic benefits provided by the state. The Artisan Statute in Italy best illustrates the structural incentives provided to small firms. Linda Weiss (1984) summarizes:

> The Italian artisan—or rather, artisan enterprise—is so defined in law, on the basis of number employed (usually up to 20 employees). Not a professional category, then, but a legal regime, membership of which entitles the owner to a wide variety of benefits, including cheap loans, loan guarantees, lower tax and employers' contributions, welfare benefits at reduced premiums, exemptions from keeping accounts and from bankruptcy proceedings. (p. 225)

This leads Weiss to conclude, "With such an impressive array of benefits at the artisan's disposal, it is easy to see how the legal classification is itself a very potent stimulus for the potential or existing entrepreneur to join its ranks" (p. 225). Lazerson (1988) also identifies the artisanal firm as enjoying advantages that make it a desirable form of economic activity. "The national contract that regulates labor relations in artisanal firms . . . allows small firms more latitude than industrial firms in dismissing employees" (p. 335).

Direct assistance for small firms through adequate financial and technological infrastructure has been vigorously offered in Italy by regional and local governments, especially in recent decades. The Italian central government has traditionally poured huge amounts of capital into large state-run firms and enterprises with the hope of reducing the regional economic imbalance between the rich industrial north and the poor agricultural south. But since the early 1970s, local and regional governments have taken a strong leadership position in facilitating the expansion of local small-firm economies. Nanetti (1988) makes the point most forcefully: "The [Italian] regions have enjoyed a locational advantage in developing policies that promote goods and services within their boundaries. . . . As a corollary to the specificity of regional policies there are two other characteristics: the small scale and the multiplicity of initiatives" (pp. 102-103). Regional governments, Nanetti argues, help to promote local products abroad, to finance applied research related to production processes, to provide access to credit, to institute vocational education for the labor force, and to foster interregional cooperation and exchange. In Nanetti's view, economic decentralization through small-firm growth and political decentralization through the 1970 institution of regional governments go hand in hand. Italy's small-firm economy cannot be understood apart from the regionalization of its political structure.

Taiwan's structural factors favoring its small-firm economy depart significantly from Italy's—the advantages of small firms in Taiwan are a byproduct of the more general set of incentives provided by the Taiwanese state and aimed at the economic policy of export-led growth. Whereas Italy's exports for 1986 amounted to 27.2% of its GDP, Taiwan's figure for 1985 was 56.1%. The economic policies of the Taiwanese state have always nurtured export-related business activities. Ian M. D. Little (1979) argues:

> The Taiwan boom has thus far been explained largely in terms of the uninhibited private response to the set of policy changes that made exporting manufactures profitable, together with (1) the restraint of government which resulted in a falling proportion of public consumption to GNP, (2) the favorable climate for private savings—low taxes and high interest rates, and (3) the rather elastic supply of labor to the industrial sector. (p. 485)

In the Taiwanese context, the facilitating factors for the establishment of small firms we observed in the Italian context are missing—accordingly, we can see the wide variation in the number of firms with fewer than 20 workers in the two countries. Italy, with a population three times Taiwan's, has more than seven times the number of small manufacturing firms (555,551 in Italy; 75,860 in Taiwan). Taiwan's firms, as observed earlier, are larger on average than Italian firms, and this variation can be explained by referring to the legal and economic advantages that in Italy accrue to artisanal firms (those with fewer than 20 workers). Taiwanese small firms, instead, lacking an equivalent set of direct incentives for staying small, are concentrated in larger numbers in the group with 20 to 99 employees per firm.

State Ideology and Small-Firm Economies

Beyond the specific economic advantages that flow to small firms, the political ideologies of the Italian and Taiwanese governments have emphasized in words, if not in deeds, the desirability of a small-firm economy. The Taiwanese government's economic philosophy is best summarized in the doctrine of Sun Yat-sen—a Cantonese doctor educated in China, Hong Kong, and the United States who is considered the ideological mentor of the Taiwanese state. Ramon Myers (1984) summarizes the Sunist doctrine as follows:

> First, most resources in society should be privately owned and managed through the market place according to traditional values, except for those resources and activities which government deems necessary to manage on behalf of society, such as defense, communications, transport and certain social services. Secondly, policies should produce sustained, high economic growth under conditions of stability. Thirdly, new wealth should not be created at the expense of others; but as benefits accrue to primary parties, similar benefits should flow to society. Fourthly, economic change should be balanced, averting scarcities or disproportionate growth of industrial sectors. (pp. 522-523)

This set of principles adds up to a government economic policy that, relatively speaking, avoids direct involvement in the national economy through financing of private firms or through strict economic planning—as is the case, for instance, in South Korea (see Chu, 1989). The official economic policy in Taiwan has always been to let market forces take their course. Commenting on the relatively small size of Taiwan's firms when compared with South Korea's, Scitovsky (1985) remarks:

> The most important factor is Taiwan's policy of helping people with entrepreneurial inclinations and know-how but insufficient capital to establish themselves as independent businessmen. . . . Taiwan has established 49 industrial parks and districts . . . which not only provide infrastructure facilities, but also enable new investors to rent rather than buy land and buildings. (p. 224)

In the Italian context, the Christian Democrats have been identified as the leading party that developed an "ideology of small ownership." As early as 1946, in their programmatic statement for a new Italian constitution, the Christian Democrats stated, "Our ultimate aim is the elimination of wage labor and the consequent servitude of the proletarians, favoring access of labor to ownership" (cited in Weiss, 1984, p. 233). Through their support of

small-firm ownership, the Christian Democrats wanted to distance themselves from both the communists' stance that economic leadership should be
provided by the state and the opposite view that the big capitalists should be
given free rein. Commenting on the characteristics of the Italian economic
miracle in the late 1950s, the Christian Democrats observed approvingly that
"the Italian social structure is moving in a direction which refutes the Marxist
hypothesis . . . progressively freeing many citizens, because the number of
people who can live by independent labor . . . or, at least, organized in small
firms, is increasing" (cited in Weiss, 1984, p. 235). Interpreting this leading
economic philosophy, Weiss (1984) clarifies:

> For Christian Democracy, the small producer is the very symbol of the inte-
> gral society: he is both employer and laborer; he works alongside his assistants
> and relates to them in a highly personal way. Consequently, in the small firm,
> the organization of work is "more human," the worker's dignity "better pro-
> tected," the sense of responsibility and collaboration more keenly developed.
> (pp. 235-236)

It is within this ideological context that Italy's Artisan Statute of 1956
emerged as the attempt of the Christian Democrats to translate their ideological support of small ownership into concrete incentives that opened up
opportunities for dependent workers who wanted to join the ranks of small
entrepreneurs.

Estrangement From and Distrust of the System

Just as structural elements can be identified that enhance the growth of
small entrepreneurship, there is a set of institutional factors in the social
structure that inhibits most small firms from growing into large corporations.
On the one hand, discussing the value system of small entrepreneurs, we have
observed the characteristic reliance on personal connections and networks
of families and friends in the creation and economic administration of small
firms. On the other hand, trust in the larger system includes confidence in its
legal, political, and financial structures—it implies confidence in offices, not
people (see Luhmann, 1979). But we have seen how in the Italian and
Taiwanese societies personalistic relations are the privileged channel for
social action.

The obverse side of an overemphasis on personalistic trust relations in both
Taiwan and Italy is a generalized distrust toward and disregard for the

system. The clearest symptom of disregard for the official economic and legal frameworks is displayed, in Italy, by the existence of an underground economy that has been estimated to account for about 20% of total GDP. *The Economist* reports:

> Italy has long been famed for its *economia sommersa*—that mysterious under-world of tax dodging, illegal employment of foreign workers and students, and civil servants who moonlight in the afternoons when their offices close. . . . In the 1970s the combination of rigid labor laws, high taxes and social-security contributions, and a general willingness to break the law gave Italy probably the biggest [underground] economy in the industrialized world. ("The Flawed Renaissance," 1988, p. 9)

The existence of such a vigorous underground economy is in good part related to the large share of self-employed individuals in Italy's labor force. Being an independent entrepreneur makes "creative accounting" a likely choice among ways to cut one's business costs. Tax evasion is a widespread habit—"total tax revenues are equivalent to 39 percent of Italy's GDP, well below the EEC average of 46 percent" (p. 9). Like the citizens of most other societies, Italians disdain politicians and bureaucrats—but perhaps they have more reasons for doing so, given that, in Italy, the national government and its attendant bureaucracy have been traditionally overstaffed, inefficient, and corrupt. Accordingly, individuals have no qualms about skirting regulations and financial burdens, because they perceive the government itself to be hardly an example of civic integrity. The weakness of system trust in Italy can be characterized as a key obstacle to firm growth. The political apparatus, the state bureaucracies, and the financial institutions are not relied upon in a universalistic fashion; accordingly, the chances of growth for many businesses that may wish to grow are greatly minimized.

There are no data on Taiwan's underground economy, but Fields (1989) describes a pattern of "public restrictions and private disregards" as being typical of the island's economic activities: "While the skirting or abuse of public financial regulations for private gain is not unique to Taiwan, entrepreneurs in Taiwan have perfected the art of outwitting (or otherwise persuading) accountants, loan officers, auditors and even financial officials" (p. 4). As Silin (1976) observes, the centrality of family and friends in business activities leads entrepreneurs to distrust the larger social system and to avoid abiding by legal rules whenever it is possible and advantageous to do so. As Fields (1989) remarks, in Taiwan, "onerous and progressive business taxes inspire a variety of creative tax evasions" (p. 11). Because the national government was until recent years entirely dominated by mainlanders, businesspeople's allegiance to the political elite has always been rather weak or totally absent. In both Italy and Taiwan, the attitude of small entrepreneurs is that establishing the independence of their business is a way to claim not only economic self-sufficiency, but independence from the rest of the system.

Absence of Centralized Economic Planning

If on the one hand individual entrepreneurs distrust the system and try to isolate themselves from it, on the other hand the system itself shows little inclination to provide strong direction for the private sector to follow. Both Italy and Taiwan are famous for economic planning that has paid little more than lip service to the role of government agencies in orchestrating the national economy. Comparing Taiwan's economic planning to that of Japan and South Korea, Thomas Gold (1986) observes:

> Whereas in Japan, regularized consultations between MITI and industry representatives helped determine industrial policy, and Korea has seen a more brutish, commandist approach, in Taiwan planners retained an aloof posture. They met to formulate policy and then relayed their decisions and attendant mechanisms to implement it to the business community and watched what happened. . . . Taiwan's private sector has been much more anarchic and self-directed than its Japanese or Korean counterparts. (p. 126)

Scitovsky (1985) clarifies the dynamics of Taiwan's small-firm economy further by arguing that the "explanation of the relatively slow growth of the size of firms lies not in the presence of policies limiting, but in the absence of policies encouraging their growth" (p. 225). And Ian Little (1979) echoes: "The main dynamic of Taiwan's growth developed regardless of any planning—unless one rather misleadingly calls the 1959-60 policy reforms part of planning" (p. 489).

Italian economic planning has also been very minimal, if not altogether nonexistent. As Russell King (1985) describes it: "Economic planning [in Italy] is regarded as a ritualistic shibboleth rather than a definite policy based on careful analysis of ends and means. Planning language is often vague and esoteric; projections are broad rather than specific; much room is purposely left for ambiguity" (p. 73). More specifically, King identifies a "cultural bias

Table 12.6   R&D Expenditure and Stock Market Capitalization as Percentage of GDP, Selected Countries

	R&D 1985	Stock Market Capital 1987
United States	2.8	50
West Germany	2.6	18
Japan	2.6	115
Britain	2.3	90
France	2.3	17
Holland	2.0	30
Canada	1.4	48
Italy	1.3	16

SOURCE: "The Flawed Renaissance" (1988, pp. 16, 22).

against planning in Italy, a lack of rapport between industrial and administrative elites." This comment, incidentally, reinforces earlier observations regarding system distrust. The successful growth of both the Italian and the Taiwanese economies has not taken place because of diligent, centralized planning; rather, it has occurred because of the entrepreneurship of the small and medium-sized firms in the private sector, in the absence of strong incentives for firm growth in either economy.

Rigidity of the Financial System

One final factor to be considered as inhibiting firm growth is the rigid structure of the financial system. In both Italy and Taiwan, the banking system is firmly under state ownership and control, and financial support beyond a minimal artisanal level is hard to come by. The state controls about 80% of the Italian banking system—of Italy's top eight banks, seven are government owned, and banking activities in Italy are the most heavily regulated when compared with Italy's counterparts in the European Community. As *The Economist* has observed, "Although Italy has built a modern industrial structure, its financial services remain medieval, and difficulties in raising finance can hold back corporate expansion" ("The Flawed Renaissance," 1988, p. 14). Similar to its banking system, as Table 12.6 shows, the Italian stock market remains largely undeveloped when compared with those of other industrialized countries. For example, consider that in Italy four industrial groups alone (Fiat, IRI, Ferruzzi, and Assicurazioni Generali) account for two-thirds of the Italian stock market's total capitalization.

Taiwan's financial system is equally rigid, and Taiwanese banks are also virtually all government owned. Fields (1989) reports: "As of 1984 there were only 24 domestic banks and all but three of them were majority government-owned. Of these 21 state banks, the top seven accounted for almost 90% of total deposits in domestic banks in 1980. The three private banks accounted for just over two percent of total deposits" (p. 19). Private businesses have difficulty obtaining bank loans and instead turn to family savings, friends, and the curb market for their businesses' capitalization. Some observers put the figure for finances obtained from family and friends at around 60% of total capitalization.

Robert Wade (1985) comments that "the rigidity of Taiwan's financial system has been a positive factor in its industrialization" (p. 106). Wade is correct that a small-firm economy has been shaped in Taiwan by the financial constraints preventing the growth of small firms beyond a certain size. At the same time, family-owned firms, both in Italy and in Taiwan, have been reluctant to go public because they want to keep total control over firm management and have therefore avoided raising capital by selling their firms' stocks. Thus the entrepreneurial independence of small-firm owners has merged with the unavailability of capitalization funds to keep the size of most manufacturing firms in a small-to-medium range.

Cross-National Comparisons and Institutional Explanations

In this chapter, I have sought to show how remarkably similar small-firm economies have emerged in Italy and Taiwan thanks to a set of parallel institutional factors drawing on cultural, economic, financial, political, and sociostructural traits—some of which enhance the development of small-firm economies and others of which inhibit the proliferation of large-scale industrial corporations. No single factor, however important, can by itself account for the creation of small-firm economies. Rather, it is the historically specific combination of factors observed in the Italian and Taiwanese cases that provides a sufficiently wide net to capture the rationale of small-firm economies in their cultural and sociostructural aspects.

The approach I have advocated rejects unilateral cultural explanations of economic action that would group economies under a uniform heading of Asiatic modes of production versus Western economic patterns. Just as the economic structures of different Asian economies vary considerably (Hamilton & Biggart, 1988), so do the economic structures of Western industrialized societies. There is no single pattern of capitalism in the West any more than there is a single pattern of capitalism in the East. At the same time, my institutional explanation of small-firm economies also rejects the market explanation of economic structures. Market forces do not exist apart from the social structures in which they operate—rather, market forces themselves are *shaped by* the societies in which they are embedded (see Granovetter, 1985). Diverse economic structures cannot be explained by a unilateral, undifferentiated market factor any more than by an undifferentiated cultural factor. More specific, context-sensitive factors need to be considered; these are what I have labeled *institutional factors*—the interstitial components of the social structure as they are formed and emerge historically in different societies.

Political factors and the role of the state have also been played up as *the key variable* explaining variations in patterns of capitalism. Weiss's (1988) most recent extension of her research on the small-firm economy of Italy has led her to claim that "in post-war Italy micro capitalism flourished because of an unusually 'sympathetic' state" (p. 161). Conversely, she argues that other state policies in France, Germany, and Great Britain led to the development of a giant-corporation economic structure in these countries. In the case of the Taiwanese and South Korean economies, researchers have also sought to reduce the explanation of these economic structures to the role played there by the state (e.g., Amsden, 1985; Cumings, 1984; Gold, 1986). Again, the temptation has been to find one single variable—one privileged actor—that can explain the observed outcome in the economic structure. This unilateral attention to the political economy of the modern state is as misguided as the strictly culturalist and the exclusively economic explanations.

On the one hand, if one looks at the individual cases of Italy and Taiwan, assessments of the role of the state in each society vary widely. For Taiwan, some authors (e.g., Little, 1979; Scitovsky, 1985; Winckler, 1984) have convincingly argued that the Taiwanese state pursued a "hands-off" policy in relation to the private sector—directly contradicting the theory of those who have identified a strong Taiwanese state. In the case of Italy, Weiss's (1988) analysis is directly undermined by Nanetti (1988), who attributes the growth of the small-firm economy in Italy in recent decades not to the Italian national government policies, but rather to the decentralized actions of regional and local administrations. Divergent interpretations for both cases undermine the political economy explanation from the inside.

On the other hand, even if we were to observe homogeneity in the analysis of the separate cases, it would be hard to put Taiwan and Italy side by side and demonstrate that similar state strategies have been at work in the two societies. The political structures of Italy and Taiwan could not be any further apart—the Italian state vigorously encouraged small entrepreneurship, whereas the Taiwanese kept an arm's-length relationship with the private sector. The Italian political leadership has traditionally been fraught with unstable governments, runaway budget deficits, and long inflationary periods. The Taiwanese state, on the contrary, has been solidly in command, boasting one of the largest reserves of foreign currency in the world and keeping inflation tightly under control. And yet the small-firm economies of these two societies have been shown to be astonishingly similar.

Clearly, one has to go beyond narrowly construed models of the social world in which discrete variables such as market forces, culture, and the state operate autonomously and exercise unidirectional pressures that determine predictable effects on the economic structure. The market, the state, and the cultural system affect and shape each other. A research approach that is more sensitive to context and that rests on an embedded understanding of economic structures can make better sense of similarities and differences in cross-national comparisons of economic structures. I hope that this chapter has provided a first round of evidence to advance the empirical understanding of small-firm economies in Italy and in Taiwan, and to strengthen the theoretical usefulness of an institutional approach to the study of economic structures.

13

Dirigiste Capitalism in France and South Korea

MARCO ORRÙ

omparative analyses of East Asian economies have allowed researchers to identify the distinctive features of business organizations in Japan, South Korea, Taiwan, and other rapidly developing economies. Japan's system of industrial cooperation among industrial firms, financial institutions, and government bureaucracies has been felicitously labeled "alliance capitalism" (Gerlach, 1992). South Korea's vertical business hierarchies and commandist approach on the part of the state have led researchers to identify a patrimonial pattern of organization. Taiwan's family-centered system of small-firm horizontal networks has led to the label of familial capitalism.

Highlighting the distinctive features of each economy's structure has helped us to understand better each case studied and to go beyond the notion of an undifferentiated East Asian economic miracle, but it should not prevent us from drawing useful parallels between these East Asian economies and other capitalist economies around the world. I have drawn attention to the striking similarities in economic structure between some East Asian and some Western European economies. In the first comparison, I pointed out the cooperation among institutional economic actors that is a central feature of business structures in Japan and in Germany (Orrù, 1993; see Chapter 11, this volume). In the second comparison, I highlighted the centrality of family-based, small-firm horizontal networks that have been the engine of economic growth in the Italian and Taiwanese economies (Orrù, 1991a; see Chapter 12).

In this chapter, I focus on a third East-West parallel by comparing two economies characterized by a central state that plays a strong orchestrating role—the national economies of France and South Korea. The label I use to describe these two cases is *dirigiste capitalism*—that is, a capitalist economy that is purposefully shaped by the central government through extensive industrial policies, the identification of industrial sectors to be targeted for rapid growth, the massive support of a few large business firms or groups of firms that are tightly integrated in a vertical fashion, close control of financial resources by the central government, and the adoption of paternalistic attitudes in both government-business relations and management-worker relations. All social organizations are characterized by some mixture of vertical and horizontal webs, but the South Korean and French economic structures display stronger vertical organizational dynamics than do their counterparts in Japan and Taiwan and in Germany and Italy.

The detailed mechanics of economic growth, to be sure, vary considerably between the French and the South Korean cases, yet the two economic structures display striking similarities in their reliance on strong state leadership and the creation of vertically integrated production sectors. Especially when compared with the partnership capitalism observed in the Japanese and German cases on the one hand and with the small-firm horizontal networks witnessed in Italy's and Taiwan's economic structures on the other, the French and South Korean cases can be confidently characterized as instances of dirigiste capitalism—capitalism from the top.

I will argue my case for dirigiste capitalism in France and South Korea in three steps. First, I present the historical background to strong states in the two countries; second, I elaborate on the key role of central governments in formulating and implementing industrial policies in the two economies;

third, I articulate the vertical organizational structure of large firms in the two societies' business activities. In the conclusion, I sharpen the typology of dirigiste capitalism by comparing its key features with two other typologies: alliance capitalism and small-firm capitalism.

Historical Background

Korea's traditions of patrimonialism, Confucianism, and regionalism set the stage for distinct organizational structures that emphasize rigid internal hierarchies, a heightened sense of duty and obedience, and strong in-group cohesion coupled with an adversarial stance toward out-groups. These traits are displayed throughout Korean society—not only in the organization of business groups, but also in political organizations and in the relations between state and private business.

Korea's dynastic state structure embodied for centuries the traits of a Confucian, region-based patrimonialism (Dobbin & Nam, n.d.). The establishment of a centralized Korean kingdom dates back to 668 A.D. For centuries, the dynastic court in Seoul ruled by extending favors to and withdrawing favors from the economically subordinate elites who lived in Korea's countryside. Unlike the feudal court of Japan, where hereditary elites had control of lands and political offices, the Korean aristocracy was at the mercy of Seoul's court; hence their insecurity kept Korea's elite clans in constant competition for privileges and prevented them from unifying against the crown. In contrast to the relative autonomy and sometimes solidarity of Japanese and European feudal retainers, Korea's patrimonial subjects were dependent and rivalrous, and Seoul's court had great power over them.

Today's Korean state is quite different from its dynastic predecessor; its government has a democratic constitution, a popularly elected president, bureaucratic ministries, and an elected National Assembly. However, behind its different appearance, the state functions in a manner reminiscent of earlier patrimonial regimes. The president wields unusual powers, and the ministries distribute and exact favors, sustaining competition among elite economic clans, now organized as powerful business groups called *chaebol*.

Most Westerners would find this autocratic system unthinkable, but Koreans accept the state's strong leadership because it accords with Confucian values and the tradition of patrimonial institutions. As Bun Woong Kim (1981) puts it: "The Koreans traditionally tended to submit themselves dutifully to any existing political authority and to equate responsibility with elitist decision-making power. . . . Koreans still view themselves culturally in hierarchical terms of authoritative rank, power, and responsibility" (p. 138).

France is a world away from South Korea, but the French state has been historically among the most centralized in Europe, at least since the absolutist monarchies of the seventeenth century, and the French nobility, like the Korean regional elites, was fragmented and under the crown's heavy control. Unlike the German landed aristocracy's ability to mobilize and shape capitalism according to their own interests, the French nobility had lost its economic clout well before the French Revolution, becoming mostly a class of rentiers. At the time, the most active economic groups were a free peasantry in the countryside and an urban-based, family-centered bourgeoisie. When capitalism spread, France's urban bourgeoisie was positioned to take advantage of the opportunities industrialization offered, while simultaneously restricting access for others. Consequently, French capitalism thrived in the economic and social structure of French cities—especially Paris.

But the French state played a leading role in the stimulation and direction of industrial development from the very beginning. Already during the reign of Louis XIV, the French minister Jean-Marie Colbert was fashioning a national policy to guarantee the emergence and growth of French industry. "The strategy combined protection from foreign competition with such incentives as monopolies, patents, subsidies, and training programs" (Stoffaës, 1986, p. 39). The minister's program was so ambitious, and its implementation during his 22-year service in the French government so extensive, that "*colbertisme* is still [today] a popular term for pervasive government initiative at the microeconomic level" (Adams, 1989, p. 46).

The state's orchestration of the French economy continued during the nineteenth century, as Christian Stoffaës (1986) reports: "The Saint-Simonian movement promoted a close association between dynamic industrialists, dynamic bankers, and the government bureaucracy. Together they would foster the development of the sunrise industries of the times: coal, pig iron, steel, waterways, steamships, and railroads" (p. 39). Government industrial planning abated somewhat during the first half of the twentieth century, but it resumed with renewed vigor after World War II, when the general feeling was that government would have to intervene if France was to hold or gain its position vis-à-vis its economic competitors. Let us, then, turn to today's economic role of central governments in South Korea and France.

Korea's Patrimonial State

An aggressive and centralized state that is actively involved in economic matters characterizes the political economy of modern Korea. Ku Hyun Jung (1989) claims that "during the high growth period of the 1960s and 1970s, the Korean government followed a policy of interventionism, the likes of which cannot be found in any other capitalist economy" (pp. 13-14). Since the end of the Korean War, the state has actively intervened in the economy by allocating financial assets and other resources, regulating entry into industrial sectors, managing major industrial enterprises, and strictly controlling Korea's financial institutions.

Beginning in the 1950s with Syngman Rhee, who was elected Korea's first president during the U.S. military occupation, authoritarianism and despotism were the distinguishing traits of the Korean state. President Rhee's successors, although not approaching his level of autocracy and corruption, continued to manage the Korean state in a patrimonial way, extending and withdrawing economic favors in a personalistic fashion. While retaining its patrimonial character, state intervention in the economy has become more rationalized and professional in recent decades. Rhee's successors, such as Park Chung Hee and Chun Doo Hwan, have pursued a strategy of development in which the government sets substantive targets for economic activity (e.g., the development of a shipbuilding industry and of an automobile industry) and then manipulates economic factors in order to achieve its goals. Still, such development strategy places control in the hands of the state and contrasts with a market approach in which impersonal economic forces are allowed to play throughout the economy (Chang, 1985).

In addition to allocating resources according to state plans, the government regulates the entry and exit of companies into new sectors of the economy. To spur the development of a market sector, the South Korean government let a few powerful business families compete for entry, echoing the competition among regional clans in dynastic Korea.

Simultaneously, the Korean state relied on public enterprise to develop essential industries and achieve economic goals. Although the size and number of public enterprises have been greater in Korea than in some socialist nations, they have tended to play not an ideological role but a strategic one (Jones & SaKong, 1980, p. 144). Infrastructure industries such as railways and telecommunications are wholly owned and managed by the state. Government-invested enterprises, at least 50% government owned, include the Korea Development Bank; government-backed enterprises, those less than 50% government owned, include the Korea Exchange Bank. In addition, there are subsidiaries of government-invested enterprises in which the government maintains some control ("The Privatization of Public Enterprises," 1989). Public enterprises played an important role during Korea's rapid-growth years of the 1960s and 1970s, accounting for about 12% of nonagricultural gross domestic product (Jones & SaKong, 1980, p. 149).

The most important source of state control over the Korean economy has been the manipulation of national finances. The management of foreign exchange under Rhee overvalued the won by as much as 50%, so that businesses with access to dollars and other foreign currencies could make risk-free profits. During the 1960s Park regime, the won was still exchanged at a 15% premium, providing excess profits to importers paying with inflated won. The state also helped large business groups by maintaining artificially low interest rates for loans to favored firms. "Except in times of war, only a few nations have used policies of selective credit control as widely and thoroughly as has Korea" (Ito, 1984, p. 453). The state maintained interest rates at below market prices from 1960 to 1980 for export-oriented activities and other projects that largely favored a few large industrial conglomerates. The state used access to subsidized funds as both an incentive and a control on business activity. Cheap loans led to strong demand for borrowed funds as a means of financing rapid growth, and large industrial firms assumed very high debt levels. Like foreign exchange rate manipulation, credit market policy in Korea gave large Korean conglomerates a source of profits denied other sectors of the economy. Thus, until very recently, small and medium-sized independent firms have been neglected by the Korean government, perpetuating the weakness of Korea's industrial infrastructure.

Overall, the relationship between the postwar Korean state and the private business community has been patrimonial, with the state actively organizing the economy and intervening in its detailed operation. Unlike the decentralized and consultative partnership model of the Japanese state and business sector, the Korean state pursued an aggressive, centralized, and particularistic policy favoring elite business clans that support the regime in power, both politically and financially. The cooperation among business groups observed in Japan is discouraged in Korea, where the state, mimicking its dynastic predecessor, has used interfirm rivalry to maintain fragmentation, thereby strengthening the state's own status as the central locus of power in society. In recent years the power balance has shifted somewhat toward private business groups, but the Korean state remains extremely powerful and directive, especially when compared with the Japanese and Taiwanese states.

France's Dirigiste State

Comparatively speaking, the French economic structure has been historically dominated by the small-firm sector, which in 1945 still accounted for more than 50% of the industrial labor force (Weiss, 1988, p. 172). After World War II, the French state embarked on a concerted effort with private industry to nurture the growth of large, internationally competitive conglomerates. After its entry into the European Common Market in 1958, the state moved rapidly to restructure the private sector. Unfettered by the lack of any antitrust tradition, as is found in the United States, the French state openly and actively encouraged corporate concentration and centralization, thereby contributing to the highest rate of mergers in Europe in the postwar period (Swartz, 1985, p. 185).

Over time, the state increased substantially its own direct and indirect involvement in the formation of large conglomerates. Beginning with the tenure of President Georges Pompidou in 1969, the French government launched a program in which so-called national champions would be nurtured in key industrial sectors. "Between 1970 and 1974 major mergers did occur. They involved consolidation of already large companies and left the fringe of small and medium-sized firms intact" (Aujac, 1986, pp. 15-16). After a decline in France's grand industrial policy during the presidency of Valéry Giscard d'Estaing (1974-1981), the French state resumed its dirigiste role with President François Mitterrand. By the early 1980s, the French public sector accounted for "30 percent of value added and 50 percent of research and development in the industrial sector" (Aujac, 1986, p. 29). Through the nationalization of banks and key industrial firms, the French state had gained "control of one-third of the country's industrial capacity" and achieved almost total control of French banking and financing.

The French government adopted a variety of instruments to implement its industrial policies. On one side, it used subsidies, public procurement, and research policies to target industrial development in key sectors such as steel, shipbuilding, aerospace, and electronics; on the other side, it adopted monetary policies, export subsidies, tax laws, and market regulations to strengthen French businesses in domestic and international markets.

With the nationalization of large industrial firms and financial institutions, the French state also sought to concentrate similar production activities in individual "champion" firms. This trend led, as in the case of South Korea, to the neglect of small and medium-sized businesses. Henri Aujac (1986) aptly summarizes the effects of French dirigisme: "Without doubt the chief beneficiaries of French industrial policy during the past fifteen years have been the state, its bureaucracy, and a few large industrial corporations" (p. 35).

The Korean State and the *Chaebol* Business Giants

A lasting legacy of Syngman Rhee's regime is the creation of the *chaebol* —large industrial groups led by elite business families in a strictly patrimonial, hierarchical fashion. Of Korea's 50 largest *chaebol,* 13 trace their origins to Rhee's sale of the spoils from Japan's colonial assets to privileged Korean families. Major Japanese *zaibatsu* such as Mitsubishi and Mitsui had extensive colonial holdings in the Korean peninsula. In 1945, when Japan lost World War II, "the Republic of Korea inherited over 2500 operating industrial and business enterprises, as well as infrastructure, inventories, real estate, and 15 percent of the nation's land" (Jones & SaKong, 1980, p. 30). Industrial holdings were distributed to friends and political allies of Rhee at 60% of their appraised value, with only a 10% down payment, the balance to be paid over 10 years. The severe inflation of the postwar era meant that the *chaebol* groups purchased Japanese assets for a pittance (Jung, 1989, p. 19). "Special bank loans, allocations of U.S. dollars at favorable rates of exchange, and capital sums imported in connection with foreign aid programs were made available by the government to those entrepreneurs who supported it" (Lee, 1984, p. 383).

The family-based industrial empires of Hyundai, Samsung, Kia, and Lucky-Goldstar, among others, were created in this era, as the elite families received countless state favors in exchange for large financial contributions to President Rhee and the regime's politicians. The successful *chaebol* gained state assistance, including cheap loans and protective tariffs, while the business developed; but favored *chaebol* could not simply go about their business, as the state routinely put politically loyal representatives on boards of directors to protect its interests. Until the early 1980s, for instance, the state set the prices that *chaebol* could charge and regulated the wages of employees. The state also barred entry into such sectors as machinery and automotive industries in 1981, because it saw too much competition in those sectors. Such a heavy-handed role for the state would be inconceivable in Japan, where the state leads, cajoles, and provides incentives, but rarely commands.

State policy toward the *chaebol* has eased in recent years, although it remains extraordinarily directive; state planners are implementing more market policies while continuing to formulate industrial plans. For example, the state targeted petrochemical production for industrial development and limited entry to selected *chaebol,* but by the mid-1980s it lifted entry and price restrictions, allowing competition between domestic petrochemical companies in an oversupplied market. That Korea is poorly positioned to compete globally in the industry "has not been sufficient to deter anyone"; rather, "corporate rivalries" and a desire to "control their own destinies" have propelled the *chaebol* into irrational all-out competition when allowed to by the state (Goldstein, 1989, p. 81).

Fortune's 1991 ranking of the largest industrial firms around the world provides a Who's Who of Korea's recently acquired industrial might. The top firms are all members of Korea's largest *chaebol.*

    14. Samsung group
    43. Daewoo group
    96. Sunkyong group
   101. Ssangyong group
   170. Hyundai Motor
   179. Pohang Iron & Steel
   213. Hyundai Heavy Industries
   246. Hyosung Group
   284. Goldstar
   350. Kia Motors

In recent years, the Korean government pursued privatization by divesting completely or reducing substantially its participation in such firms as the Korean Stock Exchange, the National Textbook Company, and Korean Airlines —often selling to *chaebol* at very favorable prices. At least 20 of the top 50 *chaebol* purchased some government enterprises (Jung, 1989, p. 19), but such major corporations as Pohang Steel (POSCO), Korea Electric Power (KEPCO), and Korea Telecommunications are still owned by, or under the heavy influence of, the Korean state. Scholars disagree in assessing the balance of power between the Korean state and the mighty *chaebol*, but they concur in considering the Korean government to be a major protagonist in Korea's industrial development.

France's *Politique de Filières* and Its Industrial Champions

Altogether, private sector capitalism in late-nineteenth-century France was characterized by small and medium-sized firms, with very little integration between economic sectors. John Vincent Nye (1987) shows that industrial firms performed quite efficiently within their economic environment, noting that France "adopted a different path toward industrialization rather than an inferior one" (p. 651). Such business networks as existed in France during this period were producer networks aiming at regulating local and regional economies. These producer networks emerged from the "mutual agreements entered into by independent firms" (Levy-Leboyer, 1980, p. 138).

As the economy expanded and the demand for capital investment increased in the early twentieth century, a second type of French business network developed—the holding company. French holding companies own shares in member firms and provide some cartel-like functions for these firms. In France, unlike in many other economies, holding companies provide chiefly a rationalization of producer cartels. According to Levy-Leboyer (1980):

> In some cases, [holding companies] were created to control the activities of a number of industrial subsidiaries, to set their prices and volume of output, and to allocate capital among them. . . . In other cases, holding companies were instituted by large corporations or financially related groups of firms to provide them with financial services such as raising capital and procuring credit. (p. 138)

In the private sector, holding companies, sometimes owned by single families, were the primary forces in the rapid postwar mergers, following a pattern of vertical integration that resembles the emergence of the South

Korean *chaebol* in the 1980s. As some firms grew prosperous and large, they began to buy out other firms in their cartels, but the resulting structure was not one of multidivisional corporations, such as those that characterize the American economy; instead, families created networks of medium-sized and large firms.

The emergence of a few very large industrial firms was made possible by the funneling of vast amounts of capital by the French state toward selected industrial sectors, and specific business firms within those sectors, targeted for rapid and sustained economic growth (Table 13.1). As Henri Aujac (1986) convincingly argues, "The [French] government has used its power over private enterprise to reinforce the big against the small" (p. 32). Available data show how the French state targeted the growth of a few industrial giants:

> Government support is highly concentrated in five large enterprises: Compagnie Générale d'Electricité, Thomson-Brandt, CII-Honeywell Bull, Dassault, and Empain Schneider. These five received nearly 50 percent of all government support of industry, as measured by R&D subsidies, export subsidies, regional development subsidies, and sectoral subsidies. (Aujac, 1986, p. 33)

Aujac and de Rouville (1983) show that for 1976, nine companies received 80% of subsidies for "industries of the future" and 70% of subsidies for "mature industries" (p. 86). Of these nine companies, three were large public enterprises, five were large private enterprises, and one was a large mixed enterprise. The French pattern of forced growth of large corporations through state financing is similar to what we have witnessed in the South Korean government's targeting of a few *chaebol* for rapid expansion during the 1980s, but in the French case the state often orchestrated industrial growth directly instead of channeling growth exclusively through the private sector. Thus 1991 *Fortune* data on the world's largest industrial corporations show that of the top 10 French industrial firms, 6 are government owned, whereas of South Korea's 10 largest industrial firms, none is owned by the government ("The International 500," 1992).

Parallel to the single-minded emphasis on financing the growth of a few very large firms, we can observe a similar disregard for small and medium-sized firms in both France and South Korea (Table 13.2). Some students of the French economy have argued that the subsidies provided to large businesses helped, in a trickle-down fashion, small and medium-size firms; the evidence, however, is that "most government subsidies flowed only as far as the subsidiaries of the large recipients" (Aujac, 1986, p. 33).

Table 13.1　French Industrial Firms by Establishment Size (1982 and 1989)

Firm Size	Number of Firms	Percentage
1982		
0-19	689,414	92.5
20-49	32,379	4.3
50-99	11,163	1.5
100-199	6,302	0.8
200 and up	5,734	0.8
Total	744,992	99.9
1989		
0-49	697,226	97.3
50-199	15,138	2.1
200-499	3,110	0.4
500 and up	1,135	0.2
Total	716,609	100.0

SOURCE: Ministère des Finances et des affaires Economiques (1982, Table 3.02-8; 1989, Table G.02-7).

Table 13.2　Korean Manufacturing Firms by Establishment Size and Number of Workers, 1986

Firm Size	Number of Firms	%	Number of Workers	%
0-29	93.7		26.9	
30-299		5.8		34.5
300 and up	0.6		38.5	
Total	189,000	100.1	2,599,000	99.9

SOURCE: Economic Planning Board (1987).

Today, family-owned business networks and densely networked public and private holding companies are the dominant organizational forms in the French economy. According to David Encaoua and Alexis Jacquemin, of the 500 largest French companies in 1974, 319 were "parent companies" of business groups that control about 8,000 other French companies. Encaoua and Jacquemin (1982) comment:

The global importance of these 319 groups is attested by the fact that their affiliated firms account for about 40 percent of total industrial employment, 50 percent of total value added, and 60 percent of fixed assets. These groups weigh heavily in most of intermediary and equipment goods industries, but are rather weak in consumer goods industries. (p. 33)

The distinctive factor in the growth of French industrial networks rests on the development of self-sufficient and strong vertical streams of production in major industrial sectors. The French government has been instrumental in devising and implementing such vertical growth strategy, called *politique de filières,* through a variety of direct investments and subsidies to both public and private industrial giants. The industrial policy of the French government was systematically developed with an eye to its capitalist competitors. The French economy, it was felt, needed large firms that could compete in domestic and international markets. The outcome of such assessment was the promotion of one or two large firms per industry—known as the strategy of national champions. A *Fortune* list of the largest industrial firms in 1991 shows France's national champions (ranked internationally within their sectors):

Aerospace	8. Aérospatiale (G)	
Building materials	1. Saint-Gobain	
Chemicals	8. Rhône-Poulenc (G)	
Computers	11. Bull (G)	
Electronics	7. Alcatel	14. Thomson
Metal products	1. Pechiney (G)	
Metals	4. Usinor-Sacilor (G)	
Motor vehicles	9. Renault (G)	11. Peugeot
Petroleum refining	8. Elf Aquitaine (G)	10. Total
Rubber and plastics	2. Michelin	

Of the 13 industrial firms listed, 10 are ranked among the 100 largest industrial firms in the world, and all are near the top ranks for their industrial sector. Of these 13 firms, 7 are government owned. Clearly the French government is not shy about promoting the bigness of one or two industries in each key industrial sector, nor is it shy in running such giant firms itself. The French government's *politique de filières*—the development of vertical streams of production in their entirety—demanded the intervention of the state to facilitate industrial regrouping. Henri Aujac (1986) describes the details of such policy:

Individual companies were asked to merge, increase spending on research and development, increase production and employment, increase ratios of exports to production, or modify product lines. In return the government agreed to finance the companies' investments, increase public training of skilled labor, increase government purchases of their products, and stimulate such purchases by parties in the private sector. (p. 18)

Whereas the Korean government identified its national champions in selected family-owned business groups and showered them with capital and incentives to push industrial growth in targeted sectors, the French government operated both indirectly, with substantial incentives to large private firms, and directly, through public ownership of numerous major industrial firms. The overall dynamic of economic expansion is still similar in the two economies, because in both cases it is the state that plans, initiates, and adopts strong policies to see that its wishes for economic growth and competitiveness reach their successful completion.

To sharpen our understanding of the distinctive features of dirigiste capitalism in France and South Korea, I will now conclude the chapter with a brief comparative assessment of the three typologies of capitalist economic structures.

Conclusion

My analysis of the economic structures in East Asian and Western European societies seeks to provide a cross-national and cross-cultural view of the various organizational patterns that have emerged throughout the modern capitalist world. These organizational patterns are shaped by each country's history, political economy, cultural traits, and social structural conditions. But beyond observing the uniqueness of each country's business organizations, I want to stress some important lessons learned from the comparative analysis of capitalist economies.

The organization of business activities in Western and non-Western societies differs qualitatively in individual economies, but also allows for similarities to be observed across cases. In Germany and Japan, the legacy of feudalism led in modern times to strong elite classes and solid alliances between private business and the state, leading to institutional cooperation among business actors. Economic alliances in both societies have maximized the range of possibilities contained within their public and private institutions. In Italy and Taiwan, where the state is much weaker and family structures are stronger, modern economic organizations ride on horizontal interfirm networks with strong cooperative traits at the level of small and medium-sized businesses. In France and South Korea, the historical tradition of a strong central state and of fragmented regional elites led to the dirigiste role of the central government in shaping each country's economic and industrial structure, embodying a patrimonial and paternalistic organizational structure for an economic development guided from the top.

Economic organizations do not develop independent of the rest of society —rather, they are embedded in, and grow out of, the social, political, and institutional forces that are in place in each society. The social groups that carry capitalism—the groups that mobilize society economically, including the state—have the power to control the economy. The manner of control, however, is determined not simply by considerations of economic efficiency and profit, but also, crucially, by the forms of social control that are historically available in each society. Accordingly, we witness a variety of patterns of collaboration within and among economic actors in each economy, depending on the set of socially instituted routines and organizational practices available in each society.

References

Abegglen, J. C. (1958). *The Japanese factory.* Glencoe, IL: Free Press.

Abegglen, J. C., & Stalk, G., Jr. (1985). *Kaisha: The Japanese corporation.* New York: Basic Books.

Aberbach, J. D., Dollar, D., & Sokoloff, K. L. (Eds.). (1994). *The role of the state in Taiwan's development.* Armonk, NY: M. E. Sharpe.

Abolafia, M. Y. (1984). Structured anarchy: Formal organization in the commodity futures markets. In P. Adler & P. Adler (Eds.), *The social dynamics of financial markets* (pp. 129-150). Greenwich, CT: JAI.

Abolafia, M. Y., & Biggart, N. W. (1990). Competition and markets. In A. Etzioni & P. Lawrence (Eds.), *Perspectives on socio-economics.* Armonk, NY: M. E. Sharpe.

Abolafia, M. Y., & Kilduff, M. (1988). Enacting market crisis: The social construction of a speculative bubble. *Administrative Science Quarterly, 33,* 126-142.

Adams, W. J. (1989). *Restructuring the French economy.* Washington, DC: Brookings Institution.

Adizes, I. (1971). *Industrial democracy: Yugoslav style.* New York: Free Press.

Aldrich, H. (1979). *Organizations and environments.* Englewood Cliffs, NJ: Prentice Hall.

Alford, R. R., & Friedland, R. (1985). *The powers of theory: Capitalism, the state, and democracy.* Cambridge: Cambridge University Press.

Allen, M. (1974). The structure of interorganizational elite cooptation. *American Sociological Review, 39,* 393-406.

Alston, J. P. (1986). *The American samurai.* Berlin: Walter de Gruyter.

Alston, J. P. (1989). Wa, guanxi, and inhwa: Managerial principles in Japan, China, and Korea. *Business Horizons, 32*(2), 26-31.

Amsden, A. H. (1979). Taiwan's economic history: A case of *étatisme* and a challenge to dependency. *Modern China, 5,* 341-380.

Amsden, A. H. (1985). The state and Taiwan's economic development. In P. B. Evans, D. Rueschemeyer, & T. Skocpol (Eds.), *Bringing the state back in* (pp. 78-106). Cambridge: Cambridge University Press.

Amsden, A. H. (1989a). *Asia's next giant: South Korea and late industrialization.* New York: Oxford University Press.

Amsden, A. H. (1989b). *Big business and urbanization in Taiwan: The origins of small- and medium-size enterprise and regionally decentralized industry.* Unpublished manuscript.

Annuario statistico Italiano. (1987). Rome: Tip. Elzeviriana.

Anonymous. (1887). Chinese partnerships: Liability of the individual members. *Journal of the China Branch of the Royal Asiatic Society,* [New Series] 22, 41.

Aoki, M. (1984a). Aspects of the Japanese firm. In M. Aoki (Ed.), *The economic analysis of the Japanese firm* (pp. 3-43). Amsterdam: Elsevier.

Aoki, M. (Ed.). (1984b). *The economic analysis of the Japanese firm.* Amsterdam: Elsevier.

Aoki, M. (1988). *Information, incentive, and bargaining in the Japanese economy.* Cambridge: Cambridge University Press.

Aoki, M. (1990). Toward an economic model of the Japanese firm. *Journal of Economic Literature, 28,* 1-27.

Aubey, R. (1979). Capital mobilization and the patterns of business ownership and control in Latin America: The case of Mexico. In S. Greenfield, A. Strockon, & R. Aubey (Eds.), *Entrepreneurs in cultural context* (pp. 225-242). Albuquerque: University of New Mexico Press.

Aujac, H. (1986). An introduction to French industrial policy. In W. J. Adams & C. Stoffaës (Eds.), *French industrial policy.* Washington, DC: Brookings Institution.

Aujac, H., & de Rouville, J. (1983). *La politique industrielle en France depuis 1945 et surtout depuis 1969.* Neuilly-sur-Seine, France: Bureau d'informations et de prévisions économiques.

Bain, J. S. (1968). *Industrial organization.* New York: John Wiley.

Baker, H. (1979). *Chinese family and kinship.* New York: Columbia University Press.

Banfield, E. C. (1958). *The moral basis of a backward society.* Glencoe, IL: Free Press.

Bank of Korea. (1987). *Economic statistics yearbook.* Seoul: Author.

Barney, J. B., & Ouchi, W. G. (Eds.). (1986). *Organizational economics.* San Francisco: Jossey-Bass.

Barrett, R. E., & Whyte, M. K. (1982). Dependency theory and Taiwan: Analysis of a deviant case. *American Journal of Sociology, 87,* 1064-1089.

Barzini, L. (1964). *The Italians.* New York: Atheneum.

Bellah, R. (1970). Father and son in Christianity and Confucianism. In R. Bellah (Ed.), *Beyond belief* (pp. 76-99). New York: Harper & Row.

Bendix, R. (1974). *Work and authority in industry.* Berkeley: University of California Press.

Bendix, R. (1977). *Kings or people.* Berkeley: University of California Press.

Bendix, R. (1984). *Force, fate, and freedom.* Berkeley: University of California Press.

Bendix, R., & Roth, G. (1971). *Scholarship and partisanship: Essays on Max Weber.* Berkeley: University of California Press.

Benedict, R. (1946). *The chrysanthemum and the sword: Patterns of Japanese culture.* Boston: Houghton Mifflin.

Ben-Porath, Y. (1980). The F-connection: Families, friends, and firms in the organization of exchange. *Population and Development Review, 6,* 1-30.

Berger, P. L. (1984, September 17-23). An East Asian development model. *Economic News,* pp. 1, 6-8.

Berger, P. L., & Hsiao, H. H. M. (Eds.). (1988). *In search of an East Asian development model.* New Brunswick, NJ: Transaction.

Biggart, N. W. (1989). *Charismatic capitalism: Direct selling organizations in America.* Chicago: University of Chicago Press.

Biggart, N. W. (1990). Institutionalized patrimonialism in Korean business. In C. Calhoun (Ed.), *Comparative social research* (Vol. 12, pp. 113-133). Greenwich, CT: JAI.

Biggart, N. W., & Hamilton, G. G. (1984). The power of obedience. *Administrative Science Quarterly, 29,* 541-549.

Biggart, N. W., & Hamilton, G. G. (1990, August). *The Western bias of neoclassical economics: On the limits of a firm-based theory to explain business networks.* Paper presented at the Networks and Organizations Conference, Harvard Business School, Boston.

Biggart, N. W., & Hamilton, G. G. (1992). On the limits of a firm-based theory to explain business networks: The Western bias of neoclassical economics. In N. Nohria & R. G. Eccles (Eds.), *Networks and organizations: Structure, form, and action* (pp. 471-490). Boston: Harvard Business School Press.

Biggs, T. S. (1988a). *Financing the emergence of small and medium enterprise in Taiwan: Financial mobilization and the flow of domestic credit to the private sector* (Employment and Enterprise Policy Analysis Project Discussion Paper No. 15). Cambridge, MA: Employment and Enterprise Policy Analysis Project.

Biggs, T. S. (1988b). *Financing the emergence of small and medium enterprise in Taiwan: Heterogeneous firm size and efficient intermediation* (Employment and Enterprise Policy Analysis Project Discussion Paper No. 16). Cambridge, MA: Employment and Enterprise Policy Analysis Project.

Bisson T. A. (1954). *Zaibatsu dissolution in Japan.* Berkeley: University of California Press.

Blau, P. (1964). *Exchange and power.* New York: John Wiley.

Blinder, A. S. (1990, October 8). There are capitalists, then there are the Japanese. *Business Week,* p. 21.

Blumberg, P. (1973). *Industrial democracy: The sociology of participation.* New York: Schocken.

Bowles, S. (1985). The production process in a competitive economy: Walrasian, neo-Hobbesian, and Marxian models. *American Economic Review, 75,* 16-36.

Brandon, R. (1983). *The other hundred years.* London: Collins.

Brandt, V. S. R. (1987). Korea. In G. Lodge & E. F. Vogel (Eds.), *Ideology and national competitiveness* (pp. 207-239). Boston: Harvard Business School Press.

Brown, F. E., & Oxenfeld, A. R. (1977). *Misperceptions of economic phenomena.* New York: Irvington.

Brusco, S. (1982). The Emilian model. *Cambridge Journal of Economics, 6*(2), 167-184.

Bunge, F. M. (1982). *South Korea: A country study.* Washington, DC: Government Printing Office.

Burt, R. (1977). Power in a social topology. In R. J. Liebert & A. W. Imershein (Eds.), *Power, paradigms, and community research* (pp. 251-334). Beverly Hills, CA: Sage.

Burt, R. (1982). *Toward a structural theory of action.* New York: Academic Press.

Burt, R. (1983). *Corporative profits and cooptation.* New York: Academic Press.

Business Korea. (1992). *Yearbook on the Korean economy and business, 1991/1992.* Seoul: Author.

Cardoso, R. H., & Faletto, E. (1979). *Dependency and development in Latin America* (M. M. Urquidi, Trans.). Berkeley: University of California Press.

Carroll, G. R., & Huo, Y. C. P. (1986). Organizational task and institutional environments in ecological perspective: Findings from the local newspaper industry. *American Journal of Sociology, 91,* 838-873.

Caves, R. E., & Uekusa, M. (1976). *Industrial organization in Japan.* Washington, DC: Brookings Institution.

Chan, C. S. (1987). *Management of chaebol: The conglomerate in South Korea.* In *Proceedings of the Pan-Pacific Conference IV* (pp. 128-133). Taipei. In *Proceedings of the Pan Pacific Conference.* Seoul, South Korea.

Chan, W. K. K. (1982). The organizational structure of the traditional Chinese firm and its modern reform. *Business History Review, 56,* 218-235.

Chandler, A. D., Jr. (1977). *The visible hand: The managerial revolution in American business.* Cambridge, MA: Harvard University Press.

Chandler, A. D., Jr. (1981). Historical determinants of managerial hierarchies: A response to Perrow. In A. Van de Ven & W. Joyce (Eds.), *Perspectives on organizational design and behavior* (pp. 391-402). New York: John Wiley.

Chandler, A. D., Jr. (1982). The M-form: Industrial groups, American style. *European Economic Review, 19,* 3-23.

Chandler, A. D., Jr. (1984). The emergence of managerial capitalism. *Business History Review, 58,* 473-502.

Chandler, A. D., Jr., & Daems, H. (Eds.). (1980). *Managerial hierarchies: Comparative perspectives on the rise of the modern industrial enterprise.* Cambridge, MA: Harvard University Press.

Chang, C. (1988). Everyone wants to be the "boss." *Free China Review, 38*(11), 10-12.

Chang, D. J. (1985). *Economic control and political authoritarianism: The role of Japanese corporations in Korean politics 1965-1979.* Seoul: Sogang University Press.

Chen, C. (1985, March). Caijia ti dajia shangle yike [The Ts'ai family gives everyone a lesson]. *Lianhe Yuekan, 44,* 13-17.

Chen, F. M. C., & Myers, R. H. (1976). Customary law and economic growth of China during the Qing period, pt. 1. *Ch'ing-shih Wen-ti, 3*(5), 1-32.

Chen, F. M. C., & Myers, R. H. (1978). Customary law and economic growth of China during the Qing period, pt. 2. *Ch'ing-shih Wen-ti, 3*(10), 4-27.

Chen, M. (1983). Woguo xian jieduan zhong xiao qiye de fudao wenti [The difficulty in assisting Taiwan's present-day small and medium businesses]. *Tianxia Zazhi, 29,* 137-141.

Chen, M. (1984). Jiazu wenhua yu qiye guanli [Family culture and enterprise organization] pp. 453-486.

Chen, Q., & Qiu, S. (1984). Qiye zuzhi de jiben xingtai yu chuantong jiazu zhidu [Basic concepts of enterprise organization and the traditional family system]. In *Zhongguo shi guanli* [Chinese-style management] pp. 487-510. Taipei: Gongshang Shibao.

Cheung, S. N. S. (1983). The contractual nature of the firm. *Journal of Law and Economics, 26,* 1-21.

China Credit Information Service [Zhonghua Zhengxinso]. (Comp.). (1983). *Taiwan diqu jitua qiye yanjiu, 1983-1984* [Business groups in Taiwan, 1983-1984]. Taipei: Author.

China Credit Information Service [Zhonghua Zhengxinso]. (Comp.). (1985). *Taiwan diqu jitua qiye yanjiu, 1985-1986* [Business groups in Taiwan, 1985-1986]. Taipei: Author.

China Credit Information Service [Zhonghua Zhengxinso]. (Comp.). (1990). *Taiwan diqu jitua qiye yanjiu, 1990-1991* [Business groups in Taiwan, 1990-1991]. Taipei: Author.

Chou, T. C. (1985). *Industrial organization in the process of economic development: The case of Taiwan, 1950-1980.* Louvain-la-Neuve: Ciaco.

Chu, Y. H. (1989). State structure and economic adjustment of the East Asian newly industrializing countries. *International Organization, 43,* 647-672.

Chung, W. K., Feenstra, R. C., & Hamilton, G. G. (1993). *Business networks in Taiwan, 1989: A database.* Davis: University of California, Institute of Governmental Affairs, East Asian Business and Development Program.

Clark, R. (1979). *The Japanese company.* New Haven, CT: Yale University Press.

Clifford, M. (1987, August 20). The price of democracy. *Far Eastern Economic Review,* pp. 53-54.

Coase, R. (1937). The nature of the firm. *Economica, 4,* 386-405.

Coase, R. (1991). The nature of the firm: Influence. In O. E. Williamson & S. G. Winter (Eds.), *The nature of the firm: Origins, evolution, and development* (pp. 61-74). New York: Oxford University Press.

Cochran, S. (1982, October). *Enterprises spanning economic time and space in China, 1850-1980: The introduction of vertical integration.* Paper presented at the Conference on Chinese Entrepreneurship at Home and Abroad, 1900-82, Cornell University, Ithaca, NY.

Cochran, S. (1984, August). *Economic institutions in China's interregional trade: Tobacco products and cotton textiles, 1850-1980.* Paper presented at the Conference on Spatial and Temporal Trends and Cycles in Chinese Economic History, Bellagio, Italy.

Cohen, M. L. (1970). Developmental process in the Chinese domestic group. In M. Freedman (Ed.), *Family and kinship in Chinese society* (pp. 21-36). Stanford, CA: Stanford University Press.

Cohen, M. L. (1976). *House united, house divided: The Chinese family in Taiwan.* New York: Columbia University Press.

Cole, D. C., & Lyman, P. N. (1971). *Korean development: The interplay of politics and economics.* Cambridge, MA: Harvard University Press.

Collins, R. (1980). Weber's last theory of capitalism: A systematization. *American Sociological Review, 45,* 925-942.

Commons, J. R. (1934). *Institutional economics.* Madison: University of Wisconsin Press.

Cook, K. S. (1977). Exchange and power in a network of interorganizational relations. *Sociological Quarterly, 9,* 62-82.

Cook, K. S. (1982). Network structure from an exchange perspective. In P. V. Marsden & N. Lin (Eds.), *Social structure and network analysis* (pp. 177-199). Beverly Hills, CA: Sage.

Council for Economic Planning and Development. (1985). *Taiwan statistical data book, 1985.* Taipei: Author.

Council for Economic Planning and Development. (1987). *Taiwan statistical data book, 1987.* Taipei: Author.

Crozier, M. (1964). *The bureaucratic phenomenon.* Chicago: University of Chicago Press.

Cumings, B. (1984). The origins and development of the Northeast Asian political economy. *International Organization, 38,* 1-40.

Daily Economic News. (1986). *Firm directory of Korea for 1986.* Seoul: Author.

Davis, L. E., & North, D. C. (1971). *Institutional change and American economic growth.* Cambridge: Cambridge University Press.

Deal, T. E., & Kennedy, A. A. (1982). *Corporate cultures.* Reading, MA: Addison-Wesley.

DeGlopper, D. R. (1972). Doing business in Lukang. In W. E. Willmott (Ed.), *Economic organization in Chinese society* (pp. 297-326). Stanford, CA: Stanford University Press.

Diao, M. F. (1983, September 1). Zhonghauminguo 500 jia daqiye [Republic of China 500 big business groups]. *Tianxia Zazhi* [World Journal], pp. 63-84.

DiMaggio, P. J. (1988). Interest and agency in institutional theory. In L. G. Zucker (Ed.), *Institutional patterns and organizations: Culture and environment* (pp. 3-21). Cambridge, MA: Ballinger.

DiMaggio, P. J., & Powell, W. W. (1983). The iron cage revisited: Institutional isomorphism and collective rationality in organizational fields. *American Sociological Review, 48,* 147-160.

Directorate-General of Budget, Accounting and Statistics. (1981). *Report on industrial and commercial survey, Taiwan area.* Taipei: Executive Yuan.

Directorate-General of Budget, Accounting and Statistics. (1983). *Report on industrial and commercial survey, Taiwan area.* Taipei: Executive Yuan.

Directorate-General of Budget, Accounting and Statistics. (1985). *1984 input-output tables.* Taipei: Executive Yuan.

Directorate-General of Budget, Accounting and Statistics. (1989). *Report on industrial and commercial census, Taiwan-Fukien area, the Republic of China.* Taipei: Executive Yuan.

Dobbin, F., & Nam, J. L. (n.d.). *The legacy of the dynasty: The nature of political continuity and the case of modern Korea.* Unpublished manuscript.

Dodwell Marketing Consultants. (Comp.). (1984). *Industrial groupings in Japan* (rev. ed.). Tokyo: Author.

Dodwell Marketing Consultants. (Comp.). (1986). *Industrial groups in the Japanese economy.* Tokyo: Author.

Domhoff, C. W. (1967). *Who rules America?* Englewood Cliffs, NJ: Prentice Hall.

Domhoff, C. W. (1970). *Higher circles.* New York: Vintage.

Domhoff, C. W. (1978). *Who really rules?* New Brunswick, NJ: Transaction.

Domhoff, C. W. (1979). *The powers that be.* New York: Random House.

Domhoff, C. W. (1980). *Power structure research.* Beverly Hills, CA: Sage.

Domhoff, C. W. (1983). *Who rules American now? A review for the 80's.* Englewood Cliffs, NJ: Prentice Hall.

Dore, R. P. (1962). Sociology in Japan. *British Journal of Sociology, 13,* 116-123.

Dore, R. P. (1973). *British factory-Japanese factory: The origins of national diversity in industrial relations.* Berkeley: University of California Press.

Dore, R. P. (1983). Goodwill and the spirit of market capitalism. *British Journal of Sociology, 34,* 459-482.

Dore, R. P. (1986a). *Flexible rigidities: Industrial policy and structural adjustment in the Japanese economy, 1970-1980.* Stanford, CA: Stanford University Press.

Dore, R. P. (1986b). *Structural adjustment in Japan, 1970-82.* Geneva: International Labour Office.

Dore, R. P. (1987). *Taking Japan seriously.* Stanford, CA: Stanford University Press.

Douglas, M. (1986). *How institutions think.* Syracuse, NY: Syracuse University Press.

Douglas, M., with Isherwood, B. (1979). *The world of goods.* New York: Basic Books.

Dow, G. K. (1987). The function of authority in transaction cost economics. *Journal of Economic Behavior and Organization, 8,* 13-38.

Dyer, J. H. (in press). Vertical *keiretsu* alliances and asset specialization: A new perspective on Japanese economic success. In W. M. Fruin (Ed.), *Networks and markets: Pacific Rim investigations.* New York: Oxford University Press.

Eccles, R. G. (1985). *The transfer pricing problem: A theory for practice.* Lexington, MA: Lexington.

The economic groups. (1991, December). *America Economia* [Special issue], pp. 48-53.

Economic Planning Board, Republic of Korea. (1985). *Report on industrial census for 1983.* Seoul: Author.

Economic Planning Board, Republic of Korea. (1987). *Report on mining and manufacturing survey, 1986.* Seoul: Author.

Economic Planning Council, Executive Yuan. (1984). *Taiwan statistical databook.* Taipei: Executive Yuan.

Economist Intelligence Unit. (1985). Annual supplement to *Quarterly Economic Review of Japan.* London: Author.

Edwards, R. (1979). *Contested terrain: The transformation of the workplace in the twentieth century.* New York: Basic Books.

Emerson, R. (1962). Power-dependence relations. *American Sociological Review, 27,* 31-40.

Emerson, R. (1972). Exchange theory. In M. Zelditch & B. Anderson (Eds.), *Sociological theories in progress* (pp. 38-87). Boston: Houghton Mifflin.

Encaoua, D., & Jacquemin, A. (1982). Organizational efficiency and monopoly power: The case of French industrial groups. *European Economic Review, 19,* 25-51.

Encarnation, D. J. (1989). *Dislodging multinationals: India's strategy in comparative perspective.* Ithaca, NY: Cornell University Press.

Ensor, P. (1986, July 24). The modest chaebol: A low-key giant. *Far Eastern Economic Review,* pp. 66-67.

Etzioni, A. (1988). *The moral dimension: Toward a new economics.* New York: Free Press.

Evans, P. B. (1979). *Dependent development: The alliance of multinational, state, and local capital in Brazil.* Princeton, NJ: Princeton University Press.

Evans, P. B., Rueschemeyer, D., & Skocpol, T. (Eds.). (1985). *Bringing the state back in.* Cambridge: Cambridge University Press.

Evans, P. B., & Stephens, J. D. (1988). Development and the world economy. In N. J. Smelser (Ed.), *Handbook of sociology* (pp. 739-773). Newbury Park, CA: Sage.

Evans, R., Jr. (1971). *The labor economics of Japan and the United States.* New York: Praeger.

Fama, E. F., & Jensen, M. C. (1983). Agency problems and residual claims. *Journal of Law and Economics, 26,* 327-349.

Feenstra, R., Yang, C., & Hamilton, G. G. (1993). *Market structure and international trade: Business groups in East Asia* (Working Paper). Davis: University of California, Institute of Governmental Affairs, East Asian Business and Development Program.

Fei, X. (1992). *From the soil: The foundations of Chinese society* (G. G. Hamilton & W. Zheng, Trans.). Berkeley: University of California Press.

Feuerwerker, A. (1984). The state and the economy in late imperial China. *Theory and Society, 13,* 297-326.

Fewsmith, J. (1983). From guild to interest group: The transformation of public and private in late Qing China. *Comparative Studies in Society and History, 25,* 617-640.

Fields, K. J. (1989). *Public finance, private business.* Unpublished manuscript, University of California, Berkeley.

Fischer, D. H. (1970). *Historians' fallacies.* New York: Harper.

500 largest industrial corporations outside U.S. (1976, August) *Fortune,* pp. 232-241.

500 largest industrial corporations outside U.S. (1980, August 31) *Fortune,* pp. 190-199.

The flawed renaissance: A survey of the Italian economy. (1988, February 27). *The Economist,* pp. 3-34.

Fligstein, N. (1985). The spread of the multidivisional form among large firms, 1919-1979. *American Sociological Review, 50,* 377-391.

Fligstein, N. (1990). *The transformation of corporate control.* Cambridge, MA: Harvard University Press.

Fligstein, N. (1991). The structural transformation of American industry: An institutional account of the causes of diversification in the largest firms, 1919-1979. In W. W. Powell & P. J. DiMaggio (Eds.), *The new institutionalism in organizational analysis* (pp. 311-336). Chicago: University of Chicago Press.

Florida, R., & Kenney, M. (1991). Transplanted organizations: The transfer of Japanese industrial organization to the United States. *American Sociological Review, 56,* 381-399.

Foucault, M. (1965). *Madness and civilization: A history of insanity in the Age of Reason.* New York: Random House.

Foucault, M. (1979). *Discipline and punish: The birth of the prison.* New York: Vintage.

Foy, N., & Gadon, H. (1976, May-June). Worker participation: Contrasts in three countries. *Harvard Business Review, 54,* 71-83.

Francis, A., Turk, J., & Willman, P. (Eds). (1983). *Power, efficiency, and institutions.* London: Heinemann.

Freedman, M. (1966). *Chinese lineage and society: Fujian and Guangdong.* London: Athlone.

Friedman, M. (1953). *Essays in positive economics.* Chicago: University of Chicago Press.

Fruin, W. M. (1992). *The Japanese enterprise system: Competitive strategies and cooperative structures.* Oxford: Clarendon.

Fuà, G. (1976). *Occupazione e capacità produttive.* Bologna: Il Mulino.

Fukuda, K. J. (1983). Transfer of management: Japanese practices for the orientals? *Management Decision, 21,* 17-26.

Futatsugi, Y. (1982). *Nihon no kabushiki shoyu kozo* [The structure of shareholding in Japan]. Tokyo: Dobunkan.

Futatsugi, Y. (1986). *Japanese enterprise groups.* Kobe, Japan: Kobe University, School of Business.

Galenson, W. (Ed.). (1979). *Economic growth and structural change in Taiwan.* Ithaca, NY: Cornell University Press.

Gamst, F. C., & Norbeck, E. (Eds.). (1976). *Ideas of culture.* New York: Holt, Rinehart & Winston.

Geertz, C. (1963). *Peddlers and princes: Social development and economic change in two Indonesian towns.* Chicago: University of Chicago Press.

Geertz, C. (1977). Centers, kings and charisma. In J. Ben-David & T. N. Clark (Eds.), *Culture and its creators* (pp. 150-171). Chicago: University of Chicago Press.

Geertz, C. (1980). *Negara.* Princeton, NJ: Princeton University Press.

Gereffi, G. (1993). The organization of buyer-driven global commodity chains: How US retail networks shape overseas production. In G. Gereffi & M. Korzeniewicz (Eds.), *Commodity chains and global capitalism* (pp. 95-122). Westport, CT: Greenwood.

Gereffi, G., & Hamilton, G. G. (1990, August). *Modes of incorporation in an industrial world: The social economy of global capitalism.* Paper presented at the annual meeting of the American Sociological Association, Washington, DC.

Gereffi, G., & Hamilton, G. G. (1992). *The social economy of global capitalism: Modes of incorporation in an industrial world.* Unpublished manuscript.

Gereffi, G., & Pan, M. L. (1994). The globalization of Taiwan's garment industry. In E. Bonacich, L. Cheng, N. Chinchilla, N. Hamilton, & P. Ong (Eds.), *Global production: The apparel industry in the Pacific Rim* (pp. 126-146). Philadelphia: Temple University Press.

Gerlach, M. (1992). *Alliance capitalism: The strategic organization of Japanese business.* Berkeley: University of California Press.

Gerschenkron, A. (1962). *Economic backwardness in historical perspective.* Cambridge, MA: Harvard University Press.

Golas, P. J. (1977). Early Ch'ing guilds. In G. W. Skinner (Ed.), *The city in late imperial China* (pp. 555-580). Stanford, CA: Stanford University Press.

Gold, T. B. (1986). *State and society in the Taiwan miracle.* Armonk, NY: M. E. Sharpe.

Gold, T. B. (1988). Entrepreneurs, multinationals, and the state. In E. A. Winckler & S. Greenhalgh (Eds.), *Contending approaches to the political economy of Taiwan* (pp. 175-205). Armonk, NY: M. E. Sharpe.

Goldberg, C. N. (1977). Spirits in place: The concept of kohyang and the Korean social order. In D. R. McCann (Ed.), *Studies on Korea in transition* (pp. 89-101). Honolulu: University of Hawaii, Center for Korean Studies.

Goldstein, C. (1989, November 30). Something must crack. *Far Eastern Economic Review,* pp. 80-81.

Goto, A. (1982). Business groups in a market economy. *European Economic Review, 19,* 53-70.

Granovetter, M. (1985). Economic action and social structure: The problem of embeddedness. *American Journal of Sociology, 91,* 481-510.

Granovetter, M. (1994). Business groups. In N. J. Smelser & R. Swedberg (Eds.), *Handbook of economic sociology* (pp. 453-475). Princeton, NJ: Princeton University Press.

Greenhalgh, S. (1988). Families and networks in Taiwan's economic development. In E. A. Winckler & S. Greenhalgh (Eds.), *Contending approaches to the political economy of Taiwan* (pp. 224-248). Armonk, NY: M. E. Sharpe.

Greif, A., Milgrom, P., & Weingast, B. (1994). Coordination, commitment, and enforcement: The case of the merchant guild. *Journal of Political Economy, 102,* 732-745.

Gross, N., with Port, O. (1990, June 15). Hustling to catch up in science. *Business Week,* pp. 74-75, 78-79, 82.

Hadley, E. M. (1970). *Antitrust in Japan.* Princeton, NJ: Princeton University Press.

Haggard, S., & Cheng, T. J. (1986). State and foreign capital in the "Gang of Four." In F. Deyo (Ed.), *The new East Asian industrialization* (pp. 8-135). Ithaca, NY: Cornell University Press.

Hahn, C. K., Kim, Y. H., & Kim, J. S. (1987). An analysis of Korean chaebols: Formation and growth pattern. In *Proceedings of the Pan-Pacific Conference IV* (pp. 128-133). Taipei.

Hamilton, G. G. (1977). Ethnicity and regionalism: Some factors influencing Chinese identities in Southeast Asia. *Ethnicity, 4*, 335-351.

Hamilton, G. G. (1978). The structural sources of adventurism. *American Journal of Sociology, 83*, 1466-1490.

Hamilton, G. G. (1979). Regional association and the Chinese city: A comparative perspective. *Comparative Studies in Society and History, 21*, 338-353.

Hamilton, G. G. (1984). Patriarchalism in imperial China and Western Europe: A revision of Weber's sociology of domination. *Theory and Society, 13*, 393-426.

Hamilton, G. G. (1985). Why no capitalism in China? Negative questions in historical, comparative research. *Journal of Asian Perspectives, 2*, 2.

Hamilton, G. G. (1989, August). *Patterns of Asian capitalism: The cases of Taiwan and South Korea.* Paper presented at the annual meeting of the American Sociological Association, San Francisco.

Hamilton, G. G. (1990). Patriarchy, patrimonialism, and filial piety: A comparison of China and Western Europe. *British Journal of Sociology, 41*, 77-104.

Hamilton, G. G. (1991). The organizational foundations of Western and Chinese commerce: A historical and comparative analysis. In G. G. Hamilton (Ed.), *Business networks and economic development in East and Southeast Asia* (pp. 48-65). Hong Kong: University of Hong Kong, Centre of Asian Studies.

Hamilton, G. G. (1992, April). *Family and big business in the industrialization of Taiwan.* Paper presented at the annual meeting of the Association for Asian Studies, Washington, DC.

Hamilton, G. G. (1994). Civilization and the organization of economics. In N. J. Smelser & R. Swedberg (Eds.), *Handbook of economic sociology* (pp. 183-205). Princeton, NJ: Princeton University Press.

Hamilton, G. G. (1995). Overseas Chinese capitalism. In W. Tu (Ed.), *The Confucian dimensions of industrial East Asia.* Cambridge, MA: Harvard University Press.

Hamilton, G. G., & Biggart, N. W. (1984). *Governor Reagan, Governor Brown: A sociology of executive power.* New York: Columbia University Press.

Hamilton, G. G., & Biggart, N. W. (1985). Why people obey: Theoretical observations on power and obedience in complex organizations. *Sociological Perspectives, 28*, 3-28.

Hamilton, G. G., & Biggart, N. W. (1988). Market, culture, and authority: A comparative analysis of management and organization in the Far East. *American Journal of Sociology, 94*(Suppl.), S52-S94.

Hamilton, G. G., & Kao, C. S. (1987a). *The institutional foundations of Chinese business: The family firm in Taiwan* (Working Paper). Davis: University of California, Institute of Governmental Affairs, East Asian Business and Development Program.

Hamilton, G. G., & Kao, C. S. (1987b). Max Weber and the analysis of East Asian industrialization. *International Sociology, 2*, 289-300.

Hamilton, G. G., & Kao, C. S. (1990). The institutional foundations of Chinese business: The family firm in Taiwan. *Comparative Social Research, 12*, 135-157.

Hamilton, G. G., & Orrù, M. (1989). The organizational structure of East Asian business groups. In K. H. Chung & H. C. Lee (Eds.), *Korean managerial dynamics.* New York: Praeger.

Hamilton, G. G., Orrù, M., & Biggart, N. W. (1987). Enterprise groups in East Asia. *Shoken Keizai, 161*, 78-106.

Hamilton, G. G., & Sutton, J. (1982, June). *The common law and social reform: The rise of administrative justice in the U.S., 1880-1920.* Paper presented at the annual meeting of the Law and Society Association, Toronto.

Hamilton, G. G., & Sutton, J. (1989). The problem of control in the weak state: Domination in the U.S., 1880-1920. *Theory and Society, 18,* 1-46.

Hamilton, G. G., & Wang, Z. (1992). Introduction: Fei Xiaotong and the beginnings of a Chinese sociology. In X. Fei, *From the soil: The foundations of Chinese society* (G. G. Hamilton & W. Zheng, Trans.) (pp. 1-34). Berkeley: University of California Press.

Hamilton, G. G., Zeile, W., & Kim, W. J. (1990). The network structures of East Asian economies. In S. R. Clegg & S. G. Redding (Eds.), *Capitalism in contrasting cultures.* Berlin: Walter de Gruyter.

Han, W. (1974). *The history of Korea* (G. K. Mintz, Ed.; K. Lee, Trans.). Honolulu: University of Hawaii Press.

Hankook Ilbo. (1985). *Pal ship O nyndo hankook ui 50 dae jae bul* [The 50 top *chaebol*]. Seoul: Author.

Hankuk kiop chongnam [Annual report of Korean companies]. (1989). Seoul: KPC.

Hannan, M. T., & Freeman, J. H. (1977). The population ecology of organizations. *American Journal of Sociology, 82,* 929-964.

Hannan, M. T., & Freeman, J. H. (1981). *Niche width and the dynamics of organizational populations* (Technical Report No. 2). Stanford, CA: Stanford University, Institute for Mathematical Studies in the Social Sciences.

Hannan, M. T., & Freeman, J. H. (1984). Structural inertia and organizational change. *American Sociological Review, 49,* 149-164.

Hao, Y. P. (1970). *The comprador in nineteenth-century China.* Cambridge, MA: Harvard University Press.

Hao, Y. P. (1986). *The commercial revolution in nineteenth-century China.* Berkeley: University of California Press.

Harbison, F. H., & Meyer, C. A. (1959). *Management in the industrial world: An international analysis.* New York: McGraw-Hill.

Hardach, K. (1980). *The political economy of Germany in the twentieth century.* Berkeley: University of California Press.

Harris, M. (1979). *Cultural materialism: The struggle for a science of culture.* New York: Random House.

Hartmann, G., Nicholas, I., Sorge, A., & Warner, M. (1983). Computerized machine-tools, manpower consequences and skill utilization. *British Journal of Industrial Relations, 21,* 221-231.

Hawley, A. (1968). Human ecology. In D. L. Sills (Ed.), *International encyclopedia of the social sciences* (pp. 328-337). New York: Macmillan.

Hayashi, S. (1988). *Culture and management in Japan.* Tokyo: University of Tokyo Press.

Helm, L., with Nakarmi, L., Soo, J. J., Holstein, W. J., & Terry, E. (1985, December 23). The Koreans are coming. *Business Week,* pp. 46-52.

Henderson, G. (1968). *Korea: The politics of the vortex.* Cambridge, MA: Harvard University Press.

Herrigel, G. B. (1989). Industrial order and the politics of industrial change. In P. J. Katzenstein (Ed.), *Industry and politics in West Germany.* Ithaca, NY: Cornell University Press.

Hirsch, P. M. (1972). Processing fads and fashions. *American Journal of Sociology, 77,* 639-659.

Hirsch, P. M. (1986). From ambushes to golden parachutes. *American Journal of Sociology, 91,* 800-837.

Hirschmeier, J., & Yui, T. (1975). *The development of Japanese business.* Cambridge, MA: Harvard University Press.

Hirschmeier, J., & Yui, T. (1981). *The development of Japanese business 1600-1980.* London: Allen & Unwin.

Ho, S. P. (1980). *Small-scale enterprises in Korea and Taiwan* (World Bank Staff Working Paper No. 384). Washington, DC: World Bank.

Ho, Y. M. (1980). The production structure of the manufacturing sector and its distribution implications: The case of Taiwan. *Economic Development and Cultural Change, 28,* 321-343.

Hofheinz, R., Jr., & Calder, K. E. (1982). *The Eastasia edge.* New York: Basic Books.

Holmstrom, B. R., & Tirole, J. (1989). The theory of the firm. In R. Schmalensee & R. D. Willig (Eds.), *Handbook of industrial organization* (Vol. 1, pp. 61-133). Amsterdam: North-Holland.

Hou, J. (1984). Xianqin rufa liangjia guanli guannian zhi bijiao yanjiu [Comparative research on management concepts in Confucian and legalist philosophy in early Ch'in]. In *Zhongguo shi guanli* [Chinese-style management] (pp. 59-74). Taipei: Gongshang Shibao.

Hsu, F. L. K. (1971). *Under the ancestors' shadow: Kinship, personality and social mobility in China.* Stanford, CA: Stanford University Press.

Hsu, Y. R. A., Pannell, C. W., & Wheeler, J. O. (1980). The development and structure of transportation networks in Taiwan: 1960-1972. In R. G. Knapp (Ed.), *China's island frontier* (pp. 167-202). Honolulu: University of Hawaii Press.

Hu, T. L. (1984). *My mother-in-law's village: Rural industrialization and change in Taiwan.* Taipei: Academia Sinica, Institute of Ethnology.

Huang, G. (1984). Rujia lunli yu qiye zuzhi xingtai [Confucian theory and types of enterprise organization]. In *Zhongguo shi guanli* [Chinese-style management] (pp. 21-58). Taipei: Gongshang Shibao.

Hwang, K. K. (1987). Face and favor: The Chinese power game. *American Journal of Sociology, 92,* 944-974.

Imai, K. I., & Itami, H. (1984). Interpenetration of organization and market. *International Journal of Industrial Organization, 2,* 285-310.

Information please almanac, 1990. (1990). Boston: Houghton Mifflin.

The International 500. (1984, August 20). *Fortune,* pp. 202-211.

The International 500. (1989, July 31). *Fortune,* pp. 280-324.

The International 500. (1992, July 27). *Fortune.*

International Monetary Fund. (1985). *Directory of trade statistics.* Washington, DC: Author.

Ishida, H. (1983). Anticompetitive practices in the distribution of goods and services in Japan. *Journal of Japanese Studies, 9,* 319-334.

Ito, K. (1984). Development finance and commercial banks in Korea. *Developing Economies, 22,* 453-475.

Jacobs, J. B. (1979). A preliminary model of particularistic ties in Chinese political alliance: Kan-ch'ing and kuan-hsi in a rural Taiwanese township. *China Quarterly, 78,* 237-273.

Jacobs, N. (1985). *The Korean road to modernization and development.* Urbana: University of Illinois Press.

Jacoby, S. (1979). The origins of internal labor markets in Japan. *Industrial Relations, 18,* 184-196.

Japan, Norinsho. (1982). *Abstract of statistics on agriculture, forestry and fisheries.* Tokyo: Ministry of Agriculture and Forestry.

Japan statistical yearbook. (1988). Tokyo: Sorifu, Tokeikyoku.

Jensen, M. C., & Meckling, W. H. (1976). Theory of the firm: Managerial behavior, agency costs and ownership structure. *Journal of Financial Economics, 3,* 305-360.

Jepperson, R., & Meyer, J. W. (1991). The public order and the construction of formal organization. In W. W. Powell & P. J. DiMaggio (Eds.), *The new institutionalism in organizational analysis* (pp. 204-231). Chicago: University of Chicago Press.

Johnson, C. (1982). *MITI and the Japanese miracle.* Stanford, CA: Stanford University Press.

Johnson, C. (1985). The institutional foundations of Japanese industrial policy. *California Management Review, 27*(4), 59-69.

Johnstone, B. (1988, August 18). Taiwan has designs on booming niche markets. *Far Eastern Economic Review,* pp. 84-85.

Jones, E. L. (1987). *The European miracle.* Cambridge: Cambridge University Press.

Jones, L. P., & SaKong, I. (1980). *Government, business, and entrepreneurship in economic development: The Korean case.* Cambridge, MA: Harvard University, Council on East Asian Studies.

Jorgensen, J. J., Hafsi, T., & Kiggundu, M. N. (1986). Towards a market imperfections theory of organizational structure in developing countries. *Journal of Management Studies, 23,* 419-442.

Juhn, D. S. (1971). Korean industrial entrepreneurship, 1924-40. In Y. H. Jo (Ed.), *Korea's response to the West* (pp. 219-254). Kalamazoo, MI: Korean Research and Publications.

Jung, K. H. (1989). Business-government relations in Korea. In K. H. Chung & H. C. Lee (Eds.), *Korean managerial dynamics.* New York: Praeger.

Kanter, R. M. (1983). *The change masters: Innovation and productivity in the American corporation.* New York: Simon & Schuster.

Kantorowicz, E. (1957). *The king's two bodies.* Princeton, NJ: Princeton University Press.

Kao, C. S. (1989). *Role of personal trust in large businesses in Taiwan.* Paper presented at the International Conference on Business Groups and Economic Development in East Asia, University of Hong Kong.

Kao, C. S. (1991). "Personal trust" in the large businesses in Taiwan: A traditional foundation for contemporary economic activities. In G. G. Hamilton (Ed.), *Business networks and economic development in East and Southeast Asia.* Hong Kong: University of Hong Kong, Centre of Asian Studies.

Katzenstein, P. J. (1987). *Policy and politics in West Germany.* Philadelphia: Temple University Press.

Katzenstein, P. J. (Ed.). (1989). *Industry and politics in West Germany.* Ithaca, NY: Cornell University Press.

Kim, B. W. (1981). Confucianism and administrative development interventionism. In B. W. Kim & W. J. Rho (Eds.), *Korean public bureaucracy.* Seoul: Kyobo.

Kim, E. M. (1988). *From dominance to symbiosis: Policy analysis of state and chaebol in Korea.* Paper presented at the annual meeting of the American Sociological Association, Atlanta, GA.

Kim, E. M. (1991). The industrial organization and growth of the Korean *chaebol*: Integrating development and organizational theories. In G. G. Hamilton (Ed.), *Business networks and economic development in East and Southeast Asia* (pp. 272-299). Hong Kong: University of Hong Kong, Centre of Asian Studies.

Kim, E. M. (1994). *Big business, strong state: Collusion and conflict in Korean development.* Berkeley: University of California Press.

Kim, K. D. (1976, May). Political factors in the formation of the entrepreneurial elite in South Korea. *Asian Survey,* pp. 465-477.

King, A. Y. C. (1991). Kuan-hsi and network building: A sociological interpretation. *Daedalus, 120*(2), 63-84.

King, R. (1985). *The industrial geography of Italy.* New York: St. Martin's.

Kobayashi, Y. (1979). *Shin kigyo shudan monogatari* [Story of the business groups] (rev. ed.). Tokyo: Toyo Keizai Shimposha.

Kobayashi, Y. (1980). *Kigyo shudan no bunseki* [Analysis of business groups]. Sapporo, Japan: Hokkaido Daigaku Tosho Kankokai.

Kocka, J. (1978). Entrepreneurs and managers in German industrialization. In M. M. Postan & H. J. Habakkuk (Eds.), *The Cambridge economic history of Europe* (2nd ed., Vol. 7). Cambridge: Cambridge University Press.

Koebner, R. (1964). German towns and Slav markets. In S. L. Thupp (Ed.), *Change in medieval society*. New York: Appleton-Century-Crofts.

Koo, H. (1984). The political economy of income distribution in South Korea: The impact of the state's industrialization policies. *World Development, 12,* 1029-1037.

Korea Investors Service. (1990). *Chaebol bunsuk bogosuh* [*Chaebol* analysis report]. Seoul: Author.

Körner, K. (1971). The social dimensions of political economy. *German Economic Review, 9*(3), 197-208.

Kosei Torihiki Iinkai Jimukyoku [Fair Trade Commission]. (1983). *Kigyo shudan no jitlai ni tsuite* [On the state of affairs of business groups]. Tokyo: Author.

Krause, L., & Sueo, S. (1976). Japan and the world economy. In H. Patrick & H. Rosovsky (Eds.), *Asia's new giant* (pp. 383-458). Washington, DC: Brookings Institution.

Kunio, Y. (1982). *Sogo shosha.* Oxford: Oxford University Press.

Kuo, E. C. Y. (1991). Ethnicity, polity, and economy: A case study of the Mandarin trade and the Chinese connection. In G. G. Hamilton (Ed.), *Business networks and economic development in East and Southeast Asia.* Hong Kong: University of Hong Kong, Centre of Asian Studies.

Kuznets, S. (1979). Growth and structural shifts. In W. Galenson (Ed.), *Economic growth and structural change in Taiwan* (pp. 15-131). Ithaca, NY: Cornell University Press.

Kyongje Kihoegwon, Chosa Tonggueguk. (1985). *Korea statistical handbook.* Seoul: National Bureau of Statistics.

Lau, S. K. (1982). *Society and politics in Hong Kong.* Hong Kong: Chinese University Press.

Lazerson, M. (1988). Organizational growth of small firms. *American Sociological Review, 53,* 330-342.

Leaman, J. (1988). *The political economy of West Germany, 1945-1985.* New York: St. Martin's.

Lee, H. B., & Kang, S. T. (1982). Development of the study of public administration in Korea. In B. W. Kim & W. J. Rho (Eds.), *Korean public bureaucracy* (pp. 18-45). Seoul: Kyobo.

Lee, K. (1984). *A new history of Korea.* Cambridge, MA: Harvard University Press.

Lee, S. M. (1986). *Management style and practice of Korean chaebols.* Paper presented at the meeting of the Decision Sciences Institute, Honolulu.

Lee, S. Y. (1990). *Money and finance in the economic development of Taiwan.* London: Macmillan.

Leff, N. H. (1976). Capital markets in the less developed countries: The group principle. In R. I. McKinnon (Ed.), *Money and finance in economic growth and development: Essays in honor of Edward S. Shaw* (pp. 97-122). New York: Marcel Decker.

Leff, N. H. (1978). Industrial organization and entrepreneurship in the developing countries: The economic groups. *Economic Development and Cultural Change, 26,* 661-675.

Le Goff, J. (1980). *Time, work, and culture in the Middle Ages.* Chicago: University of Chicago Press.

Levy, B. (1988, Spring). Korean and Taiwanese firms as international competitors: The challenges ahead. *Columbia Journal of World Business, 23,* 43-51.

Levy, B. (1991). Transactions costs, the size of firms, and industrial policy: Lessons from a comparative case study of the footwear industry in Korea and Taiwan. *Journal of Development Economics, 34,* 151-178.

Levy, M. (1972). *Modernization: Latecomers and survivors.* New York: Basic Books.

Levy-Leboyer, M. (1980). The large corporation in modern France. In A. D. Chandler & H. Daems (Eds.), *Managerial hierarchies: Comparative perspectives on the rise of the modern industrial enterprise.* Cambridge, MA: Harvard University Press.

Li, K. T. (1976). *The experience of dynamic economic growth in Taiwan.* Taipei: Mei Ya.

Li, K. T. (1988). *The evolution of policy behind Taiwan's development success.* New Haven, CT: Yale University Press.

Lim, E. M., Feenstra, R. C., & Hamilton, G. G. (1993). *Business networks in Korea, 1989: A database.* Davis: University of California, Institute of Governmental Affairs, East Asian Business and Development Program.

Lin, P. A. (1989). *The social sources of capital investment in Taiwan's industrialization.* Paper presented at the Conference on Industrial Policy and Business Organization in East Asian Capitalist Development, Tunghai University, Taichung, Taiwan.

Lin, P. A. (1991). The social sources of capital investment in Taiwan's industrialization. In G. G. Hamilton (Ed.), *Business networks and economic development in East and Southeast Asia.* Hong Kong: University of Hong Kong, Centre of Asian Studies.

Lin, X. (1984, April). Riben de qiye jingying—shehui zuzhi cengmian de kaocha [Japanese industrial management: An examination of levels of social organization]. *Guolijengjrtaxue Xuebao, 49,* 167-199.

Linder, S. B. (1986). *The Pacific century.* Stanford, CA: Stanford University Press.

Little, I. M. D. (1979). An economic reconnaissance. In W. Galenson (Ed.), *Economic growth and structural change in Taiwan* (pp. 448-507). Ithaca, NY: Cornell University Press.

Liu, K. C. (1987, August). *Chinese merchant guilds: An historical inquiry.* Presidential address delivered at the annual meeting of the Pacific Coast Branch of the American Historical Association, Occidental College, Eagle Rock, CA.

Liu, S. S., Kuo, K. M., Huang, J. Y., & Situ, D. X. (1981, Fall-Winter). Taiwan dichu guanxi qiye zhi xingcheng, yingyun yuqi yingxiang [The formation, operations, and influence of Taiwan's related enterprises]. *Qiye Yinhang Jikan* [Enterprise Bank Quarterly], *4,* 5-19; *5,* 5-23.

Lopez, R. S., & Raymond, I. W. (1955). *Medieval trade in the Mediterranean world.* New York: Columbia University Press.

Lorch, K., & Biggs, T. S. (1989). *Growing in the interstices: The limits of government promotion of small industries.* Paper presented at the annual meeting of the Association for Asian Studies, Washington, DC.

Lorenzoni, G., & Ornati, O. A. (1988). Constellations of firms and new ventures. *Journal of Business Venturing, 3,* 41-57.

Lucas, R. E. (1988). On the mechanics of economic development. *Journal of Monetary Economics, 22,* 3-42.

Luhmann, N. (1979). *Trust and power.* Chichester: John Wiley.

Magaziner, I., & Hout, T. (1981). *Japanese industrial policy.* Berkeley: University of California, Institute for International Studies.

Magnanini, S. (1988, September 12). South Korea's workers aren't taking it anymore. *Sacramento Bee,* p. D1.

Maitland, I., Bryson, J., & Van de Ven, A. (1985). Sociologists, economists and opportunism. *Academy of Management Review, 10,* 59-65.

Management Efficiency Research Institute. (1985). *Korea's fifty major groups for 1983 and 1984.* Seoul: Author.

Management Efficiency Research Institute. (1986). *Financial analysis note of top 50 chaebol of Korea.* Seoul: Author.

March, J., & Olson, J. P. (1984). The new institutionalism. *Political Science Review, 78,* 734-749.

Marglin, S. A. (1974). What do bosses do? The origins and functions of hierarchy in capitalist production. *Review of Radical Political Economy, 6,* 33-60.

Mark, L. L. (1972). *Taiwanese lineage enterprises: A study of familial entrepreneurship.* Unpublished doctoral dissertation, University of California, Berkeley.

Marx, K. (1930). *Capital.* London: Dent.

Mason, E. S. (1960). *The corporation in modern society.* Cambridge, MA: Harvard University Press.

Mason, E. S., Kim, M. K., Perkins, D. H., Kim, K. S., & Cole, D. C. (1980). *The economic and social modernization of the Republic of Korea.* Cambridge, MA: Harvard University, Council on East Asian Studies.

Maurice, M., Sorge, A., & Warner, M. (1980). Societal differences in organizing manufacturing units. *Organization Studies, 1,* 59-86.

McCullagh, C. (1984). Entrepreneurship and development. *Economic and Social Review, 15*(2), 109-124.

Menkhoff, T. (1990). *Trade routes, trust and trading networks: Chinese family-based trading firms in Singapore and their external economic dealings.* Unpublished doctoral dissertation, University of Bielefeld.

Meyer, J. W., & Rowan, B. (1977). Institutionalized organizations: Formal structure as myth and ceremony. *American Journal of Sociology, 83,* 340-363.

Meyer, J. W., & Rowan, B. (1983). The structure of educational organizations. In J. W. Meyer & W. R. Scott (Eds.), *Organizational environments: Ritual and rationality* (pp. 71-97). Beverly Hills, CA: Sage.

Meyer, J. W., & Scott, W. R. (Eds.). (1983). *Organizational environments: Ritual and rationality.* Beverly Hills, CA: Sage.

Miles, R. H. (1980). *Macro organization behavior.* Glenview, IL: Scott, Foresman.

Mills, C. W. (1956). *The power elite.* New York: Oxford University Press.

Minard, L. (1984, May). The China Reagan can't visit. *Forbes,* pp. 36-42.

Ministère des Finances et des Affaires Economiques, Institut national de la statistique et des études économiques. (1982). *Annuaire statistique de la France.* Paris: Author.

Ministère des Finances et des Affaires Economiques, Institut national de la statistique et des études économiques. (1989). *Annuaire statistique de la France.* Paris: Author.

Mintz, B., & Schwartz, M. (1985). *The power structure of American business.* Chicago: University of Chicago Press.

Miyazaki, Y. (1976). *Sengo nihon no kigyo shudan* [Business groups in postwar Japan]. Tokyo: Nihon Keizai Shimbunsha.

Miyazaki, Y. (1981). Sogo shosha soshiki no senryakuteki tenkai [Strategic developments in the organization of the general trading firms. *Soshiki Kagaku, 15,* 49-58.

Miyazaki, Y., & Fujinami, K. (1980). Jidoshagyo ni okeru ryutsu keiret suka no littai [The state of firm alignment in the distribution sector of the automobile industry]. *Kosei Tori Hiki, 355,* 24-29; *356,* 25-31; *357,* 32-38.

Mizruchi, M. S. (1982). *The American corporate network: 1904-1974.* Beverly Hills, CA: Sage.

Monthly Bulletin of Statistics. (1985, March). New York: United Nations.

Moore, B. (1966). *Social origins of dictatorship and democracy: Lord and peasant in the making of the modern world.* Boston: Beacon.

Mori, H. (1980). The behavior of general trading companies as reflected in lumber prices. *Japanese Economic Studies, 9,* 3-44.

Müller-Armack, A. (1965). The principles of the social market economy. *German Economic Review, 3*(2), 89-104.

Myers, R. H. (1980). *The Chinese economy, past and present.* Belmont, CA: Wadsworth.

Myers, R. H. (1984). The economic transformation of the Republic of China on Taiwan. *China Quarterly, 99,* 500-528.

Myers, R. H., & Peattie, M. R. (Eds.). (1984). *The Japanese colonial empire, 1895-1945.* Princeton, NJ: Princeton University Press.

Nakamura, T. (1981). *The postwar Japanese economy.* Tokyo: University of Tokyo Press.

Nakamura, T. (1983). *Economic growth in prewar Japan.* New Haven, CT: Yale University Press.

Nakane, C. (1970). *Japanese society.* Berkeley: University of California Press.

398   THE ORGANIZATION OF EAST ASIAN CAPITALISM

Nakatani, I. (1982). Risuku shearingu kara mita nihon keizai: Kigyo shudan no keizai gorisei ni kansuru ichikosatsu [Japanese economy viewed from risk sharing: A perspective on economic rationality in the business groups]. *Osaka Daigaku Keizaigaku, 32*, 219-245.

Nakatani, I. (1984). The economic role of financial corporate grouping. In M. Aoki (Ed.), *The economic analysis of the Japanese firm* (pp. 227-258). Amsterdam: Elsevier.

Nanetti, R. Y. (1988). *Growth and territorial policies: The Italian model of social capitalism.* London: Pinter.

Narushima, T. (1980). *Tokyu gurupu no subele* [The Tokyu group]. Tokyo: Nihon Jitsugyo Shuppansha.

Needham, J. (1956a). *The grand titration.* Toronto: Toronto University Press.

Needham, J. (1956b). *Science and civilization in China.* Cambridge: Cambridge University Press.

Neff, R., with Holstein, W. J. (1990, September 24). Mighty Mitsubishi is on the move. *Business Week,* pp. 98-100.

Nishikiori, H. (1975). *Sumitomo gurupu* [The Sumitomo group]. Tokyo: Yunion Shuppansha.

Nishikiori, H. (1977). *Hitachi gurupu* [The Hitachi group]. Tokyo: Yunion Shuppansha.

Nishiyama, T. (1984). The structure of managerial control: Who owns and controls Japanese business. In K. Sato & Y. Hoshino (Eds.), *The anatomy of Japanese business.* Armonk, NY: M. E. Sharpe.

North, D. C. (1981). *Structure and change in economic history.* New York: W. W. Norton.

North, D. C. (1990). *Institutions, institutional change and economic performance.* Cambridge: Cambridge University Press.

Numazaki, I. (1986). Networks of Taiwanese big business: A preliminary analysis. *Modern China, 12,* 487-534.

Numazaki, I. (1991a). *Networks and partnerships: The social organization of the Chinese business elite in Taiwan.* Unpublished doctoral dissertation, Michigan State University.

Numazaki, I. (1991b). The role of personal networks in the making of Taiwan's *guanxiqiye* (related enterprises). In G. G. Hamilton (Ed.), *Business networks and economic development in East and Southeast Asia.* Hong Kong: University of Hong Kong, Centre of Asian Studies.

Nyaw, M., & Chan, C. (1982). Structure and development strategies of the manufacturing industries in Singapore and Hong Kong: A comparative study. *Asian Survey, 22,* 449-469.

Nye, J. V, (1987). Firm size and economic backwardness. *Journal of Economic History, 47,* 649-669.

Organization for Economic Cooperation and Development [OECD]. (1988a, July). *Economic survey on Japan.* Paris: Author.

Organization for Economic Cooperation and Development [OECD]. (1988b, July). *Economic survey on Germany.* Paris: Author.

Organization for Economic Cooperation and Development [OECD]. (1989, January). *Economic surveys: Italy.* Paris: Author.

Oishi, T. (1975). *Fuyo gurupu* [The Fuyo group]. Tokyo: Yunion Shuppansha.

Okumura, H. (1982a). Inter-firm relations in an enterprise group. *Japanese Economic Studies, 10,* 53-82.

Okumura, H. (1982b). *Mitsubishi: Nihon o ugokasu shudan* [Mitsubishi: A business group that moves Japan]. Tokyo: Daiyamondo Sha.

Okumura, H. (1984). Enterprise groups in Japan. *Shoken Keizai, 147,* 169-189.

Okumura, H. (1985). *Shin nihon no rokudai kigyo shudan* [Japan's six major business groups] (rev. ed.). Tokyo: Daiyamondo Sha.

Omohundro, J. T. (1981). *Chinese merchant families in Iloilo.* Athens: Ohio University Press.

Orlove, B. S. (1986). Barter and cash sale on Lake Titicaca: A test of competing approaches. *Current Anthropology, 27,* 85-106.

Orrù, M. (1991a). The institutional logic of small-firm economies in Italy and Taiwan. *Studies in Comparative International Development, 26,* 3-28.

Orrù, M. (1991b). Practical and theoretical aspects of Japanese business networks. In G. G. Hamilton (Ed.), *Business networks in East and Southeast Asia.* Hong Kong: University of Hong Kong, Centre of Asian Studies.

Orrù, M. (1993). Institutional cooperation in Japanese and German capitalism. In S.-E. Sjöstrand (Ed.), *Institutional change: Theory and empirical findings* (pp. 171-198). Armonk, NY: M. E. Sharpe.

Orrù, M., Biggart, N. W., & Hamilton, G. G. (1991). Organizational isomorphism in East Asia. In W. W. Powell & P. J. DiMaggio (Eds.), *The new institutionalism in organizational analysis* (pp. 361-389). Chicago: University of Chicago Press.

Orrù, M., Hamilton, G. G., & Suzuki, M. (1989). Patterns of inter-firm control in Japanese business. *Organization Studies, 10,* 549-574.

Ostiguy, P. (1990). *Los capitanes de la industria: Grándes empresarios, politica y economia en la Argentina de los anos 80.* Buenos Aires: Editorial Legasa.

Ouchi, W. G. (1981). Markets, bureaucracies, and clans. *Administrative Science Quarterly, 25,* 129-141.

Ouchi, W. G. (1982). *Theory Z: How American business can meet the Japanese challenge.* New York: Avon.

Ouchi, W. G. (1984). *The M-form society.* Reading, MA: Addison-Wesley.

Ozawa, T. (1979). *Multinationalism, Japanese style.* Princeton, NJ: Princeton University Press.

Pack, H. (1992). New perspectives on industrial growth in Taiwan. In G. Ranis (Ed.), *Taiwan: From developing to mature economy* (pp. 73-120). Boulder, CO: Westview.

Palmer, D. (1983). Broken ties. *Administrative Science Quarterly, 28,* 40-55.

Palmer, D., Friedland, R., & Singh, J. V. (1986). The ties that bind. *American Sociological Review, 51,* 781-796.

Pang, C. K. (1992). *The state and economic transformation: The Taiwan case.* New York: Garland.

Park, S. I. (1988). Republic of Korea: Bank A. In *Technological change, work, organization and pay.* Geneva: International Labour Office.

Park, S. J. (1984). Labour-management consultation as a Japanese type of participation. In T. Shigeyoshi & J. Bergmann (Eds.), *Industrial relations in transition.* Tokyo: University of Tokyo Press.

Pascale, R. T., & Athos, A. G. (1981). *The art of Japanese management.* New York: Warner.

Patrick, H., & Rosovsky, H. (1976). Japan's economic performance: An overview. In H. Patrick & H. Rosovsky (Eds.), *Asia's new giant* (pp. 1-62). Washington, DC: Brookings Institution.

Peng, H. (1984). *Taiwan jingyan de nanti* [The difficult problems of Taiwan's experience]. Taizhong: Tunghai University, Institute of Sociology.

Peng, H. (1989). *Taiwan qiye yezhu de "guanxi" jiqi zhuanbian, yige shehuixue de fenxi* [Relationships among Taiwan business owners and their changes: A sociological analysis]. Unpublished doctoral dissertation, Tunghai University.

Pennings, J. M. (1980). *Interlocking directorates.* San Francisco: Jossey-Bass.

Perrow, C. (1981). Markets, hierarchies, and hegemony. In A. Van de Ven & W. Joyce (Eds.), *Perspectives on organizational design and behavior* (pp. 371-386). New York: John Wiley.

Perrow, C. (1985). Overboard with myth and symbols. *American Journal of Sociology, 91,* 151-155.

Perrow, C. (1986). *Complex organizations* (3rd ed.). New York: Random House.

Perrow, C. (1990). Economic theories of organization. In S. Zukin & P. J. DiMaggio (Eds.), *Structures of capital: The social organization of the economy* (pp. 121-152). Cambridge: Cambridge University Press.

Peters, T. J., & Waterman, R. H., Jr. (1982). *In search of excellence: Lessons from America's best-run companies.* New York: Harper & Row.

Peterson, T., with Maremont, M. (1990, June 15). Suddenly, high tech is a three-way race. *Business Week,* pp. 118-120, 122-123.

Pfeffer, J., & Salancik, G. (1978). *The external control of organizations.* New York: Harper & Row.

Piore, M. J., & Sabel, C. F. (1984). *The second industrial divide: Possibilities for prosperity.* New York: Basic Books.

Polanyi, K. (1957). *The great transformation.* Boston: Beacon.

Pollak, R. A. (1985). A transaction cost approach to families and households. *Journal of Economic Literature, 23,* 581-608.

Port, O. (1990, June 15). The global race. *Business Week,* pp. 35-39.

Porter, M. E. (1980). *Competitive strategy: Techniques for analyzing industries and competitors.* New York: Free Press.

Porter, M. E. (1990). *The competitive advantage of nations and their firms.* New York: Free Press.

Portes, A., & Walton, J. (1981). *Labor, class, and the international system.* New York: Academic.

Powell, W. W. (1990). Neither market nor hierarchy: Network forms of organization. In B. M. Staw & L. L. Cummings (Eds.), *Research in organizational behavior* (Vol. 12, pp. 295-336). Greenwich, CT: JAI.

Powell, W. W., & DiMaggio, P. J. (Eds.). (1991). *The new institutionalism in organizational analysis.* Chicago: University of Chicago Press.

Prestowitz, C., Jr. (1988). *Trading places: How we allowed Japan to take the lead.* New York: Basic Books.

The privatization of public enterprises in Korea. (1989). *Monthly Review* (Korea Exchange Bank).

Putterman, L. (Ed.). (1986). *The economic nature of the firm: A reader.* Cambridge: Cambridge University Press.

Pye, L. (1982). *Chinese commercial negotiating style.* Cambridge, MA: Oelgeschlager, Gunn & Hain.

Ragin, C., & Zaret, D. (1983). Theory and method in comparative research: Two strategies. *Social Forces, 61,* 731-754.

Ranis, G. (1979). Industrial development. In W. Galenson (Ed.), *Economic growth and structural change in Taiwan* (pp. 206-262). Ithaca, NY: Cornell University Press.

Redding, S. G. (1980). Cognition as an aspect of culture and its relation to management processes: An exploratory view of the Chinese case. *Journal of Management Studies, 17,* 127-148.

Redding, S. G. (1990). *The spirit of Chinese capitalism.* Berlin: Walter de Gruyter.

Redding, S. G. (1991). Weak organizations and strong linkages: Managerial ideology and Chinese family business networks. In G. G. Hamilton (Ed.), *Business networks and economic development in East and Southeast Asia* (pp. 30-47). Hong Kong: University of Hong Kong, Centre of Asian Studies.

Redding, S. G., & Tam, S. (1986). Network and molecular organizations: An exploratory view of Chinese firms in Hong Kong. In K. C. Mun & T. S. Chan (Eds.), *Proceedings of the inaugural meeting of the Southeast Asia Region Academy of International Business.* Hong Kong: Chinese University of Hong Kong Press.

Reynolds, L. G. (1983). The spread of economic growth to the Third World: 1850-1980. *Journal of Economic Literature, 21,* 941-980.

Robison, R. (1986). *Indonesia: The Rise of Capital.* Sydney: Allen & Unwin.

Rowe, W. T. (1984). *Hankow: Commerce and society in a Chinese city, 1796-1889.* Stanford, CA: Stanford University Press.

Roy, W. G. (1983). The unfolding of the interlocking directorate structure of the United States. *American Sociological Review, 48,* 248-256.

Roy, W. G. (1987, August). *Functional and historical logics in explaining the rise of the American industrial corporation*. Paper presented at the annual meeting of the American Sociological Association, Chicago.

Roy, W. G. (1990). Functional and historical logics in explaining the rise of the American industrial corporation. *Comparative Social Research, 12,* 19-44.

SaKong, I. (1980). Macroeconomic aspects of the public enterprise sector. In C. K. Park (Ed.), *Macroeconomic and industrial development in Korea* (pp. 99-128). Seoul: Korea Development Institute.

Samuels, R. J. (1987). *The business of the Japanese state: Energy markets in comparative and historical perspective.* Ithaca, NY: Cornell University Press.

Sato, K., & Hoshino, Y. (Eds.). (1984). *The anatomy of Japanese business.* Armonk, NY: M. E. Sharpe.

Sato, Y. (1986). Yakuin ken-nin to kigyo-kan kankei no sokutei [Measurement of interlocking directorates and interfirm relationships]. *Keizai Ronso, 137,* 22-41.

Sayle, M. (1985, March 28). Japan victorious. *New York Review of Books, 32*(5), 33-40.

Schluchter, W. (1981). *The rise of Western rationalism: Max Weber's developmental history.* Berkeley: University of California Press.

Schluchter, W. (1989). *Rationalism, religion, and domination* (N. Solomon, Trans.). Berkeley: University of California Press.

Schmalensee, R., & Willig, R. D. (Eds.). (1989). *Handbook of industrial organization.* Amsterdam: North-Holland.

Schmiegelow, H., & Schmiegelow, M. (1990). How Japan affects the international system. *International Organization, 44,* 553-588.

Schumann, M. (1990). *New forms of work organization in West German industrial enterprises.* Paper presented at the World Congress of Sociology.

Schweder, R. A. (1986). Divergent rationalities. In R. W. Fiske & R. A. Schweder (Eds.), *Metatheory in the social sciences: Pluralisms and subjectivities.* Chicago: University of Chicago Press.

Scitovsky, T. (1985). Economic development in Taiwan and South Korea: 1965-81. *Food Research Institute Studies, 19,* 215-264.

Scitovsky, T. (1986). Economic development in Taiwan and South Korea: 1965-81. In L. J. Lau (Ed.), *Models of development: A comparative study of economic growth in South Korea and Taiwan.* San Francisco: Institute for Contemporary Studies.

Scott, J. (1979). *Corporations, classes and capitalism.* New York: St. Martin's.

Scott, J., & Griff, C. (1984). *Directors of industry.* London: Polity.

Scott, W. R. (1987). The adolescence of institutional theory. *Administrative Science Quarterly, 32,* 493-511.

Scott, W. R., & Meyer, J. W. (1983). The organization of societal sectors. In J. W. Meyer & W. R. Scott (Eds.), *Organizational environments: Ritual and rationality* (pp. 129-153). Beverly Hills, CA: Sage.

Selznick, P. (1957). *Leadership in administration.* New York: Harper & Row.

Sheard, P. (1984). *Financial corporate grouping, cross-subsidization in the private sector and the industrial adjustment process in Japan* (Discussion Paper 44). Osaka: Osaka University, Faculty of Economics.

Shieh, G. S. (1992). *"Boss" island: The subcontracting network and micro-entrepreneurship in Taiwan's development.* New York: Peter Lang.

Shigeyoshi, T., & Bergmann, J. (Eds.). (1984). *Industrial relations in transition.* Tokyo: University of Tokyo Press.

Shimokawa, K. (1985). Japan's *keiretsu* system. *Japanese Economic Studies, 13,* 3-31.

Shimura, Y. (1976). Ginko kodo no nihonteki ronri [Japanese logic behind banks' behavior]. *Keizai Hyoron, 24,* 6-19.

Silin, R. H. (1976). *Leadership and values: The organization of large-scale Taiwanese enterprises.* Cambridge, MA: Harvard University, East Asian Research Center.

Sjöstrand, S.-E. (1993). Institutions as infrastructures of human interaction. In S.-E. Sjöstrand (Ed.), *Institutional change: Theory and empirical findings.* Armonk, NY: M. E. Sharpe.

Skinner, W. F. (1977). *The city in late imperial China.* Stanford, CA: Stanford University Press.

Smircich, L. (1983). Concepts of culture and organizational analysis. *Administrative Science Quarterly, 28,* 339-358.

Smith, A. (1976). *The wealth of nations.* Chicago: University of Chicago Press.

Smith, A. (1991). *The wealth of nations.* New York: Knopf.

Soref, M. (1976). Social class and a division of labor within the corporate elite. *Sociological Quarterly, 17,* 360-368.

Statistisches Jahrbuch 1988 für die Bundesrepublik Deutschland. (1988). Stuttgart: Wohlhammer.

Stigler, G. J. (1968). *The organization of industry.* Chicago: University of Chicago Press.

Stockman, F. N., Ziegler, R., & Scott, J. (Eds.). (1985). *Networks of corporate power: A comparative analysis of ten countries.* Cambridge: Polity.

Stoffaës, C. (1986). Industrial policy in the high-technology industries. In W. J. Adams & C. Stoffaës (Eds.), *French industrial policy.* Washington, DC: Brookings Institution.

Stone, K. (1974). The origins of job structures in the steel industry. *Review of Radical Political Economics, 6,* 61-97.

Strachan, H. (1976). *Family and other business groups in economic development: The case of Nicaragua.* New York: Praeger.

Streeck, W. (1984). Guaranteed employment, flexible manpower use, and cooperative manpower management. In T. Shigeyoshi & J. Bergmann (Eds.), *Industrial relations in transition.* Tokyo: University of Tokyo Press.

Streeck, W. (1989). Successful adjustment to turbulent markets. In P. J. Katzenstein (Ed.), *Industry and politics in West Germany.* Ithaca, NY: Cornell University Press.

Streeck, W. (1990, March). *More uncertainties: West German unions facing 1992.* Paper presented at the Seventh Conference of Europeanists, Washington, DC.

Sumiya, T. (1986). *Gendai nihon shihon shugi no shihai kozo* [The structure of domination in modern Japanese capitalism]. Tokyo: Shimpyoron.

Sutter, R. G. (1988). *Taiwan: Entering the 21st century.* Lanham, MD: University Press of America.

Swartz, D. (1985). French interlocking directorships: Financial and industrial groups. In F. N. Stockman, R. Ziegler, & J. Scott (Eds.), *Networks of corporate power: A comparative analysis of ten countries.* Cambridge: Polity.

Swedberg, R. (1991). *Schumpeter: A biography.* Princeton, NJ: Princeton University Press.

Swedberg, R., Himmelstrand, U., & Brulin, G. (1990). The paradigm of economic sociology. In S. Zukin & P. J. DiMaggio (Eds.), *Structures of capital: The social organization of the economy* (pp. 57-86). Cambridge: Cambridge University Press.

Swidler, A. (1986). Culture in action: Symbols and strategies. *American Sociological Review, 51,* 273-286.

Tai, L. S. T. (1988). Doing business in the People's Republic of China. *Management International Review, 1.*

Taira, K. (1970). *Economic development and the labor market in Japan.* New York: Columbia University Press.

Taira, K., & Wada, T. (1987). Japanese business-government relations. In M. S. Mizruchi & M. Schwartz (Eds.), *Intercorporate relations: The structural analysis of business.* Cambridge: Cambridge University Press.

Takamiya, S. (1982). Kigyo shudan no kadai to saihensei [Tasks and reorganization of the business groups]. *Soshiki Kagaku, 16*(3), 2-7.

Tannenbaum, A. S., Kavcic, B., Rosner, M., Vianello, M., & Weiser, G. (1974). *Hierarchy in organizations.* San Francisco: Jossey-Bass.

Taylor, J. (1983). *Shadows of the rising sun.* New York: William Morrow.

Teece, D. J. (1980). Economics of scope and the scope of the enterprise. *Journal of Economic Behavior and Organization, 1,* 223-248.

Teece, D. J. (1984). Economic analysis and strategic management. *California Management Review, 26,* 91-92.

Templeman, J. (1990, February 12). Daimler's drive to become a high-tech speedster. *Business Week,* pp. 55, 58.

Thorelli, H. B. (1986). Networks: Between markets and hierarchies. *Strategic Management Journal, 7*(1), 37-51.

Tilly, R. (1974). The growth of large-scale enterprise in Germany since the middle of the nineteenth century. In H. Daems & H. Van der Wee (Eds.), *The rise of managerial capitalism.* Louvain, Belgium: Leuven University Press.

Tong, C. K. (1991). Centripetal authority, differentiated networks: The social organization of Chinese firms in Singapore. In G. G. Hamilton (Ed.), *Business networks and economic development in East and Southeast Asia.* Hong Kong: University of Hong Kong, Centre of Asian Studies.

Toyo Keizai Shimposha. (1986a). *Kigyo keiretsu soran* [Overview of firm alignments]. Tokyo: Author.

Toyo Keizai Shimposha. (1986b). *Nihon no kigyo gurupu* [Business groups in Japan]. Tokyo: Author.

Tsurumi, Y. (1984). *Sogoshosha.* Montreal: Institute for Research on Public Policy.

Tu, W. M. (1984, October 1). Gongye dongya yu rujia jingshen [Industrial East Asia and the spirit of Confucianism]. *Tianxia Zazhi, 41,* 124-137.

Tversky, A., & Kahneman, D. (1974). Judgment under uncertainty: Heuristics and biases. *Science, 185,* 1124-1131.

Twitchett, D. (1959). The fan clan's charitable estate, 1050-1760. In D. S. Nivison & A. F. Wright (Eds.), *Confucianism in action* (pp. 97-133). Stanford, CA: Stanford University Press.

Ueda, Y. (1983). Kigyo shudan ni okeru yakuin kennin no keiryo bunseki [Mathematical analysis of interlocks in enterprise groups]. *Shoken Keizai, 146,* 25-48.

Ueda, Y. (1986). Intercorporate networks in Japan. *Shoken Keizai, 157,* 236-254.

Uekusa, M. (1977). Effects of deconcentration measures in Japan. *Antitrust Bulletin, 22,* 687-715.

United Nations. (1985, March). *Monthly Bulletin of Statistics.*

U.S. Bureau of the Census. (1989). *Statistical abstract of the United States.* Washington, DC: Government Printing Office.

Useem, M. (1979). The social organization of the American business elite. *American Sociological Review, 44,* 553-572.

Useem, M. (1982). Classwide rationality in the politics of managers and directors of large American corporations in the United States and Great Britain. *Administrative Science Quarterly, 27,* 199-226.

Useem, M. (1984). *The inner circle.* New York: Oxford University Press.

Useem, M., & Karabel, J. (1986). Pathways to top corporate management. *American Sociological Review, 51,* 184-200.

Vancil, R. F. (1978). *Decentralization: Managerial ambiguity by design.* Homewood, IL: Dow Jones-Irwin.

van Wolferen, K. (1989). *The enigma of Japanese power.* New York: Knopf.

Vogel, E. (1979). *Japan as number one: Lessons for America.* Cambridge, MA: Harvard University Press.

Wada, S. (1977). *Seibu gurupu* [The Seibu group]. Tokyo: Yunion Shuppansha.

Wade, R. (1985). East Asian financial systems as a challenge to economics: Lessons from Taiwan. *California Management Review, 27*(4), 106-127.

Wade, R. (1990). *Governing the market: Economic theory and the role of government in East Asian industrialization.* Princeton, NJ: Princeton University Press.

Wallach, H. G. P. (1985). Political economics. In H. G. P. Wallach & G. K. Romoser (Eds.), *West German politics in the mid-eighties.* New York: Praeger.

Ward, B. E. (1972). A small factory in Hong Kong: Some aspects of its internal organization. In W. E. Willmott (Ed.), *Economic organization in Chinese society* (pp. 353-386). Stanford, CA: Stanford University Press.

Watson, J. L. (1975a). Agnates and outsiders; Adoption in a Chinese lineage. *Man, 10,* 293-306.

Watson, J. L. (1975b). *Emigration and the Chinese lineage.* Berkeley: University of California Press.

Watson, J. L. (1982). Chinese kinship reconsidered: Anthropological perspectives on historical research. *China Quarterly, 92,* 589-627.

Weber, M. (1958). *From Max Weber.* New York: Oxford University Press.

Weber, M. (1961). *General economic history* (F. Knight, Trans.). New York: Collier. (Original work published 1923)

Weber, M. (1968a). *Economy and society.* Berkeley: University of California Press.

Weber, M. (1968b). *Economy and society.* New York: Bedminster.

Weber, M. (1978). *Economy and society* (G. Roth & C. Wittich, Eds., Trans.). Berkeley: University of California Press.

Weems, C. (1971). Reformist thought of the independence program (1896-1898). In Y. Jo (Ed.), *Korea's response to the West* (pp. 163-218). Kalamazoo, MI: Korea Research and Publications.

Weick, K. (1979). *The social psychology of organizing.* Reading, MA: Addison-Wesley.

Weiner, S. (1985, March 19). K-Mart apparel buyers hopscotch the Orient to find quality goods. *Wall Street Journal,* pp. 1, 20.

Weiss, L. (1984). The Italian state and small business. *Archives Européennes de Sociologie, 25,* 214-241.

Weiss, L. (1988). *Creating capitalism.* Oxford: Basil Blackwell.

Westney, D. E. (1987). *Imitation and innovation: The transfer of Western organizational patterns to Meiji Japan.* Cambridge, MA: Harvard University Press.

Westphal, L. E., Rhee, Y. W., Kim, L. S., & Amsden, A. H. (1984). Republic of Korea. *World Development, 12,* 505-533.

White, H. (1981). Where do markets come from? *American Journal of Sociology, 87,* 517-547.

Whitley, R. D. (1990a). Eastern Asian enterprise structures and the comparative analysis of forms of business organization. *Organization Studies, 11,* 47-74.

Whitley, R. D. (1990b, July). *Enterprise structures in their societal contexts: The comparative analysis of forms of business organization.* Paper presented at the annual meeting of the International Sociological Association, Madrid.

Wickberg, E. (1965). *The Chinese in Philippine life, 1850-1898.* New Haven, CT: Yale University Press.

Williams, J. F. (1980). Sugar: The sweetener in Taiwan's development. In R. G. Knapp (Ed.), *China's island frontier* (pp. 219-252). Honolulu: University of Hawaii Press.

Williamson, O. E. (1975). *Markets and hierarchies: Analysis and antitrust implications.* New York: Free Press.

Williamson, O. E. (1981). The economics of organization. *American Journal of Sociology, 87,* 548-577.

Williamson, O. E. (1983). Organization form, residual claimants and corporate control. *Journal of Law and Economics, 26,* 351-366.

Williamson, O. E. (1985). *The economic institutions of capitalism.* New York: Free Press.

Williamson, O. E. (1986). Vertical integration and related variations on a transaction-cost economics theme. In J. E. Stiglitz & G. F. Mathewson (Eds.), *New developments in the analysis of market structure* (pp. 149-176). Cambridge: MIT Press.

Williamson, O. E. (1991). Comparative economic organization: The analysis of discrete structural alternatives. *Administrative Science Quarterly, 36,* 269-296.

Williamson, O. E., & Ouchi, W. G. (1981). The markets and hierarchies and visible hand perspective. In A. Van de Ven & W. Joyce (Eds.), *Perspectives on organizational design and behavior* (pp. 347-370). New York: John Wiley.

Williamson, O. E., & Winter, S. G. (1991). *The nature of the firm: Origins, evolution, and development.* New York: Oxford University Press.

Willmott, W. E. (Ed.). (1972). *Economic organization in Chinese society.* Stanford, CA: Stanford University Press.

Winckler, E. A. (1984). Institutionalization and participation on Taiwan. *China Quarterly, 99,* 481-499.

Winckler, E. A., & Greenhalgh, S. (Eds.). (1988). *Contending approaches to the political economy of Taiwan.* Armonk, NY: M. E. Sharpe.

Wolf, M. (1983). *The Japanese conspiracy.* New York: Empire.

Wong, S. L. (1985). The Chinese family firm: A model. *British Journal of Sociology, 36,* 58-72.

Wong, S. L. (1986). Modernization and Chinese culture in Hong Kong. *China Quarterly, 106,* 306-325.

Wong, S. L. (1988). The applicability of Asian family values to other socio-cultural settings. In P. L. Berger & H. H. M. Hsiao (Eds.), *In search of an East Asian development model.* New Brunswick, NJ: Transaction.

Wong, S. L. (1991). Chinese entrepreneurs and business trust. In G. G. Hamilton (Ed.), *Business networks and economic development in East and Southeast Asia* (pp. 13-29). Hong Kong: University of Hong Kong, Centre of Asian Studies.

World Bank. (1988). *World development report.* Oxford: Oxford University Press.

Wu, H. L. (1988). A future for small and medium enterprises? *Free China Review, 38*(11), 6-9.

Wuthnow, R. (1985). State structures and ideological outcomes. *American Sociological Review, 50,* 799-821.

Wuthnow, R., Hunter, J. D., Bergesen, A., & Kurzweil, E. (1984). *Cultural analysis.* Boston: Routledge & Kegan Paul.

Yager, J. A. (1988). *Transforming agriculture in Taiwan: The experience of the Joint Commission on Rural Reconstruction.* Ithaca, NY: Cornell University Press.

Yamamura, K., & Yasuba, Y. (Eds.). (1987). *The political economy of Japan.* Stanford, CA: Stanford University Press.

Yang, G. Y. (1988). *Manpower development in Korea.* Unpublished doctoral dissertation, University of Wales College, Cardiff.

Yang, J. (1981). Zhongxiao qiye yinhang zhedu zhi tantao. *Jiceng Jinrong, 30,* 58-63.

Yang, L. S. (1970). Government control of urban merchants in traditional China. *Tsing Hua Journal of Chinese Studies, 8,* 186-206.

Yang, M. M. H. (1989). The gift economy and state power in China. *Comparative Studies in Society and History, 31*(1), 25-54.

Yasuba, Y. (1976). The evolution of dualistic wage structure. In H. Patrick (Ed.), *Japanese industrialization and its social consequences* (pp. 249-298). Berkeley: University of California Press.

Yong, P. K. (1992). *The social foundation of Chinese rubber businesses in Singapore.* Unpublished master's thesis, National University of Singapore, Department of Sociology.

Yoo, S., & Lee, S. M. (1987). Management style and practice of Korean chaebols. *California Management Review, 29,* 95-109.

Yoshihara, H. (1981). Research on Japan's general trading firms. *Japanese Economic Studies, 9,* 61-86.

Young, A. K. (1979). *The sogo shosha: Japan's multinational trading corporations.* Boulder, CO: Westview.

Yuki, S. (1985). *Sumitomo wa naze tsuyoinoka* [Why is Sumitomo strong?]. Kyoto: PHP Kenkyusho.

Zeile, W. J. (1989). *Credit-rationing as an instrument of industrial targeting: The Korean experience in the 1970's* (Working Paper). Davis: University of California, Institute of Governmental Affairs, East Asian Business and Development Program.

Zeile, W. J. (1993). *Industrial targeting, business organization, and industry productivity growth in the Republic of Korea, 1972-1985.* Unpublished doctoral dissertation, University of California, Davis, Department of Economics.

Zeitlin, M. (1974). Corporate ownership and control. *American Journal of Sociology, 79,* 1073-1119.

Zeitlin, M. (1976). On class theory of the large corporation. *American Journal of Sociology, 81,* 894-903.

Zelizer, V. (1988). Beyond the polemics of the market: Establishing a theoretical and empirical agenda. *Sociological Forum, 3,* 614-619.

Zeng, S. (1984). Yi rujia wei zhuliu de chongguo shi guanli linian zhi shentao [An in-depth discussion of using Confucian philosophy as the unifying principle for Chinese-style management concepts]. In *Zhongguo shi guanli* [Chinese-style management] (pp. 101-120). Taipei: Gungshang Shibao.

Zhao, J. (1982). Zhengfu ying ruhe fudao zhongxiao quye zhi fazhan [How should the government develop an assistance policy for small and medium businesses?]. *Qiyin Jikan, 5,* 32-38.

Ziegler, R. (1985). Conclusion. In F. N. Stockman, R. Ziegler, & J. Scott (Eds.), *Networks of corporate power: A comparative analysis of ten countries* (pp. 267-287). Cambridge: Polity.

Ziegler, R., Bender, D., & Biehler, H. (1985). Industry and banking in the German corporate network. In F. N. Stockman, R. Ziegler, & J. Scott (Eds.), *Networks of corporate power: A comparative analysis of ten countries.* Cambridge: Polity.

Zo, K. Z. (1970). Development and behavioral patterns of Korean entrepreneurs. *Korea Journal, 10,* 9-14.

Zucker, L. G. (1983). Organizations as institutions. *Research in the Sociology of Organizations, 2,* 1-48.

Zucker, L. G. (1987). Institutional theories of organizations. In W. R. Scott (Ed.), *Annual review of sociology* (Vol. 13, pp. 443-464). Palo Alto, CA: Annual Reviews.

Zucker, L. G. (1988). Introduction. In L. G. Zucker (Ed.), *Institutional patterns and organizations: Culture and environment* (pp. xiii-xix). Cambridge, MA: Ballinger.

Zysman, J. (1983). *Governments, markets, and growth.* Ithaca, NY: Cornell University Press.

Index

416   ORGANIZATION OF EAST ASIAN CAPITALISM

imperfection model of Asian-Western
    economic differences, 15, 41-44,
    122, 126
industrial organization economics, 31
institutionalization of firm autonomy,
    47-50
organizations and, 135
perfect market assumptions, 10, 15, 42
Western biases, 35-37
    See also Neoclassical economic theory
Market development:
    Asian markets, 50-51
    Western markets, 45-50
Market integration, 69
Markets and hierarchies, 16, 55-86
    background to, 57-61
    boundaries, 61-67
    Coase on, 56, 57-58, 90
    contractual/legal bases, 62-63, 90
    economic versus sociological
        perspectives, 56
    embedded networks hierarchies, 82-85
    firm-market distinctions, 58, 62
    governance structures, 62, 122
    horizontal networks, 67-68, 71-73, 78-82
    South Korean business networks, 73-82
    Taiwan and South Korea compared,
        82-85
    Taiwanese business networks, 73-74,
        78-82
    transaction cost theory, 59-61, 85-86
    varieties of, 55-57
    vertical networks, 67-71, 74-78
    Weber and, 57, 63-67, 91
Marx, K., 112
Mason, E., 10, 136
Maurice, M., 326
McCullagh, C., 357
Means-and-ends rationality, 300-301, 303
Meckling, W. H., 10
Meiji Restoration, 127, 140
Mercantilism, 46-47
Merchant class, 127
Meyer, C. A., 128
Meyer, J. W., 135, 153-154, 189, 192, 193,
    305-306, 342
M-form enterprises, 17, 42, 43
Miles, R. H., 129
Milgrom, P., 71
Mills, C. W., 189, 192

Minard, L., 115
Ministry of International Trade and Industry
    (MITI), 37, 170, 324, 330, 335
Mintz, B., 112, 188, 191, 192, 199
Mitsubishi, 38, 101-102, 195, 197-200, 209,
    210, 320, 335
    mutual shareholding patterns, 164-168
Mitsui, 38, 195, 209, 330
    mutual shareholding patterns, 164-168
Mitterand, F., 374
Miyazaki, Y., 194, 210
Mizruchi, M. S., 188
Modernization theories, 39
Monopoly, 36
Moore, B., 46
Mori, H., 210
Müller-Armack, A., 334
Myers, R. H., 115, 124-125, 127, 137, 142,
    243, 253, 360

Nakamura, T., 117, 118, 127
Nakane, C., 128-129, 312
Nakatani, I., 194, 198, 201
Nam, J., 370
Nanetti, R. Y., 323, 347, 351, 358-39, 366
Narushima, T., 194
National champions, 374-375, 380-381
Needham, J., 50, 193
Neff, R., 320
Neoclassical economic theory, 17
    as an institutional theory, 53-54
    asocial conceptualization, 36-37
    challenges to rationality and autonomy
        assumptions, 45-46
    comparing Japanese and German
        capitalism, 336-337
    ideal assumptions, 35-36
    imperfection model of Asian-Western
        economic differences, 41-44
    individual economic actors (*homo
        economicus*) and, 21, 36, 45
    not a general theory of capitalism, 44-45
    price as organizing mechanism, 57-58
    Western biases, 17, 35-37
    See also Market-based approaches
Network analysis, 188-189
Network hierarchies:
    buyer-driven versus producer-driven, 82
    demand-responsive, 82, 242, 288

About the Authors

Marco Orrù, at the time of his death at age 41, was Associate Professor of Sociology at the University of South Florida in Tampa. He was born in Sardinia and received his undergraduate education at the University of Bologna. Awarded a Fulbright Fellowship for graduate study in the United States, he attended the University of California, Davis, where he received his PhD in sociology in 1984. In addition to his writings on economic sociology, some of which are collected in this volume, he also published many articles and a book on the various aspects of sociological theory. His book, *Anomie: History and Meaning* (1987), is undoubtedly the definitive study on that topic.

Nicole Woolsey Biggart is Professor of Management and Sociology at the University of California, Davis. Her research in recent years has focused on economic sociology, and in particular on the economic uses of social relations. Her published works in economic sociology include *Charismatic Capitalism: Direct Selling Organizations in America* (1989); "Competition and Markets: An Institutional Perspective" (with Mitchel Abolafia), in *Perspectives on Socio-Economics,* edited by Amitai Etzioni and Paul Lawrence (1990); and "Labor and Leisure," in the *Handbook of Economic Sociology,* edited by N. J. Smelser and R. Swedberg (1994). She is also coauthor, with Gary Hamilton, of *Governor Reagan, Governor Brown: A Sociology of Executive Power* (1984) and numerous other works in organizational analysis that have appeared in *Administrative Science Quarterly, American Journal of Sociology,* and *Social Problems.* In 1996 she was Arthur Andersen Distinguished Visitor at the Judge Institute of Management Studies, University of Cambridge, England.

425

Gary G. Hamilton is Professor of Sociology at the University of Washington. His major areas of interest include East Asian business networks, Chinese societies, economic sociology, and historical, comparative sociology with an emphasis on East Asia. A collected volume of his writings on Chinese economies titled *Chinese Capitalism? The Economic Organization of Chinese Economies* is forthcoming. He has been awarded a Fulbright Fellowship, a Guggenheim Fellowship, and a fellowship to attend the Advanced Center for the Behavioral Sciences in Palo Alto, California.